LETTERS TO FRANCESCO DATINI

The Other Voice in Early Modern Europe:
The Toronto Series, 16

The Other Voice in
Early Modern Europe:
The Toronto Series

SERIES EDITORS Margaret L. King *and* Albert Rabil, Jr.
SERIES EDITOR, ENGLISH TEXTS Elizabeth H. Hageman

Previous Publications in the Series

MADRE MARÍA ROSA
Journey of Five Capuchin Nuns
Edited and translated by Sarah E.
Owens
2009

GIOVAN BATTISTA ANDREINI
Love in the Mirror: A Bilingual Edition
Edited and translated by Jon R. Snyder
2009

RAYMOND DE SABANAC AND SIMONE
ZANACCHI
Two Women of the Great Schism: The
Revelations *of Constance de Rabastens
by Raymond de Sabanac and* Life of
the Blessed Ursulina of Parma *by
Simone Zanacchi*
Edited and translated by Renate
Blumenfeld-Kosinski and Bruce L.
Venarde
2010

OLIVA SABUCO DE NANTES BARRERA
The True Medicine
Edited and translated by Gianna
Pomata
2010

LOUISE-GENEVIÈVE GILLOT DE
SAINCTONGE
Dramatizing Dido, Circe, and Griselda
Edited and translated by Janet Levarie
Smarr
2010

PERNETTE DU GUILLET
Complete Poems: A Bilingual Edition
Edited by Karen Simroth James
Translated by Marta Rijn Finch
2010

ANTONIA PULCI
*Saints' Lives and Bible Stories for the
Stage: A Bilingual Edition*
Edited by Elissa B. Weaver
Translated by James Wyatt Cook
2010

VALERIA MIANI
*Celinda, A Tragedy: A Bilingual
Edition*
Edited by Valeria Finucci
Translated by Julia Kisacky
Annotated by Valeria Finucci and
Julia Kisacky
2010

The Other Voice in
Early Modern Europe:
The Toronto Series

SERIES EDITORS Margaret L. King *and* Albert Rabil, Jr.
SERIES EDITOR, ENGLISH TEXTS Elizabeth H. Hageman

Previous Publications in the Series

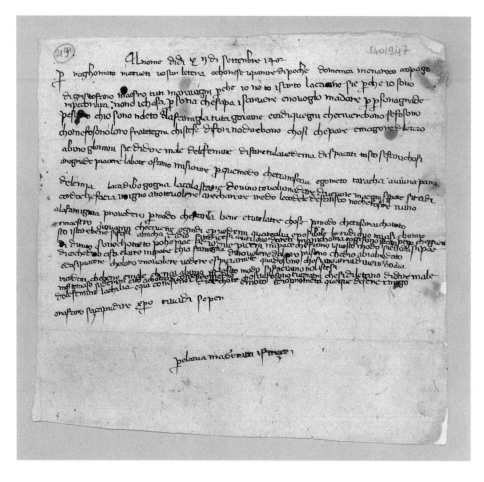

Margerita Datini (autograph) to Francesco Datini, 12 September 1402. Reproduced with the permission of the Archivio di Stato, Prato, prot. 788/28.13.10

Letters to Francesco Datini

MARGHERITA DATINI

Translated by

CAROLYN JAMES *and* ANTONIO PAGLIARO

ITER

Iter Inc.
Centre for Reformation and Renaissance Studies
Toronto
2012

Iter: Gateway to the Middle Ages and Renaissance
Tel: 416/978–7074   Email: iter@utoronto.ca
Fax: 416/978–1668   Web: www.itergateway.org

Centre for Reformation and Renaissance Studies
Victoria University in the University of Toronto
Tel: 416/585–4465   Email: crrs.publications@utoronto.ca
Fax: 416/585–4430   Web: www.crrs.ca

Iter and the Centre for Reformation and Renaissance Studies gratefully acknowledge the generous support of James E. Rabil, in memory of Scottie W. Rabil, toward the publication of this book

Library and Archives Canada Cataloguing in Publication

Datini, Margherita
Letters to Francesco Datini / Margherita Datini ; translated by Carolyn James and Antonio Pagliaro.
(The other voice in early modern Europe series : the Toronto series ; 16)
Co-published by: Centre for Reformation and Renaissance Studies.
Includes bibliographical references and index.
Issued also in an electronic format.
ISBN 978-0-7727-2116-7

1. Datini, Margherita—Correspondence. 2. Datini, Francesco, 1335–1410. 3. Women—Italy—Florence—Biography. 4. Florence (Italy)—History—To 1421. I. James, Carolyn II. Pagliaro, Antonio, 1945– III. Victoria University (Toronto, Ont.). Centre for Reformation and Renaissance Studies IV. Iter Inc V. Title. VI. Series: Other voice in early modern Europe. Toronto series ; 16

DG737.28.D39A4 2012
945'.505092   C2012-900576-2

Cover illustration:
An adaption of a donor portrait from the painting *La Trinità* by Niccolò di Piero Gerini (inv. PC 102, tempera su tavola), Rome, Musei Capitolini, Pinacoteca Capitolina, prot. 575/26.4.11.

Cover design:
Maureen Morin, Information Technology Services, University of Toronto Libraries.

Typesetting and production:
Iter Inc.

Contents

Margherita Datini: Letters to Francesco Datini

Acknowledgments

The beginnings of this project go back to 2001, when Carolyn James translated into English a selection of Margherita Datini's letters for inclusion in the CD-ROM *Per la tua Margherita—: lettere di una donna del '300 al marito mercante* (ed. Diana Toccafondi and Giovanni Tartaglione; Prato, 2002). The success of this initiative prompted us to embark on a complete English translation of the letters. We would like to thank the staff at the Archivio di Stato in Prato for their liberal help and support, especially Elena Cecchi, Diana Toccafondi, and Maria Raffaella de Gramatica. The librarians at the Biblioteca Roncioniana and our colleagues at the Monash University Centre in Prato also gave willing assistance to the project, particularly Giovanni Tarantino and Valentina Guerrieri. Much of the research for this project was done in Melbourne, and we could not have completed our task without the help of the document delivery sections of the Sir Louis Matheson Library at Monash University and of the Borchardt Library at La Trobe University. We very sincerely thank those who assisted us in tracking down sources not held in Australian libraries.

The scholarship of Jérôme Hayez has informed our work at every point, and we are very grateful to him for generously giving us copies of in-press publications and for supplying corrections to older published sources from his own more recent research. We also thank Simona Brambilla, Maria Giagnavoco, Patrizia Bertozzi, Natalie Tomas, and Diana Barnes for their help. Both the anonymous reviewer of our manuscript and Alan Crosier made many valuable suggestions and corrections for which we are grateful. We would also like to acknowledge the help and encouragement of Al Rabil, and to thank him and Margaret King for including the present volume in the series *The Other Voice in Early Modern Europe*. Carolyn James thanks the Fondazione Cassamarca of Treviso and the Australian Research Council for financial support of the research associated with the project, and the School of Philosophical, Historical and International Studies, Monash University, for contributing to the publication costs of this book. La Trobe University granted Antonio Pagliaro a period of study leave that advanced this project at a crucial stage. We also wish to acknowledge the help of Simonetta Magnani, former director of the Italian Cultural Institute in Melbourne, who gave us the opportunity to present our research at the institute's seminar.

We are especially indebted to our respective partners, Bill Kent and Annamaria Pagliaro, for their patience and assistance. Annamaria Pagliaro offered expert help in interpreting some of the more daunting passages of these letters, and Bill Kent shared his knowledge of late-medieval Italian history, even during the grueling months of chemotherapy that preceded his untimely and much-regretted death in August 2010. We dedicate this book to his memory.

Carolyn James, Monash University
Antonio Pagliaro, La Trobe University

Introduction

> I am more teased than a newlywed, and they say things
> to me that they would not even say to a new bride. If I
> am sad, they say I am jealous. If I am happy, they say
> I can't be missing Francesco di Marco. They talk such
> rubbish that if you were a young boy it would be bad
> enough. In this household all they do is joke about
> you and me [letter 1].

Margherita Datini (1360–1423) was twenty-four when she dictated
this message to be sent to her husband, the merchant Francesco di
Marco Datini, who was about twenty-five years her senior. The couple
had moved from Provence to Tuscany the year before. By the time
the correspondence opens, Francesco had established warehouses not
only in Prato, the small town ten miles from Florence that he had left
as a youth, but also in Pisa and Florence itself. The rapid expansion
of Francesco's business made it necessary for him to spend prolonged
periods away from home, during which the couple was obliged to
communicate by letter. The intriguing reference in this passage to the
teasing jokes of Florentine relatives and friends about the Datini marriage alerts us to what appears to be an unconventional relationship,
and it whets our appetite for the unfolding saga of their marital collaboration in epistolary exchanges that continued for some twenty-six
years.[1] Here is a woman who seems to conform little to the medieval

---

1. [There are two ranges of footnotes. The main range begins at letter 1; all cross-references
will refer to notes within that main range.] See *Le lettere di Margherita Datini a Francesco
di Marco (1384–1410)*, ed. Valeria Rosati (Prato: Cassa di Risparmio e Depositi, 1977), and
Le lettere di Francesco Datini alla moglie Margherita (1385–1410), ed. Elena Cecchi (Prato:
Società Pratese di Storia Patria, 1990). Margherita's letters, including a number of previously
unpublished ones, are also available on a CD-ROM. See Diana Toccafondi and Giovanni
Tartaglione, ed., *Per la tua Margherita—: lettere di una donna del '300 al marito mercante*
(Prato: Archivio di Stato, 2002). Margherita's life in Avignon before her marriage (and, to
a lesser extent, after Francesco Datini's death) can be reconstructed only in broad outline,
although the current research of Jérôme Hayez, Simona Brambilla, and Ann Crabb on unpublished Datini material may reveal more. For the most recent scholarship on Francesco
Datini, see Giampiero Nigro, ed., *Francesco di Marco Datini: The Man, the Merchant* (Flor-

stereotype of wifely virtue exemplified in its most extreme form in Giovanni Boccaccio's tale of patient Griselda.[2] Although Margherita admitted that she was not as obedient as a good wife ought to be, she regarded herself as sorely tested by an irascible and idiosyncratic husband who required her to conform to—and to go well beyond—traditional wifely roles.

Her letters to Francesco, here translated into English for the first time, provide a wealth of information about the societies of Prato and Florence, between which the Datinis divided their time.[3] Even more remarkably, the letters tell us a great deal about Margherita herself. She reveals her political views and the influence she could exert within Florentine patronage networks by virtue of her aristocratic connections.[4] She also comments in detail on her household, the tasks her husband delegated to her, and the activities and personalities of the relatives and friends with whom she socialized. The complex portrait of everyday life and social relationships in the urban environments of late-medieval Tuscany that emerges from Margherita's letters is dramatically different from the static, limited view of women's lives presented in the prescriptive texts of her period.

Although letters constitute the largest category of early writing by women of western Europe, fourteenth-century examples are scarce, especially those from lay women. Among the few that have come to light are thirty-one letters of the Florentine Dora Guidalotti del Bene, also a merchant's wife and Margherita's contemporary, and

---

ence: Firenze University Press, 2010), and Paolo Nanni, *Ragionare tra mercanti: Per una rilettura della personalità di Francesco di Marco Datini (1335ca–1410)* (Pisa: Pacini, 2010).

2. In Boccaccio's tale (day 10, tale 10), Griselda remained docile and obedient to a husband who tested her virtue with ever more inventive forms of cruelty. Giovanni Boccaccio, *Decameron*, ed. Antonio Quaglio (Milan: Garzanti, 1974), 927–39.

3. We have translated all but one of the letters that are transcribed in the CD-ROM edition of Margherita's letters to Francesco. This most complete edition dates a much-damaged letter (folio 1401879) as 3.9.1400, but it is more likely to have been written in 1398. Only the date 3 September remains. Because of the difficulty of placing this letter chronologically and its fragmentary condition, we decided not to include it here. See note 548 in letter 218.

4. On this theme see Carolyn James, "Woman's Work in a Man's World: The Letters of Margherita Datini (1384–1410)," in Nigro, ed., *Francesco di Marco Datini*, 53–72.

three written in the 1360s by a Venetian woman named Cataruza.[5] The letters of Dora del Bene share Margherita's lively, colloquial tone and her concern with domestic detail. The Datini collection, however, offers unique riches. Margherita's more extensive correspondence makes it possible to study both her epistolary voice and her relationship with her husband over time. The collection also has the advantage of breadth, because many letters written by associates, friends, and relatives in her close-knit community also survive in the same archive. This allows us to reconstruct, in unusual detail, the context for the dramas that play out in the Datini couple's exchanges.[6] For much of her life Margherita was only semiliterate, and nearly all of her letters were dictated to various scribes. Despite this lack of formal training, once she was forced by circumstance to communicate with Francesco by letter, Margherita took firm authorial control of the dictation process. Her correspondence, therefore, provides interesting evidence of how an intelligent and determined woman successfully adapted the mercantile letter—a ubiquitous, practical, dynamically evolving subgenre of epistolary writing—for her own purposes.[7]

Margherita's Early Life

Margherita's life had scarcely begun when her fate, and that of her family, was profoundly affected by the political factionalism endemic to late-medieval Florence. Her parents, Domenico Bandini and Dianora Gherardini, both belonged to ancient, knightly families that were regarded with suspicion by the major guildsmen and wealthy merchants who dominated the Florentine republic. Resentful of their

5. Three letters written by the noble Venetian widow Cataruza were preserved by the procurators of San Marco as evidence about property division within her family. The extant letters of Dora del Bene were written to her husband and sons. See Guia Passerini, "Dora Guidalotti del Bene: Le lettere (1381–92)," *Letteratura italiana antica* 4 (2003): 101–59, and Linda Guzzetti, "Donne e scrittura nel tardo trecento," *Archivio veneto* 152 (1999): 5–31.

6. See, for example, Ser Lapo Mazzei, *Lettere di un notaro a un mercante del secolo XV, con altre lettere e documenti,* ed. Cesare Guasti (Florence: Le Monnier, 1880).

7. On the evolution of merchant letters, see Jérôme Hayez, "'Io non so scrivere a l'amicho per siloscismi': Jalons pour une lecture de la lettre marchande toscane de la fin du Moyen Âge," *I Tatti Studies: Essays in the Renaissance* 7 (1997): 37–79.

exclusion from participation in government, a group of twelve magnates, including Bandini and some of his Gherardini relatives, staged an unsuccessful coup against the republican regime toward the end of 1360. Bandini and another conspirator, Niccolò del Buono, were captured and executed. The others, including Dianora's male kin, were exiled, and their property within the city was confiscated.[8] Although the Florentine government made some provision for the widow by giving her a house that had belonged to her husband in the quarter of Santo Spirito as compensation for her dowry, Dianora and her six children surely found themselves in difficult circumstances.[9]

Margherita must have been the youngest child, born only months before her father's execution, because in a letter of February 1385 Francesco Datini refers to her entering her twenty-fifth year.[10] It remains unclear how exactly Dianora Gherardini and her children fared in the 1360s. The widow might have remained in Florence until her sons reached their teens and became subject to the laws that had forced their older male relatives into exile. Margherita's sister Francesca married the merchant Niccolò dell'Ammannato Tecchini and continued to live in Florence. The rest of the family moved to Avignon, probably with the help of a relative who was already settled among the Florentine colony of merchants there. The presence of Dianora and her children in the papal capital, a city of approximately twenty thousand people, is documented from the early 1370s.[11] It was here that Margherita met her future husband.

Francesco di Marco Datini was born in Prato around 1335. His early years, like his wife's, were also traumatic. He and his brother,

8. Gene Brucker, *Florentine Politics and Society 1343–1378* (Princeton, NJ: Princeton University Press, 1962), 187.

9. Jérôme Hayez has established that this Florentine house was Bandini property, probably given to Dianora by the Florentine Commune as a refund of her dowry when her husband was executed. The widow apparently used it to raise loans. Consequently it became legally encumbered and caused familial disputes.

10. Francesco to Margherita Datini, 23 February 1385, *Le lettere di Francesco Datini*, 31–35 (34). In Francesco's 1384 tax report, Margherita is said to be 24 (Archivio di Stato, Florence, Estimo 217, folio 388v). I am grateful to Jérôme Hayez for this archival reference.

11. Jérôme Hayez, "Préliminaires à une prosopographie avignonnaise du XIVe siècle," *Mélanges de l'École française de Rome: Moyen Âge, temps modernes* 100 (1988): 113–24 (121–24).

Stefano, were orphaned after the Black Death swept through Tuscany in the summer of 1348. The brothers were cared for by their guardian and relative, Piero di Giunta del Rosso (Francesco remained intimate with Rosso's descendants all his life), and by Monna Piera di Pratese Boschetti, who took them into her home. In May 1349 Francesco was apprenticed to a Florentine merchant, but after less than a year he set off to seek his fortune in Avignon, the most vibrant financial center in Europe. The opportunities for profit and advancement in Avignon were considerable, and Francesco proved to be an energetic and talented businessman. As Luciana Frangioni has shown, he sold arms and other iron wares such as nails and needles, and he marketed various kinds of cloth and hides.[12] He also produced and sold salt.[13] These entrepreneurial activities soon made him wealthy.

In 1376, when he was about forty, Francesco finally heeded his foster mother and friends in Prato, who advised him to marry so that he might produce a legitimate heir.[14] The merchant had apparently become well acquainted with Dianora and her children. He chose the sixteen-year-old Margherita as his wife, fully confident (if we are to believe his letters home to Prato) that his friendship with her family would ensure the success of this marriage. "I know them and they know me. We have been friends for a long time and I know them better than anyone else," he wrote.[15] In many ways Francesco's judgment proved to be sound, but if he chose Margherita for the intelligence, moral integrity, and good sense that emerge clearly from her correspondence, he may have underestimated the effects of his own quick temper and strong will on a similarly disposed person. In 1381 Francesco praised his wife to his brother-in-law, Niccolò dell'Ammannato Tecchini, as respectful, obedient, and without undue pride in her no-

---

12. Luciana Frangioni, *Chiedere e ottenere: L'approvvigionamento di prodotti di successo della bottega Datini di Avignone nel XIV secolo* (Florence: Opuslibri, 2002).

13. Christiane Villain-Gandossi, *Comptes du sel (Libro di ragione e conto di salle) de Francesco di Marco Datini pour sa compagnie d'Avignon, 1376–1379* (Paris: Bibliothèque Nationale, 1969).

14. For a brief biography of Francesco Datini, see Federigo Melis, *Aspetti della vita economica medievale*, vol. 1 (Siena: Monte dei Paschi di Siena, 1962), ch. 1.

15. *Le lettere di Margherita Datini*, 4.

ble Gherardini blood.[16] Letters Margherita wrote several years later suggest that she outgrew such youthful modesty and malleability, if there was ever any truth in Francesco's boast. She was certainly aware of her aristocratic lineage and was not averse to pointing out her husband's more humble background when he annoyed her (letter 12).

Dianora Gherardini seems to have shared aspects of her daughter's robust temperament. Her amicable relationship with her son-in-law in the early period of their acquaintance was soured by later conflicts about money. In 1384 she demanded an exorbitant price when Francesco asked to rent her house in Florence. Eventually she bequeathed the property to Iacopo di Cianghello Girolli da Cantagallo, the husband of Margherita's sister Isabetta. Iacopo, or Giachi as he was known (letter 12), was in financial trouble by early 1386. Dianora's decision to leave the Florentine house to Isabetta and her spouse was probably influenced by the fact that she lived with them in Avignon and shared the consequences of the couple's ill fortune.[17] Even on her deathbed in May 1388, Dianora Gherardini remained resolute that she owed nothing to Francesco or to her other son-in-law, Niccolò dell'Ammannato Tecchini. When Giachi and Isabetta tried to sell the Florentine house after Dianora's death, their relatives in Tuscany challenged the will and impeded the sale for many years.[18] Francesco claimed that he was owed money from the disputed estate because he had never received his wife's dowry.[19] Margherita apparently felt some bitterness about the financial dealings of her natal family, whose behavior, she claimed, she could never fully reveal to her husband. In a letter of 1399 to her brother, Bartolomeo Bandini, Margherita reminded him that of all the siblings, she alone had received nothing from her father's estate.[20]

---

16. Iris Origo, *The Merchant of Prato: Francesco di Marco Datini 1335–1410* (New York: Knopf, 1957), 193–94.

17. See Jérôme Hayez, "Un facteur siennois de Francesco di Marco Datini: Andrea di Bartolomeo di Ghino et sa correspondance (1383–1389)," *Bollettino dell'Opera del vocabolario italiano* 10 (2005): 203–397 (236–37).

18. See Margherita's letters 12 and 20.

19. Francesco Datini's will mentions the fact that Margherita's dowry was never paid by her family. See Mazzei, *Lettere di un notaro*, 1:27–28.

20. Margherita's letter to her brother is translated in the notes to letter 211.

Homecoming

In late 1382, Francesco resolved at last to return to Italy. He and his household left Avignon and traveled by mule over the Alps to Italy. The party of eleven stopped to do business in Milan for a week and stayed for some days in towns along the way, such as Asti, Cremona, and Bologna.[21] In spite of the leisurely pace, traveling over rugged and unfamiliar terrain in midwinter must have been a considerable adventure for Margherita; although, as the letters show, she was certainly not the only woman in her circle to travel between Tuscany and the Provençal capital.[22] The Datini couple and their companions arrived in Prato in January 1383. Francesco immediately set about establishing a warehouse there and transforming the small house he had bought when he was still in Avignon into a splendid residence. Within two years of his return, the merchant was also overseeing a new branch of his company in Pisa and traveling constantly between Prato and Florence, where he also set up a warehouse and rented a fine house.

Margherita's first letters to her husband were sent from their Florentine home. In comparison to Prato, its tiny dependent, Florence was a sophisticated metropolis of considerable size, although its population had fallen from 100,000 to less than 40,000 following the plague outbreak of 1348. Here, back in the city she had left as a child, Margherita was reunited with her sister Francesca, her brother-in-law, their numerous children, and other relatives, including her father's sister, Monna Giovanna, the widow of Salvestro Cavalcanti. Several of her mother's brothers lived just beyond the borders of the Florentine state, and even her ninety-year-old maternal grandfather, Cione Gherardini, known as Pellicia, seems to have been still alive when Margherita returned to Tuscany.[23]

In the years following the move from Avignon, Francesco and Margherita were often apart. At first Margherita did not realize that

21. For the itinerary and other details of the journey to Italy see Melis, *Aspetti della vita economica*, 51–53.

22. Letters 3 and 4, for example, refer to Monna Beatrice's sea voyage to join her husband in Avignon.

23. Francesco Datini mentions the death of Pellicia in a letter to Margherita of 4 August 1385: *Le lettere di Francesco Datini*, 36–38.

this would be a permanent feature of their life together. Unhappy about her husband's long stays in Pisa between March 1384 and July 1385, in February 1385 she declared that she would come "not only to Pisa, but to the end of the earth" to ensure his welfare and to help him expedite his business affairs (letter 5). Her move to Pisa, discussed by the couple on numerous occasions, was however endlessly postponed, and did not eventuate. Margherita constantly reproached Francesco for living in a frenetic and disordered fashion when he was away from her. For example, in January 1386 she wrote: "You send me messages telling me to be happy and to enjoy myself but you stay awake until morning and dine at midnight and lunch at sunset. I will not be happy and will never be able to rest if you don't live differently" (letter 10).

During the 1380s, major building activity at the Datini residence in Prato often made it necessary for Margherita to stay in Florence; but as the provenance of the letters make clear, sometimes she had to live in Prato to supervise the builders and other artisans working at their house while Francesco remained in Florence (letter 16).[24] We know from the merchant's account books that in early 1387, during one of these early marital separations, Francesco fathered a male child by the fifteen-year-old servant Ghirigora, who had accompanied the Datinis from Avignon.[25] Ghirigora is mentioned by Margherita only in her first surviving letter, of January 1384. This baby died in March 1388 at six months old, and Francesco buried him with his kin in the church of San Francesco in Prato.

In 1392 Francesco had another illegitimate child: Ginevra, whose mother was a young household slave called Lucia. She is first referred to by Margherita in a letter of October 1389. Lucia was often sent to serve Francesco when he was away from home (letter 217). On good terms with her mistress (and eventually freed), in 1399 she married one of the servants and in 1401 the couple had the first of

24. On Francesco Datini's building program, see Simonetta Cavaciocchi, "The Merchant and Building," in Nigro, ed., Francesco di Marco Datini, 131–63; and Jérôme Hayez and Diana Toccafondi, *Il palazzo di Francesco Datini a Prato: Una casa fatta per durare mille anni* (Florence: Edizioni Polistampa, 2011).
25. Cavaciocchi, "The Merchant and Building," 52.

their several children together. In recognition of her long and faithful service, Francesco left Lucia and her family a bequest in his will.[26]

There are hints, such as in letter 24, that women in Margherita's circle were anxious about their husbands' extramarital sexual activities. She herself refers ironically to her brother-in-law's attachment to his maidservant (letter 7), and her enjoinder on Francesco in February 1385 to "remember what Niccolò dell'Ammannato says about women in the Marches" (letter 3) was a veiled appeal to her husband not to roam sexually. In September 1394, Francesco acquired a young female slave, and he wrote optimistically to his agent in Venice that the girl's face, "as flat as a board," could not possibly arouse his wife's jealousy.[27] His comment suggests that Margherita may not have resigned herself easily to her husband's liaisons. By now, however, afflicted for years with gynecological problems, Margherita recognized that she was unlikely to conceive a child of her own. Whatever she may have felt about the birth of Ginevra in 1392, six years later she wrote: "Don't worry about Ginevra because fortunately I don't think her sore throat will get any worse. I don't need to tell you this because I know you are convinced that I treat her better than if she were my own daughter, and I do indeed think of her as mine." This extract from letter 189 makes it clear that she not only wholeheartedly embraced the opportunity to raise her husband's child, she also lavished affection on the little girl.

Only twenty-five of Margherita's letters, and seventeen of her husband's, are dated between 1384 and 1389, suggesting that during these years the couple were together more than they would be later; and there are no surviving letters after 1389 until 1394. Lapo Mazzei, who became a friend of Francesco after 1390 and was a sympathetic ally of Margherita by 1394, provides some clues about what occurred in the early 1390s. Francesco moved his household to neighboring Pistoia in mid-1390 to avoid an outbreak of plague in Prato, and Mazzei wrote to him there between September 1390 and April 1391.[28] Husband and wife shared the same household in Pistoia, but once the epidemic died down, Francesco seems to have returned to his usual itinerant ways after mid-1391. The birth of Ginevra in 1392 suggests

26. Mazzei, *Lettere di un notaro*, 2:278.

27. Melis, *Aspetti della vita economica*, 48, n. 5.

28. Mazzei, *Lettere di un notaro*, 1:3–9.

that this was indeed the case. The complete lack of letters in these years would suggest, however, that Francesco did not stray far from home. Once his remarkable house in Prato was finally finished, he became just as obsessively focused on overseeing the building of Il Palco, his villa that looked down on Prato from across the Bisenzio River. So many men were employed on this project that Francesco had to order "a good horn" from Florence to call the workers together at meal breaks.[29] Il Palco was largely finished by 1395, but this ambitious building program was to become yet another source of tension at a difficult time in the marriage.

Three fourths of Margherita's surviving letters were written between 1394 and 1399, years in which Francesco was extraordinarily beset with worries. The fact that he had a house and flourishing business in Florence, combined with the ambiguity about whether he was a resident of Prato or Florence, meant that Florentine officials could force him, as a very wealthy noncitizen, to contribute heavily to Florence's communal tax assessments and to make substantial loans to the commune. Consequently, the merchant had to pay high taxes in both Florence and Prato. To solve this problem, which was particularly acute in the early 1390s, Francesco reluctantly became a Florentine citizen and spent eight months in the city in 1394, lobbying powerful friends who might help him to minimize what he regarded as unfair assaults on his fortune. During these months, Margherita remained in Prato, trying to protect his financial interests there by maintaining relationships with important local political figures. She also kept her husband informed about any useful gossip or news circulating in the town, and performed the administrative and domestic tasks necessitated by his absence.[30]

In April 1394, Margherita even intervened on Francesco's behalf in a less conventional way by sending two (dictated) letters to the notary Lapo Mazzei. These letters were carefully staged attempts to catch the attention of Guido del Palagio: Mazzei's neighbor in Florence, and a man of enormous prestige and political influence whose

---

29. See Cavaciocchi, "The Merchant and Building," 155.

30. See James, "Woman's Work," 65–69.

friendship Francesco was cultivating assiduously.[31] They were letters
of recommendation, albeit rather unsophisticated ones.[32] The notary
referred jokingly to Margherita as his disciple in a letter to Francesco
of 1396. It seems likely that Mazzei introduced her to the basic rules
of formal letter writing.[33] Although an accomplished writer in a mercantile context, Francesco himself felt ill-equipped to compose letters
to very important people because he had inadequate knowledge of
the *ars dictaminis*, the art of letter writing taught widely at the time.
The merchant usually asked Mazzei or one of the other notaries in his
circle to draft letters to influential political figures for him. It is no surprise, then, that the novelty of a barely literate woman even attempting to write a letter in recommendation of her husband caught the
imagination of her intended audience. Del Palagio, to whom Mazzei
showed Margherita's letters, was no doubt amused by their amateurish
lack of polish. He was also apparently delighted by the earnestly expressed declarations of friendship that were central to this epistolary
genre, and promised to bring his wife to spend Easter with the Datinis
in Prato.[34] Margherita's family and friends were equally pleased by the
success of her unconventional initiative, which further cemented relations between Francesco and a crucial Florentine ally.

Margherita had been attempting to learn to read during this
period. Although Mazzei had misgivings about female literacy, he
encouraged her—by supplying suitable religious texts with clear lettering and by writing to her in November 1395 in a large, simplified
script that she could readily decipher.[35] He knew that Margherita
would draw comfort from this spiritual sustenance; and perhaps he

31. For a contemporary view of Guido del Palagio, see Buonaccorso Pitti, *Cronica*, ed. Alberto Bacchi della Lega (Bologna: Romagnolo dall'Acqua, 1905), 75.

32. Margherita Datini to Ser Lapo Mazzei, Archivio di Stato, Prato, Archivio Datini, 1089,
folios 1402969 and 1402670. On this incident, see Carolyn James, "A Woman's Path to Literacy: The Letters of Margherita Datini, 1384–1410," in *Practices of Gender in Late Medieval and Early Modern Europe*, ed. Megan Cassidy-Welch and Peter Sherlock (Turnhout:
Brepols, 2008), 43–56.

33. Lapo Mazzei to Francesco Datini in *Lettere di un notaro*, 1:163.

34. See Lapo Mazzei's letter to Margherita Datini of 10 April 1394, in *Lettere di un notaro*,
2:179–80.

35. Lapo Mazzei to Margherita Datini, 13 November 1395, in *Lettere di un notaro*, 2:181.

hoped secretly that the examples of humble and obedient women represented in stories about the Virgin Mary and female saints would soften her willfulness. Mazzei's abundant surviving letters suggest that he was a kind person, deeply committed to Christian charity; but his attitudes toward women were conventional. He was sympathetic to the difficulties of Margherita's life, but just as ambivalent about her forceful personality and independent spirit as Francesco was. In July 1394, apparently charged by Margherita to write sternly to her husband about his wayward work habits and neglect of his spiritual welfare, the notary expressed his relief to the now-elderly merchant that she was not privy to the frivolous male jokes they exchanged in their letters.[36] Mazzei did, however, also attempt to mediate on Margherita's behalf. While regretting that she was not as patient and docile as she was wise and capable, he urged Francesco to remember how much she had to tolerate. He compared her to a monk who could hold his liquor despite drinking a whole cask of wine: "If you only knew how much she restrains herself by not responding in kind to all the domestic turmoil, you would have to admit that she is meekness itself."[37]

In December 1396, Mazzei heard rumors about Margherita's progress in calligraphy and composition. He wrote to Francesco and asked him to encourage his wife to send a letter so that he might know "whether her style was now that of a nun, or a female hermit, or that of a pedant, or just a simple woman."[38] There is no evidence that Margherita replied to Mazzei's teasing message. She had insufficient leisure to acquire dexterity with a quill and therefore continued to dictate letters as she had always done, using her own hand in less than ten of the surviving letters, when no scribe was available. Some of the autograph letters that Margherita wrote in the early months of 1399, several years after her campaign to improve her handwriting, reveal her very imperfect mastery of calligraphy. A letter of 12 September 1402 (letter 229), sent from Florence and written when Margherita was ill in bed and reluctant to seek the help of an amanuensis, is a particularly clear example of the physical effort that autograph writing

---

36. Lapo Mazzei to Francesco Datini, 12 July 1394, in *Lettere di un notaro*, 1:60–61.

37. Lapo Mazzei to Francesco Datini, 15 September 1394, in *Lettere di un notaro*, 1:71–72.

38. Lapo Mazzei to Francesco Datini, 4 December 1396, in *Lettere di un notaro*, 1:159.

still required (see frontispiece, for a reproduction of the manuscript of this letter).

The letters of 1394 explain Margherita's difficulty in finding time to improve her reading and writing. They document the diverse tasks to which she attended in Prato, during her husband's long stay in Florence. In mid-April she complained bad-temperedly: it was tactless of her husband to protest about the handwriting of her dictated letters, because he had left her to organize so many things in Prato that even the Florentine Signoria's secretary would surely have less to write than her scribe (letter 56). By May 1394 Margherita was even busier. She was nursing one of Francesco's employees who had tertian fever, taking steps to ensure that a young relative's worm infestation did not spread to the rest of the household, and attending to the slave Lucia, who had hit her head on the edge of the well. At the same time she oversaw the provisioning of the household, the builders working at Il Palco, and the collection of money from her husband's debtors. When Francesco wrote that she should pay a social visit to Lapo Mazzei's elderly mother, who lived in the country beyond Prato at Grignano, Margherita responded waspishly—annoyed that he was oblivious to the domestic emergencies and other difficulties she negotiated in his absence (letter 63)

In October 1394 the Datinis were reunited in Florence, but by March of the following year Francesco had been to Prato seven times, frequently for extended periods (letter 87). He was often at Il Palco, overseeing the final stages of work. The dates of Margherita's letters from Florence suggest she did not attend the party he hosted at the villa in March, to show off the fine frescoes he had commissioned to decorate the rooms.[39] Meanwhile, the tax situation was still unresolved; and Margherita grew increasingly worried about the effect of rumors traveling from Prato to Florence about Francesco's lavish building activities. Such intimations of great wealth would not help his case. Their dialogue remained fractious. The merchant complained about his worries and sleepless nights, while instructing his wife pedantically about every detail of her duties. He continued to expect conventional obedience from his spouse, but loaded her with

---

39. Melis, *Aspetti della vita economica*, 60.

responsibilities requiring unusual initiative and intelligence. Margherita responded with her habitual blend of concern and exasperation.

Tensions smoldered in late 1394; and in 1395, fueled in part by their months of separation, the merchant's stubbornness and distracted neglect of his wife flared into a crisis. In early June Margherita's servants told her they had been interrogated by Fattorino, one of her husband's employees, about her activities in Florence (letter 91). Francesco had heard rumors in Prato that his wife's relatives were constantly dining at his house in Florence and that Margherita had gone to nearby Fiesole with a party of women, without informing him or seeking permission. Rather than writing to Margherita for clarification, Francesco had accepted Fattorino's account. Severely vexed by her husband's lack of trust, on 3 June 1395 Margherita provided a long, angry explanation. She admitted that she had been to Fiesole, to visit the church of Saint Romulus and to take advantage of a special indulgence to mark the unveiling of a votive image of the Virgin Mary. She had also dined with her Florentine relatives, although at their house, not hers, as she explained: "I feel embarrassed, more for the sake of the others than myself, because one can do nothing without everyone knowing about it. They would be right to hold it against us but there was no revelry. No one ever dined here except Tina on one occasion" (letter 91). The tone of Margherita's letter conveys her mounting frustration over miscommunication caused by distance and rumor.

As Lapo Mazzei later informed Francesco, Margherita had sent him a message that she was at the end of her tether: "Tell Ser Lapo that I won't stay here a moment more. Any day now I will pack my bags and take myself to Prato." Apparently the notary had dismissed this threat, and had not alerted Francesco to his wife's intentions. Even if he regarded his friend's "roughened soul" and "frozen heart" as largely to blame for Margherita's distress, Mazzei underestimated her fiery resolve to end the misunderstandings with her husband by joining him in Prato.[40] Francesco should have had no need of a warning from Mazzei, because his wife had signaled her intentions in a letter of 5 June (letter 93). Three days later there could be no doubt about her mood:

---

40. Lapo Mazzei to Francesco Datini, 9 June 1395, in *Lettere di un notaro*, 1:97–98.

> I remember: when I told you at Easter I had been in-
> formed you would be away for the whole summer,
> you said it wasn't true, and it was to be only two days.
> Count how many days it has been since Easter. Your
> resolve not to keep promising to return soon without
> doing so would please me greatly, more because it
> would spare you the trouble of writing excuses than
> for my sake. [letter 94]

Francesco wrote to appease his wife on 10 June, admitting she was
partly right; but the letter probably arrived too late to prevent Margherita from packing up the whole household in Florence and leaving
for Prato. Mazzei reported that this behavior shocked the Florentine
neighbors. The scandal surrounding her sudden tempestuous departure from Florence might explain why Margherita did not return there
for some years (letter 216).

The fraught incident of June 1395 did not change the dynamic
between husband and wife. Francesco spent long periods in Florence
over the following years; Margherita remained in Prato, and his tactless communications continued to provoke her. In August 1398, for
example, Francesco unwisely assessed his marriage against that of
Guido del Palagio, whose wife, Niccolosa di Bartolomeo degli Albizzi,
had apparently never given her husband cause to be angry. Margherita
replied scornfully to Francesco's hurtful criticism, pointing out that he
could not compare himself to the exemplary Guido or imply that she
should follow Niccolosa's model of wifely virtue when the unconventional circumstances of her life in Prato made such emulation impossible: "Guido cannot be compared to other men. He treats his wife as a
lady, not like an innkeeper's wife. It is fifteen blessed years since I came
here and I have lived as if in an inn, and I don't think there is a single
innkeeper who runs the inn at the same time as organizing building
works" (letter 175). Margherita was well aware that she too was a lady,
whose aristocratic origins and connections were valuable assets that
her husband could more usefully exploit, if only he recognized the
folly of compromising her dignity and reputation by requiring her
to perform indecorous tasks. This, however, was a marital battle she
failed to win.

Several months after this exchange, Margherita finally moved back to the Florentine house, but she found that the adversity suffered by her relatives in the late 1390s had altered her relationship with them. By 1398 Niccolò dell'Ammannato Tecchini was bankrupt, and Margherita's sister Francesca was forced to take in needlework. Their daughter, Tina, who had often been a guest in the Datini household and a companion to Ginevra, now became Francesco's financial responsibility. In May 1399, Margherita's brother, Bartolomeo Bandini, appeared in Florence unexpectedly, ill and destitute. Margherita and Francesca, thinking that he might be seized and put in jail for taxation arrears and other debts, kept their distance for fear that if he were arrested, they too would be implicated. This was a painful decision for Margherita; she was torn between love for her brother and concern for her husband's interests.

To make matters worse, by the end of 1399 the plague was once more threatening Tuscany. Margherita urged Francesco to join her in Florence as quickly as possible. The larger city was a safer place to be, she argued. "Here in Florence there are better doctors than in Prato. Therefore I believe that if either of us were to fall ill, the best chance of survival would be found here in Florence" (letter 216). The situation deteriorated rapidly even there, and Francesco acted decisively, moving his household over the Apennines to Bologna, where the plague had already done its damage. Many friends who stayed in Tuscany died, and Lapo Mazzei kept Francesco abreast of news from Florence. The notary's own family was tragically struck. Two of his sons died in his arms within hours of each other, and his daughter Antonia hovered dangerously at death's door before finally recovering. Margherita's sister Francesca also died; although not from the plague, but in poverty and after a long, agonizing illness. Mazzei reported the painful news in June 1401, just months before Margherita's return from Bologna to Florence in September of that year.[41]

---

41. Lapo Mazzei to Francesco Datini, 18 June 1401, in *Lettere di un notaro*, 1:420.

Last Years

It is more difficult to reconstruct in detail the final years of Margherita's life. A letter to Francesco dated 18 May 1402 provides a rare glimpse of her feelings about the infertility that had blighted her marriage. She refers in that letter to the suffering of a woman whose baby had just died: "I think now of the favor that God has given me, since I will not have to swallow this same pill." It may be that this baby was Francesco's, his last chance to have at least an illegitimate male heir, because Margherita expresses sympathy for his sadness: "I am sorry for you because of the event that happened, both out of love of you and because I think it will grieve you in many ways" (letter 228). By now the couple accepted it as God's will that there would be no heir to the Datini fortune; they took pleasure in raising Ginevra, whose marriage in 1407 to Lionardo di Tommaso di Giunta was a splendid affair.[42]

In his last years the merchant prepared for death, turning his mind at last to the fate of his soul, as Margherita and others had been enjoining him to do for decades. With the encouragement and advice of Lapo Mazzei, Francesco made elaborate plans to secure salvation by bequeathing his entire fortune to the poor. To ensure that clerics would have nothing to do with the managing of his bequest, he established a board consisting of trusted intimates to oversee the administration of his Ceppo Nuovo ("New Fund"), named so as to distinguish it from the Ceppo Vecchio, an older source of communal charity. The board comprised Margherita, Lapo Mazzei, and several business partners such as Ginevra's husband Lionardo, and Luca del Sera, the husband of Margherita's niece Tina. Margherita's inclusion was a departure from convention: women might informally advise such bodies but rarely were members. It was a final, public recognition of Margherita's abilities and of the long, if discordant, collaboration so amply documented in the couple's correspondence. The merchant's will made careful provision for the comfort of his wife, and of Ginevra who had been welcomed into their life together. Although the two

42. See the documents regarding Ginevra's lavish clothing and the wedding feast in Giampiero Nigro, *Il tempo liberato: Festa e svago nella città di Francesco Datini* (Prato: Istituto Internazionale di Storia Economica, 1994), 219–31.

women lived in Florence, Francesco provided that La Chiusura, a property just within the city wall of Prato that was mentioned regularly in Margherita's letters, would be available for their visits.

The few letters between 1402 and 1406 suggest that relations between the Datinis were more peaceful, as age forced Francesco to concede more autonomy to his ever-capable wife. The final flurry in January 1410 reveals a confident Margherita, sure of her decisions as she prepared the house in Prato for the arrival of a cardinal and his entourage of forty-five. As usual, she reported scrupulously to her husband, sometimes more than once a day. In August 1410, Francesco died. Over her remaining thirteen years, Margherita devoted herself to good works as a Dominican tertiary. Surviving letters concerning the Ceppo suggest that she also continued overseeing her husband's legacy. She died in Florence, the city of her birth, in 1423; she was buried there in the Dominican church of Santa Maria Novella, among her aristocratic relatives, rather than with her husband in the church of San Francesco in Prato.[43]

Margherita Datini and Women's Letters

Margherita Datini's letters have been available in print for more than thirty years, but they have attracted surprisingly little scholarly attention, despite the qualities they share with the well-known collections of Alessandra Strozzi and the English Paston women.[44] Maria Luisa Doglio's important essay on Italian women's letter writing between 1350 and 1650, for example, moves from the famous epistles of Saint Catherine of Siena, written between c. 1372 and 1380, to the mid-fifteenth-century letters of Alessandra Strozzi. Doglio mistakenly de-

---

43. See Guasti's preface in *Lettere di un notaro*, 1:77, n. 2.

44. Alessandra Macinghi Strozzi, *Lettere di una gentildonna fiorentina dal secolo XV ai figliuoli esuli*, ed. Cesare Guasti (Florence: Sansoni, 1877); Alessandra Macinghi Strozzi, *Selected Letters of Alessandra Strozzi*, trans. Heather Gregory (Berkeley: University of California Press, 1997); Norman Davis, ed., *Paston Letters and Papers of the Fifteenth Century*, 2 vols. (Oxford: Oxford University Press, 1971–1976). On Margherita Datini's letters, see Ann Crabb, "'If I could write': Margherita Datini and Letter Writing, 1385–1410," *Renaissance Quarterly* 60 (2007): 1170–1206; James, "A Woman's Path to Literacy," 43–56; and James, "Woman's Work," 53–72. For earlier studies, see bibliography, this volume.

scribes the latter collection as the first surviving Italian letters by a lay woman, making no reference to the earlier letters of Margherita Datini.[45] A number of other books published during the last decade on Italian women's writing in the medieval and early modern period also ignore the Datini collection.

Several factors may explain this scholarly neglect of Margherita's letters. The most significant is that they survive in a large mercantile archive comprising 150,000 documents and six hundred ledgers, discovered in 1870 beneath a walled-up staircase in the Datini palace, now the State Archive of Prato. Generations of economic historians have pored over the archive's financial records and other papers generated by Francesco Datini's various companies. A business archive is not, however, an obvious place to look for material on medieval women's writing. In addition, Iris Origo's limited use of Margherita's correspondence in her popular book about Francesco Datini, *The Merchant of Prato*, first published in 1957, did not signal its value to social and cultural scholarship.

Also, as mentioned above, Margherita dictated the majority of her letters to various scribes, a number of whom were apprentice clerks, inexperienced at taking dictation and not sophisticated letter writers themselves. Although it was customary for busy people to dictate their letters, uncertainty about the nature of Margherita's epistolary collaborations, along with questions about the extent to which a semiliterate woman can be said to be the author of letters written with the help of a scribe, has inhibited systematic analysis of this correspondence. Only recently has the issue of scribal mediation been tackled in the study of women's letters.[46] A close reading of those

45. Maria Luisa Doglio, "Letter Writing, 1350–1650," in *A History of Women's Writing in Italy*, ed. Letizia Panizza and Sharon Wood (Cambridge: Cambridge University Press, 2000), 16. See also Gabriella Zarri, ed., *Per lettera: La scrittura epistolare femminile tra archivio e tipografia secoli XV–XVII* (Rome: Viella, 1999), and Letizia Panizza, ed., *Women in Renaissance Culture and Society* (Oxford: Legenda, 2000).

46. Deborah Stott, "'I am the same Cornelia I have always been': Reading Cornelia Collonello's Letters to Michelangelo," in *Women's Letters across Europe, 1400–1700: Form and Persuasion*, ed. Jane Couchman and Ann Crabb (Aldershot: Ashgate, 2005), 79–100; Susan Broomhall, "'Burdened with small children': Women Defining Poverty in Sixteenth-Century Tours," in *Women's Letters across Europe*, 223–37; James Daybell, "Women's Letters and Letter Writing in England, 1540–1603: An Introduction to the Issues of Authorship

presented here suggests that Catherine of Siena was not alone in using dictation to communicate coherently and effectively despite limited literacy.[47] Indeed, Margherita comments on some of these very
issues. Her correspondence explicitly discusses her independence
from—and collaboration with—her male scribe, her gradual mastery
of aspects of epistolary technique, and the contrasting attitudes of
husband and wife regarding what could be put into their letters. The
evidence suggests that what James Daybell and others have discovered
about the fifteenth and sixteenth centuries applies to the preceding
period: women with various levels of formal literacy used epistolary
forms with dexterity and confidence. Letters were a more important
area of female activity in the fourteenth century than scholars have
previously thought.[48]

Another possible reason for the neglect of Margherita Datini's
letters is that scholars may have been wary of their characteristically
dense domestic detail and the blurred, even chaotic, boundary between private life and business or public affairs. This intermixing may
be a consequence of the circumstances of composition. Margherita
frequently dictated her letters hurriedly as the bearer was waiting to
depart for Florence, Pisa, or Prato, and the Datini correspondents
were sometimes deliberately cryptic to limit damaging gossip by the
scribe. They did not need to spell out all the matters they discussed,

and Construction," *Shakespeare Studies* 27 (January 1999): 161–86. In relation to women's
writing, see Lynn Staley Johnson, "The Trope of the Scribe and the Question of Literary
Authority in the Works of Julian of Norwich and Margery Kempe," *Speculum* 66, no. 4
(1991): 820–38; Julia Boffee, "Women Authors and Women's Literacy in Fourteenth- and
Fifteenth-Century England," in *Women and Literature in Britain, 1150–1500*, ed. Carol M.
Meale (Cambridge: Cambridge University Press, 1993), 159–82; and Margaret W. Ferguson,
"Renaissance concepts of the 'woman writer,'" in *Women and Literature in Britain 500–1700*,
ed. Helen Wilcox (Cambridge: Cambridge University Press, 1996), 143–68.

47. On writing and orality in Catherine of Siena's letters, see Karen Scott, "'Io Caterina':
Ecclesiastical Politics and Oral Culture in the Letters of Catherine of Siena," in *Dear Sis-
ter: Medieval Women and the Epistolary Genre*, ed. Karen Cherewatuk and Ulrike Wiethaus
(Philadelphia: University of Pennsylvania Press, 1993), 87–121, and Jane Tylus, *Reclaiming
Catherine of Siena: Literacy, Literature and the Signs of Others* (Chicago: Chicago University
Press, 2009).

48. James Daybell, ed., *Early Modern Women's Letter Writing, 1450–1700* (Basingstoke: Palgrave, 2001).

because they communicated frequently via letters and oral messages. In the mid-1390s they sometimes wrote every day, in running conversations resembling our own use of e-mails.

Some social and economic historians of the period value Margherita's pragmatic information; but this attention to prosaic detail tends to miss a compelling epistolary voice. Her frequent shifts from domestic routine to more intimate concerns are striking. Margherita made effective use of her letters for self-representation, recognizing intuitively that physical distance enabled more forthright communication about important issues, particularly Francesco's neglect of his health and spiritual welfare and her own desire for marital companionship. Conventional notions of wifely decorum could be set aside in letters, as Margherita herself observes. She sometimes relishes the medium's potential for cathartic release (in letter 12, for example).

Dictation and Collaborative Writing

Francesco first wrote of being struck by his wife's distinctive way with letters in January 1386. He wrote teasingly to her from Pisa: "Yesterday I received a letter from you that was very well dictated. I can't explain this. It made me think that you must have a friend who is teaching you to express yourself so well."[49] Francesco did not believe that Margherita had in fact composed the letter and was curious about who the scribe had been. In a letter to her that does not survive, and another to his employee Piero di Filippo Milanesi, Francesco asked whether Milanesi had composed the letter on Margherita's behalf. Margherita was pleased at first by her husband's praise, but became infuriated by his assumption that someone she regarded as untrustworthy had composed her letter (letters 11 and 12). Her angry reply left Francesco in no doubt: she was firmly in charge of the dictation process, and was determined to choose a scribe at her own discretion. He hastened to placate Margherita, writing that if the first letter was well composed, the next so clearly captured her voice that he could be in no doubt about its authorship. In typical fashion, he then mused that this realization made him proud but also afraid. According to popular wisdom,

49. Francesco to Margherita Datini, 19 January 1386, in *Le lettere di Francesco Datini*, 40–41.

Margherita's inexplicable, miraculous ability to dictate letters so well meant that she would surely die soon.[50]

This exchange raises interesting issues. What was it about Margherita's letter of 16 January 1386 (letter 10) that alerted Francesco to her ability to use the scribe as a passive amanuensis rather than as the actual composer of her letter?

> You tell me not to remain forever a girl and say that we will be rewarded in accordance with the good we do here on earth. You are right. It is a good while since I left girlhood behind but I would like you not to remain the Francesco you have been since I first knew you, someone who has done nothing but inflict tribulation on his body and soul. You say, indeed you preach, that you will live a virtuous life, and every week of every month it is the same story. You have said this for ten years and now it seems to me that you intend to rest less than ever. (letter 10)

Francesco must have heard, through the dutiful transcription of a junior scribe, the exasperated lecturing and the intimate style of his wife's authentic voice. Margherita made the situation quite clear: if she did not have the apprentice Simone d'Andrea Bellandi to write her letters she would dictate to her brother-in-law, Niccolò dell'Ammannato Tecchini: "Only to those two would I reveal my secrets and to no one else" (letter 12). In his apologetic response, the busy merchant declared himself defeated.[51] However, he remained uncomfortable about such candor, and worried about the semipublic nature of their exchanges. Margherita, on the other hand, felt less inhibited: "Francesco, I acknowledge that I have written to you too freely and have demonstrated too much independence from you in telling you the truth. If you were here beside me I would not have spoken so boldly" (letter 12).

There is evidence in the letters of tension between Margherita and her scribes, and finding anyone competent to read incoming letters was often difficult. Frustration over such reliance may have

50. Francesco to Margherita Datini, 22 January 1386, in *Le lettere di Francesco Datini*, 41–45.

51. Francesco to Margherita Datini, 25 January 1386, in *Le lettere di Francesco Datini*, 46.

prompted her in the 1390s to improve her literacy. Of course, producing letters in her own hand did not necessarily mean that she wrote more intimately or freely; the labor of writing was more inhibiting than the ease of dictation.

Epistolary Conventions

Margherita's capacity for intelligent improvisation, joined with her determination to master the rules of formal letter writing, made her an adept dictator of clear and sometimes eloquent communications, adapted to the conventions of mercantile writing. Her letters are carefully dated, they acknowledge incoming correspondence, and they indicate to which letter or letters she is replying. In spite of her more emotive, unmeasured style that often intrudes on the standard template, she reports systematically on significant domestic matters and news from acquaintances. Margherita exceeded the simple delivery of information that Francesco expected, borrowing from an epistolary culture that combined pragmatic business concerns with the consolatory discourse of male friendship. There was an expectation that men would unburden themselves to their friends in letters; but there was little precedent for such written confidences with a wife, especially because low levels of female literacy called for mediation through scribes.

Nevertheless, the prescriptive advice with which the Datinis negotiated their relationship was laced with a kind of literary rhetoric. The elegant letters of Lapo Mazzei to Francesco show his familiarity with Latin culture and early Florentine humanist circles; but Margherita takes part also in the notary's pious sermonizing. The two campaigned together to reform Francesco, striving to convince him of the wrongheadedness of his approach to life. Their admonitory style suggests that they were both influenced by contemporary preachers such as Giovanni Dominici, whom we know they heard (letters 217, 230, and 232), and by spiritual advice from religious texts. Letter 84 provides a particularly notable example:

> Why is it that in this, and other matters, you don't do
> as you say you would with your children, if you had
> any? You say that if God took them away, you would
> accept your fate. If we were to place all our faith in
> Him, and accept what came, we wouldn't be subject
> to such passions. If we thought about death, and how
> little time we have on this earth, we wouldn't worry as
> much as we do, and we would allow ourselves to be
> guided by Him and accept everything that happens.

In contrast to her consolatory but reproving tone, the merchant preferred to instruct his wife directly on how to behave. He could not wean himself from this prescriptive mode, even when she was a mature woman who took such needless instruction amiss. Both husband and wife, however, recited the narrative of health and illness that was a perennial feature of Latin letters between friends, and related genres. Statements of concern for a correspondent's physical well-being were a familiar epistolary trope, demonstrating affection and caring for the absent body; and for the Datinis, they were an expression of marital love.

In other ways Margherita's language departs radically from the models available to her: the letters and learned talk of educated male contemporaries. The speed of written exchanges with her husband encouraged a strongly reactive mode, usually reflecting everyday speech more than the patterns of literary and spiritual rhetoric. Margherita's letters express a wider range of emotion than her husband's do, and many more examples of open anger. While Francesco occasionally teased and even deliberately provoked his wife, on the whole he preferred not to conduct a marital quarrel by letter. On the other hand, Margherita was frequently stung into a spirited rejoinder to the gossip that reached Francesco, through his networks of factors and associates. She could be cuttingly ironic, with sharp-tongued colloquial phrases calculated to demolish her husband's excuses.

Margherita was interested enough in contemporary epistolary conventions, and in challenging traditional expectations of women's capacity to participate in written culture, to maintain a clear sense of authorship in her letters and to try her hand at composing two formal letters of recommendation. There are, however, few dramatic or consistent stylistic differences between the early letters to her husband and the later ones, and there is little evidence that Margherita strove self-consciously to compose more elegant or well-crafted epistles as her literacy improved. The majority of her letters were written for pragmatic purposes, even if she readily took the opportunity to speak her mind. Her letters, extemporized at moments when the domestic routine slackened or was put to one side for the sake of urgent communication, capture a maturing voice and persona. Their tone becomes increasingly confident and authoritative, reflecting Margherita's awareness of her essential role in almost every aspect of her husband's life. Today's readers of her letters will encounter in them an unusual and impressive woman.

Carolyn James

A Note on the Translation

The letters of Margherita Datini present the modern translator with daunting challenges. The most obvious of these is the difficulty of finding an appropriate register in contemporary English to convey her lively and colloquial late-fourteenth-century Tuscan. As discussed above, Margherita was largely self-educated. Although her active role in her husband's affairs and her shrewd intelligence gave her an intuitive grasp of epistolary communication, the results of her linguistic improvisation as she dictated range from the strikingly articulate to the somewhat chaotic. The poor calligraphy of letters in Margherita's own hand, particularly the very early example of February 1388 (letter 17), was from lack of formal training; but the variations in spelling and grammatical forms were not. As Luca Serianni points out, from at least the eleventh and twelfth centuries the fluctuating influences of Lucca and Florence on Prato's linguistic development encouraged linguistic polymorphism, even in documents from the same hand.[1] Both Margherita and her scribes, themselves sometimes inexperienced as letter writers and likely to write colloquially, used elements of competing dialects rather erratically. Sometimes it is a matter of educated guesswork to identify subject and object in a sentence, or the correct attribution of adjectives whose suffixes do not distinguish singular and plural, or masculine and feminine. For verbs, there is sometimes no distinction between first and third person in the present tense; some first-person plurals coincide in present and perfect tenses; and uses of the conditional are often problematic.[2]

1. See Luca Serianni, *Testi pratesi della fine del Dugento e dei primi del Trecento* (Florence: Accademia della Crusca, 1977), 94–98.

2. A number of these linguistic differences, characteristic of early Italian, are explored in "Linguistica e italiano antico," a special issue of *Lingua e stile*, ed. Lorenzo Renzi and Antonietta Bisetto, 35, no. 4 (2000). Also important to our interpretations were Serianni, *Testi pratesi*; Neli Radanova-Kuseva and Maria Kitova-Vasileva, "L'espressione della posteriorità nell'italiano e nello spagnolo del Trecento," *Studia slavica hungarica* 35 (1989): 133–47; Neli Radanova-Kuseva, "Sui valori del condizionale nell'antico italiano (il Trecento)," *Rassegna italiana di linguistica applicata* 19 (1987): 55–65; and Outi Merisalo, "L'omissione del relativizzatore che nel toscano del fine Trecento alla luce delle lettere di Francesco Datini," *Neuphilologische Mitteilungen* 101 (2000): 279–85.

The everyday vocabulary used in these letters has been little studied. A significant number of the words do not appear in Salvatore Battaglia's authoritative multi-volume dictionary, the *Grande dizionario della lingua italiana,* or in the still-incomplete online dictionary of early Italian, the *Tesoro della lingua italiana delle origini* (TLIO). For the sake of readability, we have not been too fastidious in interpreting passages where such words appear. We have sometimes had to blur the contrasts between eloquent passages and those that are less assured; a number of letters have therefore been rendered more smoothly and coherently in English than in the Italian. It would, in any case, be folly to attempt replication of mistakes and irregularities from the original text, or to mimic those paragraphs that are, in effect, long single sentences with many "ands." Such are the inevitable features of hurriedly dictated, unrevised letters. These long, breathless passages conjure the atmosphere of bustling household activity and the haste characterizing their composition; but they do not make for easy reading, so we have broken some of them up while retaining others to give a sense of the original. We have also judiciously summoned up colloquialisms to convey idiomatic flavor. English has lost its native distinction, observed with great subtlety by Shakespeare, between optional second-person singular forms; so we could not mirror Italian's familiar *tu* ("thou") and polite *voi* (a borrowed plural; "you, ye"). Margherita's choices of pronoun are erratic in any case, and the variations are not necessarily significant. Margherita used *tu* to address her husband, but sometimes the scribes, especially Francesco's more senior associates, wrote *voi* to be more formally correct.

Costume historians might find the translation somewhat lacking in precision, where our decision to use current English ruled out exact English equivalents from the specialized vocabulary of fourteenth-century clothing. We have preferred generic words such as "overgown" for the familiar *cioppa* seen in contemporary paintings of both men and women. Those interested in the precise details of clothing and textiles from this period must return to the Italian text.

We have left most terms for currency and weights and measures untranslated, as well as common titles indicating rank and occupation. General meanings will be clear from the context, supplemented by Appendix 1 and Appendix 2. There are many references to time of day in the letters. Margherita's contemporaries used the traditional seven canonical hours as marked by the ringing of church bells: matins, prime, terce, sext, nones, vespers, and compline; but they also increasingly referred to solar hours. We have preserved the distinction between these two systems, and given some details in Appendix 2.

One needs to be both a period historian and a linguist to penetrate some of Margherita's more elusive meanings. Sometimes the text becomes intelligible only in light of information from Francesco's replies, or from other correspondence such as Lapo Mazzei's.[3] Occasionally the difficulties defeated us, despite generous help from colleagues—especially from Jérôme Hayez, whose own archival research on the vast Datini collection resolved a number of perplexities for us as we unraveled the comings and goings of the many characters.

We hope our English translation of Margherita Datini's letters will bring this rich correspondence to the attention of a wider public, and increase awareness of the lives, education, and aspirations of women of the mercantile class in the late-medieval period, through a rare view of one woman's use of the epistolary genre. All translation is interpretation; but we trust we have interpreted this unique collection in a way that is true to its lively essence.

Carolyn James and Antonio Pagliaro

3. Although we have included some excerpts from Francesco's letters in the footnotes, these are necessarily brief and do not give a full sense of the couple's exchanges over time. Antonio Pagliaro is translating Francesco's letters to Margherita so that the complete Datini marital correspondence will be available in English.

MARGHERITA DATINI

LETTERS TO
FRANCESCO DATINI

Letter 1 (1401880)
23 January 1384
Florence

In the name of God. Amen. Written on the 23rd day of the month.[1]

Margherita commends herself to you and hopes very much to see you as well and as happy as she is. I have had Master Giovanni examine Ghirigora.[2] He has lanced her boil which was the biggest she has ever had and now she should be fine. I gave the doctor a florin. I had Bartolomea examined for the same problem and we'll do whatever has to be done.[3] The carter has been here and brought a load of

1. [The main range of footnotes begins here; all cross-references will refer to notes within this range.] From January 1384 until the spring of 1386, Francesco Datini was often in Pisa, where he had set up a branch of his company (letters 1–15). Pisa was important to his import and export business because it facilitated communication northward with Genoa and the rest of the Mediterranean. Francesco had to spend long periods there due to the difficulties associated with establishing his company in the city's volatile political climate and against fierce commercial competition. At first he suggested that Margherita join him in Pisa, but their continuing discussion about this proposition in the early letters came to nothing, and they were sometimes separated for weeks at a time. Margherita was occasionally in Prato but mostly in Florence during this phase of their correspondence. In this first letter, Margherita stresses the dangers that overwork and the lack of a proper domestic routine posed for Francesco's health, a theme that will become familiar in their exchanges. Not until letter 7 does Margherita sign off explicitly at the end of her dictated letter: "From your Margherita, in Prato". The letters shift between the voice of Margherita herself and the scribe's, referring to Margherita in the third person. These shifts will be noted only where they are of independent interest.

2. Ghirigora, a young servant who had accompanied the Datini couple from Avignon, bore Francesco's son in September 1387. The merchant provided her with a dowry and arranged her marriage to Cristofano di Mercato di Giunta, his distant relative, when she was in the early stages of pregnancy. The baby died at six months and was buried in March 1388 among Francesco's ancestors in the church of San Francesco. See Monte Angiolini's letter of 5 March 1388, informing Francesco of the child's death, transcribed in Enrico Vivarelli, "Aspetti della vita economica pratese nel XIV secolo: con trascrizione delle 459 lettere di Monte d'Andrea Angiolini di Prato" (*Tesi di Laurea*, University of Florence, 1987), 568. The doctor, Giovanni di Banduccio, often treated members of the Datini household. Francesco provided financial help to Giovanni's son, Bandino, during his medical studies. See Melis, *Aspetti della vita economica medievale*, 1:91, n. 3.

3. Francesco regarded the slave Bartolomea as unreliable and in need of constant supervision. Bartolomea is also mentioned in letters 3, 7, 9, 10, and 17, and in Francesco's early

wood from Prato and said he will bring another on Monday. I asked him how the work was going at Prato and he said the fireplace was finished and they had started the whitewashing.[4] The carter also said that they want the flour that was sifted in Florence taken there. In my view it would be better to leave it here; but if they insist, it should be taken to the farm. Bernabò was here and said that the mason had started work on the walls. I asked him if he was giving the mason an allowance for meals. He replied that he was providing breakfast and a snack and he thought it was necessary to give him dinner. It seemed to me that you had said the opposite.[5]

I asked Bernabò about whom he had left the key to the wine cellar with and he told me he had left it with Monte.[6] It seems to me you should write to Monte and tell him to lock up that wine so it can't be accessed easily, since I think Bernabò would be a poor guardian. You have sent me a message to keep a close eye on the household goods. I have looked after them better than you could have wished; but I urge you to do the same there since there is no need to worry about things here. If you are worried, I would advise you to come back and watch over them yourself, since you would watch them better than anyone. That's what my heart would tell me to do in order to have peace of mind. You sent a message that it seems to you a thousand years until it

letters. See Cecchi, ed., *Le lettere di Francesco Datini.* Hereafter, this edition will be cited as FD, followed by the letter number. Francesco sold Bartolomea in May 1388 for fifty-six florins. This met with the disapproval of his aunt, Monna Tina di Betto Ridolfi, who seems to have lived near the Datini residence and often supervised Bartolomea. Monte Angiolini to Francesco Datini, 6, 22, and 29 May 1388, in Vivarelli, "Aspetti della vita economica pratese," 624, 631–33.

4. Margherita refers here to the enlargement and embellishment of the Datini residence in Prato, which continued for the rest of the decade. See Cavaciocchi, "The Merchant and Building."

5. Domenico di Giovanni Golli, known as Bernabò, was Francesco's employee from 1376 to 1406. He owned some land in Prato and spent periods of time in Rome between 1383 and 1392. See letters 13, 14, and 100. Discussion about preventing theft from the house in Prato during its construction is perennial in the correspondence.

6. Monte d'Andrea di Ser Gino Angiolini, from an old Pratese family, was Francesco's business associate in Prato between early January 1384 and 15 March 1390, when he was murdered in Pisa. Monte was married to Lorita di Aldobrandino Bovattieri. See his letters transcribed in Vivarelli, "Aspetti della vita economica pratese."

is Carnival time. I feel the same; if you can stay here a little longer once you get back, I don't think it would do any harm. I would be surprised if [Pisa] were more than a day's travel from here.

You sent a message saying it was midnight when you wrote that letter, and if you had there what you are used to, you wouldn't have stayed up so late. But that is nonsense. It seems to me that you always used to stay up later than anyone and you have never worried about it as far as I know. I am more teased than a newlywed, and they say things to me that they would not even say to a new bride. If I am sad, they say I am jealous. If I am happy, they say I can't be missing Francesco di Marco. They talk such rubbish that if you were a young boy it would be bad enough. In this household all they do is joke about you and me.

Don't keep wearing yourself out and having dinner at midnight as you usually do, or at least have some consideration for the rest of the household. I won't say anything else. May God protect you. I commend myself to you. Greet Monna Bartolomea and tell her from me that she is doing penance for her past. If she is regretting it, tell her I would probably have acted as she did.[7] I didn't send for Sera's and Stoldo's wheat because it has a musty taste and makes dark bread. We got only one *moggio*. If you want us to get the rest let me know. I think we need to buy twelve bushels of the finest that can be found for Lent. If you celebrate Carnival take care not to get gout again. Written by Michele in Florence.

To Francesco di Marco da Prato himself, in Pisa.
Received from Florence, 31 January 1384. Answered.

---

7. Monna Bartolomea seems to have been Francesco's housekeeper in Pisa. Margherita may refer here to the difficulties that Bartolomea faced in trying to serve her exacting and irascible master.

Letter 2 (1401892)
4 April 1384
Florence

In the name of God. Amen.

Francesco, Monna Margherita commends herself to you. It seems to me that these guardians are inclined to take a different view. They don't want to cooperate at all and are insisting that Mattea agree, this very day, to their guardianship; so we have lost no time in summoning you.[8] Therefore, I really beg you to come without inconveniencing yourself as soon as you can. This I beg of you.

I have nothing else to add.

To Francesco di Marco in Prato.
Received from Florence, 5 April 1384.

Letter 3 (1401715)
7 February 1385
Prato

In the name of God. 7 February 1385.

Francesco di Marco, Monna Margherita commends herself to you. The reason I write this letter is to ask whether you would like me to send Simone back to you, because I don't need him here.[9] Let me know if you want him. You should know that the evening you left Pra-

---

8. Niccolò d'Uguccione, his wife Mattea, and their children were living in Florence at the time of Niccolò's death in 1384. Francesco first knew the family in Avignon, and Monna Margherita di Michele Barducci now asked him to help her daughter Mattea, by ensuring that she and her children received a proper share of Niccolò's estate (Archivio di Stato, Prato, Archivio Datini, 1095, 134897; hereafter cited as ASPo, D; information provided by Jérôme Hayez). This brief letter implies that the widow Mattea was involved in a dispute with Florentine officials over their attempt to assume the guardianship of her children and perhaps the administration of her husband's estate.

9. Simone d'Andrea Bellandi, Francesco's cousin, worked in the warehouse in Prato as a young apprentice for three years after March 1384. See Melis, *Aspetti della vita economica medievale*, 1:284. He was often Margherita's scribe in this early period of his career.

to, Nero and all his family arrived here at the Ave Maria. This evening the wet nurse of Monna Beatrice's boy, who was very ill, visited us.[10]

We will offer hospitality to everyone on your behalf. Dolce and Nero are here, and they take care of everything we need; so if you need Simone, write to us, and we will send him.

I have bought a twelve-yard length of linen costing a florin; the man we bought it from did not have any more.

We will buy the rest as soon as we can. For my part, I want to beg you to look after your health and avoid this staying up till all hours, because at this stage you shouldn't worry yourself so. May God protect you. Commend me to Niccolò dell'Ammannato and to Giachi.[11] Greet Francesca for me, and all her children.[12] Remember what Niccolò dell'Ammannato says about women in the Marches.[13] Greet Bartolomea for me, and tell her from me to make sure that she serves

---

10. Nero di Vanni da Vernio and his family arrived at the Datini household in Prato at about seven in the evening. Nero and his daughter-in-law Beatrice were preparing to travel by boat from Pisa to Avignon, where Beatrice's husband, Iacopo del Nero, worked as an apothecary. The family had been briefly united in Prato between January 1383 and March 1384. On Iacopo del Nero, see Jérôme Hayez, "'Tucte sono patrie, ma la buona è quela dove l'uomo fa bene'. Famille et migration dans la correspondance de deux marchands toscans vers 1400," *Eloignement géographique et cohésion familiale (XVe–XXe siècle)*, ed. Jean-François Chauvard and Christine Lebeau (Strasbourg: Presses Universitaires de Strasbourg, 2006): 69–95. See also letter 4. Both Monte Angiolini and Francesco undertook to ensure the well-being of Iacopo's relatives in Prato during his stay in Avignon. See Jérôme Hayez, "'Veramente io spero farci bene …': Expérience de migrant et pratique de l'amitié dans la correspondance de maestro Naddino d'Aldobrandino Bovattieri médecin toscan d'Avignon (1385–1407)," *Bibliothèque de l'École des chartes* 159 (2001): 425.

11. Niccolò dell'Ammannato Tecchini was married to Margherita's sister Francesca, while Iacopo di Cianghello Girolli da Cantagallo (or Giachi, a Provençal form of Iacopo) was married to Isabetta, her other sister. Giachi had accompanied the Datini couple from Avignon to Prato in 1382. By 1386, he was in financial trouble and required Francesco's help to return to Avignon. See letters 12 and 14, and Melis, *Aspetti della vita economica medievale*, 52.

12. Margherita refers to her sister.

13. Niccolò dell'Ammannato wrote to Francesco that the women in the Marches region of Italy said to their husbands at parting, "Remember your home!" See Origo, *The Merchant of Prato*, 174.

you well. The neighbors say that it is very quiet here without Bartolomea.[14] The bearer of this letter is Guccio d'Alesso.[15]

To Francesco di Marco da Prato, at the Loggia of the Tornaquinci.

Letter 4 (1401882)
23 February 1385
Prato

In the name of God. 23 February 1385.

Francesco di Marco, Margherita commends herself to you. We are all well by the grace of God.

We are sending to you, with Argomento, the overgown, the purple mantle, a pair of your shoes, and also some pills.[16] We would have sent you some peas and chickpeas if Argomento had been able to stay longer. If you need any let us know. I beg you not to stay up late and not to be too anxious. Make sure that you look after your health during Lent.

Greet Monna Beatrice and everyone else there. May God protect them all.

With this letter you will receive two others addressed to Monna Dianora.[17] Give them to Monna Beatrice and tell her to look after them well, because I wouldn't feel like doing them again for a year. We are sending some clothes wrapped in a sheet. Make sure you send the sheet back here. Tell Monna Beatrice that I am going to visit her daughter this morning.[18]

14. The troublesome slave Bartolomea had moved to Florence to serve Francesco.

15. This is Guccio d'Alesso Pratesini Sassoli. On the Sassoli family, see Fiumi, *Demografia, movimento urbanistico e classi sociali in Prato*, 454, 477–78.

16. Argomento di Perotto was a regular carrier of letters and goods between Florence and Prato until at least 1408. He was an ex-slave who had been freed by Francesco.

17. Margherita refers to her mother, Dianora Gherardini, who lived in Avignon.

18. On 25 November 1384, Monna Beatrice bore a daughter who was baptized with the names Piera Caterina, after one of her godfathers, Piero Borsaio, and Saint Catherine of Alexandria, on whose feast day she was born. Francesco was another of the godfathers.

May God protect you.
Written on 23 February.

To Francesco di Marco, in Pisa. Delivered.
Received from Prato, 23 February 1385.

Letter 5 (1401881)
27 February 1385
Florence

In the name of God. 27 February 1385.

I, Margherita, received your letter and read it gladly. You wrote
to me as well as to Monte; because we received your letter before Monte received his, he will let me know your latest instructions. I gather
that you would be happy if I were there with the whole household you
have entrusted to me. You are far too kind, because I am not worthy
of such honor.[19]

I am completely willing to come, not only to Pisa, but to the end
of the earth if it makes you happy. You say that we would be better off
together than one here and the other there. This is true for several rea-

---

See Monte Angiolini to Francesco Datini, 28 November 1384, Vivarelli, "Aspetti della vita
economica pratese," 92–93. The child was left in the care of a wet nurse when Beatrice left
Prato to join her husband in Avignon. Margherita undertook to keep an eye on her. See
letter 5. The boat in which Beatrice traveled from Pisa was attacked by pirates, delaying her
arrival in Avignon. See a reference to this incident in a letter of 5 June 1385, from the doctor
Naddino d'Aldobrandino Bovattieri to Francesco Datini, in Hayez, "'Veramente io spero
farci bene … ,'" 433 and 486. For another letter concerning the same incident, see Robert
Brun, "Annales avignonnaises de 1382 à 1410: extraites des Archives de Datini," *Mémoires de
l'Institut Historique de Provence* 12 (1935): 79–80. Naddino (whose family originated from
Vernio, just north of Prato) sent news from Avignon regularly. See his letters published in
Hayez, "'Veramente io spero farci bene … ,'" *passim*.

19. Margherita refers to a letter that Francesco wrote to Monte Angiolini, in which he said:
"Tell Margherita that she is as she is and people may say what they like; but I am not about
to leave or to remain anywhere without her, and whatever anyone says I don't feel myself
without her." Francesco to Monte Angiolini in Prato, 13 March 1385, ASPo, D.347.6/4011.
See also FD 1. Monte replied to Francesco that when he read this section to Margherita, the
servant Ghirigora laughed heartily. See Vivarelli, "Aspetti della vita economica pratese," 128.

sons: because of the expense, because it is true that we spend a fortune here and there, although that would not matter if you were content. It seems to me that to finish off your business there it would be best if I joined you soon so that you could more easily concentrate on your affairs. I believe that you are poorly looked after there, and so it seems necessary that I should come urgently to ensure that you are looked after properly. When you are attended to as you should be, you can better dedicate yourself to your affairs. I am very worried about you because it is Lent and because of the bad air there, so I have decided to come to make sure you are as well looked after as you are accustomed to be.[20] It would be very easy for you to catch yet another illness if you are not cared for properly.

My main concern is to ensure you remain in good health, because as long as you are healthy we will prosper and be able to sustain any great expense. This is why I cannot wait to be there, so you will be able to live more happily. So I will come. You write that if I did not wish to come there, you would come here at Easter and travel back and forth as necessary.[21] Apart from being very dangerous, such coming and going would make you waste time and prolong your stay there. So, also because of the bad air there, I would like to come immediately.

That would allow you to finish what you have to do. Whatever else might happen, I would not like you to be there when the weather is very hot, because every year there are deaths. About this I will say no more. You are wise and will make the best decision. Remaining there or coming here is your decision.

Concerning your foster mother, I have spoken with Monte, and he tells me that he will organize things in consultation with the Prior of San Fabiano, Arriguccio di Ser Guido, and with you.[22] I said I was willing to agree with them on whatever sum they want to spend, be-

---

20. Pisa was notoriously unhealthy because of the marshy areas around the city and had been depopulated in 1382 by a serious outbreak of plague.

21. See FD 1.

22. Francesco's foster mother, Monna Piera di Pratese Boschetti, looked after him and his brother after the death of their parents during the plague of 1348. She died on 1 February 1383. Margherita refers here to arrangements for Monna Piera's tomb in the twelfth-century abbey of San Fabiano in Prato. It was to be organized by Arriguccio di Ser Guido Ferra-

cause I believe they want to do it honorably. In my opinion, you can agree with what the Prior wants to do because he must act honorably. Should he do anything else, I think it would bring them little credit, and it would be a disgrace to bury her as if she were just anybody. There have been bigger [tombs] but it seems to me it would be sufficient to do what is usually done. You will be here and can do as you see fit.[23] Concerning your aunt and all the others I won't reply because I hope you will be here soon and I will tell you my opinion in person.

You don't need to worry about the women in the household here. I supervise them more than you would do yourself.[24] They have behaved themselves exceedingly well. I pay more attention to Bartolomea than I would to you if you were here. I decided not to send you any of the things that you need there because it seemed better to send everything together.

When you are here you will have a clearer idea of what has to be done. I received a letter from Niccolò dell'Ammannato. He puts himself at my disposal. I wrote to tell him that you wanted me to be with you, and I asked him for his opinion because I said I would follow first your commands and then his. I did this to honor him like a father.

Monna Dianora has sent a power of attorney for you and for Niccolò because she wants you to sell the house and to know whether I agree. I replied that I did not wish to lose the right to it under any

---

cani (Gonfalonier of Justice of Prato in that period), Monte Angiolini, and the prior of the church.

23. Monna Piera's bequest of her house to Francesco to pay for her burial was contested by the prior of San Domenico, the executor of her husband's will, which left this property to the hospital. In a letter of 23 February 1383 to Francesco, Monte Angiolini refers to the burial of Monna Piera as costing thirty-six *lire*. Vivarelli, "Aspetti della vita economica pratese," 3–4. The Magistracy of the Eight Defenders in Prato appointed Messer Manetto to examine the matter, and it appears that Francesco's claim was considered weaker. See Monte d'Andrea to Francesco, 12 October 1384, Vivarelli, "Aspetti della vita economica pratese," 59–61. In November 1384, Monte referred to the continuing debate about who would pay this money. See Vivarelli, "Aspetti della vita economica pratese," 84–86.

24. In his letter of 23 February 1385 Francesco wrote: "Now don't make me get angry with you. You can't go wrong if you keep a close eye and it won't be difficult for you. But take care of everything and pay attention to the house and the servants, not to the loom or needlework which couldn't make up in a hundred years what you might lose in an hour. Now try to be a woman, not a girl. Soon you'll be entering your twenty-fifth year" (FD 1).

circumstances, but it was not my decision, and I would be satisfied by what you and Niccolò did about it.[25]

I presented your compliments to all the people you indicated, and I was particularly courteous to Messer Giovanni di Lippo.[26] Everyone received me very graciously. I am sending you a lot of things; the list of all the items that I am sending is with this letter. That's all I have to say. I saw Beatrice's children and made a fuss of them and told them to consider themselves my own children.[27] As for what you say about the herrings, I don't think I should do it, because there will be plenty of time for us to give them away later. Monte says the quality is rather inferior. I am well, as is the rest of the household. Think of me. Please don't overdo it. Work at a pace you can keep up.

May God protect you always.

To Francesco di Marco da Prato, in Pisa.
Received from Florence, 29 February 1385.

Letter 6 (1401891)
1 March 1385
Prato

In the name of God. Amen. 1 March 1385.

I am sending to you with Argomento the carter half a quart of chickpeas, half a quart of peas, half a quart of beans, a good quantity of capers, a quart of chestnuts, plenty of figs, a jar of raisins, four hand

---

25. Dianora Gherardini's house in the quarter of Santo Spirito in Florence was a source of tension within the family. Francesco tried to rent it from her in 1387, but she demanded an exorbitant price, and her son-in-law found another house. It was eventually bequeathed to Margherita's sister Isabetta and her husband, Giachi Girolli; but Dianora's will was contested by other family members, and Isabetta was still trying to sell the house in 1395. See Naddino's letters to Francesco published in Hayez, "'Veramente io spero farci bene ...,'" 510–11, 526–27.

26. Giovanni di Lippo Benamati acted as Francesco's lawyer in the dispute over Monna Piera's will.

27. See note 18, above.

towels, two sets of underlinen, a large towel, and a set of Simone's underlinen.

If you need anything else, let me know. I await your arrival.[28] May God protect you.

Your wife Margherita commends herself to you.

To Francesco di Marco himself, in Pisa.
Received from Prato, 2 March 1385.

Letter 7 (1401716)
31 July 1385
Prato

In the name of God. 31 July 1385.

Francesco, Margherita commends herself to you. You sent a message with Niccolò telling me to prepare myself to come there and to sell the wine. I haven't yet found anyone who wants either the white or the red wine. I remind Bettino every day; you know what he is like.[29] It would be necessary for Bartolomea to be here before we could leave, because there is a lot of dirty washing that must be done because there are so many mice here that they would do too much damage. Since you have decided to stay there, the sooner we are together the better. We will be better off together than one here and the other there. I would not be happy to stay here without you.[30] Be careful what Bar-

28. In a letter of 10 March (FD 2), Francesco promised to come to Prato as soon as possible to discuss with Margherita whether she should return with him to Pisa. He kept his promise, but on 23 March he left for Pisa without his wife, remaining there until 18 July. See Melis, *Aspetti della vita economica medievale*, 173–95. Letter 7 suggests that she did not join him in Pisa. See also note 30, below.

29. Francesco responded to this letter on 4 August, saying that he only put up with Bettino for the sake of Bettino's wife, Monna Tina, who was Francesco's aunt (FD 3). Francesco employed Bettino to supply firewood, wine, and other household commodities. He seems to have been often in debt and was harassed by the authorities for insolvency.

30. Francesco reassured his wife that he was not content to live without her: "It is certainly my intention that Bartolomea should go soon to Prato to do the washing and put everything in order. We will stay here in Florence until mid-September and then we will return to Prato

tolomea does with my lengths of cloth. She is as likely as not to ruin them. I would have asked for Simone if I thought you would send him, but I know he is needed there to look after the key. I would have had him sell this wine by sending him out and about, because I have no one else to send.

Try to come as soon as you can. Remember your home and what Niccolò dell'Ammannato said so that I may have peace of mind.[31] Tinuccia is better now.[32] I have nothing else to add for now. May God protect you always. Commend me to our friends and answer this letter, telling me which day you are arriving, because I want to welcome you properly. You could bring Niccolò dell'Ammannato, although he would not leave his serving girl behind.

From your Margherita, in Prato.

To Francesco di Marco da Prato at the Loggia of the Tornaquinci in Florence.
Received from Prato, 3 August 1385. Answered.

Letter 8 (1401883)
17 December 1385
Florence

In the name of God. Amen. 17 December 1385.

Francesco, Margherita sends you her greetings from Florence. I am writing this letter because I really want to know what you did about that business relating to Paolo da Pistoia.[33] Please avoid wor-

---

and stay there until All Saints' Day. Then, if it pleases God, we will go to Pisa. This time I want to give us the opportunity to rest. You can see how matters are going" (FD 3). Francesco moved to Pisa without Margherita before 16 December 1385.

31. See note 13, above.

32. Tinuccia may be Margherita's niece Caterina (Tina) di Niccolò dell'Ammannato Techini. She later joined the Datini household (see letter 28, for example) and was betrothed to Francesco's partner Luca del Sera on 20 May 1403.

33. Paolo d'Andrea della Torre was a merchant who had worked in Avignon. Francesco had a lawsuit against him in Pisa.

rying about it as much as you can, though these things always bring anxiety. You must act in accordance with your conscience. This is more important than all the things we must put up with. I will say no more about this. Try to control yourself. Leave justice to the Lord God, who knows better than we how to sort out such matters. You will be vindicated once more, just as you were in the past when others wronged you. Above all, I beg you not to get angry, because we are doing well and it is not right to throw away so much good to satisfy that man. That would be doing a favor to a person who wishes us ill. God has shown us great favor. May God bestow His grace on us, and may we be thankful.

We are all well. Monna Giovanna and Tieri's niece are here with me, and I had the mantle for Tieri's mother made and the overgown for his niece.[34]

Commend me to Monna Parte and to Michele; embrace Tina for me.[35] Ask Monna Parte if she wants me to send her the cloth as it is, or to wait until the weather improves because it hasn't stopped raining here. What does she want me to do?

Monna Giovanna and Francesca send a hundred thousand greetings. I'll put Bartolomea in charge of grooming the mule. It will do fine that way. It often has such heavy loads that the poor thing looks as if it has been in the wars. I've nothing else to add. May God protect you always.

I tried to send you some underlinen, and I sent one set to Prato, but you had already gone. I will try to send you a set there [in Pisa] if I can find someone to bring it, because you must be in need of it.

To Francesco di Marco da Prato himself, in Pisa.
Received from Florence, 18 December 1385.

34. Monna Giovanna was Margherita's aunt. She was the daughter of Donato Bandini and widow of Salvestro di Cantino Cavalcanti. Tieri di Benci da Settignano worked for Francesco Datini in Avignon from 1371 and became his partner in 1382. See Melis, *Aspetti della vita economica medievale*, 136–41.

35. Monna Parte, Michele di Carlo, and the couple's daughter Tina (or Caterina) (see letter 9, and FD 4), were friends who lived in Pisa. In his letter of 16 December 1385 (FD 4), Francesco refers to the mother and daughter spending the night of his return to Pisa in his house, presumably to cook for him. Margherita returned the favor by organizing the dyeing of some cloth for Monna Parte.

Letter 9 (1401884)
10 January 1386
Florence

In the name of God. Amen. 10 January 1386.

Francesco di Marco, Margherita commends herself to you and hopes you are happy and well. The reason for this letter is that we have received a flask of Corsican wine from Prato, delivered by Trincia, and from another carter we have received a basket containing oranges, two rounds of parmesan cheese, and hazelnuts. Tell us what you want done with them, and we will do as you say. We are sending some of the Corsican wine to Lorenzo and to Niccolò dell'Ammannato, and we drank the rest. If you want me to send back the flask to you for refilling, I will do so willingly. It was very good. Monna Lapa thought it particularly good. She says it is such an appealing wine that she would drink it in abundance.[36]

When you get a chance to write, tell me what you did about that matter concerning Paolo.[37]

I have sent Monna Parte's cloth off to be dyed. I haven't received the other cloth back yet.

Commend me to Monna Parte, and embrace Caterina for me. After you left here, Argomento went off to Prato and has not been back since. I don't know why. I believe he is following your instructions. I have nothing else to tell you. May God protect you always.

To Francesco di Marco da Prato himself, in Pisa.
Received from Florence, 11 January 1386.

---

36. Lapa was the daughter of a tavern keeper and wife of the master dyer, Niccolò di Piero di Giunta, Francesco's cousin and business partner. Lapa was visiting Margherita in Florence. See letter 13, which refers to her eagerness to return to her family in Prato. Corsican wine was imported in large quantities during this period and arrived regularly at Pisa. It was expensive, suggesting that the quality was high. See Federigo Melis, *I vini italiani nel medioevo*, ed. Anna Affortunati Parrini (Florence: Istituto Internazionale di Storia Economica "F. Datini" di Prato, 1984), 78–79.

37. For Paolo d'Andrea della Torre da Pistoia, see note 33, above. Francesco's answer to this request is not extant.

Letter 10 (1401885)
16 January 1386
Florence

In the name of God. Amen. 16 January 1386.

In the last few days I received two of your letters, and because I was unwell, I didn't reply. I do so here.

As for closing the outside door well, we do that and we rise early. You say that you would be displeased if anything unusual were to happen. I would be even more displeased. Bartolomea never goes out except to the bakery.[38] She is the sort of woman I wouldn't let out of my sight. You know her better than I do. I would prefer to supervise any of the others. I don't want you to think she has behaved worse than usual, because she has always been a devil and will always be so. We are cautious with her and allow her to do what she likes provided that she doesn't go out of the house. Francesca has bought a slave, so Bartolomea doesn't need to go out now except once a week to the bakery. Sometimes I have her accompanied, and because of this, much to our great amusement, she does nothing but complain.

About this matter, don't worry, as I will make sure you are content.

Niccolò was here on Saturday and did the things you told me about, and Lapa slept in the room with the bed curtains. Argomento drained the cask and put it in the cellar above the benches where it was before, and he put a *metadella* of white wine in it. We reminded Argomento several times about the locks. He said the keys were not ready yet.

As for telling you when I go to church, I have told him and her. They will confirm it, if they do the right thing.[39] I have gone out very little because of the wet weather and because I was unwell. If it weren't for Lapa, I would have gone out even less. You tell me not to remain forever a girl and say that we will be rewarded in accordance with the good we do here on earth. You are right. It is a good while since I left girlhood behind but I would like you not to remain the Francesco you

38. This is the slave Bartolomea. See note 3, above.

39. Margherita probably refers here to Niccolò di Piero di Giunta and his wife, Lapa. See note 36, above.

have been since I first knew you, someone who has done nothing but inflict tribulation on his body and soul. You say, indeed you preach, that you will live a virtuous life, and every week of every month it is the same story. You have said this for ten years, and now it seems to me that you intend to rest less than ever. This is your fault. God has given you knowledge and the power to act and has done for you what he hasn't done for a thousand others. You think you can continue to concern yourself with honor and profit before turning to a virtuous life.

But if you wait any longer, you will never achieve this virtuous life. If you wish to say: "Look at the difficulties that assail me every day, there is no escape from them in this life," [I would reply] that this shouldn't prevent you from living a life that is good for the soul and for the body. I have a good mind to curse whoever is to blame for your business dealings in Pisa. On this subject I will say no more.

Monte was here on Sunday and told me that you need to stay in Pisa longer.[40] You well know that I would be glad to come there, given the many discussions we have had about how unhappy I am about you staying there while I remain here. It is pointless to talk about this any further. If you were to decide that I should come there, I know that you would have to return here first, and you could then best decide if I should come or not. I am always happy to do what you want. Your behavior does not suggest to me that you intend to rest. In vain I remind you that you are now, like Monte, almost fifty years old, and you have always served the world. Now it is time to begin to serve God. I don't want you to think that I say this so I can rest too. I don't regard a person as good who does not cherish both the soul and the body of a loved one. You may as well follow the example of the person who threw his money in the sea because he couldn't do what he wanted with it. You may as well do the same. If I have said something that displeases you, I beg forgiveness. My great love makes me say it.

You send me messages telling me to be happy and to enjoy myself, but you stay awake until morning and dine at midnight and lunch at sunset. I will not be happy and will never be able to rest if you don't live differently. For the sake of Monna Lapa I will strive to be cheerful

---

40. Francesco had returned to Pisa in December 1385. He promised in his reply to remain there for no more than a fortnight (FD 5).

and to help her pass the time as well as I can. If only you would do the same.

Piero di Filippo sent a message to say that you wrote to him that I should send a whole parmesan cheese to Giovanni d'Arrigo, and I sent him a basket of the finest oranges available.[41]

Messer Niccolò Cambioni hasn't returned.[42] Don't send us any oranges that are no longer edible. The cheese that we sent to Giovanni is excellent. For now I cannot think of anything else to tell you.

Chiarmonda has requested that I ask you to send a lot of lemons.[43] Let me know if I can have some.

Today we received Monna Parte's cloth. It has been dyed very well. They said it would always be a pleasure to serve you. We will send it to you as soon as possible.

I will say no more. May God protect you always.

Monna Margherita sends you her greetings from Florence. Monna Francesca and all the others send you greetings.

To Francesco di Marco da Prato himself, in Pisa.
Received from Florence, 18 January 1386.

Letter 11 (1401886)
20 January 1386
Florence

In the name of God. Amen. 20 January 1386.

Today I received your letter, written on the 19th, to which I reply here as required.[44]

---

41. This is Piero di Filippo Milanesi from Prato. See letter 12. Giovanni d'Arrigo Rinaldeschi, a relative of Francesco's friend and neighbor in Prato, Piero di Paolo Rinaldeschi, was a banker and Piero Milanesi's father-in-law.

42. Niccolò Cambioni was the brother of Bartolomeo Cambioni, with whom Francesco went into partnership when he set up his bank in Florence in the late 1390s. See Melis, *Aspetti della vita economica medievale*, 297.

43. Chiarmonda was a Florentine relative of Margherita's.

44. See FD 5.

You say that the letter I sent you was well composed. I don't know if you meant it, but if so, I am pleased.

In my opinion it seems that neither Boninsegna nor I have advised you well, because you have never wanted to do anything that he has told you to do.[45] I won't mention myself because I am a woman, and a man shouldn't follow a woman's advice.

I am pleased about your return here.[46] Please come as quickly as possible. You will do me a great favor. I beg you to avoid an attack of gout this Carnival. It would be very inconvenient just when you have so much to do. Don't keep adding to your worries, and stop claiming that I don't care at all that you are always so anxious. I don't mind if you say this to me in person, but don't write it.

You have left two fellows in charge of the warehouse here in Florence who don't have half a brain between them. You know how your partner leaves whenever he likes.[47] One day the bell rings at vespers and another day not at all. On Saturday, when it is most necessary, it doesn't ring. Imagine how your affairs are going. You send us letters often, and between having them sent over to him there and then having the others delivered, the warehouse remains closed half the day. During the day a lot of people come there to do business and find the door barred. It seems a place run by children. I would suggest that if you have another incompetent over there, send him here, because this is how you seem to prefer to do things. You can stay up and write letters of four or five pages to that associate of yours, and it doesn't matter at all to him to whom they are addressed. He has two tutors who help him to read them. His mother and daughter read them, as well as the women who work in the warehouse and all the others. These are some of his other feats of intelligence. You keep on revealing your affairs to everyone. I don't see that it is necessary to write to your friend all about your worries and every detail of your business. You might say to me, "How do you know what I write to him about?" I don't, but knowing you as I do, I can well imagine it.

45. Boninsegna di Matteo Boninsegna was Francesco's senior partner in Avignon. Francesco said he was always well advised by Boninsegna and Margherita (FD 5).

46. Francesco had promised to return to Florence within two weeks (FD 5).

47. Stoldo di Lorenzo di Ser Berizo Ormanni, the experienced head of the Florentine branch and Francesco's partner, was in Avignon during this period. See letter 15.

Simone tells me that you write him letters of three or four pages—I can't believe they are all about business—and that day after day you send him those tomes.[48] You must be unburdening your soul to him about some worry that you have, but I wouldn't place any more trust in him than the others.

This is because, with the exception of Boninsegna and Tieri, there isn't anyone who hasn't been cheating you twelve times a day.[49] It's happened to you before, and you know whether I'm telling the truth or not, so look out for that man more than anyone. He can deceive you better than anyone because he's had a lot of practice.[50] I wish to God that I was lying through my teeth about his dealings, although it is very unusual for me to tell a lie. If you had been respected as much as you are disliked, that would be your good luck, since there are a hundred people who dislike you, though they used not to, and I am telling you this because I am upset about the things I hear, because I feel that your shame is mine. I trust in God that you will see through him, as you did with the others. I will say no more about this. I beg you not to behave the same way you have other times. This will just create too much hostility and end up completely ruining you. I beg you to behave calmly with him and all the others until you have overcome these worries of yours, and afterwards you can treat them as they deserve. For God's sake, don't let yourself slide down to this level or you will ruin yourself completely. Give them plenty of assurances and promises until you have arrived where you want: a man kisses a hand first when he would like to see it chopped off.

I understood many things from another letter of yours, and what worries me most is that you seem to have been extremely melancholy, though you refuse to tell me anything. I think you are do-

---

48. On 15 January, Francesco wrote a letter of six pages to his associates in the Florentine warehouse (ASPo, D.675, 1179440). The letter is not addressed to a particular person, but it is likely that Margherita refers here to Piero di Filippo Milanesi, whom she distrusted. See letter 12. Simone di Andrea Bellandi was Margherita's scribe on this occasion. See note 9, above. Francesco replied that he was impressed by the youth's handwriting (FD 5) and pleased that he was learning to write well (FD 6).

49. Tieri and Boninsegna had assumed responsibility for the firm's branch in Avignon in 1382.

50. Margherita refers to Piero di Filippo Milanesi.

ing it with the best intentions, and I am grateful. I wish you would do the same with others—you would be praised more than you are. I am worried that you will come back here in worse health—this is my main concern—because for many reasons you made me pass the worst day of my life, although perhaps the situation was not as bad as I imagined. Try to live in a way that allows your affairs to prosper. They will if you desire them to. I will say no more about this. Please burn this letter when you have read it. I beg you to do me this favor. Lapa and all the others send a hundred thousand greetings. May God protect you always.

Your Margherita, who commends herself to you, from Florence.

To Francesco di Marco himself, in Pisa.
Received from Florence, 22 January 1386.
Answered.

Letter 12 (1401887)
23 January 1386
Florence

In the name of God. Amen. 23 January 1386.

I received two of your letters that don't need a detailed response, so I will answer briefly.[51]

You told me in your two letters, and the one you wrote to Piero, that I cannot have composed those letters myself but that Piero di Filippo must have composed them. Excuse me, but he never composes my letters, neither he nor anyone else. You very much underestimate me in thinking that I would get him to compose my letters.[52] If I don't have Simone, I go to Niccolò dell'Ammannato, who seems to me more

---

51. Margherita refers to his letters of 21 January (not extant) and 22 January. The letter to Piero di Filippo Milanesi is in ASPo, D.675, 117 9442.

52. Margherita's poor opinion of Piero di Filippo Milanesi was vindicated in 1397 when he spread damaging rumors that Francesco was bankrupt. See Francesco's letter of 21 April 1397 to Bindo Piaciti, ASPo, D.1115, 9300486 (reference provided by Jérôme Hayez).

suitable than Piero di Filippo, or else to Lorenzo.[53] Only to those two would I reveal my secrets and to no one else. Francesco, I acknowledge that I have written to you too freely and have demonstrated too much independence from you in telling you the truth. If you were here beside me, I would not have spoken so boldly. Slap me in the eyes or on the head or wherever you will. I don't care. I will always speak the truth as I know it. I have said nothing to you that I haven't already said at least once a month, and when you are here perhaps I don't speak so directly, although I see you do things that make me swell with anger twelve times a day. I may have a bit of the Gherardini temper, not that I'm proud of that, but I cannot work out yours! I don't know what need there was for you to write that to Piero. You have upset me greatly and it is not the first time. It seems to me, if you wanted to clarify this matter, you should have waited for my answer because, according to the women, you found me slightly dishonest, a little fond of pleasure, and a bit too friendly with the friars. I have been with you now for ten years, and I have spoken with them twice a year at most, and from now on I will have nothing to do with them. I don't collect godmothers and godfathers of every sort like you do.[54] You are well ahead of me there! I am not going to excuse you any more.

Until now I have answered you calmly because I've seen letters of yours that were not to be taken lightly, and I have tried to reply to the best of my ability. From now on I will do the opposite. Let's descend to the trivialities that you seem to be looking for. It will be a relief to me. Concerning your affairs, you seemed such a reformed character that I imagined you would rather not celebrate Carnival in order to avoid observing Lent. I never thought the day would come when you and I would find it necessary to discuss such trivialities since I was never so immature as to like them. However, I am going to have to learn to do so because I see that is what you are after. Now you will realize that I composed this myself. On this subject I have nothing more to say.

On Monday at nones Iacopo Girolli arrived looking very troubled and worn out. I regret that I neither invited him for a meal nor to sleep the night because of what you once said, and I admit that you are right. I asked him where he was going, and he said that he had taken a

---

53. This is Boninsegna di Matteo Boninsegna's brother Lorenzo.

54. Margherita implies here that her husband cultivated people for business reasons.

small house and inside there was nothing, not even a bed. He told me it was a bad day and had tears in his eyes. I'm not used to disobeying any of your instructions: not for him, nor for any other person. Nor do I want to worry you more than necessary, because I have such faith that you will do what should be done.

He told me that Bernabò came with him as far as Siena. If you need a good employee for Avignon, or for any other place, he would be suitable. Don't let him slip through your fingers, but first I want to send for him so he can write me two or three letters.[55]

You tell me to let you know how Argomento is behaving.[56] From what I have seen up to now I can't say other than quite well, although they seem to think he's not as careful as they would like. Unless I change my mind again, I'm not going to give you the facts about every item of your business. Argomento left here last Thursday. We can't tell you how the mule behaved because he didn't return here afterward.

There are other things that I could tell you. I won't write them because I don't see the need and they will only annoy you. You let me know that you stay awake until midnight. I believe it is worse than you say. If you never leave any work for others, they will work less than you do, and you'll be worse off. You should know that it's no advantage to you to leave them idle, because those you don't leave idle will try to get out of working, and I would too, if I worked for you. For the love of God, don't let them do this. Believe a little in others, not only in yourself. I laugh at the idea that you will ever live a good life. I will say no more about this.

Monna Giovanna, Monna Chiarmonda, and Monna Francesca were here on Sunday for dinner and supper. They all send a hundred thousand greetings.[57] Monna Lapa likes staying in Florence very much. We are all well, as I think you are. May God protect you always.

Your Margherita, who commends herself to you, from Florence.

55. Iacopo (or Giachi) di Cianghello Girolli da Cantagallo was bankrupt. His situation continued to deteriorate, and he seems to have fallen ill. See letter 14. Francesco apparently took up Margherita's suggestion to help Giachi in a limited way, because he returned to Avignon by June 1386. See also note 25, above.

56. For Argomento di Perotto, see note 16, above.

57. These are all Florentine relatives of Margherita's.

To Francesco di Marco da Prato himself, in Pisa.
Received from Florence, 24 January 1386.

Letter 13 (1401888)
28 January 1386
Florence

In the name of God. 28 January 1386.

I received two of your letters very recently, and I will deal with the items I regard as most important.

It is true that Lapa keeps saying that she would like to leave, the reason being, I believe, that she quite rightly loves her husband and the rest of the family. You know that Monna Gaia is in poor health, and Niccolò is having a very difficult time.[58] It does men good, too, to find things done and to see their own woman in the house when they return home. I can't think of any other explanation. I, at least, try to make her as welcome as I know how, and I've begged the whole household to obey her more than me. You ask me whether I know if Monna Gaia is to blame for her wanting to go home. I don't know, as I have heard nothing.

I won't tell you what I think about Argomento now, or about anyone else, because I hope you will be here soon, and I will tell you in person my opinion about everything.

I am writing very little in response to the matters you've asked me about because I am very upset that you didn't go to bed after you arrived there and did not have dinner. I gathered from what you also wrote to Niccolò di Piero that you prepared a will and a dozen other things as well that weren't necessary and involved a lot of time. Everyone has to occupy themselves with the reams you write.[59]

You think everyone enjoys doing what you do. If you have a tired hand, you have only yourself to blame. You send messages telling me to enjoy myself and be happy. I have nothing in the world to be happy

58. Monna Gaia, who was Matteo Bellandi's daughter and the wife of Francesco's guardian, Piero di Giunta del Rosso, was mother-in-law to Lapa, who had been in Florence with Margherita since early January. See note 36, above.

59. At this point the manuscript is damaged, but the general meaning is clear.

about. You could make me happy if you wanted to, but you're not interested in your own happiness or anyone else's. Every evening when I go to bed, I remember that you have to stay awake until morning, and then you tell me to enjoy myself! Why don't you enjoy yourself more since you have the means, and allow others to enjoy themselves? If I had my way, I would relieve you of so many worries.

I will not respond to the things you write about, except the fact that you are wearing yourself out. This concerns me; the other things I don't care about at all. But I don't believe anything you write. About everything else I would swear that you have never told me a lie, except about living properly. I would swear that you never once told me the truth about that. Don't try to say anything else about it because the more you say the less I believe. I will never get tired of telling you this.

Bernabò was here and came to see me and said he would like his book back. I told him I didn't know where it was but that I would write to you about it. If you don't want us to give it to him, let us know.

You wrote to Piero that I should give him the key to the chest, and you've written nothing about it to me.[60] I didn't want to give it to him because when you left you said I was not to give it to anyone; then I decided I would. He found the documents you asked him for. Niccolò di Piero, Simone, and I were present, and we put every sheet of paper back inside, so everything is in order. I will keep the letter in Niccolò dell'Ammannato's hand.

I haven't seen Iacopo Girolli since he arrived […][61] when you have to be here for Lapa, whom I assured you'd be here soon. I begged her to stay until […].[62]

Tell me if you have received Monna Parte's cloth and if she is satisfied. Send her my greetings and, if you are happy to do so, you could bring me any money you receive that is mine.

I like the idea of making peace with you. I have never been at war with you. I don't know what it is you say you will bring me. I can't guess. When I have it, I will say: "How generous." You don't usually bring me many things when you come back here. I should say what you have said to me in the past—"Life is short"—but I console myself

60. This is Piero di Filippo Milanesi. See note 52, above.

61. On Iacopo di Cianghello Girolli's situation, see note 55, above.

62. The letter is too damaged to reconstruct the meaning here.

with the fact that I don't believe that at all. We will still live for a good while yet in exactly the same way. Enjoy the time that we have been given, and use it well for the sake of body and soul because we can't take anything with us. Note please that this was dictated by a woman.[63] I will say no more. God protect you always.

From your Margherita.

Tell Benvenuto the bread man that not everyone who managed to make you laugh should be a jester.[64]

Letter 14 (1401889)
30 January 1386
Florence

In the name of God. Amen. 30 January 1386.

I received your letter of 27 January. I respond here.

Concerning our relative, I know that you are right about everything, and I want the same as you do. I will pay the expenses and the doctor very willingly. If only this business were over, because it is one of my greatest sadnesses. I have not seen him since the day he came. If I see him, I will tell him my opinion, and I won't be afraid to let him know it.[65]

You tell a little story about Bernabò, that as soon as he arrived in Florence he was often taken for a citizen of Prato. He boasts about it and says he has an inn in Rome better than the one Felice has in Bologna.[66] He went on and on about it to me as well and to everyone else. About you he says what you deserve.

As for the preserves, I have decided not to make any. You have eaten too many preserves, and even if you could digest them, they

63. See letter 11.

64. The postscript is elusive. The Italian reads: "Di' a Benvenuto dello pane ne' chovorebono essere tutti gulari e furono mai in franca a farvi ridere."

65. Margherita refers to her brother-in-law, Iacopo di Cianghello Girolli.

66. See note 5, above.

would seem very different now from when Monna Piera made them.[67] They are very expensive to make; but if I thought you would be able to eat them, I would make them.

[…][68]

As for what you are going to bring me, I'm completely at a loss. Anything you bring me would please me as long as you return in good health. I have written any number of letters about how I feel. Now I will sit back patiently to see if what you say is true; even half true would do.

I would like to know if you are sleeping alone or not. If you aren't, I would like very much to know who is sleeping with you. If you say who it is and ask me why I want to know, I will tell you.[69]

You are always telling me to enjoy myself, and yet you want to keep toiling away. You say that's what you thrive on, since you have calluses on your hands from hardship and you are used to it. I understand that you deliberately tease me in every letter, but I don't mind. My anger has damped down a bit, but I have faith that it will revive soon, so look out!

I only wanted to talk of trivialities in this letter to keep the peace. I won't say anything else. May God protect you always so that I may have peace of mind.

Your Margherita, greetings, from Florence.

I haven't sent the cheese to Messer Niccolò Cambioni. Tell me if you want me to send it to him. If not, I will divide it and we will eat it. Don't send any more because we have enough to last until Carnival. Unless you want to give it to someone else, don't send any more in the meantime, and remember that the woman you gave the fish to last year said that there would be duty to pay on it.

I know about the lemons. I'm glad you bought them. Send them with the first messenger.[70] Again may God protect you.

---

67. Monna Piera had apparently made very good turnip preserves during Lent. See FD 181 and Melis, *Aspetti della vita economica medievale*, 46.

68. The paragraph here is too fragmentary to reconstruct. It concerns the return of one of the female household servants to Florence.

69. In the manner of the times, Francesco was sharing his bed with a male companion in whom Margherita hoped he would not confide.

70. The lemons were for Margherita's relative, Monna Chiarmonda.

To Francesco di Marco himself, in Pisa.
Received from Florence, 1 February 1386.

Letter 15 (1401890)
5 April 1386
Florence

In the name of God. Amen. 5 April 1386.

On 2 April I received your letter written on the 31st of last month. I reply here.

I haven't yet received the parcel of chickpeas and herrings. I don't know why. As soon as they arrive, I will let you know. I am happy that you gave some to Monna Parte and to our other friends.

I have now decided that I don't want any Malvasia wine. As the Romans say: "When one is fasting, medicine is useless," so I don't want any this Lent.[71]

I regret that you don't have the comforts we do, but if a person seeks out difficulties, he finds them. Sometimes it's good to experience discomfort so you can appreciate when you're well off. It might be said that these discomforts do the soul good, because what seem discomforts to us are not regarded as such by many people.

I've heard about the favorable responses Niccolò Pentolini has given you.[72] May it please God that this is so.

Certainly, from what I can see, God has granted you more favor than anyone else I can think of, and you have succeeded in ways that none of your friends ever imagined. May it please God that we are grateful for this. Certainly, if you don't decide to change your way of life and leave aside the things of this world and pay attention to your soul and to some extent your body, I'm afraid your fortunes will change. I know that you stay awake until midnight and eat at strange times. You just never stop! You should try to eat at the proper time for

---

71. On Malvasia wine, see note 121, below.

72. Niccolò di Francesco Pentolini da Montemurlo seems to have owed Francesco money. See FD 6.

your own sake and that of your household. They will be happier that way.

I beg you to live in a more ordered way during this long period, because I know that you are living badly. Do not fast at all because I am fasting for us both; and if I had the means to give alms, as you do, I would never fast, because at the moment there are so many good indulgences for those who can take advantage of them that you could sleepwalk into heaven. I believe, however, that you will miss out. All the almsgiving in the world will do you no good if you don't capitalize on it. This is the way we will live until death. I'll not say any more about it.

Stoldo's mother, Monna Lionarda, has complained to Aunt Giovanna because I haven't made the usual fuss of her. It has entered her head that Stoldo must be dead, and when she sees me she does nothing but cry. Write to Stoldo and tell him to send her a letter if he wants to, and tell him how she is behaving.[73]

Because it is Lent, I will write briefly and only occasionally because I don't have much of a brain even when it's not Lent, and a good deal less when it is, so please excuse me. A thousand greetings from Monna Giovanna, Francesca, and all the others. Give my regards to Monna Parte and to everyone else. May God protect you always.

From your Margherita, in Florence.

To Francesco di Marco da Prato himself, in Pisa.
Received from Florence, 6 April 1386.

---

73. Stoldo's mother, Monna Lionarda, was worried about her son, who was in Avignon. See Hayez, "Un facteur siennois de Francesco di Marco Datini," 319, 329. For Monna Giovanna, see note 34, above.

Letter 16 (1401717)
31 March 1387
Prato

In the name of God. 31 March 1387.[74]

Since you left here fifteen days ago, you haven't sent a single letter or any messages, so I won't inform you about what has been done here—because you have so many junior and senior employees, although I am worth all of them put together. There is no one who knows about your welfare or looks after your reputation as well as I do, because it is my duty. I remember things better than anyone else, and there is no one who knows more than I do what you like and don't like. Having lived with you for ten years, it would be a disgrace if I didn't know your ways. I would like you to be the Francesco you say you are, rather than someone who can make a fuss about lighting a small candle while at other times keeping a torch lit when there is no need. You have left me here for three weeks with builders in the house. You are not as attentive to all this as you think you are, and I believe it would be more decorous and a greater comfort to your family, to those who love you, if the construction work could stop when you are not here; and I believe you would be more praised for it. I don't say this because of the builders, who have carried on as usual, but because the main door has to remain open, as is the case on any building site. Anyone at all can come in or go out, and sometimes this cannot be avoided. But if you are as afraid as you seem, take away the materials so there'll be no need for anyone to be here when you are away. As if this house had to be built with gold! I will say no more about this. Your job is to command and mine to obey, and in my view I act in such a way that

---

74. Letters 16–25, sent between March 1387 and October 1389, were prompted by separations associated with building work at the Datini residence in Prato. In this letter, Margherita complains that she had been left in charge of the house and the workmen for three weeks with little contact from Francesco. As building intensified and technical and logistical problems arose on site during the following months, Francesco was often forced to intervene personally. On 20 September 1388 he even lent a hand, when he arrived in Prato in the rain to find the house unroofed. "I acted as laborer again to get it sorted out," he wrote; cited in Cavaciocchi, *The Merchant and Building*, 147. The elaborate extensions and beautification of the residence placed considerable strain on Francesco and caused conflict with Margherita.

I need not fear your reproaches. Tell Stoldo from me that I wish the best for him and grace be with him for the good of his soul and body.[75]

We are waiting to go to confession and to prepare ourselves for Pentecost.

Give my greetings to Niccolò and to Francesca. May God protect you.

From your Margherita, greetings from Prato.

I will make a new bag for all the letters and notes you have sent me.

To Francesco di Marco himself, in Florence.
Received from Prato, […] April.

Letter 17 (10891:3302781)
20 February 1388
Florence[76]

In the name of God. Amen.

I received your letter and was glad to have it.[77] I will send you what you ask for when I have a messenger, despite my misgivings, as you have chosen a terrible moment for building. Even if it costs me my life I will tell you the truth—and I always have. I think that you have made a bad decision to stay there during this dangerous season

75. Monte refers to Stoldo's troubles in a letter to Francesco of 1 April 1387. See Vivarelli, "Aspetti della vita economica pratese," 446. Francesco also refers to his anger about risky business transactions that Stoldo had undertaken, especially during an earlier mission in Sicily, in letters from 1385 and 1386 (Tieri di Benci to Stoldo, 2 December 1385: ASPo, D.182, 317344; 15 December 1385, D.186, 317348 and 25 January 1386, D.184, 317347). Two of Tieri's letters to Stoldo appear in Luciana Frangioni, *Milano fine trecento: Il carteggio milanese dell'Archivio Datini di Prato* (Florence: Opuslibri, 1994), 2:93–94 and 2:96–97. See also Tieri di Benci to Francesco Datini, 25 June to 2 July 1386 (ASPo, D.621, 110262; archival references supplied by Jérôme Hayez).

76. This is the earliest letter in Margherita's hand and was only recently identified. Jérôme Hayez kindly provided his transcription. Parts of the original are difficult to decipher because of Margherita's uncertain script.

77. See FD 9.

because it is difficult enough to remain healthy during Lent. I wish that God would give me the grace to worry [about others] as little as they worry about me. You understand what I mean. I keep imagining you in the courtyard in your cloak when in fact you are not there. Even if you decided to become compassionate, you would make a vow to Saint Anthony and all the saints to make your enemies happy and those who love you sad. You will always be the same Francesco. It is a wretched person who spends a pound to save a penny. That is the sort of person you are. I'm afraid that this house will be the thing that destroys both your body and soul. It will deprive you of rest in this life and the next because it has made you lose all common sense, and well you know it. You know how little good it will do you to stay there, and meanwhile time goes by from one day to the next and all you gain is more worry.

I won't say any more as I am a little angry with you for your own good. Please don't destroy your health all the time. Try to look after yourself and stay well. Remember, it is a risky time for those who have had a sickness like yours, as Master Giovanni says.[78] Make sure you are in bed by midnight, because the doctors say there was never such a dangerous season as this one. You are wise and know what you should do. You are not a child and it is a long time since you were a ward. However, if I had power over you, as you have over me, I would give you a guardian because sometimes you need one. I suspect that there in Prato they told you that I had been sick, although you make no mention of it in your letter. I am amazed, although I am not worried on my own account. Perhaps they did not report it, as I told Iacopo da San Donnino on the day that you left.[79] You will remember that I told you in the morning that I did not feel well. At nones I had a bad turn when I was in the dining room, although, thanks to God, I was able to call out.[80] I lost my senses and the power of speech, and so I remained. My condition caused great concern to all who love me. I never believed I would die as much as at that moment, and it would have been for the best, even if such a sudden death would have been

78. This is Giovanni di Banduccio, the Datinis' doctor. See note 2, above.

79. Iacopo di Matteo da San Donnino was a stonemason and carpenter who also supplied Francesco with timber.

80. See Appendix 2.

too cruel. May God protect me and those who love me from such a death. May it please God to do so. Please return as soon as you can. If it wasn't for this weather I wouldn't mind. All the household is well.

Bartolomea is as mad as she usually is, and she will never improve. Lorenzo comes here once a day without fail. I am still eating minced chicken. Since you left the doctor has not explained this episode to me nor the sickness that I have. It seems to me that it comes from my head because I am still feeling dizzy. Margherita commends herself to you. Niccolò and the household send their greetings.

The bearer of this letter is our baker Meo from Prato. May God protect you.

Your Margherita commends herself to you, 20 February 1387.

Received from Florence, 21 February 1387.

Letter 18 (1401893)
18 August 1389
Florence

In the name of God. Amen. 1389.

I am astonished that you have not written me a line since you left. I don't know what the reason might be. According to Niccolò di Piero, you said the reason was that no one from the warehouse came when the wine was being sold. On the morning you left […] came and I sent Andrea to get Stoldo, who was in bed, and he came here […]. The other morning the vintner came again and I sent Andrea to the warehouse.[81] Papi came with a message that they would take away some white wine, but I didn't want to let them because you said nothing to me about white wine.[82] Papi said that the […] barrel of white wine belonged to them. The other day the carter came, but I didn't send Andrea because Monna Giovanna was there.[83] They didn't do

---

81. The servant Andrea is mentioned frequently in the letters of 1389, but seems to have left the Datini household by the end of the year.

82. This is probably Papi di Michele, an employee in Pisa.

83. This is Margherita's aunt.

as well as you would have liked about the wine, but in the end it was done.[84] I worried about it and will continue to do so until you answer me and tell me what you are thinking, because I believe this is the reason you have not written to me. As for the white wine you sold to the *Podestà*, he has taken four barrels and two of the red.[85] We gave him the other two and because it was after [dinner] and Monna Giovanna, Monna Francesca, and Cilia were there, I told […] to go to the warehouse. I don't know what they have written. This is the truth about the wine. Write to me if you want him given more or not. We will follow your instructions.

Michele del Campana was here, and he brought cloth for Giovanna […].[86] I have shown Cilia hers; she thinks it a little too [light] and I agree; she would like it a bit darker.[87]

I have been told that you are building very busily indeed.

On Monday Federigo di Bindo left Venice at vespers […] between the twenty-third and twenty-fourth hour, and he caught a fever at Firenzuola and died of the plague. He did not confess or go to communion, so his family had [no] comfort from his [death].[88]

It seems to me to be the time to put one's affairs in order, [particularly] someone who has worked as much as you, because I think

---

84. Here, and later on in the letter, there are a number of lacunae, and the translation can only be approximate.

85. Prato had been under Florentine rule since 1351. It had retained some of its own institutions, however, such as the Gonfalonierate of Justice and the Magistracy of the Eight Defenders. These operated with a certain independence from Florence, although always under the watchful eye of the Florentine-appointed *Podestà*, who in this period was Agnolo d'Uguccione Tigliamochi. Francesco was keen to cultivate good relations with the men who came to Prato to take up this six-month office, and often sent them gifts of food or supplied them with wine at a favorable price. See Jérôme Hayez, "Le rire du marchand: Francesco di Marco Datini, sa femme Margherita et les *gran maestri* florentins," in *La famille, les femmes et le quotidien (XIVe–XVIIIe siècle): Textes offerts à Christiane Klapisch-Zuber*, ed. Isabelle Chabot, Jérôme Hayez and Didier Lett (Paris: Publications de la Sorbonne, 2006), 455.

86. Michele del Campana regularly carried letters and money for Francesco and supplied him with paper.

87. Margherita regarded her servant Cilia as trustworthy and Giovanna as unreliable. See letter 19.

88. Federigo di Bindo was the son of Margherita's cousin, Bindo Piaciti. There are numerous lacunae in this paragraph.

that a person who dies in that way dies in the worst possible way if he does not have God's mercy. I pray to God to look after our friend, and may He be pleased to forgive him.

[…] was here and says that Stoldo claims you sent a message to ask why he had not done the key for the door. He says that you did not tell him to do it and asked if you had told me. As far as I remember, you did not tell me.

Send my greetings to Monna Simona and Monna Tina and everyone else.[89]

I have no more to say for now. May Christ protect you. Try to come soon. I would have written to Monna Simona if it had not been for this sad event.

From your Margherita in Florence, greetings, 18 August.

To Francesco di Marco, Prato.

Letter 19 (1401894)
23 August 1389
Florence

[…].[90] You say you will send the horses on Tuesday evening so I can come on Wednesday. I don't see how this can be done because, as you know, on Wednesday I am expecting those pains of mine. If I have them on Wednesday, I could not come before Sunday without great difficulty. You know how well I am. In the meantime we will see what happens about Lisa.[91] For various reasons I don't think Giovanna should stay here. They are uncouth women, and it is not the moment

---

89. Piero di Paolo Rinaldeschi, and his wife Simona, lived across the street from Francesco in Via Rinaldesca on the corner of Via Tinaia. See Simona Brambilla and Jérôme Hayez, "La maison des fantômes: Un récit onirique de ser Bartolomeo Levaldini, notaire de Prato et correspondant de Francesco Datini," *Italia medioevale e umanistica* 47 (2006): 75–192. Their names, and that of their daughter Caterina, appear regularly in the correspondence.

90. The first page of this letter (which responds to FD 11) has not survived. The first sentence of the second page of the letter is too fragmentary to translate.

91. Monna Lisa di Niccolò was ill. See note 96, below.

to leave the house in the hands of people like that. They are women likely to turn out like the Provençal proverb: "Opportunity turns men into thieves and women into prostitutes." I think it would turn out like that for her, because even a man has his work cut out to supervise her and to keep her busy all the time. It seems to me that the best person to leave is Cilia. She is a trustworthy woman, and we have found out through experience that there is no reason to worry about her. Andrea would stay with her because it would be better than leaving her alone.

Didn't Matterello tell you about the straw that you ask about?[92] My bed is as full as necessary. I had the beds of these women emptied and filled with the straw that you sent. Andrea's is full and so is Bernabò's. I had the rest put in the stable loft.

I intend to air the clothes here until Sunday and to clean the house, so there will be no need to air them further when the cold weather arrives.

You tell me to bring only my Sunday clothes. I will bring as little as possible; but I think I could find the linings and the other bedcovers for winter, because we usually spend six or seven months in Prato.[93] I don't mind, however, because I am as happy there as here. From Sunday on I will be ready at any time you wish, even when the porcupine is awake and the birds are singing loudly.[94]

We have only drawn a *metadella* of red wine from the full barrel on two occasions. Write to tell us what to do about this and all the other things you want done.

There is still enough Vernaccia wine left for Cilia and Andrea. We don't drink other wine.

The *Podestà* has only taken one barrel of the wine. There are a hundred barrels. He says he wants to keep it all for himself, and the

92. Bartolomeo di Giovanni, known as Matterello, worked for Francesco as a farm laborer at Il Palco and in many other capacities in town. He appears regularly in the correspondence.

93. Francesco interpreted Margherita's intention to bring winter bedding from Florence to Prato as a veiled attack, evidence that she thought they would spend much longer in Prato than he had promised. On 25 August, Francesco responded: "On this matter I say that you have not understood my intentions at all; because you should believe that it is as certain as death that I have decided to behave in a different way, and to conduct a different life from what I did in the past so that, God willing, I can ensure you live happily. Don't believe that I want to continue being as I was in the past, nor do many things that I used to do" (FD 12).

94. Margherita means that she could leave even at dawn or early in the morning.

stronger it is, the happier he is. He always comes with the same barrel. He says we will recognize it, and that you have also seen it and can measure it. If it holds more, he is happy to pay more.

Monna Giovanna and Cilia are here and everyone is well. Niccolò, Monna Francesca, and Monna Giovanna send greetings. Send my regards to everyone. I have nothing more to say for now. May Christ protect you always.

Your Margherita sends you greetings, 23 August.

Francesco di Marco, in Prato.
Received from Florence, 24 August 1389.

Letter 20 (1401895)
26 August 1389
Florence

In the name of God. Amen. Written on 26 August 1389.

I received your letter of 25 August. I received it on 26 August, and I respond here as required. About Master Naddino, it will be done as you say.[95] Monna Lisa is still in the same state.[96] I have had my pains, and in fact they were not too bad given the circumstances.

I will expect you on Sunday evening if I don't hear otherwise. It seems to me that you have made the right decision to remain in Florence until the fair is over.[97] I think it will be best because of all the

95. Naddino di Aldobrandino Bovattieri, Monte's brother-in-law, was a doctor who had emigrated to Avignon in 1386. He returned to Tuscany in July 1389 as part of a papal delegation from Pope Clement VII. Francesco had instructed Margherita to serve the doctor the best wine if he visited Florence (FD 13). On 18 July 1389 Naddino had written to Francesco explaining that his official and family duties had prevented him from visiting his friends. For this letter and a detailed analysis of Naddini's life, see Hayez, "'Veramente io spero farci bene ... ,'" 517.

96. Francesco refers to Lisa di Niccolò as Margherita's relative (FD 63 and 69). Jérôme Hayez has found a reference to a Lisa dell'Ammannato Tecchini who was Monte da Uzzano's widow and the sister of Margherita's brother-in-law Niccolò dell'Ammannato Tecchini (Archivio di Stato, Lucca, Diplomatico, Altopascio, 1 December 1386).

97. The fair in Prato began on 8 September, the feast of the Virgin's birth.

people. I was asked if I would be in Prato for the fair. I thought I really wanted to come, but for God's sake let's avoid this nuisance if possible, because it is money thrown away and we don't have adequate provisions. Let's stay here.[98]

These last two days I have drunk Stoldo's wine because our wine is too strong. I wouldn't care if it weren't for these pains. You should drink our wine if you want to.

Let's talk about the things to buy at the fair another time because it hurts me to speak given the bad night I just had, when I lay awake in pain. I don't want to say anything else for now. May God be your protector and companion.

From Monna Margherita, wife of Francesco di Marco. Nanni di Domenico di Cambio in Florence.[99]

To Francesco di Marco himself, in Prato.
Received from Florence, 27 August 1389.

Letter 21 (1401896)
28 August 1389
Florence

In the name of God. Amen.

This morning I received your letter from Niccolò di Piero, and I have understood what you say about the wine. I have not answered you about Gherardo Becchi because he is in the country. Niccolò has written three letters to him and hasn't received any reply. When he does I will tell you.[100]

I will let Stefano know what you've said about the wine.

I will send Papero's bag with Niccolò or someone else.

---

98. Margherita and Francesco agreed to remain in Florence during the annual fair in Prato to avoid having to offer hospitality to visiting notables.

99. Margherita's scribe, Nanni, was the son of Domenico di Cambio, a business associate of Francesco's in Florence.

100. Francesco wanted to buy wine from Gherardo Becchi. See FD 13, and Margherita's letter 22.

As for your remaining there in Prato until Thursday, you can do as you please because you are the master, which is a fine role but one that should not be taken too far.[101] But if the master weren't as occupied with the fair as he is, I would not still be in Florence for dinner on Monday. I don't know who it is I am meant to be looking after here. I am ready to do anything in order to be together, God willing, and you should not keep on saying that it would be too much of a burden for me. I am right, and don't try to take away that fact by shouting.

I don't understand the need for you to send a message every Wednesday saying that you will be here on Sunday. It seems to me that every Friday you change your mind. At least send me a message on Saturday evening so that I can do some quick shopping, and that way we will be better off on Sundays! I had found someone to keep me and these women company, so it worked out well. Unhappy the person who trusts you! You think you can trick everyone, but the joke is actually on you! You have the judge there. I don't know if it is he who advises you to leave your wife all alone in August. I believe that if you follow his advice, some of it will be good, but a portion will be extremely bad. If only he were presiding here! Youth excuses a great many things! Ser Bartolomeo is really on your side.[102] He passed through here, and I asked him what you were up to. He acted as if he had not even seen you. If only I could believe it! I wish there were more like him, and that judge you have there. I am really surprised that Monna Simona has not stood up for me, but I believe in the end

---

101. On 26 August Francesco had written that he expected to be in Florence on Sunday evening (FD 13); but two days later he decided to stay in Prato until the following Thursday: "I will be brief because I expect to be there soon. But while I plan to be there in Florence until the fair is over, it could still be that I will stay here until Thursday which is the market day for buying flax. If I can get it at a good price, as I still believe I can, I will be in Florence sooner and will leave Monte and Barnaba to look after everything" (FD 14).

102. Here Margherita suggests that Francesco was delaying his departure for Florence because he was having far too good a time in Prato entertaining his neighbor, the lawyer and judge Piero Rinaldeschi, and the notary Bartolomeo di Nicola Levaldini. Both friends came from magnate families and enjoyed considerable political influence and social prestige; hence Francesco's efforts to cultivate them. See Brambilla and Hayez, "La maison des fantômes," 88–128.

she will, because I am always pleased to see her and new faces.[103] May God recompense her for the past and give her something to be happy about, as I wish for myself.

Commend me to Messer Piero and to Monna Simona. That's all for now. May Christ protect you.

From your Margherita, who commends herself to you on 28 August.

To Francesco di Marco, in Prato.
Received from Florence, 29 August 1389.

Letter 22 (1401897)
30 August 1389
Florence

In the name of God. Amen.

Yesterday I received your letter, delivered by Biagio d'Alesso, but I won't answer it because you have said you will be here on Monday evening. A letter has arrived addressed to Stoldo. I sent Andrea at once to find out why you weren't coming. He said he didn't know why and that he believed you wouldn't be here, even by Tuesday. How right he was!

You say that you worked until the seventh hour. This is hardly a novelty, and now we've even taken to plastering on Sundays![104] You say that you write to me so that I won't worry. Has it occurred to you that I don't worry about what you imagine but rather because you will never change? Every day you say that you won't be the same Francesco any more.[105] Do you think I can be very happy when you send a message to say that you worked until bedtime because you had so much to do?

103. Piero Rinaldeschi's wife, Simona, was Margherita's friend and neighbor. See note 89, above.

104. Francesco had admitted in a letter of 29 August (FD 15) that he had been slaking lime so that it would not be wasted and had emptied the well to prepare for building works at the house in Prato. On this theme see note 74, above.

105. Francesco had promised to change his ways only a week before. See note 93 above.

It is this that upsets me, because I wouldn't object if you worked like that only when you saw it was necessary, but I see this is not so. You cannot be building and doing other things elsewhere at the same time. It's time you did something apart from building, because I think your main worry is the time you've wasted. If there were ever any time to waste, it's certainly not now, since everyone is expecting the plague to arrive.[106]

You write that you have had many misfortunes. Don't make me laugh. May it please God that no man has had as few as you. I thank God for all the favors that he has granted you. You ought to come on Saturday evening to look after your household because God says that you must steal rather than let us die of hunger.[107] If I could only know what these misfortunes were, I would fast even on the Monday of the feast of Saint Catherine so she would give you grace and consolation in your sorrows.[108] But I have been told exactly the opposite: that you are happy and are having a good time, which is very unlike you. I will repeat what Porcellana once said: "Good will come to those who do good—this is Porcellana's motto."[109]

Since I wrote we have had a reply about the wine from Gherardo Becchi.[110] He hasn't got what we require. Stefano is not here.

We have the flask of rose water.

For now there's nothing more. May Christ protect you.

Your Margherita commends herself to you from Florence 30 August.

To Francesco di Marco, in Prato.
Received from Florence, 2 September 1389.

---

106. The plague eventually arrived in Prato, and Francesco moved his household to Pistoia from July 1390 to May 1391. See Brambilla and Hayez, "La maison des fantômes," 105–6.

107. This reference to Francesco's duty to look after his household bears some relationship to Proverbs 6:30.

108. Margherita probably refers here to the popular saint Catherine of Alexandria, whose feast day was 25 November. The meaning of the statement seems to be that she would give up the usual culinary treats associated with this feast day.

109. Giovanni di Lotto degl' Angiolini was known as Porcellana. He was married to Monna Sandra. See Melis, *Aspetti della vita economica medievale*, 67.

110. See letter 21.

Letter 23 (1401718)
16 October 1389
Prato

In the name of God. Amen. 16 October 1389.

I am sending you the keys with Matterello; the key of the large box and that of the chest, because I forgot to give them to you. Send me two of my dark-colored hoods that are in the chest, because I need them, and two skeins of raw thread that are in the same chest, and look in one of the chests for a piece of gray cloth belonging to Lucia, and send it to me.[111]

And send me a pair of combs that are on the shelves in the carding room. Send me the long scarlet overgown that is in the box beside the little bed. If I want anything else I will let you know.

Send my regards to Niccolò and everyone else. Remember to get my pills made up, and if there is any cumin, send me some. If not, try to procure it from somewhere.

As for the large flask that is in the cupboard, take out half of the infusion with one of those small flasks that are in the cupboard full of infusions that I had made. Top up the large flask, and our friend can have it, because it is worth nothing. One of the flasks contains burdock and the other fennel. They are to be mixed in equal portions.

From your Monna Margherita, in Prato.

Francesco di Marco da Prato, in Florence.
Received from Prato, 17 October 1389. Answered.

---

111. The slave Lucia was the mother of Francesco's only surviving child, Ginevra, born in 1392. See Mazzei, *Lettere di un notaro a un mercante del secolo XV*, 1:229 and 1:353.

Letter 24 (1401719)
20 October 1389
Prato

In the name of God. 20 October 1389.

On Tuesday morning, 19 October, I received many things from you, delivered by Nanni di Luca da Santa Chiara. At the same time I received a complete list of the goods, and nothing was missing.[112]

The first letter that I received from Monte asked about the fastenings taken off your overgown. I took them off because I needed some for the overgown that I made from your mantle, since I didn't have any. Antonio the tailor knows this because he took them off.

The thread that you sent me is the one I wanted. I thought it was raw but it is finished, so don't look any more.

I would like you to buy two linings there: one for Giovanna and one for Lucia. Lucia's should be thin and inexpensive because she will soon spoil it; Giovanna's should be heavier because she is more careful, and buy half a yard of black cloth to make caps for them.

I still haven't received the flask of Malvasia wine that you told me you would send. I received a flask containing an infusion. I don't know if it is half of the big flask or what it is. I would like to know what it is before I use it. Send it to me a bit at a time, from the large flask as well as from the other, and then I will have a better idea of its quality.

If you agree, we will stay here until All Saints' Day. Let me know, and I think we will enjoy ourselves.

The women from Niccolò's household are amazed that Niccolò is not coming. They are upset and would like to know the reason for various rumors they hear about him here. Tell Niccolò to write them a letter in his own hand, giving them some news that they will know is from him.[113]

Look among the Perpignan hose to see if there is a decent old pair for Andrea.[114] They would be stronger.

112. Margherita is responding here to FD 17.

113. This is Niccolò di Piero di Giunta del Rosso.

114. Perpignan is a woolen jersey cloth, a specialty of the Catalan town of Perpignan, and was not made in Florence before 1418. See Hidetoshi Hoshino, *L'Arte della lana in Firenze nel basso medioevo* (Florence: Olschki, 1980), 235–36.

Tell Domenico di Cambio to buy me two samite wimples, fine enough to wear under hoods.

If you want to buy linings for the girls, I will send you the measurements.[115] I will send you Giovanna's and Lucia's house gowns. You should have them made according to these models.

I will send you thirty loaves of bread with the first available carrier, because Nanni da Santa Chiara hasn't found any pack animals. Nanni will bring the wine on Friday. When Nanni arrives tell him when you want him to bring the letters. He says he is always available. I told Monna Nanna about the lining.[116] Make sure it is beautiful and in a fashionable color.

I have no more to add now. May God protect you.

From your Monna Margherita, in Prato.

Francesco di Marco da Prato, at the Tornaquinci Loggia in Florence. Received from Prato, 21 October 1389.

Letter 25 (1401720)
23 October 1389
Prato

In the name of God. 23 October 1389.

On 21 October I received your letter from the carter Nanni di Luca. I answer here.

I am sending you the measurements for the linings for Giovanna and Lucia with Matterello. The one for Giovanna is tied with white thread, and the pattern for the collar is the small piece within it. Lucia's is tied with black thread and indicates the size she wants it. The collar pattern is the smaller piece of cloth.

---

115. As the cold weather approached, Francesco wished to provide undergarments of fur, or perhaps something cheaper, for Giovanna and Lucia.

116. Monna Nanna was Barzalone di Spedaliere's wife.

Matteo showed me the black cloth, but it is not suitable.[117] If you have any of that white cloth, use it, or buy the English one and Niccolò will dye it black.[118]

I am sending with Matterello two lengths of linen that I got from Biagio d'Alesso, as you requested.

I am sending with Matterello twenty loaves of bread in a small sack. There are twelve for you that are marked; the other eight are not marked.

Yesterday evening I received on your behalf from Nanni di Luca two gold florins for expenses, and two pounds of cumin for Michele. Today I received a flask of Malvasia wine from Matterello. I received a bed canopy and a horse blanket.

I am sending you an ounce of rhubarb extract with Matterello, and that seems plenty to me. In my opinion this one seems by far the best. I am not sending the curtain with Matterello because it seems to me that the packhorse is overloaded. On Monday I will redo the packages in my own way and send them to you with the first carter.

Today I received a cartload of vine cuttings from Giovanni the saddler, and there are two hundred bundles. They didn't seem to us to be of good quality. We put them up in the storeroom where the grain was and spread them over the room so they would dry.

I didn't ask you about the shoes. It isn't usual for important merchants to open letters addressed to other people and read the messages of their agents.[119] I answered two letters concerning those matters, as seemed appropriate. I won't say any more for now, so as not to give you more problems, because it seems to me you have enough of them.

Send my regards to Niccolò, Francesca, and everyone else.

From your Monna Margherita, in Prato.

Francesco di Marco, in Florence.
Received from Prato, 24 October 1389.

---

117. This is probably Matteo di Andrea di Matteo Bellandi, Monna Gaia's nephew and a distant kinsman of Francesco.

118. This is the master dyer Niccolò di Piero di Giunta del Rosso.

119. Francesco seems to have opened a letter from Margherita addressed to her sister Francesca, regarding shoes. See FD 17.

Letter 26 (1401721)
6 February 1394
Prato

In the name of God. 6 February 1394.[120]

Since you left here I haven't written to you because there was no need. This is just to let you know about the wines, because yesterday morning Niccolaio Martini, Biagio, Ser Chimenti, Barzalone, and Bernabò were here and they all agreed not to touch any of them until they hear from you. Barzalone will tell you everything that should be done because he was with them. Bernabò tasted both the Razzese and

---

120. After a long gap, the correspondence resumes in February 1394 and gathers momentum from this point on. Three quarters of Margherita's letters were sent between early 1394 and the spring of 1400 (letters 26–217). The mid-1390s were particularly difficult for the Datinis; hence the density of the couple's exchanges as they cooperated closely to protect their financial and other interests. As a citizen of Prato, the merchant had to pay the *libra* or *estimo* tax, decided by the local Magistracy of the Eight and paid by inhabitants of Florentine territory who were not citizens. At the beginning of 1394, however, because of his long periods of residence in Florence, the citizens of his district (the Gonfalone of the Red Lion) began a campaign to make Francesco a citizen so that he might contribute in a substantial way to that administrative district's tax levy and thus lessen their own contributions. Florence was divided into sixteen districts (*gonfaloni*); Under this regime, individual tax payments within each Gonfalone were allocated by a committee of its residents. Florentines had to pay the *prestanza*, or forced loan, which was likely to be more costly than the *estimo* of Prato. A person could become a citizen after six months' residence, but Florentine citizenship was meant to be voluntary. It is clear that Francesco was being pressured to become a citizen because of his wealth; hence the questions about his periods of residence in Florence. Francesco resisted the campaign to force citizenship on him because he paid less tax in Prato and could influence the Eight more easily than he could influence the officials of the Red Lion. Eventually he had to capitulate, become a citizen, and pay the *prestanza*. Francesco's Florentine friends—the notary Lapo Mazzei, and Guido del Palagio—did their best to defend the merchant from excessive tax assessments in Florence, but Francesco remained bitter about his treatment by the citizens of his Gonfalone. In May 1394 he complained to a friend and fellow merchant in Milan about "the great wrong done me by a Gonfalone where I have stayed only once. Whether I like it or not, they want to make me a citizen, to get at my money.... They say I am rich and have built a fine house in Prato." See Frangioni, *Milano fine trecento*, 1:588. On the Florentine taxation system in this period, see Giovanni Ciappelli, "Il cittadino fiorentino e il fisco alla fine del Trecento e nel corso del Quattrocento: uno studio di due casi," *Società e storia* 11, no. 46 (1989): 823–72, particularly pages 828–44; and Dale V. and Francis W. Kent, *Neighbours and Neighbourhood in Renaissance Florence: The District of the Red Lion in the Fifteenth Century* (Locust Valley, NY: Augustin, 1982), 57–59.

the Malvasia wines and says that they will not be spoilt if they are left alone until your return.[121]

The flour for the household is running out. Tell us what we should do.

Niccolaio has been to see me and told me that a citizen of the Red Lion district [of Florence] had been here. He asked a friend of Niccolaio how long we had owned the house there; when had we returned from Avignon; why had we been charged such a small amount of tax; and if he had ever heard that you wanted to become a citizen of Florence.[122] This all seemed childish to me. There are people there who know when you returned from Avignon and whether you want to become a citizen [...]. Niccolaio seems really to want someone else to enroll you, and he is warmly encouraging others to do so. I questioned him about who the Florentine citizen was. He said he would tell you if you were here, but he refused to tell me.

I would really like to know how far you've followed the matter and the other one to do with the Genoese business [...], which worries me more. I beg you to let the matter drop and let others set up in Genoa. Don't you do it just because you do everything. You were doing things [...] to help others rather than yourself, and it seems to me that you can be excused from this before God and the world. Niccolaio and the others do not doubt that you or Stoldo wish to go ahead, but I am one of those who believe that Stoldo doesn't wish to take any risks. I believe that what he did was prompted by good intentions, and I don't know who could have foreseen that this would then happen. Everyone says: "He is making a fuss because of this business." These things are difficult to endure and so I feel anxious because I sense that you're not as patient as I would like. In that place beware of

---

121. The early-ripening *razzese* grape was cultivated in Liguria and produced a full-bodied wine drunk especially in winter. See Melis, *I vini italiani nel medioevo*, 79. Malvasia was an aromatic, sweet wine imported from the Peloponnesian peninsula by Venetian merchants. See Maria Giagnavoco, *Mercanti a tavola: Prezzi e consumi alimentari dell'azienda Datini di Pisa (1383–90)* (Florence: Opuslibri, 2002), 286–87. Margherita's cousin Bindo Piaciti, who operated as a merchant in Venice, seems to have sometimes supplied the Datini household. See note 500, below.

122. Niccolaio Martini, a draper and close friend of Francesco, was prominent in Pratese politics. Francesco replied to Margherita that he knew who the person was and told her not to worry (FD 18).

others trying to infect you with their problems. And remember what Tina always says. Please answer me about these concerns so that I may be a little happier.[123]

Nannino has returned and says that you told him to sleep here this evening; and so he will, and he is looking after the animals, as you told him.

Cristofano and Nannino are working on the lower enclosure toward the Bisenzio River, and Nanni di Santa Chiara is fetching the sand. He was told to bring some rocks, and he says that rocks can be found anywhere but not sand.

Brancaccio, Meo, and Cecco and the garden hand have finished the trench and are now working on the vines. Nannino says they are doing their best, as if you were here.

Tell us what we should do with the oil barrels you bought which we have here.

As for the tasks that you left to be done both here and at Il Palco, we will do all we can to satisfy your wishes, and you need not worry at all about matters here.

Remember to speak to Monna Taddea, and ask Domenico di Cambio to send the table napkins if they are already sewn.[124]

Commend me to Niccolò and to Caterina, and greet Monna Francesca and everyone else there.

I've nothing more to add. May God protect you.

Your Monna Margherita, greetings from Prato.

To Francesco di Marco himself, in Florence.
Received from Prato, 6 February 1394. Answered.

---

123. In 1393, Stoldo and his cousin Andrea del Bonanno persuaded Francesco to invest 500 florins in a joint venture with the Florentine wool processor Nofri di Michele di Mato. Nofri set up spinning and weaving equipment in Genoa and recruited skilled artisans from Florence, starting production in September 1393. Stoldo seems to have secretly invested more than 2,000 florins of Francesco's money in the business, which failed to flourish. On 6 February 1394 (FD 18), Francesco wrote to Margherita that the partners had determined that Nofri should cease processing wool in Genoa and return to Florence within six months. See Melis, *Aspetti della vita economica medievale*, 232–36.

124. For Taddea Pucci, see note 308, below.

Letter 27 (1401722)
8 February 1394
Prato

In the name of God. 8 February 1394.

On the 6th of this month I wrote you a letter, and I haven't had an answer from you.[125] The reason was to explain why I am sending you Matterello, who says he wants to come and see you. Piero sent us news that he had a fine castrated sheep that had been milk-fed and a stuffed pocket of six-month-old veal. It was not of the best quality. I sent it to you, however, because I don't believe they are as good in Florence.[126]

Nanni has recovered the money that you wanted him to collect; that is Antonio di Forese's fifteen florins. He has recorded that Paolo di Bertino is the debtor and Antonio is the creditor.[127] I sent for the rest of the money, and he said that it wasn't due until the end of January. Nanni replied that if he gave it to him by the last day of the month, that would be satisfactory, but in the end he [Paolo] promised to give it to me on market day.

Our young servant came back from collecting the money and was returning through the piazza. He says that there were two men walking in front of him who were talking about the Florentine *prestanza* tax. One said he had dined with Nofri di Palla degli Strozzi, and that he had asked Nofri, "What's Francesco doing? I saw him speaking with you in the New Market." And Nofri had replied that you were there for the Florentine *prestanza*, and the man from Prato then said that you were a taxpayer at Prato. Nofri replied that the *prestanza* had priority, and the man from Prato replied that the first priority was the *libra* tax at Prato and you would defend yourself strongly because you had many friends and you were well liked. Nofri answered that it was what you deserved. He had to pay fifty florins, and he claimed you had more money than Prato was worth—what kindness, eh? The man

---

125. FD 18 had not yet arrived.

126. This pocket of veal, stuffed with tripe, bread, and herbs, was a Genoese specialty.

127. The reference is to the double-entry accounting system, in which debits and credits are registered side by side. See Melis, *Aspetti della vita economica medievale*, 391–424. Paolo di Bertino Verzoni was a money changer from Prato. See Fiumi, *Demografia*, 500.

from Prato answered that you did not have one fiftieth of the wealth that they claimed, and Nofri replied, "There are very few gentlemen who live as he does." This is how he and the other citizens of Florence judge you.[128] In the meantime I and my whole household are turned into servants when they come to stay with us. I remind you that the various *Podestà* stay with us so they can save the expense of their servants. I won't even mention the time when Messer Guelfo brought his daughter-in-law![129] I will always be ashamed of the things Messer Guelfo did to make me stay that evening, and you, in order to honor the Florentines on their arrival, sent me to scavenge for provisions, because you know I do that so well. There would be many such stories: the arrival of the lord of Mantua and other similar events happen all the time.[130] This is the sort of work I do. At least I should be able to speak a little when the company arrives, and you should listen to me a little more willingly. It would turn out better for us, because we would obtain the best friend that we can have in this world. In my opinion, today this friend is money; because if you had received a return to match all the money you have spent entertaining these guests, they would be your best friends.

You know that this servant has been with us for a short while, and he doesn't know anyone yet. I asked him how tall the man was. He said he was small and thickset and that he saw him go into the house that is beside Nofrino the tailor and has a doorway with three steps, and, according to the boy, he has a beautiful wife. From everything

128. The Strozzi family was one of the richest and most powerful in the Red Lion district of Florence. On Francesco's tax situation, see note 120, above.

129. Guelfo di Simone Pugliesi, a leader of the Prato Ghibelline faction, became a Florentine citizen in 1375. He was a major political figure, holding prestigious judicial posts throughout Italy. See Fiumi, *Demografia*, 458–59. The faction opposing the Pugliesi was led by Francesco Mainardi, one of the Guazzalotti, and the jurist Niccolaio Migliorati. The Pugliesi and Guazzalotti families had been hostile to each other for at least forty years. In 1388, approximately one hundred members of each faction engaged in a series of hostilities. See Brambilla and Hayez, "La maison des fantômes," 91. See also Margherita's letter of 28 February 1394 (letter 36), which compares the wealth of Francesco Datini, Piero Rinaldeschi, and Guelfo Pugliesi.

130. The Lord of Mantua, Francesco Gonzaga, visited Prato and dined at the Datini palace on 21 June 1392. See Melis, *Aspetti della vita economica medievale*, 73.

the boy says, I think it must be Ser Francesco di Ser Alberto.[131] I heard it said among the women that this man is taking up office with Nofri degli Strozzi. I have told you this against my better judgment because it is not my habit to pass on gossip. I have always been against people who do pass it on to you so that you won't feel enmity for anyone. But I do this to inform you, because I think that you had greater trust in Nofri than anyone. But I excuse him somewhat because he has to pay up, and he is considered a bit of a miser. If you were to behave that way, you would confirm their suspicions. Pardon me if I am making a mistake, but I say it because I'm upset. May God protect you.

Greetings from Margherita, in Prato.

Letter 28 (1401723)
14 February 1394
Prato

In the name of God. 14 February 1394.

Yesterday I received your letter from Castagnino.[132] I respond here promptly to what seems most urgent.

Bernabò did not receive his letter before mine, but it seems that mine says the same as his, so I will organize what I think is required. We had the mule shod and attended to. I am sending Castagnino to you with the mule, and soon I will be sending Nannino, who says he is happy to do what you want. He would go to the end of the world, not just to Pisa. Nannino seems best to me because he looks more presentable and better dressed than Matterello.

I am sending you Nanni da Santa Chiara with our three pack animals and with his donkey. I am also getting him to bring you all the fruit that there is and thirty-three eggs. The ones that are marked came from our hens on Thursday and Friday, and I am sending you twenty loaves of bread. They are not as good as I would like. I am not sending you any poultry because the hens are all thin and every day

---

131. The notary and judge Francesco di Ser Alberto Cianfanelli. See Fiumi, *Demografia*, 347–48.

132. FD 19. Castagnino was another of the regular carriers.

they are laying eggs, which I have gathered. Because the hens are small and skinny, buy them there if you need any.

I am not sending you the female donkey, as I have been advised not to, and we are not sure whether Nanni da Santa Chiara could lead so many animals there. Meo says that he can get four and a half florins for her, and Nanni da Santa Chiara and others who understand such matters say he should sell her because she will never be any good. Tell me whether you want me to sell her—yes or no?

Domenico Santini came here and spoke to me about various things. Among other things he said that Ser Chimenti has asked him for money owing to the wool guild. According to what Domenico says, Nanni di Guiduccio also asked him. Domenico says that whenever he took any goods, you said to Matteo, "Put it on my account." So I sent for Ser Chimenti and asked him to be so good as not to take any further action until we had heard from you, especially in relation to the master artisans who have been working for you this year.[133] It seemed to me the best thing to do, so reply to Ser Chimenti however you like.

Castagnino has told me you told him to tell Meo that if the cuttings were being planted, there was no need for more than one worker. Cristofano will finish preparing the cuttings tomorrow. According to what Nannino tells me, there is still enough work for three days. So it would seem best to me that it was finished, so I will arrange to get it done unless I have any instructions from you to the contrary. A lot more could have been done if others were employed, but if you don't want them, that's that.

Bernabò has told me to inform you how much work it has been possible to do. Everyone I have sent there tells me that the work was done as well as if you had been present. I simply ask Nanni to do what's needed, and it is done.

Niccolaio Martini came to see me yesterday, and he told me that Giovanni Panciatichi was in Prato and that he had passed on your

---

133. Nanni and Domenico di Guiduccio Santini dal Montale were builders. See letters 29, 97, and 107. The notary, Chimenti di Ser Leone, first mentioned in letter 26, increasingly acted as Francesco's debt collector.

message to him.[134] I asked him if he would be in Florence tomorrow and he said no.

From what he tells me, everyone there says that you are right. I am very pleased. May God grant that you are treated as you treat others.

With this letter there is also one from Pisa, as well as one from Pulicciaio and one from Barzalone.

Tell Niccolò that I tried the chickpeas, and in my opinion they are very good. So he should send me a lot; that is, as many as he can. I don't remember the price that he told me I had said, so let me know. I have made preparations to sell what I can on Monday, when the market is being held. I think that one can't go wrong in selling them. If they were mine, I would do this: I would set a flexible price to sell them quickly.

Tell Francesca to order twenty-six yards of those ribbons for me in the next few days. They should not be any wider than the last ones. They are for Chiarito's daughter.[135] She wants them here within a week, without fail.

I sent Tina to the baptism of Domenica's child.[136] She said she didn't want to go on foot and that if you were here, she wouldn't have to walk. Despite her protests I sent her on foot, with Bernabò and Monna Piera.[137] She found Castagnino at Mercatale. She knew how to flatter him so well that he put her on the mule. A man asked whose daughter she was, and she brazenly said she was Francesco di Marco's daughter. She is more arrogant than you. This is because you insist on spoiling her. She says, "If Francesco were here you wouldn't be-

---

134. The Panciatichi family were influential and very wealthy Florentine magnates. See Lauro Martines, *The Social World of the Florentine Humanists 1390–1460* (London: Routledge & Kegan Paul, 1963), 63–65, 76–77.

135. Chiarito was a poor, distant relative of Francesco. One of his daughters was about to marry, and Margherita concerned herself with the girl's trousseau. Francesco provided dowries for four of Chiarito's daughters. See FD 9, 18, 21, 45, and his will in Mazzei, *Lettere di un notaro*, 2:277.

136. Tina, Margherita's niece, was living in the Datini household. The baptism was probably that of Domenica and Saccente's child, Nanna.

137. Monna Piera was a servant whom Margherita regarded as unsatisfactory. See letters 50 and 51.

have like that." It would be better if she stayed with her mother. She wouldn't be so proud. I have no more to add. May God protect you.

Give my regards to Niccolò, and greet Monna Francesca and everyone else there.

Margherita sends you greetings from Prato.

Francesco di Marco da Prato, in Florence.
Received from Prato, 14 February 1394. Answered.

Letter 29 (1401724)
17 February 1394
Prato

In the name of God. 17 February 1394.

Nanni da Santa Chiara has been here and says he must go to Florence with two pack animals loaded with the dyed cloth and a load of wood; he says you told him to bring it. I asked him if he had a load for three animals, and he said he only had a load for two; so I am keeping the horse, which also needs shoeing. I will have it shod, and I am using it today to carry wood and manure for the kitchen garden. Cristofano will be working there as well as Matterello and Giorgio, and they will finish as quickly as they can. I did not send Nannino to Il Palco yesterday because we could not get that white wine until it was very late. In fact it was only delivered at nones. I sent Nannino to Filettole and the barrel has been filled, so that has been taken care of. I had him bring the broad beans to Ser Chimenti's house and got him to carry the materials that Nanni di Guiduccio asked for to build the fireplace, and for the rest of the time I had him making lime.[138] So today Nanni will find everything ready, and I gave him orders to use that lime.

Meo was here yesterday with Schiatta.[139] I asked him what they were doing. Schiatta advised that all the cuttings be planted this year.

138. This is Nanni di Guiduccio Santini dal Montale. See letter 28.

139. Schiatta, often referred to as Tantera di Niccolò, was an agricultural laborer who worked on Francesco's farms and orchards at Filettole, above the villa Il Palco. See FD 20.

If they are not done in a particular way, they will die, according to him. The method is this: a little hole is made for each cutting, and he wants it to be filled with pigeon manure; so I told Meo to follow his instructions. I asked him how long this would take, and he said that it would be completed in a day, so I ordered him to do what Schiatta says. I invited Schiatta to dine with me, and I urged him to look after these vineyards of ours properly. It seems to me he has great love for you and serves you gladly. He promised me that he will be here next week and he will look after them better than if they were his own.

Three and a half bushels of Niccolò's chickpeas were sold for forty-eight *soldi* a bushel. I think it would be better if you gave him the money there in Florence, or do you want me to send it to him? I think that this was the best way of selling them. So if you are happy, send me many bushels.

I am not sending you apples or pears because we couldn't find any. I will deal with the matters you left me to do as best I can.

Nanni says he has the twenty-five florins owed by Antonio Forese. Paolo di Bertino received them.[140]

That is all for now. May God protect you. Give my regards to Niccolò and send my greetings to everyone there.

From Margherita, in Prato.

Francesco di Marco da Prato, in Florence.
Received from Prato, 17 February 1394. Answered on the 17th.

Letter 30 (1401725)
18 February 1394
Prato

In the name of God. 18 February 1394.

Nanni di Santa Chiara brought me your letter, which requires only a short reply. The reason I did not send you three pack animals is because the black one had a sore front right hoof. It's not serious. We

---

140. See letters 27 and 53.

made him a poultice, and I think he can be used tomorrow, but I think it would be better to leave it on for one or two days until he gets better.

Cristofano di Ser Francia asked Nanni for a florin. He answered, as he had been told by me, that he only collected money, and it seems Cristofano asked Barzalone for money for a pig. I think that he is asking for too much. I don't think he intends to work much for us but rather is thinking of going to the monastery to do the work that he had promised. If he asks for money from me, I will tell him that I have orders from you not to give money to anyone. Barzalone will write to you about it, as he promised Cristofano.[141]

Nanni says he collected twenty *lire* from Lodovico di Ser Iacopo, and perhaps today or tomorrow he will get approximately another fifteen *lire*.[142]

Tell Niccolò that I found the twelve rabbit skins that Matterello brought when he came from Florence. He says he told me they were rabbit. I didn't pay attention because of those pains of mine. Lucia thought they were gloves and threw them in the big chest. So Niccolò shouldn't be surprised that I didn't answer that I had received them. I don't know why he sent them. When he was here I asked him what they were worth. He didn't want to tell me. I told him not to send them to me. Find out what they cost him and give him the money, and if he doesn't want it, I will send the skins back because I don't need them. Remind Cristofano that he should read the list of goods that he took with him and send us the things that we need.

May God protect you.

Give my regards to Niccolò and send my greetings to everyone there.

From your Margherita, in Prato.

To Francesco di Marco from Prato, in Florence.
Received from Prato, 18 February 1394. Answered on the 18th.

---

141. The carpenter Cristofano di Ser Francia made constant requests for money. Francesco regarded these requests with some impatience, especially as he did not have a high regard for the carpenter's skills. See FD 21.

142. Lodovico di Ser Iacopo di Messer Leo Villani da Prato was a money changer. See letter 38. For the Villani family, see Fiumi, *Demografia*, 503.

Letter 31 (1401726)
19 February 1394
Prato

In the name of God. 19 February 1394.

This morning your letter was delivered by Castagnino, and this evening I received your other one from Nanni di Santa Chiara.[143] I will answer here about the matters that are most urgent.

I sent immediately for Niccolaio Martini and Ser Schiatta, and I told them your wishes and I asked Ser Schiatta to go to Florence.[144] He said that, if necessary, he would get himself carried there to you and he would come if it killed him, but I think he is in a bad way, so I didn't insist. He told me one reason why he doesn't think his presence is necessary. He thinks it is more necessary on Monday, and both he and his friend are determined to come as required and to stay there until the *signori* are chosen.[145] We decided together that Niccolaio and Ser Baldo should go, […][146] they are happy to go because it is necessary. It was agreed this evening to […] make an application, and their requests were approved. They are going to Florence tomorrow morning, and they have obtained permission from their commune to accompany Messer Torello, and they will present the case to assist the commune of Prato.[147] So have the petition written meanwhile and prepare everything that you consider is necessary. Make sure that Niccolaio Martini has his mantle at the Lion Inn, which is opposite Piazza della Signoria and down the street of the scissor makers, so he does not have to send for it.

I was amazed the other time that they rode to the house of Niccolò, because it was not a prudent thing to do. People are keen to demonstrate your connections with Niccolaio and Ser Baldo, so be careful

143. FD 21 and 22.

144. Ser Schiatta di Ser Michele Mei de' Ferranti (1351–1400) was Francesco's preferred notary. He owned property at Filettole, much of which ended up in Francesco's hands. See Fiumi, *Demografia*, 369.

145. Margherita refers to the Florentine priors, the elected chief magistrates of Florence.

146. The manuscript is damaged at this point. Francesco's representatives, Baldo di Vestro Nucci and Niccolaio Martini, were to testify regarding his residency in Prato and Florence.

147. This is Torello di Messer Niccolaio Torelli.

not to be seen drinking with or speaking to them in a place where you may be seen.[148] Leave the horses belonging to Domenico di Cambio and Niccolaio Martini at the stables. You might as well keep them there as anywhere else. If you need to send for anything else, it would be better to use animals that belong to people from Prato. It would assist you for various reasons. At the present moment, it's not a good idea to worry about economizing on a cart or a horse. The tax could end up costing you as much as the cartage costs for an entire year.

I am sending you the horse with Castagnino so it can stay there in Florence because I don't want us to have to deal with these animals arriving every day. With regard to the goods we receive, I had intended, if the packhorse hadn't returned with Niccolaio Martini, to hire a cart horse that was in good condition. Various people here at Prato agree, because our horse is too well known and so it creates too many risks. You can leave Domenico di Cambio's horse because it is used to rough conditions.

I am getting Castagnino to bring you two new sets of underlinen. Give Castagnino the old ones that I shortened, as he needs them badly.

I will answer you about the other matters in another letter. May God protect you.

I am sending you scarlet and pink cloth. Tell Francesca to make me eight cloth buttons, just as in the drawing, the most beautiful she can. If possible, she should have them ready for me by Saturday when Nanni returns here.

From Margherita, in Prato. Greetings.

With this there is a letter to you from Niccolaio Martini.

Francesco di Marco da Prato, in Florence.
Received from Prato, 20 February 1394. Answered on the 20th.

---

148. Margherita was worried that Francesco's witnesses would be perceived to be too close to him and therefore not impartial.

Letter 32 (1401727)
23 February 1394
Prato

In the name of God. 23 February 1394.

I received your letter from Cristofano and Castagnino. I didn't answer because it wasn't necessary, and I will be brief because I know that you are busy at present with your affairs and have many problems. Things will turn out for the best, God willing.

I am sending you a pair of capons with Nanni da Santa Chiara, and I am also sending you two loads of wood and twelve loaves of bread. I did not send them to you on Saturday because I thought you might be coming back, and so I had only a small quantity made. I have packed the bread and you will receive it on Tuesday if someone goes to Florence.

Tell Francesca to make the buttons as if they were for herself.

I am sending you the overgown that I had made for Castagnino. I heard from Filippo that you gave the horse to Messer Bartolomeo. I am pleased, and it seems to me you have done very well; at this stage you can't go wrong by looking after him and people as powerful as he is. We have no better remedy nowadays, and there is no damage that cannot be repaired if we look for such opportunities and spend on them, because if it were not for events like these we would be in need of very little. I trust to God that this affair will give us more profit than loss; so please worry about it as little as possible, and trust in your own good sense. If you were anywhere else, I would be more concerned than I am because, as Cristofano says, they are treating you so well that I'm afraid you'll be completely spoilt. I'll find out about it, even if they don't want me to.

I won't say any more in this letter but I'll write again soon. May God be pleased to give us good news.

Ser Chimenti was here and told me that Niccolaio Brancacci had asked for some Corsican wine, because he had heard that we had some.[149] I told him the truth, that is that we had had two small barrels of Malvasia wine and that we had given one to Master Matteo

---

149. Niccolaio di Bartolomeo Brancacci was a wool merchant from an emerging Pratese family associated with Francesco's bank. See note 151, below.

and still had the other, which was not clear or ready to drink.[150] We hadn't treated it properly because of the other troubles you have been having. I thought it would be a good idea to buy some and so did Ser Chimenti and Cristofano, and that was what we did. And afterward Ser Chimenti thought we should send them a flask of the wine that we are drinking. And I didn't agree because it didn't seem good enough. I wanted him to open a new barrel, and Ser Chimenti didn't want to. He sent Baronto to us for this flask. I did it my way. I opened the barrel that we are due to drink after the present one and had two flasks filled for them, and I sent word to Niccolaio Brancacci that if he and his friends wished, I would tap it today and they should let us know how much they wanted. I also said to tell him that if he wanted to order any Corsican wine, we would order some from Pisa. He is a man who likes these things. I am told he was pleased. You can't go wrong if you stay on good terms with everyone.[151]

Yesterday we got a letter from Pisa addressed to you and also advice of a consignment of a hundred pounds of washed wool from San Matteo inside a metal trunk. We will have it brought here. I will forward the letter to you and keep the consignment note.[152]

May God protect you always.

From Margherita, in Prato.

Francesco di Marco da Prato, in Florence.
Received from Prato, 23 February 1394. Answered on the 24th.

---

150. This is the doctor Matteo di Giovanni Giuntini, from Prato. See letters 62, 63, and 66.

151. Niccolaio Brancacci must have been one of the Magistracy of the Eight Defenders in Prato. Francesco approved of Margherita's decision to send wine to the Eight. See FD 25.

152. Francesco told Margherita to send the wool to Francesco Bellandi. See FD 25.

Letter 33 (1401728)
25 February 1394
Prato

In the name of God. 25 February 1394.

I received your letter from Nanni da Santa Chiara and have understood enough to send you a brief reply.

In regard to what Niccolò di Piero told you, I think you must have passed a bad night and a bad day. I didn't have a better one myself, worrying about your anxiety. […][153] Niccolò di Piero and Ser Chimenti have visited, and Cristofano has arrived from Florence, and they all offered their opinions: and according to one view we have lost, according to another we have won. And people here think that representatives will probably come from the Gonfalone.[154] If they do, I think that they are likely to be people well disposed to us, more from fear than love, because they are in disarray according to what one wretch said. We are in the middle of this assessment for the *libra* tax that everyone is trembling about, and there is no reason to be surprised or worried, because those against them are very powerful. Anyway it would be good to hear if they are coming here. I don't feel there are people able enough to make a response to them if they do, but if he wanted to help, in my opinion Messer Bartolomeo would be the best person of all.[155] There is no need to be frightened about this or to retreat. I am amazed that these tax assessors, who are considered such good men, haven't settled the matter. But I suspect that some of them are trying to please the Gonfalone and make you do what they want by gently explaining to you that it is to your advantage. I will tell you my opinion: I would hold out, and they would not get a kind word from me. So lobby as much as you can, keep those counselors there and whoever else you need. Don't let them imagine they can start celebrating Carnival.

I wanted Nanni to come to you in time to keep you informed and to relieve you of as much worry as I can. Cristofano will stay here

153. A sentence has been omitted here because of holes in the manuscript. This letter is concerned with Francesco Datini's battle to resolve the tax issue referred to in note 120, above.

154. The representatives of the Gonfalone were from the district of the Red Lion in Florence.

155. This is Bartolomeo Panciatichi. See note 134, above.

to do what is necessary; if anything new happens, you will be told about it. These other people will advise you what to do better than I can. Martino, Niccolò, Ser Chimenti, and your other friends are doing what is necessary.[156] May God protect you.

From Margherita, in Prato.

Francesco di Marco da Prato, in Florence.
Received from Prato, 26 February 1394.

Letter 34 (1401729)
27 February 1394
Prato

In the name of God. 27 February 1394.

This is to let you know about the visit here of the representatives of the Gonfalone. I realized it was them when I heard the bell ringing as they passed. As soon as they heard it, Ser Nicola and your other friends came here. I sent for them because I had realized who had come. We decided to go to Messer Piero, and this morning, before they came, all the necessary preparations were made in case they arrived. Everything is ready. Messer Piero says that one could not do better than to send someone to you, and he said this would resolve your problems. I have no time to say anything else. May God protect you. You will be informed by Niccolò about who they are.

From Margherita, in Prato.

Francesco di Marco da Prato, in Florence.
Received from Prato, 27 February.

---

156. These are Martino di Niccolaio Martini, Niccolò di Piero di Giunta del Rosso, and the notary Chimenti di Ser Leone.

Letter 35 (1401730)
27 February 1394
Prato

In the name of God. 27 February 1394.

After we told you that those three representatives from the Gonfalone of the Red Lion came here, I went to Messer Piero and asked him how matters stood.[157] He said he was with the Eight this morning. He found them very fearful and suspected that they had lost all courage. Messer Piero told me that he had won over most of them, and one stood up and answered in this way: "It seemed wrong to treat Francesco poorly and to harass households such as his because they would always remain enemies of the commune."[158] Messer Piero replied that they should always observe justice, and, while showing that they were serving their commune, they should make it clear that they did not have any prejudice against you, because this was their duty. He insisted that this could never bring them harm or shame, and if they did not do this they would not be serving justice. He said to me that among the Eight there were very few who had much character, except Niccolaio di Bernardo and Ser Amelio. Niccolaio di Bernardo is not there today. I was told that the other time, when they wanted him to attack Francesco, he refused. When Ser Amelio sent for him, he replied to the messenger who was going to the piazza that he knew what they wanted and that he did not intend to stand up in the commune to speak against Francesco di Marco, because it was a disgraceful thing. He had been sent many times by the commune to Figline and other towns. They had always been allowed to send their own representatives and one would expect no less for a fellow citizen of Florence than for someone from the country. Then, after hearing that the Eight had lost courage, I sent for Carlo di Francesco.[159] I reminded him of the long friendship between you and his family and asked him to remind Ser Amelio of the love and trust that you have for him and for his brothers. I said that you had been told by me about all the efforts he

157. This is Piero Rinaldeschi.

158. The commune of Prato.

159. This is Carlo di Francesco Mainardi Guazzalotti. On the political factions led by the Guazzalotti and Migliorati families in Prato, see note 129, above.

made in regard to Francesco's affairs and he should be willing to show it today as he had in the past, and if a consultative committee was held, he should pay attention to Francesco's friends. [...] It was said to me by one who saw them in the piazza that he went straight to Arriguccio and made an appeal to him about this matter.[160] Later they went into the piazza and they said the most disgraceful things that were ever said and they received nothing from the commune, as Ser Baldo will tell you.

After the meeting was held, four were called in to give their answer to the Eight, and they are with them now. Messer Piero and Arriguccio were among them, and they said very loudly what a great honor they had from this event.

They went back to confer four times and said they were not satisfied with the answer. They stayed there for more than five hours, and it seems that they did not get the answer they wanted. Now they are going down the street looking as if they are about to burst! As I have no time, I won't say any more. Ser Baldo will tell you all about it in a letter he is sending.

I will send the mule tomorrow.

From Margherita, in Prato.

To Francesco di Marco da Prato, in Florence.
Received from Prato, 28 February 1394.

Letter 36 (1401731)
28 February 1394
Prato

In the name of God. 28 February 1394.

I didn't send the mule with Nanni because he left here after the twenty-fourth hour had rung.[161] I decided he should leave for Florence

---

160. Arriguccio di Ser Guido Ferracani was an influential political figure who was appointed Gonfalonier of Justice on several occasions. See letter 49.

161. The public clock in Prato was completed by 1388 and was maintained by Michele di Falcuccio, who is mentioned in letter 48 and is called the trumpeter. See Nigro, *Il tempo*

without it so he could get back here earlier tomorrow morning. I don't think it can do any harm. I will send the mule to you with Cherichero because you say you want to come here. Make sure it is the right thing to do. If it were up to me, I wouldn't leave until the matter was over.

The people from Florence made such a bad impression that I am very happy; and this was said, I think it was by [Guido] del Palagio, in front of Messer Piero.[162] He said that you had thirty thousand florins capital and five *lire* of tax, whereas Messer Piero, who had twenty thousand, had six, and Messer Guelfo, who had thirty thousand, paid six *lire* tax, and they argued and maintained this line.[163] Most of the assessors went into the piazza to say as many bad things as they could, and the entire town gathered there.[164] Each of the assessors said his piece, and our people replied to every point. Bernabò responded more than anyone. They said that when you returned to this town you had twenty thousand florins. Bernabò answered that he would like to have as much capital as you had debts, and he would never ask for any more. They asked him if he was a relative of yours, and he said no. They asked him what his trade was and if he was your employee. He said he had none and said to them, "What would it matter to you if Francesco had no tax to pay? Have you received a penny less than you should have had from this commune?" They replied no, and everyone said his piece. Furthermore, when Filippo was coming back yesterday evening, they were at Ferro's inn.[165] These words were being said to the large crowd that was there: "Come to the Gonfalone of the Red Lion when you want a favor. There are many noble men in that city who can

---

liberato, 15–21.

162. Guido del Palagio, from a prominent Florentine aristocratic family, was described by a diarist around 1390 as "the most important and respected man in Florence." See Pitti, *Cronica*, 76. He was twice Gonfalonier of Justice and served as a Florentine ambassador. He was also a member of a pious Florentine protohumanist circle that included Lapo Mazzei. See Simona Brambilla, *Itinerari nella Firenze di fine Trecento: fra Giovanni dalle Celle e Luigi Marsili* (Milan: Edizione Cusi, 2002), *passim*.

163. See letter 27.

164. Many people in Prato were upset about the excessive taxation imposed by Florence on the subject population because it had reduced some residents to abject poverty. See Veronica Vestri, "Istituzioni e vita sociale a Prato nel primo Quattrocento," *Prato, Storia e Arte* 84, supplement (1993): 17–21.

165. This is Filippo di Francesco. See letters 32, 38, 48, and 50.

do what they like and leave the tax burden to the poor." I think that they have been so discredited that everyone in this town is annoyed with them, especially the most prominent people.

I am not worried about the other minor details, because they seem more like smoke than fire. I am writing this because it looks like good news for you. I wish they had been unwise enough to attack someone. I am telling you this because I think that it will be useful to you. May God help those who are in the right.

I say no more. May God protect you.

From Margherita, in Prato.

To Francesco di Marco da Prato, in Florence.
Received from Prato, 28 February 1394.

Letter 37 (1401732)
5 March 1394
Prato

In the name of God. 5 March 1394.

I am sending you three peacocks with Matterello, as well as ten loaves and some figs for Maso and the serving maid (that is, half of the good ones we had). I am also sending a jar of raisins for you and there are some figs, a jar of grapes, and some chickpeas for Monna Giovanna.

I have been with Messer Piero because I believe he has a great love for us.[166] I spoke to him about the matter we were discussing, and indeed the more I deal with him the better he seems. He said you must recall that, when you wanted advice about whether you should get representatives from the commune to go there on your behalf, he said no. He saw that they could be of no use to you, and even harmful, especially if the tax was to be revised. He said you told him that Messer Guelfo and Niccolaio Martini had advised you to do so. He told you to follow the advice of Messer Guelfo and Niccolaio Martini, but if it were his decision, he would not want them involved. He thought that

---

166. Margherita refers to the judge Piero Rinaldeschi, her neighbor.

you could defend yourself better than they would because he knows their evil minds and says that they act out of envy.[167]

I spoke to him about whether it was best to stay in Florence or come here. Messer Piero says he was very sorry that you thanked the Eight. Although it would have been bad for you to do otherwise, he would have preferred you to have done the following: not to have come back here until the matter had been concluded, or in the event you did, not to thank them at all because they didn't deserve it, and by this stage nothing could have done your affairs any harm. He says he would have come back when the matter was concluded and the decisions made; then he would have persuaded them to call a council of the people and that whole lot. He would have complained to them about their poor treatment of you, saying that previously you had been told that they didn't love you as you used to imagine, but that you could not believe it. If you had known that they were so ungrateful, you would never have undertaken the struggle against such powerful families and borne the cost and damages that you did, as well they knew. He would also have said, "I did it all for love of you, because you treated me as a fellow citizen, not just someone from the provinces. It harmed me little because, as you knew perfectly well, I can afford to bear the cost."[168] He says it would have been best for you to conclude by saying, "I have sorted out this business. Now I am satisfied and can make the decision I please. Anyway, I don't intend to trust you because I see I cannot. I have heard gossip that you are threatening to impose too much tax on me and so I am not obliged to keep any agreement with you. You didn't keep yours with me, so I'll suit myself, because that is what you do when people are ungrateful." I think everyone would start to say that these people had favored you more for their convenience than for love of you. However, Messer Piero says that you shouldn't be alarmed about this. Even if you had twenty thousand florins at Avignon, twenty thousand at Genoa, and twenty thousand at Milan, he would undertake to defend you in court, because you could never be

---

167. Despite being common enemies of the Guelf faction led by the Guazzalotti, Piero Rinaldeschi's distrust of Francesco's friends Guelfo Pugliesi and Niccolaio Martini suggests that there were tensions within the Ghibelline faction in Prato.

168. Presumably this is a reference to Francesco's having previously paid the Florentine *prestanza* as a citizen and now still being asked to pay the *libra* tax in Prato.

forced to pay for more than the visible portions of your property. On this point he says you can trust him to argue your case before all the judges of this world. In his view, even if you were to take no further action, you could only be condemned for the words you said in Florence and here in Prato. He would be more concerned about what you said in Florence than here; so he says you should try to resolve the matter because you are there, and when you return to Prato, he thinks he will give you such good advice that you will be pleased whatever course of action you decide to follow.

Ser Chimenti will send you his opinion and Ser Schiatta's, and you will see which one of these you like better. May God give you the grace to choose the one that is better for body and soul. May God protect you.

Tell Niccolò to send some chickpeas if he can.

From your Margherita, in Prato.

Francesco di Marco da Prato, in Florence.
From Prato, 5 March 1394. Answered on the 5th.

Letter 38 (1401733)
10 March 1394
Prato

In the name of God. 10 March 1394.

Today Castagnino brought me your letter, which I now answer.

I sent Filippo to the *Podestà* immediately to give him the message you sent me. He said that if he wanted anything, he would let us know.

I sent your letter to Giovanni di Simone. He wasn't home—he was in the country—but today I will send someone to ask for the money as you say.

I spoke to Nannino about it, and he says that he is ready to do what we advise. It doesn't seem to me that he should be working with the baker. I will give you my opinion. I think you should look there for a boy like the young baker who was with us, who is used to working at the bakery, who knows the trade well and who could stay with him for two weeks while he taught him. I spoke about it to Nannino. He likes the idea; he is pleased about it. A decision needs to be made quickly.[169]

I sent Checco Bondì and Bernabò to the hospital to see the wheat that Paolo had promised to give me willingly.[170] He said exactly the opposite to them: that they had no grain to sell. He passed by here. I said I was surprised that he had told me there was plenty of wheat of various qualities to sell. He told me that they had made the decision not to sell. I understood precisely why he said this to me. I said that if he didn't want to give me the grain, he should give me the money he owes us and I would buy it elsewhere. He said he did not know that he owed you money.[171] I replied that they had to give us the money Monna Ghita owed us.[172] He said the hospital was not obliged to pay for what you gave to Monna Ghita, and you should have the money from her and not from them. I said that if my memory was correct, you had lent the money in agreement with the other hospital wardens. I answered that I would send Francesco di Matteo Bellandi, who knew all about it.[173] I sent him there and they said they couldn't settle the matter. Then Francesco said that what I had said was true. I will try and get the money if I can.

I heard that Lodovico was in prison. I thought that it was for debt. I went to Messer Piero to find out whether there was a way of keeping him there. Messer Piero said that he was there for another reason and that he could not be kept there for debt.[174] The reason turns out to be this: the council was holding a public meeting and it had to be decided whether to impose a *libra* tax or not. It seems a cobbler rose to speak on the podium, and he must have said something against the rich. It appears that Lodovico found him later at Appianato, and

169. See FD 31.

170. This is the money changer Paolo di Bertino Verzoni.

171. See letter 27.

172. This is the servant Monna Ghita, wife of Matteo di Ghetto Guizzelmi.

173. Francesco di Matteo Bellandi was a warden of the Misericordia hospital in Prato. Lapo Mazzei describes him as a man of steel, because he had witnessed the wills of so many plague victims admitted to the hospital but had survived unscathed. See the letter from Lapo Mazzei to Simone Bellandi in Mazzei, *Lettere di un notaro*, 2:337.

174. Lodovico di Ser Iacopo Villani owed Francesco money.

it seems he and his brother beat him up.[175] It seems that the cobbler was waiting for the council meeting the other day. He appealed to the *Podestà* and to the Eight about what Lodovico had done. Everyone was upset, and it was thought to be a disgraceful act. The *Podestà* was most upset of all, and if he had not been defended immediately, he would have been sent to Florence, and what's more, they say that they threatened to send him to the captain of the Balìa. I am writing this to you so you can know what happened but please don't say anything. This is from Messer Piero who doesn't speak nonsense and thinks [Lodovico] did a disgraceful thing by assaulting someone who rose to speak on the podium.

They are beginning to work on the vineyard at Il Palco. Nanni da Santa Chiara is there with the animals carrying the canes. Nanni has completed the entire kitchen. Some lime is left over. He is preparing the bedroom on the *loggia*. I will get him to use up the lime, and after that he won't do any more unless I hear from you.

I had Bernabò see to the wine, and it is rather sour. I had him put the tap in and began to send some to Il Palco by the half cask.[176] I still haven't been able to get anyone to taste the other wines for me. They promised to come today, but they haven't come yet. I told them that you had sent me a message saying that if there was any wine available, I should buy another [barrel] because you wanted to send it to Florence. Niccolaio Martini has promised to take it there. In my opinion, I think, if you agree, the best thing would be to send a barrel to Florence, because I think that Niccolò was only speaking of his personal needs. You can see that every day there are issues to settle, but we can solve everything except for the wine, so it would be good to have some. Answer me and I will tell you what wines there are.

175. Lodovico's brother Tommaso was married to Caterina di Iacopo de' Guazzalotti, from a Guelf family. The cobbler was probably on the Ghibelline side of the factional divide in Prato, led by the Pugliesi and Rinaldeschi families, but his criticism of the rich could have been motivated by poverty.

176. For the cask and all other measures see Appendix 2.

I sent half a sturgeon to Messer Piero.[177] He was very pleased. Castagnino tells me that Fattorino's cloth is at the warehouse.[178] I am surprised you haven't sent it. Send it immediately if possible.

Remember to tell Francesca that she should let me know if some capable woman who could help us turns up.

I sent you with Nanni da Santa Chiara a half quart of chickpeas that I got from Iacopo da San Donnino's brother.

We can't find anyone who wants the packhorse. They say it is old and that you have made it so used to plenty of food that it would die as soon as it was left short of barley.

That is all. May God protect you.

From your Margherita, in Prato. Greetings.

With this there will be a letter from Messer Guelfo to Guido di Messer Tommaso [del Palagio], as well as a letter from Florence.

Letter 39 (1401734)
11 March 1394
Prato

In the name of God. 11 March 1394.

I received your letter from Castagnino, and I have understood what you say. I am answering the urgent matters, and tomorrow morning I will write about the rest.

From the said Castagnino I received ten tench, and I did with them as you said; that is, I sent two to Messer Piero, two to Ser Schiatta, two to Niccolaio Martini, and two to Ser Baldo: this is what I did with them.[179]

Tina tells you to remember to send her the dice she told you about when you were here.

---

177. The sturgeon is a large fish that was highly prized for its flavor and texture. It was therefore a worthy gift for Margherita's influential neighbor in Prato, Piero Rinaldeschi.

178. Fattorino was the nickname of Giovanni di Luca Bencivenni, a Florentine whom Francesco employed in the warehouses of both Prato and Florence.

179. Tench, thick-bodied freshwater fish similar to carp, were welcome gifts during Lent.

I received Fattorino's cloth from Castagnino.

I sent Nanni to take the letter you sent to Giovanni di Simone and got him to ask for the money. He said he would write you a letter.

Because a relative of Niccolaio Martini is very unwell, he could not bring Biagio, but I think he will bring him tomorrow.

That is all. May God protect you.

From your Margherita, in Prato.

To Francesco di Marco da Prato, in Florence.
Received from Prato, 11 March 1394.

Letter 40 (1401735)
12 March 1394
Prato

In the name of God. 12 March 1394.

I wrote about what I thought was important in a letter sent with Castagnino. The reason I am writing this is that Nanni da Santa Chiara is going to Florence. I am sending you eighteen loaves of bread and half the mushrooms that I got from Pisa. Don't send any more tench because they are starting to arrive here.

Fattorino's overgown has been cut, and there was only enough material for the gown. He has urgent need of hose. Tell me if you want me to get them here or if you want to send them from Florence.

I can't answer you about the wine yet. The reason is that Niccolaio is very upset because they are also saying that his relative is dying and will leave his three daughters destitute. I think Niccolaio is looking after them.[180]

I understood that the baker was to stay some months with Nannino and was sending his family elsewhere, but I didn't think it was a good idea to talk to the baker about it. Do you think the baker would want to teach Nannino, or anyone else? I think that if he knows any dishonest tricks, he would pass them on, and it would be his greatest pleasure if some poor common criminal were to come along who

180. This is Niccolaio Martini.

could take the blame. If the bakery were mine, I would get rid of him promptly before sending anyone else here in his place. I wouldn't worry about the money he owes you. Don't imagine you'll ever see any of it. When you find an apprentice that you think is better than the baker, the best thing to do would be to tell us how you want us to go about dismissing him. I heard that the baker went to Florence today. I think he must have gone to see you because he heard something, so keep me fully informed. I think that if he has been able to convince you to keep him on a little longer, it would be best to keep the shop closed. The longer he stays, the worse it will be for you and for him. After he stops eating up the bread he will start on the cooked beans, plenty of which are now coming in. I would like Francesca to obtain twenty-eight yards of gold ribbons like the other ones she sent us.

I'll say no more. May God protect you. Pass on my greetings to everyone.

From Margherita, in Prato.

To Francesco di Marco da Prato, in Florence.

Letter 41 (1401736)
15 March 1394
Prato

In the name of God. 15 March 1394.

I haven't written to you since you left, as I haven't seen the need. This is to inform you that today we got back the packhorses you lent to Messer Filippo Corsini. He brought back the black horse injured; the others must have been well looked after, because they are in good condition. He wanted to take the horse back with him and keep it until it recovered. He was sorry about it and very upset. He said he had six packhorses to take back there. I told him that if any of them were unfit, he could leave them with me and I would look after them as if they were ours. I said what seemed appropriate.[181]

---

181. See FD 28 and 29.

The mule is getting much better, and we'll do what needs to be done for the black horse. Don't be upset, because we'll take care of them as if you were here. If there weren't risks, there wouldn't be favors.

I chose some of the bowls that you left me to send to Ser Lapo. I sent him ten of different sizes. There aren't many, so I could not send him any more. And I sent him a half quart of chickpeas. I thought of sending him two tench if any good ones came in.[182]

Regarding the wine, I await your instructions. Tomorrow is the market, and we will buy the things we need.

I sent word to Piero di Monna Mellina, the brick maker from Filettole, to pay us or we would take action. I said we hoped we wouldn't have to. He should be here on market day and he will pay me every last penny.[183]

At Filettole nothing can be done until the weather improves. Nannino and Meo have almost filled in the ditch as you said, and while it was raining they pruned the willows.

Niccolò di Piero told me that you think that your tax problems will be resolved soon. I can't wait for the day that will happen. May God in His grace deliver us. If you can, write to Fattorino with news about his brother because he is very worried about him.

I have no more to say. May God protect you. Give my regards to Niccolò and greet Francesca for me.

From your Margherita, in Prato.

We are missing Nannino's hooded cloak, which was in the room where Castagnino sleeps. I began to imagine that Castagnino must have taken it. Just the same, we were worried, Nannino more than anyone. To cheer him up, I sent for the baker and asked him if he had seen Castagnino wearing it, and he said yes. If you're born a rogue, there's no remedy. He could at least have said to me, "I'm taking Nannino's hooded cloak." May God give him his just deserts![184]

To Francesco di Marco da Prato, in Florence.
Received from Prato, 16 March 1394. Answered on the 16th.

182. See note 179, above.

183. Piero paid twelve *lire*. See letter 43.

184. See FD 33.

Letter 42 (1401737)
17 March 1394
Prato

In the name of God. 17 March 1394.

This morning I received your letter; with it was one addressed to Marco di Tano. I sent it on to him immediately. I understand about the business concerning Falduccio. I'm afraid he might behave like the sailor. Now that you are looking after this matter, it would be good to fix that one too.[185]

As for reminding Ser Chimenti, I did what you say, and he came here to see me and he spoke about the matter to everyone. I think he is not looking after this business very willingly. I told him that this time he has to do it, whether he likes it or not, but that next time, if you get yourself into this sort of situation, he should let you recover the debts. I told him that if no one went now, we could say it was our own fault that we lost the money. Lodovico and all the other debtors make empty promises and in the long run are hoping that nothing will be done.[186] He promised me he would see to it tomorrow without fail, and I told him to do so. I will urge him on and ensure that everyone gets what he deserves. I said to Ser Chimenti that it seemed to me much better to follow up this matter when you were not here and we have the good excuse of this tax problem. Ser Chimenti liked this idea very much. From the way he speaks, I don't think he is worried.

I told you about the mule and the packhorses in the letter I gave to Argomento, and they are getting better every day.

No good barley was available and very little bad, so I did not buy any. I told Meo to keep all the barley that Stefano da Filettole has at a reserve price of twelve *soldi* a bushel, and the weight per bushel is forty-four pounds. The selling price was at fourteen and fifteen *soldi* a

185. Falduccio di Lombardo da Spugnole was Francesco's partner in Florence. Lapo Mazzei considered him difficult. Mazzei, *Lettere di un notaro*, 2:223–25. In a letter of 20 November 1394 from Barcelona, Luca del Sera advised Francesco to break with Falduccio. See Melis, *Aspetti della vita economica medievale*, 85. In FD 32 Francesco reported that Falduccio had forgiven him without explaining what he had done to require forgiveness.

186. Francesco asked Chimenti to put pressure on his debtors, such as Lodovico di Ser Iacopo, who is first mentioned in letter 30. See FD 31 and 32.

bushel and it is not good quality; we paid twenty *soldi* for wheat grain. I did not have much bought because we won't get a great deal from it.

We bought twelve bushels of spelt. I passed on the message you sent me in the letter brought by Meo di Niccolaio Martini. He says that he will send one of his packhorses there tomorrow.

I am sending you twelve loaves of bread and a total of fifty-six apples and pears with Nanni da Santa Chiara. I am also sending you walnuts, a half quart of shelled broad beans, and a half quart of beans and some peas. I am sending you small quantities of everything because it was a poor market and there was very little of anything.

I will wait for your instructions about the wine, and I will tell you about the animals once they have rested.

Send us the trimmings for Monna Vanna di Chiarito's daughter. We need twenty-six yards similar to what she sent for Monte's girl. Send them as soon as possible. That's all I have to say. May God protect you. Send my best wishes to everyone there.

From Margherita, in Prato.

Francesco di Marco da Prato, in Florence.
From Prato, 17 March 1394. Answered on the 18th.

Letter 43 (1401738)
18 March 1394
Prato

In the name of God. 18 March 1394.

I sent a reply to the two letters I received yesterday with Nanni da Santa Chiara. It dealt with what was most urgent. For this reason I will say little here because I know you have received it.

Ser Chimenti came here to see me and thinks he will recover a good sum this week. And from Piero di Monna Mellina I received twelve *lire* today, and he says he will pay the rest this week.[187]

The mule has recovered now and so has the black horse. The other horses are well.

187. See letter 41.

I get Nannino to groom the animals early every morning and afterward I send him to Il Palco with the pony and every evening I get him to return so he can look after them again. It is really necessary to do this because he looks after them better than anyone. I beg him every day to ensure that they stay in good condition.

Nanni di Guiduccio sent to ask for five *lire* and said you would agree to it. He has a high fever. Send a message offering him all our assistance. In the meantime I sent a message to reassure him about whether I would give him the money or not, and to say that I would never refuse him since he was in that state. Tell us whether we should give any more if he asks for it.[188]

Monna Simona offered me a *moggio* of superior-quality wheat. It seems that Monna Simona must have had a discussion with Messer Piero as to whether he owed you money. He told her not to interfere between him and you, but he said if we needed wheat, we should send for a *moggio* or even two. This information comes from Monna Simona and not from me. I wanted to send him the money but Monna Simona said not to pay him [for the wheat]. She says that if he owes you money, he does not want you to give him any, and if he didn't owe money he wants us to keep it for Caterina's belt. I said that I didn't ever hear from you that Piero owed you anything; I will take a *moggio* anyway because it is good and it is also cheap.

Try to sell Monna Simona's cloth as soon as possible.

I know you received the things I sent you with Nanni da Santa Chiara. If you need anything else, let me know.

I will not bother to tell Cristofano which letters are for him, as he reads everything; the only other letters that come here are his. I would like you to tell me if he has any buckskin at Barberino for carrying chestnuts, because I understand he wants to wait until May. I would order two loads for you. Perhaps that would be a mistake, because you may have already sent for them there because you like them. If that is so, I am happier than if they were to be sent here. I will send some fish to Ser Lapo's mother as soon as we get some and anything else that I think she would like.[189] Give my regards to everyone.

---

188. Francesco gave Margherita permission to lend Nanni up to fifty florins (FD 35).

189. Monna Bartola, Lapo Mazzei's elderly mother, lived at Grignano, in the countryside not far from Prato.

I received Nannino's hooded cloak from Nanni da Santa Chiara, as well as five small bags.[190]

May God protect you.

Francesco di Marco da Prato, in Florence.
From Prato, 18 March 1394. Answered on the 18th.

Letter 44 (1401739)
19 March 1394
Prato

In the name of God. 19 March 1394.

Yesterday I received your two letters: one delivered by the servant of Messer Rinaldeschi and one by Nanni da Santa Chiara. I won't answer every question here, since I will reply in full later.

I am sending you the gray horse courtesy of Barzalone. One of his workers is bringing it, and I am sending you twelve loaves because the bread is fresh.

There are few squabs; only a couple of pairs are good enough to eat. We will choose the best we can. I cannot tell you how much barley there is. I will tell you tomorrow since Nanni is coming back this evening and I will find out from him.

I told Ser Chimenti what you said to me in your letters. He has hopes of recovering the money from everyone except Lodovico, who is not here.

It seems to me that Ser Chimenti is reluctant to press him, because he says he wouldn't want to be the first to take action; but he has promised he will if it becomes necessary. Lodovico has promised to give Ser Chimenti forty florins between now and Saturday. I told Ser Chimenti to wait until Saturday. If Lodovico doesn't pay, he will get what he deserves and there will be no mercy for him.[191]

---

190. Castagnino had taken Nannino's hooded cloak without permission. See letter 41.

191. Lodovico di Ser Iacopo appears regularly in the correspondence as a man reluctant to repay money borrowed from Francesco. Ser Chimenti may have been wary of pressing him

With this letter there will be another from Ser Chimenti, which tells you about Lodovico and all your debtors.[192]

I wrote to Ser Lapo's mother and I sent her two tench and offered her all our assistance; and apart from that I said what seemed appropriate.[193]

Regarding the forced loan and the loss involved, there is nothing to be done. May God by His grace help us.

We sent you the gray packhorse with Barzalone because it was in better condition than before and Barzalone wanted to leave immediately.

The spelt that I bought weighs thirty-five pounds in the sack, and costs eight *soldi* and eight *denari*.

I have no more to add. May God protect you.

From Margherita, in Prato.

Francesco di Marco da Prato, in Florence.
From Prato, 19 March 1394. Answered on the 20th.

Letter 45 (1401740)
21 March 1394
Prato

In the name of God. 21 March 1394.

I received your letter from Niccolaio Martini's son, Martino. I have understood what you say and will now answer.

Try to get the trimmings for the lowest price you can. If you can't do any better, go ahead and buy them.[194]

---

for the money he owed Francesco because Ludovico had recently demonstrated his violent temperament. See letter 38.

192. See letter 42, and FD 32.

193. This is Monna Bartola. Margherita sent fish, such as tench, as gifts to her neighbors and friends during Lent. See letters 39 and 41.

194. Francesco had quoted four *lire*, fifteen *soldi*, and four *denari* for the trimmings. They were for the wedding of Chiarito's daughter, as were the items listed in the following paragraphs. See letter 42, and FD 36.

I would like you to have someone buy for me two and a half ounces of buttons for Chiarito's daughter, the same size as the one included here. If you can find some secondhand ones, she would prefer them to new ones, to save money. If you find old ones, provided they are not too small and are not too varied, buy them whether they have a loop attached or not.

She would also like a used belt costing between six and seven *lire*. She doesn't care if it is not in fashion, but make sure it is not too broad, as she is a young girl. If you find one—provided we can send it back if she doesn't like it—send it and the buttons and the trimmings as soon as possible.[195]

Tina has read the Psalter; she needs a small prayer book that has the seven psalms and the Office of the Virgin with good lettering.[196]

With this I am sending you an ounce and a half of silver buttons. Have them sold. Look for those other things on Monday because the letter will arrive so late that it won't be possible to do it today.

I should like to know what decision you will make with those people about that tax business. I will tell you my opinion anyway. In my view, if no good alternative presents itself, you ought to go ahead and commit yourself in the way that was advised by those who understand these matters. This is because the people here think they have done you so many favors that you have no hope of repaying them. Since they have done nothing for you, I wouldn't want it to happen that after spending all that money and creating so many enemies to get out of this impasse, you find yourself in even more trouble here in Prato as time goes by. You will be held in too much contempt for having done what was necessary to stay in with them. It is very wise to make decisions on reasonable grounds when you have to. In my opinion, considering what must inevitably happen, it would be best for you to be in Florence. As for all the other things that could happen, it would be better to be a citizen of Florence than a country yokel in Prato.[197] That certain friend you know who gives me good advice

195. On the marriage of Chiarito's daughter, see note 135, above.

196. Margherita's niece Tina was learning to read. The seven psalms were the liturgically important Penitential Psalms: 6, 32, 38, 51, 102, 130, and 143 in the modern numbering.

197. Francesco decided to follow the advice of his Florentine friends, Guido del Palagio and Lapo Mazzei, to accept Florentine citizenship. He would then pay tax only in Florence. See

likes my idea.[198] I spoke about it with him yesterday evening, and he says I could not suggest anything better for your advantage than this. He went as far as to say, and he says he won't say it again, that people here are very ill-disposed. He knows it. He tells me that if indeed you happen to come here, he will tell you face to face what he thinks you should do. I begged him to tell me the truth, as in my opinion he always has in the past. He said he would tell me, and he said that if it were his affair he would certainly do exactly what I had advised. That is what he would do and what he was saying to himself. Just between you and me, he did not want to write to you, because he said: "The letter could go astray." I gathered that he would write to tell you that you should be assessed there if it is to your benefit. Indeed it could only be to your benefit.

I am sending you with Nanni da Santa Chiara twenty apples that Bartolomea di Ser Naldo sent me, and some chestnuts that Dettora's son sent to me in a basket. I have nothing to add. May God protect you. I am sending you the small packhorse with Nanni, because he says he wants to sell it. May Christ be your guardian.

From Margherita, in Prato.

Francesco di Marco da Prato, in Florence.
From Prato, 21 March 1394.

Letter 46 (1401741)
27 March 1394
Prato

In the name of God. 27 March 1394.

I didn't write to you with Meo because I waited for the council meeting to finish in order to tell you about what is happening here, and for this reason I kept back Castagnino. Ser Chimenti will inform you about everything, and has told Messer Piero what to do. It seems the

note 120, above.

198. Probably Piero Rinaldeschi, whom Margherita was consulting regularly. See letters 37 and 46.

matter has been entrusted to Guido di Messer Tommaso [del Palagio]; and let him do what he likes as long as it is what you and those of the Gonfalone want. There could have been no victory if it had not been for Messer Piero. He presented them with many arguments, including that it was being done for this commune, for your own reputation, and in order to remain at peace with the Gonfalone—and it would bring them great credit. They did it more out of fear than for love.

Meo heard that Brando has received a letter.

I sent for Messer Piero yesterday evening. I told him on your behalf that you would be glad to have some advice from him about how you should deal with these matters, and that you would have written to him if it had not been for the reasons you told me. He told me face to face what he thought. I begged him to put it in writing, and so he did before he left. He was glad to visit me so he could find out from me what you thought. I said that you remained in Florence unwillingly, but that you had decided to do what Guido wanted and what he and his other friends had advised. He was pleased. He said he would adopt one course of action if you wanted to remain here and another if you wanted to remain there. You were wrong not to send him a letter so he could know what you thought, and what would have made you happy. He did not know what to do, because he says that others are changing their minds from one moment to the next. I informed him of what I knew.

When I arrived here I sent the letter to Messer Guelfo. He came here immediately and read me some of it. It was written by Ser Lapo. Messer Guelfo seems to have a great love for Ser Lapo. He spoke of how Ser Lapo had conducted your business and the risks he ran in doing it. He also told me about the risks he himself ran when he went to Florence. I thanked him on your behalf as best I could, but not as much as he deserves. I will tell you two things that Ser Lapo's letter to Messer Guelfo said: that if it had not been for Guelfo, well supported as he was, even if there were only three issues a year like this it would be enough to ruin him, and that you would keep this in mind. He would be relieved if he never had to take on a more difficult task than this. Say to him whatever you think appropriate.

Ser Chimenti came to see me. I think he is ready and willing to give everyone a good shake-up without my intervention. Ser Chimenti had that blacksmith who is a relative of Matteo arrested, and got a good deal of information out of him. According to him, Matteo told the other debtors that the action against him was not at your bidding and that Chimenti was fleecing people.[199] He is slandered by many. People came to tell me that Matteo has received a large sum from Carmignano, but he pretends he is yet to receive it. I know for a fact that he has, and I wouldn't say it unless I was certain. Ser Chimenti is so much abused that I am sorry. For love of Ser Lapo he doesn't want to collect the money, and he won't let anyone else collect it. If little fish could talk they would say that Matteo has tricked you. You know that I once had evidence about it from that woman from Carmignano; but let it be. For love of Ser Lapo I told Ser Chimenti not to abuse him and not to remind him of his failings, since you would take it too much to heart, considering what Matteo is to Ser Lapo. Ser Chimenti says he would like to arrest Matteo, ask him for the money, and not let him off until he gave a security and went to collect the money himself. Most people say there is little money to collect.

Messer Piero says that the town statutes don't allow you to hold anyone in prison for debt, unless there is a written contract. When you have [Florentine] citizenship you will be able to prosecute him there, and it will be done for you without any appeal being allowed.

I am sending you the key of the room with two beds. I am sending you Villana's mantle as well as Francesca's, and an overgown of Messer Piero's Caterina.[200] Have them forwarded immediately.

Send me back the oil barrel, because the one that is here holds two extra pounds, and that one holds exactly the right amount.

When the capers arrive, send me plenty so that I can forward a generous amount to Messer Piero.

Send me Monna Vanna's bill because I want to settle her account; don't get the belt made.[201]

---

199. Matteo d'Andrea Bellandi was related to both Lapo Mazzei and Francesco. See Mazzei, *Lettere di un notaro*, 2:218–37, and Brambilla and Hayez, "La maison des fantômes," 116–17. See also letters 48 and 49.

200. Margherita refers to Stoldo's wife, Monna Villana, her own sister Francesca, and Caterina Rinaldeschi.

201. Monna Vanna was the wife of Chiarito, and mother of the girl whose wedding preparations Margherita and Francesco were organizing. See also letters 28 and 45.

With this letter you will find a note written in Messer Piero's hand—some advice, which in his opinion you should keep close beside you. He is still convinced that you have guarantors from that Gonfalone who are not exactly your friends. He said another Gonfalone would be better than that one. Nevertheless, he says he believes your petition to the Florentine government should succeed. I would say that you can't go wrong by making them obliged to you.[202] With this there will be a letter from Ser Schiatta and one from Ser Chimenti.

Send my regards to everyone.

From Margherita, in Prato.

Francesco di Marco da Prato, in Florence.
From Prato, 27 March 1394. Answered on the 28th.

Letter 47 (1401742)
28 March 1394
Prato

In the name of God. 28 March 1394.

I sent a letter to you with Castagnino about what was needed. I haven't had a letter from you since then, so I will not say much here.

I am sending you with Nanni da Santa Chiara half a bushel of chestnuts, twenty-two loaves of bread, and the […] chickpeas available—and tied onto the sack a pair of shoes that belong to Messer Piero's Caterina.[203] Send them to her immediately.

Give Nanni the key to the room with two beds for me, and send me Fattorino's washing if there is any. If possible, have Resi fetched and let him know how his brother is. Send me back the same sack and the towel in which the mantles are wrapped and everything else there that is ours.

---

202. In Piero Rinaldeschi's view, Francesco would have been better treated had he not been resident in the Red Lion district, where even citizens who were not openly critical of him, such as Nofri Strozzi, could hardly be regarded as friendly allies. See letter 27.

203. Caterina Rinaldeschi was about to marry Stefano Cepperelli.

That is all. May God protect you.

From your Margherita, in Prato.

Francesco di Marco da Prato, in Florence.

From Prato, 28 March 1394. Answered on the 28th.

Letter 48 (1401743)
29 March 1394
Prato

In the name of God. 29 March 1394.

I received your letter from Michele di Falcuccio, the trumpeter. I did not receive the herrings.

Niccolò di Piero has been here, and he gave me the key of the bedroom. He says he read the letter I sent you. He asked me if I knew which debtors Matteo had told that it wasn't your desire that he pursue them vigorously. There was no need to ask, as he knew better than I. He pretended he didn't know. I said to him that Paolo di Bonaccorso was one of those he told. I said that I did not remember the others, but that Ser Chimenti said there were three. Before he left, Ser Chimenti arrived and I told Niccolò to ask him who the others were. Ser Chimenti said to him: "You know who they are because I told you," and he named them all. I think they won't be happy that all their relatives will find out, but I don't care.[204]

Matteo went to Filippo and asked him if Cristofano is to come tomorrow or not. You haven't told us anything, so I don't know where they found this out.

It is not Brando, but someone else here, who is asking for the return of a mattress and a vest, which he lent to the man he was working with when he returned to Monna Ghita.[205] He is also asking for fourteen *soldi* in rent for every month the man kept the mattress. I sent Ser Chimenti there to find out how the matter stood. It seems that the person who is asking for it is in the right. The other man has kept

204. For Matteo d'Andrea Bellandi's slanders of Ser Chimenti, see letters 46 and 49.

205. Monna Ghita was the wife of Matteo di Ghetto Guizzelmi.

the mattress for more than eighteen months, and must give back the mattress along with the money he owes. He has kept it and can't avoid the debt because he entered into a contract. I then had words with him, because I had told him on several occasions that he should give it back if it was not his. He always claimed it was his. He lied through his teeth. He said he had often wanted to give it back but you hadn't wanted him to do so. It would serve him right if he died in prison.[206]

I can't give you any information regarding your representatives because the Council hasn't come out yet and it is three hours after dark. You will be told everything by Ser Chimenti. Tell us what to do about this matter of Matteo.

That is all. May God protect you.

From Margherita, in Prato.

Francesco di Marco da Prato himself, in Florence.
From Prato, 30 March 1394. Answered on the 30th.

Letter 49 (1401744)
1 April 1394
Prato

In the name of God. 1 April 1394.

Yesterday evening Nanni di Santa Chiara delivered your letter. The reason I didn't answer was that Messer Giovanni Panciatichi's sister Monna Lionarda, and her daughter Monna Sandra, arrived here at the twenty-fourth hour, and the son of Monna Sandra was with them.[207] They stayed the night and in the morning they ate here. I tried to provide the best hospitality I could but it was not possible to do this very well because in the morning, to my misfortune, all the fish smelt bad. Niccolaio Martini's son went as far as Cervello's place but

---

206. See FD 39. The person who borrowed the mattress was Meo. For the sequel, see letter 49.

207. See footnote 134, above.

we could not get any more.[208] We did our best to serve them honorably with other food.

About Nanni da Santa Chiara's arrival, I did not know that he was coming empty-handed. I won't send the packhorse with Nanni. It is needed here because today I had all the oranges in the kitchen garden picked. I sent all the manure to Il Palco and I had Meo work in the kitchen garden, as he can stay here for three days because of the market. Tomorrow I will get him to empty the stables and carry the manure up there. On Thursday I will make him bring […] to the small garden. I had a search made at Il Palco for some doors for the entrance to the kitchen garden from the direction of Serraglio, but they are not to be found anywhere. Chiarito's wife, Vanna, says that Antonio di Vitale came to her place and brought the measure with him to see if there was anything wide enough [to reach] to the drains. He said he had taken a [door] made of chestnut wood to Chiarito's house that was just right, but you could not find it. I think it must be in use because it can't be found. As it is, the kitchen garden is in a bad situation because anyone who wants to enter can do so through the place where the canal runs. They have not been able to do any damage so far. It is not bad at present. I thought of doing this: taking those old gates and barring the entrance to the canal very securely so that there can be no access through this opening. According to what they tell me it is only necessary to change the metal reinforcements of the gates. Chiarito and Nanni di Guiduccio would do it. They say they will be able to make it secure in an hour. I will get it done if you approve.

As for chickpeas, it is true that they are the ones Niccolò sent me, because I had them in my room. They were in a box and we were writing the letter and I said, "Go and bring half the good chickpeas here," but the girl brought some bad ones, and this explains how it happened.

Matteo was here with me yesterday, and I told him what I had written to you. He excused himself very much and said it wasn't true that he had ever said those words. He told me that he always wanted to remain like a son to us, and I said to him that I forgave him, con-

208. Piero di Giovanni da Coiano, known as Cervello, was a miller. See Brambilla and Hayez, "La maison des fantômes," 110–11. Margherita presumably hoped that, as Cervello lived by a river, he might have some fish.

sidering his relationship with Ser Lapo. I think that it was Lapo's idea, because he is the wise person there. I answered as well as I could for love of him.

Regarding the matter of Meo, this is what I did: I was polite to him and I told him to wait for your return and that you will do what has to be done, and I told him to tell Ser Chimenti this. I don't think there could be a better solution than this one of mine.[209]

The representatives did not come because they are waiting for the new Eight to take up office. Arriguccio is the Gonfalonier of Justice.[210] You will be told everything by Ser Chimenti.

We received the herrings and I sent them immediately to Gherardo;[211] and we received the sack.

I am sending you the doublet and twelve loaves with Nanni da Santa Chiara, as well as a pannier with some mushrooms. I was not unhappy to send them. That is why I am sending them, and don't be surprised that they have been cleaned because I intended to cook them. [Make sure] that you eat them, because they were very expensive. […] find a large quantity so you could send them to Ser Lapo […] if chickpeas come in, you will get some.

As for the packhorse, Antonio Micocchi [came] to me and asked me about it. […][212] He told me that he had to be in Florence at this time and he would speak to you about it. Tell him what your opinion is. He is one of the Eight, and he needs to be treated well.

I am sending you some good chickpeas. Send back the small basket, as it belongs to Monna Fia.[213]

I am using the pony and the black horse for the next two days, and afterward I will order the wheat at Il Palco to be weeded with a

---

209. See letter 46.

210. This is Arriguccio di Ser Guido Ferracani.

211. This is Gherardo Becchi.

212. The next sentence is fragmentary, but Francesco's reply reveals that the carpenter Antonio di Michele Micocchi, or "Bicocchi," wanted to borrow a packhorse. Francesco was reluctant to oblige and approved of Margherita's handling of the matter.

213. Monna Fia was Baronto's wife and a tenant of one of Francesco's houses in Via del Porcellatico. See Melis, *Aspetti della vita economica medievale*, 61; and Brambilla and Hayez, "La maison des fantômes," 125, n. 171.

hoe because now is the right time. There is nothing to be done to the vines until May, so I had the vineyard at Filettole dug over.

That is all. May God protect you.

From Margherita, in Prato.

I am also sending you a pair of blue hose because I know you need them.

Francesco di Marco da Prato, in Florence.
Received from Prato, 2 April 1394.

Letter 50 (1401745)
2 April 1394
Prato

In the name of God. 2 April 1394.

I received your letter from Nanni da Santa Chiara as well as several other letters that I had sent on.

I understand what you say about the loss.[214] May God in His mercy give us, as well as Niccolò, the grace to resign ourselves to it.

About the business of Lodovico di Ser Iacopo and Giovanni di Simone the furrier, I can't do any more than Ser Chimenti is willing to do. Every day I remind him, and every day he says that he has written to you, and he says Cristofano must come here. In the meantime, if he came here the day after tomorrow, he should do it because he would do it better than anyone else. If he can't come, you could make Filippo your representative, and in this way it would be possible to solve the matter. There is no other solution.

Nannino could not stay here, though I would have kept him willingly. Meo will be leaving this evening because he is not needed here any more.

There was no business in the piazza yesterday. We bought thirty bushels of spelt for the animals, and it is worthwhile for us to send for it. It is four miles away, and costs eight *soldi* and eight *denari*. It grew

214. Margherita refers to news that both Francesco and Niccolò dell'Ammannato Tecchini had lost money because of the bankruptcy of debtors in Florence and Pisa. See FD 41.

among wheat. Ser Chimenti says it is as good as quality barley. The barley was sold to us at fourteen *soldi*.

I did not forget to send you anything. Nanni da Santa Chiara left some things at the dye works because his loads were too great. He says he will bring the rest to you tomorrow.

Monna Piera left me yesterday evening. I don't care much because she was so unpopular that I was ashamed for her to be seen in my house; and also I doubted that she was loyal, as I told you when I saw you. I was ashamed for her to come with me anywhere and I did not want to let Lucia go alone with her.[215] I did not leave the house after my return because of this leg of mine, as the doctor told me not to tire it too much. I am getting much better now. I will keep Monna Lorita, Monna Ghita, or one of our friends with me and you will be pleased with the outcome.[216] Tell Francesca that if she finds a good maid suitable for me she should keep her for herself, and I will see if I can find one here.

Ask Francesca about a knife with two silver rings on it belonging to Ser Schiatta's wife, Monna Nanna, who says she left it at table. Try to find it and send it to me, as she does not want Ser Schiatta to find out.

I sent half the capers you sent me to Messer Piero.

Together with this is a letter to you from Messer Piero, and one from Ser Chimenti.

That is all. May God protect you.

From your Margherita, in Prato.

Francesco di Marco da Prato, in Florence.
Received from Prato, 2 April 1394.

---

215. The servant, Monna Piera, first mentioned in letter 28, had given Francesco an account of her grievances (FD 42). Margherita regarded her as unsatisfactory. See also letter 51.

216. Monna Lorita was Monte's wife; Monna Ghita was the wife of Matteo di Ghetto Guizzelmi.

Letter 51 (1401746)
3 April 1394
Prato

In the name of God. 3 April 1394.

Nanni delivered your letter, and I have understood what you say. I will respond to some items now.

I lent the black horse and the pony to Messer Piero because he doesn't want the mule. They are coming to Florence.

About the matter of the doublet: as you know you sent a message requesting a new one for Nanni da Santa Chiara, and I said I would give him a new one. It was the fault of Filippo, who said to Nanni that it was old without asking me whether it was old or new.[217]

The mule is well, as are all the packhorses; it is not necessary to tell you so in every letter. We look after it as Filippo the farrier instructs and we keep the animals here, not at Il Palco.

Filippo the farrier has asked me for a pair of hose for this Easter.

You tell me Monna Piera did not want to supervise Lucia any more; and I tell you I didn't want to supervise [Piera], because I found she needed it more than Lucia. She gave you that excuse, but she wanted to go off and do different things from what she was supposed to do. [Lucia] is better off alone than in bad company.

Don't worry about this household because it is managed in such a way that you will never hear scandal. That is why I sent Monna Piera away, as she is old in years but has a childish mind.[218]

I think I told you that Nannino is working his land and we do not need him, because Fattorino and Filippo will look after these animals well. I would not like Nannino or anyone else to come here before you return. Filippo never sleeps at the dye works, because Niccolò doesn't want him to do so while you are not here.

Meo is doing what needs to be done in that garden at Filettole. Tomorrow and Monday he will stay at Il Palco again; he will hoe all the wheat, and guard the place.

---

217. See FD 42.

218. Monna Piera was in her early fifties. See also letter 50.

I will say no more because Messer Piero wants to leave. May God protect you.

From Margherita, in Prato.

Francesco di Marco da Prato, in Florence.
Received from Prato, 3 April 1394.

Letter 52 (1401747)
9 April 1394
Prato

In the name of God. 9 April 1394.

Yesterday Monna Simona delivered your letter.[219] I understand what you say in it and respond here as necessary.

I will get the things done that you have told me should be done and, as necessary, I will inform you once they are done.

I will send you Stoldo's small mule today, if I find someone I can trust.

I am sending you a full donkey-load of vinegar with Nanni di Santa Chiara, and the jar of grapes, eighteen loaves, and a flask of that Trebbiano wine that you asked for.

Ask Cristofano where the key is to the chest containing his underlinen.

Buy me two and a half yards of guarnello cloth for Monna Fia.[220] It should be beautiful.

Buy the buttons for Tina when you can and get the same sort that you got for Monna Vanna's daughter, which were sixteen in the ounce, and get several ounces because we can't make do with less.[221]

Tell me about the matter you were asked about, concerning Ser Piero Cepperelli's son, and whether things went ahead, because that

---

219. This is Monna Simona Rinaldeschi, Margherita's neighbor.

220. Guarnello was a cloth made of flax and cotton. For Monna Fia see note 213, above.

221. Francesco bought two and a half ounces. See FD 45.

friend I talked to about it regrets it already and has not returned.[222] Don't say anything to anyone.

From Margherita, in Prato.

I won't say any more. May God protect you always.

To Francesco di Marco da Prato, in Florence.
Received from Prato, 9 April 1394.

Letter 53 (1401749)
14 April 1394
Prato

In the name of God. 14 April 1394.

Nanni di Santa Chiara brought me your letter. I respond here as necessary.

About the woman promised me by Niccolaio Martini, I spoke to her yesterday, and she promised she would come to me when she had finished looking after a woman who is about to give birth. It seems to me, as far as I can tell, that she is a good woman. She has no husband or children. Keep this other one waiting until I answer you, and tell me what her situation is.

Regarding Prizzi, we should pursue him as much as we can.[223] We received Tina's buttons in a bag.

I will try to obtain the amount you are owed by Paolo di Bertino.[224] I wrote to you about the wheat and how I got it. Because Matterello is there, it is being milled today.

We can't find anyone who wants the wine. You will be here for these holidays. You can decide about it then. I can't find anyone who can come to do the plastering because they are all busy.[225] Nannino got his mantle back.[226]

---

222. See letters 55 and 56.

223. See note 235, below.

224. See letters 27 and 29.

225. See letter 56.

226. See letter 46.

I have decided not to send a letter to Guido, and I don't want you to forward any from him to me here.[227]

Yesterday morning I received a letter from Ser Lapo that says you detained him there in Florence for two days, and he said that he showed my letter to Guido. It was a letter written in such a way that I decided many times I would not answer him. Afterward I did answer him, thinking he was at Grignano.[228] I sent him wine, a pannier of chestnuts and hazelnuts, and on top there were many mushrooms. I told him about the events concerning Guido so he will be able to say that I am not in a position to reply to Guido. I entrusted him with this matter, but Fattorino tells me he had left Grignano. The letter remained with his wife. Don't say anything about it to him if he doesn't raise the matter with you because I know he will show it to you.

I did not send you any bread because I don't have any suitable flour.

I will send you a flask of wine if Nanni can carry it.

We received a jar of green ginger from Pisa.

That is all. May God protect you.

From Margherita, in Prato.

To Francesco di Marco da Prato, in Florence.

Received from Prato, 14 April 1394.

227. Here Margherita refers to Guido del Palagio. She was apparently embarrassed by the prospect of having to answer such an important man.

228. Lapo Mazzei wrote to Margherita on 8 and 10 April. See Mazzei, *Lettere di un notaro*, 2:178–80. On 10 April, Margherita replied in a letter addressed to him in Florence and, on 13 April, with another addressed to his small farm at Grignano, near Prato. ASPo, D.1089, 1402969, and 1402670. No response to Margherita's letter of 13 April survives.

Letter 54 (1401748)
14 April 1394
Prato

In the name of God. 14 April 1394.

Concerning the maidservant, send her if you can. I don't think I can have that other one. And also send me a black samite cushion.[229] Make sure it is beautiful. Get Domenico di Cambio to buy it for me.

I have retrieved the letter that I sent to Ser Lapo at Grignano.[230] Give it to him and not to anyone else, and don't read it until Lapo has read it first. I have no time to say anything else, as Michele wants to leave.

May God protect you.

From Margherita, in Prato.

To Francesco di Marco da Prato, in Florence.
Received from Prato, 14 April 1394.

Letter 55 (1401750)
15 April 1394
Prato

In the name of God. 15 April 1394.

The reason I am writing this is to let you know that yesterday evening at the second hour, Messer Piero married his daughter Caterina to the son of Ser Piero Cepperelli.[231] The only people present were Messer Piero and Monna Simona, myself, and Caterina. May God's will be done in heaven and then on earth, and may it bring comfort to those who love her!

Considering the status and possibilities of Messer Piero, I think he has done extremely well and will profit greatly from it. Keep it secret because neither Giovanni nor anyone else knows it yet. I was told

229. Samite is a type of silk.

230. See note 228, above.

231. See letter 52.

that Messer Piero will send someone to Florence to tell everyone. If Giovanni or anyone should talk about it to you, say that Messer Piero has done well, because he has indeed.

As regards the debts to collect here, we are recovering as much as we can. I have nothing to add. May God protect you.

From Margherita, in Prato.

Francesco di Marco da Prato, in Florence.
Received from Prato, 15 April 1394.

Letter 56 (1401751)
15 April 1394
Prato

In the name of God. 15 April 1394.

I received your letter, delivered by Castagnino. I have understood everything and reply here as necessary.

Nanni di Guiduccio and Nannino are here today to do the plastering in the baker's house. I want the hood for myself.

You didn't explain whether you need those letters from Pistoia urgently or not. I decided to send someone immediately. He will be there this evening. Next time, tell me if you need them or not. It was just as well that I sent the letters, because Ser Chimenti told me that it would have been impossible to find anyone who was going there for the market.

I have twice sent someone with a message to Cristofano di Ser Francia, but both times he said he couldn't do anything before Easter. I have decided to send the eggs there on Friday with the cheese. If Nanni is coming your way I will send them to you on Friday.

Messer Piero cannot give us any wheat because he has none. I will buy some tomorrow at the market along with the other things you have listed. I'll do everything in my power to get it for the reason that you mention, and I won't be put off by the price. The same goes for the chickens and capons if any can be found.

I have asked Checco Bondì if he knows where we might find some grain. We still have twenty-eight bushels of wheat we haven't touched, all of it first quality. There will be no shortage if we buy at least a *moggio*. This business about the need for grain and chickens does not mean that you should be here tomorrow, because I will see to it that everything is bought (if it is to be found). It would be better to go to Fiesole to pray to God for yourself and for me and then come here tomorrow evening. I have understood about the wheat problem even if you haven't given me an explanation. With a little over a *moggio* more we will have enough. I will make sure it is bought.

Messer Piero begs me to lend him the black packhorse tomorrow for the business you know about. I will send you the mule so you can let them know there. Don't bother to send sweetmeats because there are plenty already; we need sweet spices. There are no candles except for a few wax ones.

I just now received your letter, and the one for Niccolò di Piero that I have had given to him. I have understood everything you say and reply below.

The letter for Messer Guelfo's son Nanni was taken by Fattorino and put into Messer Guelfo's own hands. He says that he will send the packhorse tomorrow morning.

We have twelve wax candles, so for now there is no need to buy any. Send us some oranges for Easter. Come quickly, because Tina says she wants her husband. She says he does not want to remain there any longer and to avoid returning to Florence he will get a house and stay here.[232]

As for the fact that my scribe's handwriting is getting worse, I am sorry but it is no surprise because he is being directed by a woman. You have really left me to organize so many things that they would be more than enough even for a man; the secretary of the Signoria never had as much to do as mine.[233] We attend to everything but I don't think this will last much longer because both my scribe and I are being driven mad.

232. Caterina Rinaldeschi had just married but had not yet moved to her husband's household. See letter 55.

233. See FD 42, in which Francesco complained about the handwriting of the letters dictated by Margherita.

Send me an ounce of silkworm eggs so that when those youths you sent on Sunday return I can give them some.

Send me two yards of ribbon and do it tomorrow; I include the width here. As for the maidservant, I will find a way to secure either Piera or her mother so that we will be well attended. Remember me to everyone there. When you return I will show you the letter Ser Lapo sent me.[234]

With this letter I include another sent to you by Prizzi ordering that tomorrow you be given ten florins.[235] May God protect you.

From Margherita, in Prato.

To Francesco di Marco da Prato, in Florence.
Received from Prato, 15 April 1394.

Letter 57 (1401752)
27 April 1394
Prato

In the name of God. 27 April 1394.

I am sending you with Nanni da Santa Chiara twenty-four eggs, eighteen loaves of bread, and a flask of wine.

Remember to send me Monna Nanna's account and Monna Simona's ribbons. That's all for now. May God protect you.

From your Margherita, in Prato.

Nanni da Santa Chiara tells us that Stoldo has bought eighteen sacks of woad for us, so we would like you to organize its collection and to send some loads to us, as it would be useful to mix with the other dye that Niccolò got from Prizzi.[236] Send us a message with Do-

---

234. Margherita refers here to Mazzei's letter of 10 April. See Mazzei, *Lettere di un notaro*, 2:178–80.

235. Prizzi di Messer Bartolomeo Visconti was a wool merchant originally from Pistoia, who lived in Prato and supplied dye to Francesco. See letter 57. See Fiumi, *Demografia*, 506.

236. Woad is a blue dye prepared from the powdered and fermented leaves of *Isatis tinctoria*.

menico di Cambio to say whether this should be charged to you separately or to Francesco di Marco and Associates. May God protect you.

To Francesco di Marco da Prato, in Florence.
Received from Prato, 28 April 1394. Answered on the 28th.

Letter 58 (1401753)
29 April 1394
Prato

In the name of God. 29 April 1394.

Nanni da Santa Chiara brought me your letter as well as letters for friends. I sent them on. There was one among them to Messer Piero's Monna Simona. She has told me what she wants.

She says she wants fifty yards of ribbon of the type that you say will cost more than four *soldi*. She does not want them to cost much more.

She would also like twenty yards of trimming: ten black and ten blue. She would like the blue to be as close to this color as possible, the sort that is used doubled over, as broad as possible.

And she says she also wants up to two ounces of those small buttons. If you can't find two, get one; that is, up to two ounces of whatever you find. If they are different—either bigger or smaller—get them anyway, as long as they are white.[237]

Ser Andrea will go to Florence on Friday if he can, so give him these things when he returns here.

I sent the ginger to Niccolaio Martini and to Ser Lapo's mother. I also sent the lengths of timber to Antonio Micocchi, and I reminded Ser Chimenti about the anvil matter.[238]

Meo has told me that the baker will come to teach Nannino whenever we wish. I will wait for you to come, so you can give orders about the baker's departure.

---

237. These items were probably for Simona's newly married daughter, Caterina. See letter 55.

238. See FD 51 and 54.

Monna Simona says to sell the linen for what you can, and to draw up the account for the belt and whatever these things cost and to let her know the price. That is all. May God protect you.

From Margherita, in Prato.

To Francesco di Marco da Prato himself, in Florence.
Received from Prato, 29 April 1394. Answered on the 29th.

Letter 59 (1401754)
30 April 1394
Prato

In the name of God. 30 April 1394.

Benedetto from Milan, the brother of Giannino who worked for you in Avignon, has arrived here.[239] I am writing this so he can find you because he says he needs to speak with you.

Enclosed here there is a letter that came from Pisa today.

We bought three pairs of pullets and no more because they were dearer at this market than at the other.

We also bought two sacks of millet. That is all. May God protect you.

From Margherita, in Prato.

Francesco di Marco da Prato, in Florence.
Received from Prato 1 May 1394.

239. In the summer of 1384, Giannino di Iacopo da Milano had been recruited in Milan by Tieri di Benci to work in the firm's branch in Avignon (information supplied by Jérôme Hayez).

Letter 60 (1401755)
1 May 1394
Prato

In the name of God. 1 May 1394.

I sent you a letter with Castagnino and I haven't yet received your reply, so I will be brief.

I am writing this only to let you know that they have elected the representative to go to Florence. He is Ridolfo di Niccolaio.[240] No one else is going with him. He is one of the tax assessors. Everyone is pleased because he is a friend of this Gonfalone.

Send back the small packhorse with Nannino because we need it.

That is all. May God protect you.

From Margherita, in Prato.

To Francesco di Marco da Prato, in Florence.
Brought from Prato by Nannino da Volterra, 1 May 1394.

Letter 61 (1401756)
6 May 1394
Prato

In the name of God. 6 May 1394.

Filippo the farrier delivered your letter. I understand what you say in it and respond here as necessary.

Regarding the wine from Il Palco: before you left here it seemed to have deteriorated, but I did not want to say so in case you would say I was too fussy. The wine is being drunk, but there is not much of it. There is no reason for not using it, because Ser Lapo's wife liked it and so did her children who have been sick with rubella. It's not that they ever asked for it; but I sent a flask every day, and some meat when good meat was available. I also sent this wine to the custodian at San Francesco. He had some every day. We had very little of it.

---

240. Ridolfo di Niccolaio Manassei was a Pratese notary.

There is no need to remind me about Filippo.[241] I am only doing for him what I would do for myself, or even for a cat, in such circumstances. I keep Monna Vanna just for him because she can look after him as he needs. Sometimes I also call Monna Ghita so she can give him enemas because she is older than Chiarito's wife, Monna Vanna. I will make sure he is well looked after so you will be content.

Niccolò di Piero sent Lapa to us on the day that you left. I wanted to keep her with me as you said. She did not want to stay because she had her niece at home. Niccolò sent me a message through Filippo on Friday that you would be happy for Lapa to stay here until you came back. You sent me word on the same day through Nannino that you would be coming back on Saturday; I told Filippo this, but only so that he and you could be certain that I was happy. Niccolò sent her on Sunday after lunch. I wanted to keep her here and pressed her very strongly to stay, although I had been invited to a dinner to be attended by many distinguished ladies, at the house of Messer Piero, in honor of his daughter.[242] Messer Piero came for me in person while Lapa was here. Thinking I would be keeping her, I refused to go. It seems to me that she has good reasons to leave because Monna Gaia is in the country and she has to serve her husband and children and look after everyone who comes and goes and, Filippo says, every morning she must prepare food and wine for the workers. Monna Vanna was better than Lapa when Filippo was sick, because I could send Monna Vanna to places where I could not send her. Similarly, I have Chiarito, who is not busy. I send him for the doctor, or to wherever else I need him to go, because Fattorino has not been very well and, although he is not in bed, he is still not better. For this reason I kept them on because it seems to me they like looking after him.

I do not wish to bother others when I find people who are happy to do it and earn something for themselves. You know that Monna Vanna and Chiarito do not have much to do, but write to me about what you want just the same.

I am glad that you said you wanted to speak to me face to face. We have made peace after greater wars than this one. You mocked me when I wrote to you: "I will always follow the road to which I am ac-

---

241. Filippo di Francesco, Francesco's employee in Prato, had tertian fever. See letter 62.

242. Caterina Rinaldeschi had married in April. See letter 55.

customed and I will never stray from it, whatever is said to me. I will do to others as I would like to be done to me and I will never knowingly stray from this."[243]

There is no need for you to worry about the affairs of this household, and you don't need to tell anyone except me, because it concerns me more than anyone and I don't think I am less clear sighted than those people you trust more than me.

About this tax matter of ours: I don't know what to say except may God do what is best for our body and soul.

No woman turned up here. Look for one there, because I can't find anyone here who wants to come and stay with me.[244]

Monna Simona wants a yard of blue trimming and a yard of black, because she doesn't have enough, and an ounce of used buttons. If you can't find old ones, buy new ones. Try and send them tomorrow if you can.

I won't write any more because Fattorino is not feeling well.

Tomorrow evening we will write about the rest. Together with this there are letters from Piero. Have them delivered.

That is all. May God protect you. Send my greetings to everyone.

Send me the account for the purchases you made for Monna Simona.

From Margherita, in Prato.

Francesco di Marco da Prato himself, in Florence.
Received from Prato, 6 May 1394. Answered.

243. On 5 May 1394 (FD 53), Francesco referred to a letter from Margherita of 3 May that is not extant. It may have been destroyed for confidentiality. Apparently in it Margherita gave him news about a tax assessment that concerned her.

244. See letter 62 regarding the arrival of the servant Monna Giuliva.

Letter 62 (1401757)
7 May 1394
Prato

In the name of God. 7 May 1394.

Nanni di Santa Chiara delivered your letter. I understand what you say in it. Now I will answer.

The steward of the new *Podestà* was here to see the wine. Bernabò showed it to him. He had with him the steward of the Eight, who supplies them with wine. Bernabò explained that we had bought it at twenty-five *soldi* a barrel and refused to agree with them on a price. They told him they wanted to come and speak to me about it. I told Bernabò that the steward knew the price was twenty-five *soldi* but if they wanted a present it would be our pleasure to present it. If you were here, you would rather give it to them than sell it, but I would not set any price on it because he knew the price we had paid. He said that he wanted it for twenty-two *soldi* because it was not worth any more. I said I would be happy to oblige him, whether he paid or not, as they preferred. This is the worst wine and he said he would pay us the best possible price. I offered him our respects on your behalf.

I will make sure that you are happy about the matter concerning Ser Lapo's wife. Paolo di Bertino got the money for the salted tuna from the former *Podestà*.[245]

Filippo has the worst tertian fever possible. Master Matteo is treating him and looking after him well.[246] He has promised to say by today how many days it will last. You do not need to worry about him. If only every friend of ours were treated like that!

Send us some sugar because the time is coming to use it.[247] A woman called Monna Giuliva, who says you sent her, arrived here. Write to tell me what agreement you made with her and whether I should send her to the bakery or anywhere else I need.[248]

---

245. This is Paolo di Bertino Verzoni.

246. This is Matteo di Giovanni Giuntini, the doctor from Prato.

247. See FD 54.

248. Monna Giuliva, a fifty-year-old woman, had worked for Niccolosa, wife of Guido del Palagio. Francesco had reservations about employing her as a servant because she was married and had children. See FD 53 and 54.

At Il Palco they are hoeing the vineyards. The buttons that Monna Simona wants should be small and suitable for threading, and she also wants four yards of trimming, two black and two blue. Send it to us this evening if you have anyone coming; otherwise send it tomorrow.

I think everything is all right on the outside of the garden gate, because things are now safe. Let me know what you think about it.

Ser Chimenti is looking for preserved oranges. If they are nice, we will buy what we need.

I received thirty-five *lire* from Tarpuccia, and we needed the money badly.[249]

If you approve of buying two or three bundles of wood at the market, we will buy them; otherwise we won't. Write to tell me what you want me to do.

Many of the young silkworms are dying. I don't know if Fattorino recognizes the disease. I have asked him to write to you, and I will get him and Tina to do what he thinks best. May God protect you.

From Margherita, in Prato.

Francesco di Marco da Prato himself, in Florence.
Received from Prato, 7 May 1394. Answered.

Letter 63 (1401758)
8 May 1394
Prato

In the name of God. 8 May 1394.

Niccolò di Piero sent me a message saying that you would be happy if I were to go to Grignano, with Monna Gaia and Monna Lapa.[250] It was not necessary for you to say so to him, or to me, because

---

249. The cobbler Domenico di Giovanni di Puccino, known as Tarpuccia, bought leather from Francesco on credit and supplied him with firewood. See letters 128 and 250, and FD 43.

250. Francesco was keen for Margherita to accompany Monna Gaia and her daughter-in-law Monna Lapa, on a social visit to Lapo Mazzei's mother, Monna Bartola, who lived at

if I had found the time to go I would have gone. It amazes me that you send a message that I should go to Grignano when Filippo has tertian fever; and so has Fattorino, who despite being unwell continues to go about, won't lie down, and collapses all the time. As well as all this, yesterday we thought that Chiarito's little girl would die from a worm infestation. I have never been so afraid. I arranged for Master Matteo to prepare a worming syrup for them, and they must all take it during the next few days. According to the doctor, Filippo had a higher temperature today than ever before, and he lies there trembling violently and crying so loudly that we are all busy heating up cloths. Another crisis will come on Sunday, so I don't see how I can go there for many days yet.

I am taking the syrup and intend to have the enema on Monday—that is, both Filippo and I, because Monna Vanna will be here to give it to me and to him. I don't have anything wrong with me, but I want to purge myself while there is time to do it.

And what's more, Lucia hit her eye on the top edge of the well, pulling up a bucket of water, and I thought that she had lost the sight in it. I put a poultice on it, and I'll attempt to draw the blood off on Saturday, after advice from Master Matteo, because it is a little swollen. I'm telling you this so that you won't say that I have an objection to going to Grignano. I'm sending them some meat and wine, and yesterday I sent them a quarter of a really fine goat as well. It seems from what Fattorino says that they truly appreciated it, as much as if I had gone there myself. Nevertheless, write to me if you still want me to go there on Sunday and I will leave everything and go. I must admit that I'm very reluctant to do so. I am just not in the mood to amuse myself because it seems to me that this year there is no time. This year, I've gone neither to Il Palco nor to church since your departure, except for when Monna Simona sent for me on Wednesday to restring Caterina's pearl necklace, and I wouldn't have gone if Monna Vanna hadn't been here.

Today they finished working on the vines at Il Palco. I am sending you two sets of linen for yourself, two for Castruccio, a set that belongs to Castruccio, and two new caps for you. I am also sending you a small coif to wear under the hood, and two small kerchiefs. And

---

Grignano. The visit finally took place more than two weeks later. See letters 70 and 71.

the week after next I will make the hood and anything else I discover you need.

I am sending back a towel that Castruccio brought that belongs to Monna Nanna di Ser Schiatta. Return the basket and the cloth in which the eggs were packed, and send back those white hose (that I know you don't wear) because Meo needs them. And return the flasks to us and anything else of ours.

I am not sending you any squabs because they are too small and we eat them one at a time. Buy some cockerels for yourself because here in Prato they cost more.

Send us a few bottles of vinegar, and if what I sent you has turned out well, I will send some more. I've nothing else to say. May God protect you.

From Margherita, in Prato.

To Francesco di Marco da Prato, in Florence.
Received from Prato, 8 May 1394. Answered.

Letter 64 (1401759)
8 May 1394
Prato

In the name of God. 8 May 1394.

I am writing because Monna Simona is sending you her servant because she needs an ounce of buttons for threading, the same as the other time, and four yards of black trimming and two of blue.

I sent you a letter yesterday morning, and Nannino says he gave it to two friars of the Carmine. I don't know if you got it. I don't think so.

This morning I sent you an order with Nanni da Santa Chiara. Make sure that it is dispatched with one of those boys so that it will be here by nones because I have to go to a dinner on Sunday. With this there is a letter to Ser Chimenti, which Nanni da Santa Chiara forgot to collect.

May God protect you.

From Margherita, in Prato.

Francesco di Marco da Prato himself, in Florence.

Received from Prato, 8 March 1394. Answered on the 9th.

Letter 65 (1401760)
9 May 1394
Prato

In the name of God. 9 May 1394.

I received the letter addressed to Niccolò di Piero from Lapo di Toringo, and Niccolò said there was nothing for me.

The *Podestà* is taking the wine he bought by the half barrel. Fattorino is keeping a written record and is decanting it as they require it.

About the wood, I will do as you say. I have heard about the woman who is to come from Lucca. I will do as I have been advised, and I won't go out for any reason to ensure I am here when she arrives. If she comes here, I will get someone to meet her so she is well looked after.

About that woman you sent us: as soon as I saw her I knew what she was like, and I said to Monna Simona that she had the face of a featherbrain. She loves to sing and dance, and there is not a dance that she doesn't know. When she is tired of this she knows how to play cards. Her name is Monna Giuliva, and she is aptly named because she is blithe of spirit and lighthearted. She talks to people she has no business talking to, and there is always something to burst out laughing about. I should have had her twelve years ago, because now I am not easily amused; but if you come back here, she will teach you how to smile. I get cross with her and so do Caterina di Bernabò, Cilia, and Niccolosa; and Tina also gets very cross with her. I have never seen a woman with so little sense. One can tease and laugh at her as much as one likes, and she doesn't take offence.[251]

251. For Monna Giuliva, see note 248, above. As for the aptness of her name, still in current Italian *giulivo* means "joyous, happy," or even "birdbrained."

I would like to remain pleasant, as you prefer. I have never been one to make nasty remarks either to you or to anyone else, and you know that I try to do unto others as I would have them do unto me. When people don't understand that, I get very upset, and it makes me suffer more than anything else that happens to me.

About your long letter to me, I'm not displeased about staying at home. It would not show respect for you to do anything else, considering that you are there full of worries. I don't want to say any more about this because it will seem that I am chattering on.

Nanni di Santa Chiara brought the bundle you sent us, tied with a towel, in which there was your lined overgown, a lined doublet, two hoods, two caps, and a pair of white hose. You ought to have another pair of new hose that you wore one time you came here that were intended for Meo. As for the little vegetable garden, I will do whatever is possible.

Filippo has tertian fever, as usual; the doctor says it will last ten or twelve days, may God's will be done. Tell me if I sent you three coifs or not because I wrote to you about two and I thought I sent three. That's all for now. May God protect you.

From Margherita, in Prato.

To Francesco di Marco da Prato himself, in Florence,
Received from Prato, 9 May 1394.

Letter 66 (1401761)
11 May 1394
Prato

In the name of God. 11 May 1394.

The reason I am writing this is that I am sending you three pairs of squabs so you can taste them, because they are from the new dovecote.[252] They are not big. I am also sending you three rounds of cheese. Send one pair of squabs and one cheese to my aunt. I am sending you

---

252. The squabs arrived dead. See FD 56.

little cheese because it will not keep. I am also sending you twenty-two eggs from our hens.

I had the garden secured so it is safe. I did have the expenses that you mentioned, but I forgot to tell you about it.

Draw up the account for what you bought and did for Monna Simona.

I sent the letter to Grignano, but Lionardo was not there.[253] He had left, so I am sending it back to you.

Regarding Monna Giuliva, although she sings and dances, she seems to me a decent person and we can let her stay until we have someone one who is really perfect; otherwise don't bother about it.[254]

Filippo is still the same. Master Matteo treats him properly mornings and evenings, and looks after him well. I have not given him anything, because of the Malvasia wine we gave him this year. But it seems to me you should write him a letter when you have time and say whatever you think is appropriate, although it is not necessary. But it is good to do such things sometimes.

Send us some sugar. Nothing else is needed for now.

Niccolò di Piero showed me a letter from you that does not require an answer. Because I am having the enema tomorrow, both myself and Filippo, I will say no more.[255] May God protect you.

From Margherita, in Prato.

Francesco di Marco da Prato, in Florence.
Received from Prato, 11 May 1394. Answered.

Letter 67 (1401762)
12 May 1394
Prato

In the name of God. 12 May 1394.

Nanni da Santa Chiara delivered your letter. I reply here.

253. Lionardo Mazzei, brother of Lapo.

254. See letter 65.

255. See letter 63 for reference to the enema to be administered by Monna Vanna.

Before Niccolò di Piero left, I gave him the letter you wanted taken to Grignano. I also sent Monna Bartola wine and the things I had bought for her. Fattorino says he read the letter to her, and she told him we should send it back to Florence and so we did.

I have sent you the squabs so you will believe me that they are not good.

I still have not had the opportunity to talk to Monna Simona in the way you suggested, because I have never been alone with her to say it properly. I have touched on the matter a few times, but not as I wish because I have not had the opportunity. When an occasion presents itself, I will tell her my opinion.[256]

I received from Nanni the sugar, the small basket, and the apples, and also the pigeon cage.

About the milling, I don't dare send wheat to that mill because in my view it turned out no better than unsorted and uncleaned wheat. I wonder whether the mill is working properly. If you think I should change millers, tell me and afterward we will arrange to send the wheat for Monna Taddea there.[257]

About reading the letters, we read them once, twice, and three times, so we don't make mistakes.

About your worries, I think you have more than you write to me about. This fretting about problems you can't fix simply makes matters worse and wastes more time. One needs to take stock and think about others who have far greater worries; recognize the favors that God gives to people in this world and think about death; then one can be at peace about everything.

I am surprised that you do not return sometimes and that you haven't told me why or how your tax matter is proceeding. I am very worried that Ser Lapo has not come back because it seems to me that it has happened at a bad time for you. May God in His mercy send him back soon.

---

256. See FD 56 for the message to Monna Simona.

257. Taddea Pucci was the mother of Francesco's young employee Priore, and sister-in-law of Boninsegna di Matteo Boninsegna. Her husband, Lorenzo di Matteo Boninsegna, had died in May 1392. Francesco helped her to buy grain and other essentials. See also letter 95.

About the sugar, I will let you know next time what the price is here.[258]

I will send you a small basket of dry chestnuts among the roses, and I will send you a pair of big cockerels. They are to caponize and are good. I won't send you any more because I don't have any. If I had looked at those squabs I would not have sent them to you, but I did not look at them because they came in late yesterday evening and Meo had told me they were good. May God protect you.

From Margherita, in Prato.

Francesco di Marco da Prato, in Florence.
Received from Prato, 12 May 1394.

Letter 68 (1401763)
13 May 1394
Prato

In the name of God. 13 May 1394.

Nanni da Santa Chiara delivered your letter. I will answer now although it is not necessary to say much. I will immediately do the things you say in the letter.

The person who had to bring the woman from Lucca brought her. Today they are going to Florence. I decided to send them on horseback because in my view it reflects better on you. The woman was unwell and had no maid to accompany her.

I am keeping Monna Giuliva because I need her and she is a very respectable person, in my opinion, and she doesn't seem either a glutton or a drunkard. As far as I have seen up until now, I don't think I can find any fault with her except that she is very simple. I don't think I will send her away until I have someone else.[259]

---

258. See FD 56.

259. Margherita's correspondence documents the perennial difficulties associated with finding reliable and capable household servants. The woman from Lucca whom Margherita refers to had traveled to Prato to be interviewed as a replacement for the recently arrived but

I am sending Matterello with the woman from Lucca, and he will bring the horses back here. He sleeps here every night. Filippo will be happier, if only because Matterello wakes up much earlier than Nannino. This is for no other reason than that Nannino is less alert than Matterello.

If Ser Lapo does not arrive, come and stay here a few days.

I did not send anyone else to accompany this woman because her husband is coming with her, and I think that is enough. She is a woman who deserves good treatment because she is a virtuous person. If that uncle of hers comes to thank you for anything, look after him. May God protect you.

From Margherita, in Prato.

Francesco di Marco da Prato himself, in Florence.
Received from Prato, 13 May 1394.

Letter 69 (1401764)
24 May 1394
Prato

In the name of God. 24 May 1394.

We enclose several letters received from Pisa.

That is all. May God protect you.

From Margherita, in Prato.

Francesco di Marco da Prato himself, in Florence.
Received from Prato, 25 May 1394.

---

eccentric Giuliva. Margherita was still looking for a suitable servant in August (letter 75). Probably the ill health of the woman from Lucca made her unsuitable for employment.

Letter 70 (1401765)
26 May 1394
Prato

In the name of God. 26 May 1394.

Yesterday I sent you several letters received from Pisa with Giovanni Barnetti.[260] I imagine you have received them.

You should know that we went to Grignano on Sunday morning and stayed until the evening. I sent one of the fine baby goats there, as well as some bread and wine. Those women treat us with great honor. Monna Simona would have come but she was unwell.

Tarpuccia bought us eighteen donkey-loads of wood and has put them away. They don't add up to a cartload, and they cost five *lire*, four *soldi*, and eight *denari*. I told Schiatta to bring us a cartload to see which is better value, and when you are here you can see for yourself.

Barzalone has bought a cartload of kindling. It will be loaded on Friday and be here on Saturday.

Barzalone's son, Piero, has returned and brought two of your letters, which I am forwarding with this.

Filippo is getting better, and we are all well.[261] And the animals are still all well. That is all. May God protect you.

From Margherita, in Prato.

Francesco di Marco da Prato himself, in Florence.
Received from Prato, 26 May 1394. Answered on the 26th.

260. Giovanni Barnetti was a Pratese notary.

261. See letter 63.

Letter 71 (1401766)
28 May 1394
Prato

In the name of God. […] May 1394.

I did not tell you who came to Grignano, but I entrusted Ser Lapo's brother with telling you, thinking he knew.[262] Lapa, Francesco's wife, Monna Francesca, Bernabò's Caterina, Messer Piero's daughter, Caterina, and all our household went. I left Matterello with Filippo and barred the door on the stairs.

I had the large wine cask at Monna Tina's house tapped. The *Podestà*'s steward did not keep the promise he made when he bought the other—that he would take this one as well. He says it is not true that he promised to buy it. He says he will buy a few small barrels. I told him to take what he liked. I did not want to fight with him because it is better not to. The other large cask has been finished.

I sent some of the ginger to Niccolaio Martini, and a shoulder of cured meat to Ser Lapo's house. I asked for his daughter to be sent, and she came. I will get her to do the tasks I need her for. There is also the daughter of the *Podestà*. He sent her to us, and she spends time with Tina and Lapo's daughter when she wants to. Yesterday I kept her for dinner and overnight. Don't be surprised if people you know boast of being of the Cavigliati family. The *Podestà*'s daughter said she was a Strozzi, and Ser Lapo's daughter said, "If you are a Strozzi, I am a Cavigliati," and Tina said, "I'm not anything."[263]

Meo bought two bushels of barley for the mule at Filettole. We bought two bushels here from Paolo Marcovaldi, and he has four bushels left, which we told him to keep for us. It costs thirteen *soldi* a bushel; so the animals have had all they needed.

I spoke about it to Schiatta and I asked him to bring a load as soon as he can. He has not brought it yet. When he does, we will do with it what you say.

262. On Margherita's visit to Grignano, see note 250, above.

263. The Cavigliati were Bolognese merchants, and the Strozzi were a very prominent and wealthy Florentine family. Tina di Niccolò dell'Ammannato Tecchini lived with Margherita and Francesco. See letter 28, which reports an incident when Tina claimed to be the daughter of Francesco.

Barzalone had bought the kindling and had made an agreement with the carter to bring it to Florence on Saturday. Barzalone says he requires fifty *soldi* for transport and five *soldi*, three *denari* for tax.

The hospital money has been received, and Ser Chimenti will tell you about it all. The money from Michele di Falcuccio has not been received yet. Ser Chimenti says he is expecting it any day now. Bosco's money has been received.[264] Ser Chimenti will tell you about the 100 *lire*. Apparently it has not been paid yet.

Schiatta has asked me for four florins and wants them on market day. Tell me if you want me to give him the money.

I think that there will be enough vine branches until you are here. Just the same, I will look into it.

I asked Bernabò if he had taken the tonic. He replied he had not. Every day I remind Paolo di Bertino to prepare the account. He says he will do it immediately.[265]

We received the torches, and they are mounted on poles. Master Matteo prepared them. I told Niccolò di Piero not to give money to Guidalotti, but he says that he has already been given it.[266]

I spoke to Nanni da Santa Chiara. He thinks he will go to Florence on Saturday with two beasts without a load. If that is so, I will send you the oil and load the animals with the things that I think are needed.

The wheat produced seven and a half bushels of flour. I will have some bread made and see how it turns out. We are eating some squabs to economize. They are not good enough to send there. I won't send any to you until there are better ones.

I am sending you one pair of hose because I have not had any more made. I will make some and send them to you. I am also sending you the shoes, the spectacles, and the two covers—the red and the blue.[267]

---

264. Michele di Falcuccio and Bosco owed money to Francesco.

265. See letters 27, 29, 54, and 62.

266. Francesco instructed that no money was to be given to Giovanni Guidalotti (FD 58).

267. On the use of spectacles in this period, for which the Datini correspondence provides valuable evidence, see Vincent Ilardi, *Renaissance Vision from Spectacles to Telescopes* (Philadelphia: American Philosophical Society, 2007).

Monna Simona says to sell that cloth for the best price you can and to act as if it were yours.

We had the black horse bled before Castagnino came, because Filippo thought it was necessary. He says the mule does not need it because it has been bled twice this year. Castagnino thought he would get the horse shod there in Florence.

I received the oranges and the cherries, and I sent some of them to Ser Lapo's family.

We had the hay restacked by Bernabò so it is in order. I sent the chain for the mule and the collar of the black horse.

I received the clothes and all the things belonging to Ser Lapo's daughter.

The meat is still better up there than down here. When I think it is ready to be transferred, I will see to it.

About going to Florence, I will wait for you, and we will do what pleases you. Barzalone went to the country with his family. I will wait for the day he comes and tell him what you say about the florin that Piero borrowed.

Filippo is so-so; at least the fever is gone. The doctor thinks the sickness is still inside him even though the fever has disappeared. He says he has never seen urine more foul than his, and he is as yellow as a crocus. I will tell you privately what I think.[268]

I had the letter delivered to Agostino Giovannelli. I sent a message that if he wanted to reply he should send the letter to us, and I also had the letter delivered to Niccolaio Brancacci and to Cambio di Ferro.[269]

Niccolò di Piero thought he would go to Florence later, and he will borrow a horse that he will bring here afterward. This arrangement will be more convenient for you because you can keep the horses, which need shoeing.

Schiatta has promised to bring me a load of wood tomorrow. I will have it stacked beside the others. When you come you will see it.

---

268. Filippo di Francesco had been ill since early May. See letters 61 and following.

269. Niccolaio di Bartolomeo Brancacci was a wool merchant in Prato, and Cambio di Ferro was an innkeeper.

Ser Lapo sent his Parenzino to us so we could send him on to Florence.[270] Send my regards to Bindo and Nanna and say I would have liked very much to see them before they left.[271]

That is all. May God protect you.

From Margherita, in Prato.

Francesco di Marco da Prato, in Florence.
Received from Prato 29 May 1394. Answered.

Letter 72 (1401767)
8 August 1394
Prato

In the name of God. 8 August 1394.

Yesterday I sent you a letter with Nanni di Ser Iacopo di Pagno, and with it there were two letters from Stoldo. That is, one from him and I don't know who the other was from. Included with the letters from Stoldo there was one addressed to Pistoia. I sent it this morning with Michele del Campana, and I also had the others delivered.

Niccolaio di Giovanni da Carmignano, the brick maker from Tavola, was here to see Monna Margherita, and he says he has sent seven cartloads of terra-cotta guttering. He says he wants to borrow twenty-five or thirty *lire* from you. Write what you want us to do. If you want us to lend him the money, tell us from where we should get the money. He also says he will send the bricks on Tuesday or Wednesday without fail. Answer as soon as you can because he says he will come for the money on Monday.

I sent Monna Giuliva away and paid her at the rate of eight florins per year.[272] She was so sick with worry and great sorrow that she was most unhappy. She has not been happy for a long while because of

270. FD 62 shows that Lapo Mazzei planned to return to Prato with Francesco. Parenzino was probably his mule or horse.

271. Margherita refers to her cousin Bindo Piaciti, who was a Florentine merchant based in Venice, and his daughter Nanna.

272. See letter 62.

her problem. After you found out about that matter, she was so upset that she didn't want to be here when you returned. She begged me to let her go and so I did.[273]

I'll say no more. May God protect you. Send my greetings to everyone.

From Margherita, in Prato.

I cut up one of the cheeses that came from Filettole, and I don't like it. Just the same, I will send you three of them. Taste them and tell me what you think.

Francesco di Marco da Prato himself, in Florence.
Brought from Prato by Castagnino, 9 August 1394. Answered on the 11th.

Letter 73 (1401768)
12 August 1394
Prato

[…]

Niccolò di Piero was here on Sunday and came for Tina because they wanted to go to the festivities at Gonfienti.[274] I did not let her go because I was alone and you were not here. I would have let her go if you had been here. I will have a look at the letter you sent today with Castagnino and I will write today, although I will not be able to send it unless I dispatch Fattorino. Niccolò di Piero and his wife have just come back from the country. I sent him a message that if he wanted to reply to the letter, he should write it, because Castagnino is leaving.

Regarding the cloth for Monna Bartolomea di Ser Naldo, do not buy it there unless it is well-finished. If you write telling her there

---

273. The source of Monna Giuliva's unhappiness is not revealed.

274. The first page of this letter has not survived. Evidently the top of page two refers to gathering produce from the fields; however, the precise situation cannot be reconstructed. Therefore, we have omitted these lines. Margherita refers here to her niece Tina, and to Niccolò di Piero di Giunta. The Assumption of the Virgin Mary was celebrated on 15 August and coincided with the summer festival of Ferragosto.

is no very fine cloth, she has decided to reply that if you can't find a beautiful one, you should buy the best there is. In the meantime write your opinion as soon as you can, because she has an urgent need of it.

Tell Cristofano da Barberino on behalf of Puccino the furrier that he wants to hear from him because no furs of any sort have come in.

I have no more to say for now. Tomorrow we will write in more detail. May God protect you.

From Margherita, in Prato.

Francesco di Marco da Prato, in Florence.
Brought from Prato by Castagnino on 13 August 1394. Answered on the 13th.

Letter 74 (1401769)
13 August 1394
Prato

In the name of God. 13 August 1394.

Checco hasn't bought the two *moggia* of wheat. If he does buy them, we will do what you say.

As for the bowls, buy twenty-four small ones and others as you please. We need big bowls more than normal ones.

We arranged for the wheat to be ground.

Nanni di Guiduccio will finish his tasks at Il Palco tomorrow. They have finished cutting the wood, and Meo says Messer Giovanni went there and reported that they have stacked it properly. Messer Giovanni says that he can't go there again before Monday because he has to visit the parish priest of Filettole on Saturday.

The only wine we have sold was that which you gave to Nencio. Meo says we will sell some barrels tomorrow for the approaching feast day.

We received 420 bricks and fifty tiles from Piero di Monna Mellina.

We saw the pigeon man. He says they are not good to eat yet.

There are thirty loads of sand at the kitchen garden. We will not have anything else brought there until we know whether Nanni is to come or not. We could not find out this evening because he came back so late that he did not take the road past here.

Ser Chimenti returned from the baths. He is not going outside and is unwell.

We reminded Antonio several times what you said. I told you about Cristofano in the letter that I sent you with Castagnino. It informed you about what he had done for us. I will see to this and to the wood. I will look for Monna Taddea tomorrow.

We will tell Nanni di Guiduccio what you say about the […] and we will pass on your message to Meo.

We have bundled up the mantle and the linen in a towel, and in a cloth belonging to Francesca. I will give it to Nanni da Santa Chiara tomorrow if he can bring it. If not, Niccolò di Piero will bring it.

I am not sending you any bread because I did not get your message in time to have some baked. No work will be done from tomorrow on, unless you send orders to the contrary. I will send Meo to stay at Il Palco with Filippo for this feast day, which they say will be celebrated throughout Prato because the parish priest has invited many visitors. If you don't want Meo to go, let us know. I felt it was better for him to stay there for these two days. That is all. May God protect you.

From Margherita, in Prato.

With this there is a letter from Ser Chimenti.

Francesco di Marco da Prato, in Florence.

Received from Prato, 14 August 1394. Answered on the 14th.

Letter 75 (1401770)
14 August 1394
Prato

In the name of God. 14 August 1394.

I received your letter of the 13th, today at nones. It was not possible for us to do what you said about sending the horses there to Florence, as you can understand given the time that we received the letter. Simone was here today. I gave him your message. He said he would wait for Niccolò to return, and if you sent for him he would come.

Nanni di Guiduccio has done the window that Lotto made; that is, he has laid bricks around it and finished it off.[275] I spoke to him and asked if he could work at the kitchen garden. He told me that he must work four days at the convent of San Domenico, and afterward he will work there as you wish. It seems that this will be all next week, so if you are not returning now, let me know whether we should have the lime slaked or not.

The other cartload of bricks has arrived. We gave the carter three *lire* and six *soldi* for transport, in accord with what the brick maker wrote to us.

We gave the wheat to Cervello to be ground. Together with this letter is the copy of the account for the twelve bushels, as you asked.

I don't know what the tax official wrote to you, but I do know that as soon as I received the letter I went to his place and he was not there. I returned home and stayed there a little while, and then I looked all over Prato. I finally found him and I told him about it.

We gave that woman five *lire*, as you instructed. Monna Simona asked her to come and stay with me after she has married her daughter. She promised she would, provided you are happy for her to do so. She lives opposite Ser Schiatta. She worked for his sister for eight months, and I will ask them about her, because I have not done so yet. She was the wet nurse of Niccolò di Piero's child who died. She is the sort of person we need. I can find out about her from many people because she is from Prato.[276]

I am amazed that you think I am so unintelligent as to reveal that you were not here. May God preserve us. Meo has come back every evening; he stays the night and then leaves.

---

275. Generally windows were fitted with waxed paper, although Francesco ordered an expensive glass window for the luxurious bathroom, complete with a steam bath, built in his Prato residence. See Cavaciocchi, "The Merchant and Building," 151.

276. Margherita sought a suitable servant to replace Giuliva, who had left the household in Prato (letter 72).

I went to see Michele di Campana, and I told him what you wrote. He says he sent two bales of paper to Pisa and that Manno received the money you mentioned.

We are sending you twenty-five loaves with a boy who is bringing back Simone's packhorse. The bread is in a sack with a pocket for books.

Together with this is a letter for Monna Simona's sister. Have it delivered to her immediately.

From Margherita, in Prato.

Francesco di Marco da Prato, in Florence.
Received from Prato, 15 August 1394.

Letter 76 (1401771)
21 October 1394
Prato

In the name of God. 21 October 1394.

Yesterday evening I received your letter. I have understood it and reply here as necessary,

Arrigo the painter was here.[277] He told me today that he has completed the work at San Francesco and asked me to write and find out what you want him to do about the other painting. He has spoken to you about it, and says he wants at least five florins for it. He says if you think he is being greedy then you should ask in Florence about prices. So write to him this evening about how much you want him to do, and he will do it. And say if you want the scaffolding taken down.

Meo will tell you the length of the lining that we require. It is for a belt, which means it should be as long as a belt and as wide. The barrels are all full and in good order.

---

277. This painter, Arrigo di Niccolò (c. 1370 to c. 1444), worked for Francesco between 1394 and 1404. See Mazzei, *Lettere di un notaro*, 2:410–14.

We can't find any Raveruschio wine.[278] I asked Barzalone about it, and many other people, and there is none to be found.[279] Nor can Tarpuccia find any. Barzalone says that since they had mixed old and new wine there is no need for Raveruschio—nor for mountain wines, which he considers of poor quality and thinks we can well do without. I will show Barzalone how much wine from the plain there is and he will advise me what to do, if you agree. Zaccheria is working at Gonfienti. The *moggio* of lime has been slaked. Nanni di Guiduccio is working with Ser Maggio. This evening he will tell me when he intends going to Il Palco, and I will inform you immediately.

I am sending Meo to Florence this evening, and tomorrow I will send you what is still to come. I will organize the other household matters properly so you will be happy.

There is no time to say any more. Tell Cristofano to give me the key to his chest, so I can get out various things from it and send him what is his so it won't be left here. May God protect you.

From Margherita, in Prato.

Francesco di Marco da Prato, in Florence.
Received from Prato, 21 October 1394.

Letter 77 (1401772)
22 October 1394
Prato

In the name of God. 22 October 1394.

Meo delivered your message yesterday. I will follow your orders as best I can. You send him back here so late that he arrives just before the gates close; the horses have to run, as does he. This is not good, and between sending the carpenters here and there I have no choice but

---

278. Raveruschio is a wild grape used to sharpen the taste of wine or strengthen its color.

279. Barzalone was entrusted with finding and purchasing fine wines for Francesco, and he frequently traveled around Tuscany for this purpose. See Melis, *I vini italiani nel medioevo*, 154.

to stay awake until midnight. I think it is your fault, not his, since you always imagine it is terce when it is evening.

As for the things of mine which are to be sent to Florence, I will make sure you lack nothing, and I will send you pillow cases and whatever is necessary for your comfort. Nanni di Guiduccio is going to work at Il Palco tomorrow. If he can bring a companion, he will. It would be best if Meo did not return to Florence for two days. I do not think there is any need for him to go, because there are no urgent loads to send and he should stay up there at Il Palco. Make a list tonight of the most urgent items, and Nanni will bring them to you tomorrow.

Domenica's mattress would not be big enough for Lucia's bed, so I have decided to send you one of those that were made from that old cloth. I will send you the smaller one because I think it will be very suitable. The other one will be fine for the bedroom with the two beds, once we get them back. I am sending you the mattress that Domenica had, but I cannot send you any others because there aren't any more. We are also sending you an old cover with lilies, and the two bed hangings that were at Filettole.[280] We are also sending you the pink hanging wrapped inside the bed cover. Iacopo di San Donnino says he wants at least five *lire* for those two beams that you want for the bed canopy, and Antonio Micocchi has nothing suitable for that. Tell Cristofano that in the sack where the bed cover is there are five sets of underlinen and three pairs of his underdrawers, and beneath there is another sack with several things belonging to Monna Villana.[281] We are not sending you pomegranates because there aren't any.

That is all. May God protect you.

From Margherita in Prato.

Francesco di Marco da Prato, in Florence.
Received from Prato, 22 October 1394.

280. Francesco had several houses at Filettole, including a tower bought from the Guazzalotti. See Melis, *Aspetti della vita economica medievale*, 65–66.

281. Monna Villana was Stoldo's wife.

Letter 78 (1401773)
24 October 1394
Prato

In the name of God. 24 October 1394.

Barzalone laid down the wines as he thought best. He tasted all the wines, and he does not think it is worth sending you any of the old and new wine. It was a waste of money. He thinks that we can make money from the wine when the present glut has passed somewhat, and he wouldn't send it to Florence under any circumstances. Regarding the Razzese wine, he says that if the white is to be drunk, you should start drinking it from the flask this winter or it will deteriorate.[282]

It will be good to drink two months or so from now. The wine from Arsiccioli is sound, and he thinks the one from La Chiusura is a fine wine, and also the one from the pressing that you made with those grapes belonging to Piero di Guidaciaglia. All the others are in good condition. The decision should be made at the right time to sell the former and drink the latter.

The painter is still doing the work he undertook. I think he will have done most of it by All Saints' Day, but he won't take on anything else before he completes it. He also asked me for twelve *lire* for what he did around the oculus of the church. Tell me if you want me to give it to him, as I received some money from Tarpuccia.

Today, while I am waiting for Il Palco to be swept, I am putting some things in order here. As soon as Il Palco is ready I will go off there with the entire household. When I am there you will be able to come here. I would not be going otherwise. That is all I have to say. May God protect you.

From Margherita, in Prato.

Francesco di Marco da Prato, in Florence.
Received from Prato, 24 October 1394.

---

282. For Razzese wine, see note 121, above.

Letter 79 (1401898)
30 October 1394
Florence

In the name of God. 30 October 1394.

This morning Piero di Monna Mellina brought a letter from you that says while going over the accounts with him you found a note that he should be paid for 150 tiles: that is, 125 delivered on 23 October and twenty-five on 24 October. Filippo wants to remind you that Pagliaio brought 225 tiles; that is, he did three trips with his two donkeys and with one belonging to Niccolò di Piero, and each donkey carried twenty-five at a time. Just the same, you can clarify with Pagliaio if it is as I say, and whether on the 24th Nanni brought twenty-five tiles with Schiatta's donkey. In total that makes 250.

Filippo says that Meo Saccente did not bring any lime at all after you left Prato. He also says that Filippo and the baker went to get a *moggio* of lime on 20 October. They brought it on Schiatta's donkeys, as well as the one belonging to Piero, and they slaked it. As for the quantity that Saccente says he brought, since you left he has not brought any.

I have understood what you wrote to me in the letter Filippo delivered. You think there is a mistake about the number of tiles. I urge you to look at the papers and see whether the same is written there as in the book, because I'm sure that we have received 250 tiles from him. I may be wrong, as you say, and I would be happy to be there to receive the punishment from you that I deserve, because I think it would be good for me. In the meantime I beg you to forgive me this time, and next time I will make the matter so clear that you will be quite content with it.

You say that the *moggio* of lime we received hasn't been noted down yet. I am amazed at this. If it is as you say, I say you have as much reason as possible to punish me. But you are very forgiving, so I beg you please to forgive my mistake, and in the future I will do better than this time.

Yesterday a man called Gaspare came to see me and asked me to write to Nanni di Giusto in Prato to find out when he wants to go to Avignon.[283] He says it is early and he says to ask if Nanni wants him to come to Prato and then proceed to Avignon, or does he want Gaspare to wait for him in Florence and leave for Avignon from here. Get Nanni to tell you his answer and let us know.

Yesterday we received from Nanni di Santa Chiara the various things you sent us, except for the sewing needle, and today we also received the things you sent us with Nanni and Matterello.

That is all. May God protect you.

From Margherita, in Florence.

To Francesco di Marco, in Prato.
Received from Florence, 30 October 1394.

Letter 80 (1401899)
17 December 1394
Florence

In the name of God. 17 December 1394.

I have not written to you since you left here because there was no need.

I am writing this only to remind you that on Sunday you must go and have dinner with Giovanni di Ser Dato, who is preparing this meal specially for you, and if you are not going he would not buy the food. That is all. May God protect you always.

From Margherita, in Florence.

Francesco di Marco, in Prato.
Received from Florence, 17 December 1394.

---

283. Nanni di Giusto di Borgo da Prato worked at the branch in Avignon.

Letter 81 (1401900)
18 December 1394
Florence

In the name of God. 18 December 1394.

This morning we received your letter from Nanni di Santa Chiara, together with the various things you sent us. We received everything you listed in your letter.

With Nanni we are sending you eleven sacks of flour, and we are also sending the flask of medicine for which you asked. I say no more, as time is short. May God protect you always.

From Margherita, in Florence.

Francesco di Marco, in Prato.
Received from Florence, 18 December 1394.

Letter 82 (1401901)
21 January 1395
Florence

In the name of God. 21 January 1395.

Since you left, I have only had two letters from you: one yesterday and the other on Wednesday, in which you said that you would send us a cut of castrated kid to go to Ser Lapo. We received the piece of meat the day before yesterday. In the same letter you said that you would send a flask of Malvasia wine that had to be taken to Giovanni Guidalotti. We received that the day before yesterday, with the meat; so I sent it to Giovanni and the letter was delivered to him the day before he got the goods. So, apart from the meat and the Malvasia, we received a flask of white wine and, as well, the small flask of Malvasia that you sent to Monna Margherita.

Don't be surprised that I haven't written to you, because we were expecting you every morning and then every evening. Each time Nanni arrived, I wasn't there. I was looking for him or someone else from Prato to deliver the silkworms and the dried herbs from Monna

Simona. The other morning I was looking for someone to take a letter that had to go to the *Podestà* in Prato. It was a letter written by Ser Lapo, so I sent it with Ridolfo di Niccolò.

I want to let you know about something, but I don't know how to do it as I would like to. However, I will tell you as best I can. On Tuesday night there was a council meeting here and, from what I have heard, there was a letter from the Marquis of Ferrara saying that Marquis Azzo is fighting against him, and everyone says there will be a war. They also say that the count is recruiting as many soldiers as he can have in the Marches.[284] He has sent Conte Corrado here as his envoy, and they say he will stay here to try and recruit as many soldiers as possible. May God bring peace to the world and may everyone acknowledge His might. They also say the Lord of Coucy wants to come this way to take Arezzo, so people are preparing defenses here against all the misfortunes threatening us.[285]

I'll tell you what I think about Zanni's girl. I like her, and I have never heard a girl's virtues praised as much as hers. She comes from very good stock because people in Prato know who her mother and sister were. Generally people care more about who the mother is than the father. She is strong, healthy, and attractive—and just what our friend is seeking. May God bring about what is best.

About your remaining there with Messer Piero, I am satisfied. You have chosen well because I know that it will be a great comfort to them. I will send the things that you asked me for as soon as I can.

I am very pleased that Barzalone is sleeping with you. Make sure that working late doesn't tire you both out. As for Monna Nanna, I think she is like me because when you are in a happy mood, so am

---

284. Niccolò III d'Este's succession as Duke of Ferrara in 1393 was contested by Azzo X d'Este (1344–1415). Many people in Tuscany suspected that Giangaleazzo Visconti of Milan supported this challenge because it helped his campaign of destabilization geared to making him lord of all Italy. See Gene Brucker, *The Civic World of Early Renaissance Florence* (Princeton, NJ: Princeton University Press, 1977), 150–53. Giangaleazzo Visconti was known as the Count of Virtue (Conte di Virtù).

285. Enguerrand VII, Lord of Coucy (1340–1397), occupied Arezzo in 1384. Florence bought the town from him for 40,000 florins. In 1394–95 Enguerrand was in Liguria in the pay of Louis, Duke of Orleans, who tried to intervene in Italian affairs in alliance with Giangaleazzo Visconti. See Brucker, *Civic World*, 104–5.

I, as long as you take care of yourself properly.[286] I am convinced that you will come back in a dreadful state because of a dream I had. I will scold Barzalone as well when he comes here since he is in charge.

I still haven't received those two doors you said you were sending. When I have them, I will do what you requested in your message.

Don't worry about the cloth for Fattorina because I don't need it at the moment. When I come there, I will do it for her. Send me those pieces of linen cloth that I spoke of to Barzalone. He knows where they are.

Send me the box the painter gave back to you. The two sacks of flour that Saccente said were the whitest amount to just over six bushels, and the one for the house amounts to five and a quarter bushels. We have put the white flour in the larder, because it will keep well there, and the flour for the household in a large crock.

About the lard there is nothing else to say, except that you had it done by someone who knows what he is doing. You have done the right thing about the ham, and if I were you I wouldn't cure any more.

Finish up as soon as you can, and take care not to start something that will keep you there longer than you anticipated.

There is nothing more to say here. May God protect you always. Remember me to everyone there.

Your Margherita, in Florence

To Francesco di Marco himself, in Prato.
Received from Florence, 22 January 1395.

Letter 83 (1401902)
22 January 1395
Florence

In the name of God. 22 January 1395.

This morning, with the brother of Nanni da Santa Chiara, we sent you a letter written by Stoldo and two written by me. Shortly af-

---

286. Margherita refers here to the fact that Barzalone's wife, Nanna, was happy that her husband and Francesco were working together harmoniously in Prato.

terward we received several letters from you and one to Ser Lapo. He received it at once, and his answer is with this letter. We also sent you the overgown and various other things with Nanni's brother. Ser Lapo says you can stay until Monday.

There is not time to say anything more. May God protect you. From Margherita, in Florence.

Francesco di Marco, in Prato.
Received from Florence, 24 January 1395.

Letter 84 (1401903)
23 January 1395
Florence

In the name of God. 23 January 1395.

After the departure of Nanni di Santa Chiara's brother, we received a letter from you that has made me very anxious, because I see that you are very worried, although I don't really know the reason. But, whatever it is, why dwell on it so much that you harm both body and soul? Why is it that in this, and other matters, you don't do as you say you would do with your own children, if you had any? You say that if God took them away, you would accept your fate. If we were to place all our faith in Him and accept what came, we wouldn't be subject to such passions. If we thought about death and how little time we have on this earth, we wouldn't worry as much as we do, and we would allow ourselves to be guided by Him and accept everything that happens. God doesn't like people who ignore Him. Remember the books that you read when you are here, and don't worry so much. I don't think there is a man or woman more fortunate than we are, because we have received much bounty from God and we are not afflicted by the problems of this world. We haven't acknowledged enough the bounty we have received, because it could happen that things won't go well for the two of us, even though we are patient when little things go wrong. Let's think about those who have great misfortunes to put up with and who can't escape them; let's entrust everything to God and let Him decide what He wishes about people and property. Whoever acts in this way won't have so many worries.

Remember me to Messer Piero and to Monna Simona and to anyone else you think appropriate, and remember to observe the feast day well. May God protect you always.

From Margherita herself, in Florence.

To Francesco di Marco, in Prato.
Received from Florence, 23 January 1395.

Letter 85 (1401904)
17 March 1395
Florence

In the name of God. 17 March 1395.

The reason for this letter is that the painter is going to Prato with the gray horse that belongs to Domenico di Cambio, because he could not go on foot and I could not find anyone who had horses that they wished to send back.[287] Domenico lent us his to help us out, so have it sent back tomorrow.

Send us a few capons for Monna Margherita, if you have bought any, since all we have here is one hen.[288]

I have no more to say in this letter. May God protect you always.

The painter is bringing two hundred pieces of gold.[289]

From Margherita, in Florence.

Francesco di Marco, in Prato.
Received from Florence, 17 March 1395.

---

287. On the painter Arrigo di Niccolò, see letter 76.

288. Margherita was ill and did not dictate this letter or the next. The scribe, probably Niccolò dell'Ammannato Tecchini, therefore writes in her name, referring to Margherita in the third person and to himself in the first.

289. The gold leaf was for paintings commissioned by Francesco.

Letter 86 (1401905)
18 March 1395
Florence

In the name of God. 18 March 1395.

This morning Piero di Barzalone delivered your instructions and we also received Domenico's horse from him. We have understood what you say.

I went immediately to Ser Lapo and told him what you wrote about the papers.[290] He says that there has been too long a delay in submitting them, but just the same he says it would still be good to submit them if it is possible.

Monna Margherita has seen all these documents, and there are no more than two that are correct. So she can't give you a proper reply until they are all correctly done. The two correct ones were written by Ser Lapo, but this evening he will write a full reply that will be rather more moderate, as it should be.

Monna Margherita says she thinks you and Barzalone and Niccolò di Giovanni paid so much attention to putting in the posts at Il Palco that you did not remember the documents. It's just like you to ignore big things for little ones. May God protect you. Stoldo cannot reply to you today. When he can, he will.

From Margherita, in Florence.

Francesco di Marco, in Prato.
Received from Florence, 18 March 1395.

---

290. See note 292, below.

Letter 87 (1401906)
18 March 1395
Florence

In the name of God. 18 March 1395.

Today we sent you a letter with Nanni di Santa Chiara; and because there was not much time to write, we didn't answer everything as we should have. I'll explain why and answer more fully here.[291]

As soon as I received your letter this morning I went immediately to the warehouse to see Stoldo and gave him his letter, which he read straight away. We both then went to Ser Lapo with the letter you had sent him. He read it at once and understood what you said about the documents, and also what we told him. He said it was a mistake to have delayed so in sending them, but that nevertheless they should still be submitted. I immediately took the documents (there were three of them including the one you sent), and I went to the warehouse and showed them to Stoldo. It turned out that one of them was wrong: the one in Niccolò's handwriting. I had Nanni di Domenico recopy it immediately, and it is fine now and without error. So now we have three: two done by Ser Lapo and one by Nanni di Domenico.

Today Stoldo gave one to Tommaso Rucellai and asked him to return the other one, as you instructed in your letter. Rucellai said that he didn't know when he would be able to find it among the many it was mixed up with.[292] The request seemed strange to him. For quite a few reasons that would take too long to explain, you should think about whether it is a good idea to ask for it. So when the others are handed over, which will be tomorrow, we won't pursue the matter.

I have heard it said that the Office of the Ten want to speak to you. This has made me extremely worried because with these bad times all sorts of thoughts have passed through my mind, and I can't imagine that someone who is well off won't be taxed. If you are agreeable, it would be a good thing to stop building works that aren't necessary, and even those that are, given these bad times. I have been told

291. Unlike the two preceding letters, this one is clearly dictated by Margherita.

292. Margherita refers here to documents presented to tax officials by Francesco. Tommaso Rucellai was an influential figure in the Red Lion district of Florence with whom Francesco communicated. See Kent and Kent, *Neighbours and Neighbourhood*, 59.

that you go to Il Palco every day and return late in the evening. I can well believe that there is work going on, whether it's building walls or erecting beams. Don't imagine that it's not talked about by people from Prato who come to Florence. It would be best to leave this alone, and anything else that gives you the reputation of being rich. It's also a good idea to lie low when times are troubled.[293]

Though it is five months since we came here to Florence, you have already gone to Prato seven times; and if you think about it, you have stayed there a third of the time. If you want to tell me that you can't do otherwise, remember that for four years you didn't come here to check a contract or a business matter because there was nothing more serious to attend to than what you had to do in Prato.

For the love of God, I beg you not to continue any activity you have started until you see that these blessed taxes are sorted out. I just can't understand what is to become of this business. If what you say is true about wanting to build there this year, you are really going too far and this is because you have always behaved this way. Everyone should be able to enjoy moments of pleasure at the appropriate time. A person who doesn't do this can't ever relax, and you are just like that.

We haven't any sturgeon in the house. I sent to every supplier for some but there is nothing of good quality to be found. I would like some to please Barzalone and Monna Nanna, because I know that you don't eat it.

When you come, bring the small blue hose for me because I need them.

As for the black horse, I have nothing else to say except that I paid the dealer a florin. I have also paid the tax, and they didn't want to give me a receipt because they said it wasn't their usual custom unless there was a problem. Niccolò from the warehouse registered it in the book, so there is nothing to worry about.

Don't worry about the capons. When I want some, I will find a way of getting them.

---

293. Building at the villa Il Palco was almost complete. See Melis, *Aspetti della vita economica medievale*, 60.

I am sending sweet and hot spices with the carter. Monna Margherita has now fully recovered.[294] May God be praised.

I will write to Barcelona and to Avignon about what you say. There's nothing more for now. May God protect you.

I tried everything to persuade Piero to come back to us, but he didn't want to.

From Margherita, in Florence.

To Francesco di Marco himself, in Prato.
Received from Florence, 19 March 1395.

Letter 88 (1401907)
22 March 1395
Florence

In the name of God. 22 March 1395.

Schiatta and his wife were here on Sunday.[295] He came to get a baby [for his wife] to wet nurse, but he didn't come to an agreement with anyone. He left word that they should come to speak to me for further information because he is one of our workers, but no one came to give me a reply. He has left it to me to search for a baby but I haven't done so; and I won't, because it would be wrong and shameful. The woman is old and the milk too abundant, despite the fact that she says she has very little. So tell him to try in Prato and be careful that Saccente doesn't find out, because he would tell Schiatta immediately that I didn't want to help him. Schiatta said to me that Saccente told him that you wanted him to be godfather to the little slave girl, and Schiatta was to go with him for the baptism. I know nothing about this either. You know that when you left here the girl wasn't well; and on Sunday she was worse, and again during the night, so that Monna Ave decided to baptize her on Monday and she went ahead. Monna

---

294. This addition seems to have been made by the scribe, to assure Francesco that Margherita had now recovered from her illness.

295. This is the agricultural laborer Schiatta di Niccolò, also known as Tantera.

Ave, Caterina, and Fattorino baptized her. May God give her the grace to be a perfect and good Christian, and may we be granted the same.

As for the need for women to be prudent, I want to behave as you would like and as I should. In future I will be more prudent and I won't write what I don't see. I trust that God will help me to continue in the same spirit in which I am writing.[296]

There is nothing else to say here. May God protect you.

From Margherita, in Florence.

To Francesco di Marco, in Prato.
Received from Florence, 23 March 1395. Answered.

Letter 89 (1401908)
29 May 1395
Florence

In the name of God. 29 May.

I received two letters from you to which I told Niccolò to reply, and it seems he did so. We had your reply today and he read it to me. Concerning the person from whom you are seeking redress, I am at a loss to know what to say to you other than that you will know better next time. He did what he usually does. When you are here you will be told who he is and about his dishonest ways.

Concerning the sons of Niccolaio Martini, Domenico has done what you entrusted him to do, and we have done likewise, although there is little need for advice because they take after their father. They have hardly had a sheltered existence, and you might think that they were from Paris.[297] Piero brought me the mantle this morning. I had him tell you to bring it because I thought you were coming today and were bringing me that and the other things, because that is what we decided before Easter.

---

296. Margherita refers here to her reprimands in letter 87 regarding her husband's building activities. Francesco's response to her angry letter does not survive.

297. Niccolaio's sons were Martino and Piero. See Brambilla and Hayez, "La maison des fantômes," 110.

I have the mantle but I have neither a bag nor a hood. If you could, I would like you to send Fattorino with them tomorrow because I should go to dine with Piaciti. If you send him, I want my silk overgown and the long scarlet one I have and my hoods. If it is inconvenient, don't send them to me. I don't mind, because it is very risky to send them the way you did this morning.

Although the mantle came in good condition, it wouldn't have done so with a less prudent carrier. Give my regards to Niccolaio Martini, and tell him I am hoping and praying that God's will be done at the right moment and that it will bring salvation to his soul and body and peace to all. Remember me to our friends and anyone else you see.

I won't say any more for now. May Christ protect you.

Greetings from Margherita, in Florence.

To Francesco di Marco da Prato himself, in Prato.
Received from Florence, 29 May 1395. Answered.

Letter 90 (1401909)
3 June 1395
Florence

In the name of God. 3 June 1395.

I received your letter, which I have understood, and I reply here. It doesn't matter that you didn't answer my letter, and I am happy about your decision to stay there all this week. I don't believe it is necessary for you to come here just for a day, unless you have other business. I beg you to free yourself as quickly as you can, because we are halfway through summer without seeing each other.

I suffer a lot because of your staying there in Prato, for the many reasons we have discussed in the past. I beg you not to continue staying up and living so immoderately—as much for your sake as for your household there—because a bad night followed by a bad day is worse than a month of winter. I will send you the flask of wine with Monna Fia. I will watch the cat as carefully as possible once I have her. I do little reading because I have so much else to do.

I have sewn the cover as you asked. The flour came to about twenty bushels. As for making sure to close the main door securely, you needn't worry. I will check that everything is fine. I go to bed early; if only you would do the same, as we should both be in bed by midnight!

About the anxiety you suffer, I am sorry but there is nothing I can do. You could do something about it if you wanted to. I want my clothes: the three indoor overgowns and my mantle and my two hoods; one is blue and the other red. I also want my overgown, if you intend to stay here this summer, and send me my linen undershifts and my light overgowns that are in the middle chest. They are up there, because I saw them—and those scraps of lining that are next to them. Tell Monna Simona that I will get the bowls and bigger dishes made for her, and if Domenico and I like them I will send them with Michele once they are finished. My scribe is Guido, who works in our warehouse.[298] I have nothing else to say at the moment. May Christ protect you. Remember me to everyone and greet them for me.

From Monna Margherita, in Florence.

To Francesco di Marco da Prato, in Prato.
Received from Florence, 3 June 1395.

Letter 91 (1401910)
3 June 1395
Florence

Just after I finished the letter I was sending you, I was so amazed by what Monna Ave and Lucia told me Fattorino had asked them that I don't want to repeat it to you, out of respect for those he asked about.[299] For love of you, a man who worries about every little thing, I will explain the whole matter. The day I came here I lunched and dined

298. Guido di Sandro Pieri da Firenzuola (d. August 1411 in Pisa) was first employed as an apprentice by Francesco in January 1394, and rose steadily in the firm. Francesco regarded him as diligent and trustworthy. See Melis, *Aspetti della vita economica medievale*, 206–7.
299. This letter is a long postscript to the preceding one.

at Niccolò's house. I didn't want to dine there, but so that the capon didn't die in vain I did stay on with my whole household; and in the evening I returned here and had all the rugs and the covers beaten because they really needed it. On Wednesday I refurbished the mattress and ate at the twentieth hour; as you know, when I begin something I can't put it down until it is finished.[300] On Thursday I did the feather quilts, two beautiful ones for the beds because they were needed, and during all this I had my usual stomach pains; and between Friday and Saturday Lucia sifted twenty bushels of flour. These are the revels we were engaged in! On Sunday morning I went to Piaciti's house, and returned Monday evening.[301] I couldn't refuse because they had come here many times. On Monday evening Bellozzo's wife and Francesca and Caterina slept here with me, so that we could get up early.[302] We managed to do so and went off to see that holy icon and other reliquaries. We and all our women went off together, and we lunched on the bacon that Fattorino had preserved. We ate together and then went to Fiesole, where there was a special indulgence, the biggest one of the year, and we received it and saw the unveiling of the holy image of Saint Maria Primerana.[303] I went in once for you. We returned that evening tired, and everyone went to their own house and we were all in bed early. This is the way we have lived since we came here.

I feel embarrassed, more for the sake of the others than myself, because one can do nothing without everyone knowing about it. They would be right to hold it against us, but there was no revelry. No one ever dined here except Tina on one occasion.

I beg you to reply at once because I am worried about this; and if you can, write and let me know how it came about. Please do so, because I have told you the whole truth. And Stefano, the son-in-law

---

300. See Appendix 2.

301. This is Bindo Piaciti. See letter 71.

302. Margherita refers here to Monna Bartolomea (also known as Monna Mea, and as Bellozza because she was the wife of the spice dealer Bellozzo Bartoli), her own sister Francesca and her niece Caterina.

303. The tiny church of this name in the cathedral square of Fiesole was built on the site where the Virgin Mary appeared to Saint Romulus, patron saint of Fiesole, and told him of his impending death.

of Messer Piero, was here.[304] I told him to tell Monna Simona that they were making her bowls. He replied that she had already bought some, and so when they are ready I will leave them. They were supposed to be finished this week. I wouldn't buy them myself, because the design wasn't beautiful and I would have had them made in a design I liked. Domenico would have bettered the price by more than twenty *soldi*.

To Francesco di Marco, in Prato.
Received from Florence, 3 June 1395. Answered.

Letter 92 (1401911)
4 June 1395
Florence

In the name of God. 4 June 1395.

I received a letter from you at vespers; and because Piero wants to leave, I will be brief. When Fattorino said I told him I wouldn't go to Fiesole, he spoke the truth. I thought it would not be good for me because it was so hot, and I told him this so you wouldn't worry; but I also did have reason to go, because of my devotion to the sacred image being shown that day.[305]

And if he said I told him anything else, he is a liar.

Fattorino asked Monna Ave: "Tell me the truth about what people in Prato have been saying"; and Monna Ave said, "I will tell you." He said he had been told that Niccolò and all the family were always eating and drinking at our house. But Monna Ave said they had never eaten nor drunk here, and that this was the truth; and he said, "Good, I'm pleased you have told the truth so I will know what I must say."

And I, imagining what you might have been told, and knowing it was not the truth, felt wretched; it made me really upset, more for your sake than mine. On the other hand, I was amazed at just how despondent you were about this, and also at how anxious your letter seemed. Since you asked me who my scribe was, I thought you were

304. See letter 52.
305. This was a votive image of Saint Maria della Primerana. See letter 91.

afraid that Francesca was reading my letters.[306] For this reason, I decided that you were not being frank, no matter how straightforward [your letter] appeared. I concluded that, when you said I should not devote myself to reading, you had that incident in mind; and because you didn't know who would read me my letters, I decided you were afraid to speak your mind. About what is going on here, you needn't worry in the least; and if I had known that you hadn't heard all that, I would not have written to you about it, knowing that you would distress yourself—not because I was here, but because you would assume that if I had company I wouldn't attend to the household duties as you wish. These anxieties of yours weigh me down and fill me with regret. I just can't get used to them.

If I had known you would remain in Prato so long, and if you had foreseen all the work that would keep you there, I would never have come here. I don't want to stay, because I moved here later than I should have and it is too hot.

I'll not say anything else. May Christ protect you.

To Francesco di Marco da Prato himself, in Prato.
Received from Florence, 4 June 1395.

Letter 93 (1401912)
5 June 1395
Florence

In the name of God. 5 June 1395.

I received the cat and the twelve rounds of cheese from Nanni da Santa Chiara. We will do our best to take good care of the cat. You tell me not to send squabs. If you can't find the cheese, we will make do here as well as we can. I am amazed that you question me about the linen from Lapa. You must believe me: if I had any, I wouldn't ask you to buy it.

It is four years since Lapa made me that length of linen, and I will tell you what was made from it: I had twelve undershirts made

306. See FD 65.

for you this year and eight for me, and most of them were sewn by Fensi's wife; but since I had an argument with her about her charges for carding the cloth, I gave the rest to the convent of San Niccolò, and Monna Ghita di Matteo knows I did. She can vouch for the truth of this, and there are people in the house who must know it. I don't know the people who spin it.

Last year I gathered fifty pounds of raw linen. Domenica knows what I did with it, and I left all the skeins with the weaver down there; this year I have had two dozen skeins of linen bought through Filippo that I have kept here with me, and I had them woven today. Take half for yourself, and the other half you will find here, if you want to see them. Last year, as Domenica knows also, I had thirty towels made by Monna Vivola and twenty-four large ones by Monna Ghita. And last year, Marco made me twelve fine towels that you will find there in Prato, not counting the four that are here; and I had tablecloths made, all twelve of which I have here for my own use and the rest of the household. Last year I had five pairs of large sheets made. Monna Ghita sent them to be sewn at the convent of San Niccolò. I can assure you that none of our women spun a single length of thread. Rather, I gave orders for it all to be spun away from here, because our women spin very little, as Domenica can testify. Since she came into my household she hasn't spun two pounds, nor have the others, because they couldn't. I make every effort to give you a detailed account of everything, but it really upsets me when you interrogate me needlessly about trivialities, making it clear that you have no faith in me. I could repeat what you said to me in one of your letters: that your problems were almost enough to be the death of you. It seems to me indeed that you are at that point. In your letters—which are a great comfort to those who receive them—I would have appreciated it if you had told me the source of Fattorino's stories. Because you don't mention returning in your letter, I will wait and see. I will arrive with these women on Sunday, Monday, or Tuesday, and you can have it out with me in person. You have been there three months. I don't know why I need to stay here, because I arrived so late to attend to what I needed to do that I no longer want to do it. I don't know what you mean about the medicines or about staying there. I beg you, if you return, to try to do penance for the good of your soul and your body. If linen underdrawers can't be found there, they will be here. Even though you have a pair, I will have another made for you. I am having your linen cuffs made. No more for now. May Christ protect you.

From Monna Margherita, in Florence.

To Francesco di Marco, in Prato.
Received from Florence, […] June 1395.

Letter 94 (1401913)
8 June 1395
Florence

In the name of God. 8 June 1395.

I received a letter from you to which I am replying with Niccolaio Martini as my scribe. I received eight squabs, and they were in such wretched condition that they were barely alive. I gave them away to the poor because I didn't think they would survive. Don't send any more like that, because they were not suitable to be presented to anyone of note. About sending Stoldo there, I will leave the decision to him. In my opinion he doesn't seem organized enough to leave immediately. I am going to need my lighter gowns and bodices because you can see how warm it is. In any case I had the idea that you would be returning just before Easter, so I didn't push you to hurry up; but you still haven't finished washing down the table.[307] It seems to me that your table is like a chalkboard that children draw all over, wash down, and then start again, and this is why your work is never done. It is not this that upsets me, but rather that when someone else says it, you deny it. I remember: when I told you at Easter I had been informed you would be away for the whole summer, you said it wasn't true, and it was to be only two days. Count how many days it has been since Easter. Your resolve not to keep promising to return soon without doing so would please me greatly, more because it would spare you the trouble of writing excuses than for my sake.

---

307. Or "clearing the decks," as we might say.

My own suspicions don't do me any harm, but those of other people harm both body and soul.

Regarding Niccolaio Martini, I have begged him to come back here for dinner and to stay the night. He says he can't because he is here as an ambassador. In the meantime I am sewing the cuffs, and I may give them to Niccolaio if he doesn't leave too soon. He advised me to come to Prato with him, but I have resolved to stay here for a few more days. I am doing this for the sake of my household, as I would not want them to be anxious; but if Stoldo decides to go there I might come with him, if he agrees to take me, and I would like to see if I can manage to stay there for a month after you come here. Then you will see how many suspicions I will sow, and you will have to reap them; so this is what I want to do this year and my heart tells me to be resigned to these things. You can answer me when you see me. I am content to stay here. There are no twigs or straw for our bed for the summer. If you are planning to pass summer here, you had better send some rather than leave them there. Tell Domenica to remind my weaver about the table napkins, because we really need them, and she knows how much trouble I had to go to twelve years ago to keep the tables supplied. I need some strong flax from Vernio, to spin the thread for embroidering the napkins. Send it to me as soon as you can, because the napkins can't be started until I provide her with thread. When I left there, Niccolò gave me three *lire*. I have spent them. Send me some more please; I want to rely on Barzalone, who is sensible, and I don't want it written down in the firm's account books.

Get someone to find my amber rosary beads that I left hanging from the bedstead in the room with the two beds.

I sent the panniers and the cage to you with Nanni di Santa Chiara, as well as a flask of white wine for Monna Fia. You have sent us a fine sort of cat! If we tie her up, she goes mad; if we leave her free, she runs away. Monna Ave had to search for her for a whole day, and she jumped from the window down to where the chickens are. We surrounded her, and she got into the chicken coop; she won't be coming out until you return because I would rather have her there than worry about her further. It would be even better if you took her back because one day we will lose her. We need some herbs to wash the bowls. I have nothing more to say. May Christ protect you. About your not eating and not drinking, I believe you; and this is my complaint: that at least when I am with you there is no such disorder and we are all better off together.

From Monna Margherita, in Florence. Greetings.

To Francesco di Marco da Prato, in Prato.
Received from Prato, 9 June 1395.

Letter 95 (1401914)
9 June 1395
Florence

In the name of God. 9 June 1395.

I am writing this because Monna Taddea was here this morning and says that one of those in charge of levying the taxes came to visit her.[308] She says she doesn't know him, but he is a linen draper and a good man. He told her that if she didn't get someone to put in a good word for her with those in charge of reviewing the tax levy, she will be badly treated. He said that one of those submissions that are done through intermediaries had been presented, and she said she never sent anything. She went to speak about it to Master Giovanni da Santo Giovanni, who told her that she needed to submit three written statements to them, as is the usual custom, and if she doesn't do it, he thinks they will have to treat her harshly, even if they would be sorry to do so. If she had to do one on her own account, she would know to say that she only has household chattels.

---

308. Taddea Pucci, the Florentine widow of Lorenzo di Matteo Boninsegna, would inherit the estate of her brother-in-law, Boninsegna di Matteo Boninsegna (d. 1397), when her son Priore, who had inherited his uncle's estate, also died. Later, from 1403 to 1406, she was involved in a long lawsuit to recover money that she thought Francesco owed to the estate of Boninsegna. It was pursued at the Mercanzia in Taddea's name by a relative, Bartolo di Iacopo di Banco Pucci. In December 1405 Lapo Mazzei acted as an intermediary and resolved the dispute. See Mazzei, *Lettere di un notaro*, 2:42–43 and 56–58, and Jérôme Hayez, "L'Archivio Datini: de l'invention de 1870 à l'exploration d'un système d'écrits privés," *Mélanges de l'école française de Rome*, 117 (2005): 178–81. See also note 257, above.

And so she says she told everyone with whom she talked about it; but she is worried about the matter of Boninsegna and his son, because she knows that it is all too easy to allege that people are rich, and it happens all too often.

She would like you to put into a statement what you think should be said about the affairs of Boninsegna and his son. She leaves this task to you because you know her situation, and Boninsegna will be happy about whatever you do. Her affairs are straightforward, since she has nothing, and she won't submit any statement before she gets a reply from you. If you will do it, she will have it copied by someone else, as you see fit. She has sent someone a number of times to ask if you had returned without explaining why she wanted you, and I say to her every time: "He will arrive tomorrow," or "He will arrive the day after tomorrow." So send the reply at once because they are in a hurry to have the submissions. I am sending you four handkerchiefs belonging to Monna Ghita that came back from the seamstress. Tell her I guessed how she would like them done, and if I have made a mistake I will make up for it next time. Monna Taddea discussed this business with Giovanni di Ser Dato, and he says that in his view she shouldn't include Boninsegna because, he says, "It is such a long time that people won't remember him," but I scoff at this. I leave the matter to you to resolve as you see fit.

Monna Lisa has been unwell for a long time, as you know from Niccolò, and she has tried every doctor and is worse than ever. The wife of Niccolò de' Cerchi was unwell for a long time and says that she was cured by a woman brought to her by Niccolò, and Monna Lisa has also been put under her care. I don't know how she will fare. I am very concerned about Lapa di Niccolò, because from what I hear her illness is like theirs; and Niccolò says that the woman is coming to Prato on Tuesday to visit one of the sick and she should remain until Friday. I don't know where she is staying, but one hears news so quickly in Prato that Lapa will find out if she asks. I would advise Lapa to go to her—and if she decides to go, to do it respectfully because she is a woman who will serve her better if she is treated with respect. I am only saying what I have heard but I know nothing else. Lapa could explain her problem, listen to what she says, and tell her that she wants to be treated by her. I would wait to see how Monna Lisa fares. She is only charging for medicines, so Lapa shouldn't hesitate to go there. I wouldn't do anything until I see what she can do for other people. Tell her quickly because the woman told Monna Lisa that she has to leave on Friday. I won't say any more. May Christ protect you.

From Monna Margherita, in Florence.

To Francesco di Marco da Prato, in Prato.
Received from Florence, 9 June 1395.

Letter 96 (1401774)
21 July 1395
Prato

In the name of God. 21 July 1395.

The reason for this letter is that Barzalone was here today and he read me a letter from you. It was astonishing to me that you were amazed that I hadn't written to you. I'm not angry with Fattorino or anyone else, and I wonder what provoked all this. Niccolò di Piero was here, saying you had written requesting that he ask how the household was behaving. I told him the truth, that in my opinion everyone had done very well. Fattorino has written to you a number of times when it was necessary, and every evening he has returned very late, as you must know is normal for those who work outside the walls; and you know it was necessary for Meo to sleep at Il Palco and La Chiusura until the grain was brought home, and in the evening he has to feed and see to the animals.[309] The nights are short, and I haven't seen the need to write to you as I normally do. I have been less dutiful than usual; but this is why I haven't written to you. If there had been some news, I would have written, even if it meant staying awake until morning. I beg you to distress yourself as little as possible, and me the least you can, because I can't stand it any more. I feel sad, and you know

309. This property was near the gate of Santa Trinita in Prato. The name La Chiusura ("The Enclosure") suggests that it incorporated a walled garden. In his will Francesco stipulated that this property should be preserved for Margherita's and Ginevra's use on their visits to Prato. The agricultural laborer, Meo, is sometimes referred to as Saccente.

the state I was in when you left, and the condition I suffered from; this summer it hasn't given me a minute's peace. Francesco, I have to tell you, it seems to me that you can afford to live without any thought or worry about the household tasks, because I see to them and I dedicate myself to them more than when you are here. I believe that I act and keep the house in such a way that in my opinion, may it please God, I need never be embarrassed about anything.

I sent the house gown for Monna Ave to the dyer, and I am having them do it black; Lucia says she doesn't want it. I made one for Fattorina in recent days. We have gathered four bushels of beans, less half a quart, and a bushel and a half of vetch from Il Palco; and we have brought all the harvest in safely.[310] You have had eight pairs of squabs, and we have eaten seven pairs. I told you there were several pairs because I don't know how to exaggerate as well as Saccente and Fattorino. I would have sent you some tomorrow but it is Thursday.[311] I think you'll be provided for. I'm not worried that a few pairs have gone. I keep the keys of the dovecote with me, and I have sent Fattorino there twice. You write that I should tell Meo to come to Florence on the feast of San Iacopo; but to judge from your letter, I don't think you realize it is a Sunday. Tomorrow, which is a holiday, I will get Meo to speak to the people he thinks would be good at handling that business, and on Friday morning I will let you know how they want to proceed and who will come, and you can say on Friday evening whether or nor you are happy.

In Saccente's view, and mine also, the keys should be taken away from Piero di Schiatta because he has no more work to do. I will see to it. During the harvest they have behaved satisfactorily. Goglia will do the threshing on Saturday, or so he has promised, and if Meo goes there, I will make sure Fattorino stays, after which we will be finished with this harvest.

As for getting the vats out of the warehouse, if it can be done we will do it before your return.

I made a visit to Niccolaio Martini on your and my own behalf. I offered my sympathy and declared that you were ready to serve him in every way; and I said, as you instructed me to, that you would drop

---

310. Vetch is a legume used as fodder; it was frequently eaten by the poor.

311. The squabs could not be eaten on Friday (the day for eating fish).

everything to pay him a visit. He thanked me profusely and said there was no need. He has had a really high fever, and now they think he is a little better. I will go often to visit him, and inform you daily about how the household is getting on. He thinks he came down with this illness after getting very upset, because he is one of those who put the mice in the bag.[312] These factions are ready to kill each other and, from what I have heard, Iacopo di Messer Biagio Guasconi came to the aid of Ser Migliorato, because they don't want a bastard to have one of the communal offices and it is obvious that the faction leader, Stefano Bernarducci (who is the son-in-law of Ser Iacopo di Messer Leo), has equipped your faction so that it is more able to defend itself. He defends it with his sword drawn and the whole town is volatile, so I haven't pressed you to return. Those people have never come and only rarely have I seen them pass, because they are so busy with their mouse catching and they have no time for diversions.

Fattorino told me that the customs official asks him every day when you will be here. He is one of those leading the mouse catchers and so is Croca. It seems it will be a long process because those from Prato can't come to an agreement. The Florentines are pleased about this and are doing very well. The situation is that every day they receive twelve florins, so that with the salary and expenses, they want to be employed for life.[313] You had better come some time, if it doesn't cause you problems, and then make a decision about whether to stay here or not. I will send your message to Messer Piero.

We gave your message to Niccolaio Martini about making sure that the rhubarb liquor isn't stolen. Because it is nones we will stop

---

312. The following passage seems to concern a fraught moment in the electoral politics of Prato. The particular reference to Martini's role is difficult to interpret. Possibly he was a scrutineer responsible for placing eligible names in the electoral bags. Francesco's letter to Margherita of the same day (FD 70) refers to Piero Rinaldeschi's undertaking of such an electoral role. However, Margherita's references to "mouse catchers" do not sit very easily with this reading. For the factions in Prato politics at this time, see Brambilla and Hayez, "La maison des fantômes," 88–128; and for their survival into the fifteenth century, see Francis W. Kent, "Prato and Lorenzo de' Medici," in *Communes and Despots: Essays in Memory of Philip Jones*, ed. John Law and Bernadette Paton (Aldershot, UK: Ashgate, 2010), 193–208. Francesco seems to have tried, somewhat uncomfortably, to straddle both factions.

313. This is probably a reference to Florentine officials, sent to oversee the electoral process in subject towns such as Prato.

here; tomorrow we will send you back the wine flask if you need it.[314] Argomento apologizes. May God protect you always.

From your Margherita, in Prato.

To Francesco di Marco da Prato, in Florence.
Received from Prato, 22 July 1395.

Letter 97 (1401775)
22 July 1395
Prato

In the name of God. 22 July 1395.

This evening we received two letters from you. We will answer both briefly this evening because there is nothing very pressing. Tomorrow we will answer you about the rest. I am pleased you received the hood. We sent Master Matteo's letter immediately.

I am keeping the keys of Il Palco and of the dovecote, and will do so in the future. As for coming there, I would be pleased to since this is your wish, just as I would be happy to stay here this summer. Meo made the haystack at Il Palco today and returned at nones. I had ordered that they should be back at nones, together with Cristofano di Ser Francia, with Nanni di Guiduccio and Domenico, and so they were. They replaced all the vats and the barrels. Because they are dry, it was not the sort of job you would let just anyone do. They carried them carefully and they arrived safely. None of the bands came off. Cristofano set up the barrels and he also set up the vats on trestles as if for the pressing, and he dragged all three vats to a place facing our *loggia*, and on the other side he set up the barrels, and they put two planks and several chairs underneath them so that they would not touch the ground. I think you will be satisfied they are safe. I had them do that today so you couldn't say they were idle. Barzalone went this morning to see about the timber needed for the raised platform that has to be built above the vats, and he did not come to an agreement because he was so worried about paying too much that he did not buy anything.

314. See Appendix 2.

I asked Cristofano what the price for the timber was. He said it costs between twenty and twenty-four *soldi*. I decided not to leave the platform incomplete when such a small amount was involved, because it is necessary. I sent Barzalone back there this evening and made him get the timber. I am doing it the best way possible because you can't afford to go wrong in such matters. It is urgently needed for Domenica's sake and for the hay, which is not stored properly at present. Tomorrow morning Cristofano must be there to build it. He claims we owe him expenses. We'll let him have his way. Meo will bring the timber tomorrow. I sent for Antonio Micocchi and he came to me, and I told him what I thought was needed. Regarding the beam that he has to deliver to you, he said to give them two days' notice and they will bring it to you directly. They ask this because they are up there cutting timber. He says you know well that he wasn't the one who promised it to you. The person who promised it did not bring it because he was busy cutting timber, but he thinks that he can provide what Cristofano needs.

As for those coming to Florence to carry the crucifix, Nanni and Domenico di Guiduccio are willing to come, and the other two will be Saccente and Nannino. I pointed out to them that two of them are tall and two are short. They say it doesn't matter because the two tall ones will go first and the two short ones behind. They would be happy to go on Saturday night and return here on Sunday. They would not waste time because it won't affect Monday. Answer me and tell me what you want done.

I will send you some squabs. They don't think Niccolaio Martini is any worse. If you see rain, don't worry about the hay or the flax because everything is under cover.

We will send you some kindling if possible. I passed on your message to Antonio Forese: that is, that you don't want Dettera's promissory note. He says he will find a way to give it back to him immediately.

I told Matterello about the twelve florins. He says he can't sell his calf, and if you want it he will give it to you willingly. Between one excuse and another he says he can't come to Florence. That is all. May God protect you always.

From your Margherita, in Prato.

Piero di Niccolaio passed by this morning and he says last night went very well for him.

Francesco di Marco da Prato, in Florence.
Received from Prato, 23 July.

Letter 98 (1401776)
23 July 1395
Prato

In the name of God. 23 July 1395.

This evening Argomento delivered a letter from you, as well as three others […]. We carried out your wishes; and we also received from him a flask of white wine. I sent it to Messer Piero, and he says it seems the best wine he has had. Tomorrow we will see if it lasts in the flask, because tonight it is very hot, and then I will tell you how good it is.

Today we brought the wood from Arsiccioli, and then we were to bring the bedstead that Antonio Micocchi had. Matteo da Faltugnano had Saccente arrested, and Saccente escaped from them and fled to our house and barred the door. It was agreed that he could stay in the house today because Matteo was at one of his properties. This evening I got Messer Piero and Arriguccio to speak to Matteo, and he promised them that for the next week he won't take any action. I spoke yesterday to Cristofano di Ser Francia and with the others who should be going to Florence. They discussed the matter and Cristofano thought it best to go there and look at the crucifix for himself, to assess its weight and how it could be transported and to make a decision.[315] I lent him the horse because we had ordered the mule to be shod tomorrow, and that is what we will do. Cristofano did not want to wait for the mule because he counts on being back here at nones, so I will not send it to you. If he does not come back, or if you decide that Cristofano should

---

315. Saccente was supposed to go to Florence to help carry the crucifix. His arrest made this impossible; hence the calculations about whether three men would be sufficient to bear the weight of the cross. See letter 97.

come back here, let me know whether I must send you the mule with him or not. You can find out about Il Palco from Cristofano. I am not sending you any squabs because I did not have any caught, believing it best to send them to you tomorrow with the others.

They think Niccolaio Martini has improved. I think God will do him this favor. I did not get the mule shod today because of the incident involving Saccente. Fattorino went to Filettole because he has finished threshing with Saccente, and in all we got seven bushels of wheat and we gave one to Tantera. We have told you twice that we gave the letter to Master Matteo.

Saccente will be released tomorrow at nones. May God protect you always.

From Margherita in Prato.

Francesco di Marco da Prato, in Florence.
Received from Prato, 24 July 1395.

Letter 99 (1401777)
26 July 1395
Prato

In the name of God. 26 July 1395.

The reason for this is that Niccolaio Martini is worse; he never seemed to have improved to me, but I didn't want to say so because there were those who said one thing and those who said another. He has had a continuous fever and now he has developed hiccups, which I am afraid might change matters for the worse. May God grant what is best for his soul. I think it would be best if you came here this evening when you have organized to have the crucifix sent, as he would be happy to see you, and his children dearly wish you to come. These are things that must be done, and if they aren't it will never leave the minds of the family who survive. I would have written this to you days ago; but as you know, I have made excuses for you with these people by repeating that you have very important business there. I have said the same things to Niccolaio's sons and to anyone else who asked me. It seems from what I hear that they will be leaving here tomorrow morning to have dinner with the parish priest of San Giusto, and from there they will make their way to Florence. If I were you, I would arrive here at the ringing of the Angelus.[316] I would then go to visit Niccolaio, because I have said that you are coming to Prato for this reason, although you have important business to see to in Florence, and that if it were not for your love of Niccolaio, you would have sent for me. For their sake, I think that you must have no hesitation in coming, even if they would excuse you. Come at once for Niccolaio's sake. He asked me if you would buy a jar of Vernaccia wine, the best that can be had, and also if you would send Iacopo di Messer Biagio home and get him to buy a small flask. Have it filled with Vernaccia, and explain why. Enclosed with this letter of mine there is one from the prior of San Domenico, who wants you to forward it on to Rome by a secure method. We have just had your letter of the 25th. We can't reply now, so we will do so tomorrow. Francesca will be sent a little prayer book of the Office of Our Lady. Monna Gemma was here yesterday evening with a friend of hers; she gave the neighbors and me the best evening I have ever had, because she is such an angel. She will send that little book to Francesca, and if she doesn't, have Maso fetch it and don't forget to bring it to me.[317] I am sending you a purse. Give it to Monna Giovanna di Paolo Mattei and tell her this is the type they make for widows. We received the shovels from Gonfienti. The white wine was better than the first day. May God protect you.

From your Margherita, in Prato.

To Francesco di Marco, in Florence.
Received from Prato, 26 July 1395.

---

316. In this period the Angelus was said in the evening at approximately 7 p.m., rather than at midday, as it is today.

317. See letter 98.

Letter 100 (1401778)
12 August 1395
Prato

In the name of God. 12 August 1395.

    Yesterday I received a letter from you that I got Bernabò to read. He labored over it a great deal, and I couldn't understand what it said very well; so I had the son-in-law of Messer Piero read it, and still I could hardly understand. I had your doublet mended. Do as you please about the little prayer book, but above all make sure that it has good lettering that is large and easy to read. As for Tina, don't be surprised that I don't want to send her.[318] I have thought a lot about the matter and the reason why she shouldn't go. I'll explain when I see you. I received the sugar, and I sent it to Niccolaio Martini with Argomento, because it arrived at nightfall and I had no one else to take it. In my opinion, I'm badly off here with seven women, none of whom is reliable enough for errands, as you know. It seems to me that the situation is worse for you because, if you send me letters in the evening, Bernabò is barely able to read them. It was pitch dark when Argomento turned up last night; and you can't expect a reply from me if you don't at least tell Fattorino to get here in the evenings to read your letters, and then to write replies in the mornings if that is necessary. I will tell Cristofano that you will expect him on Sunday, and if he wants to come he can use the pony. We will do the other things you mention. I will stop here because Fattorino has come for the wine, and I have had him write this quickly because he wants to go back with it. I don't want to hold him up, because you said he should stay at Il Palco. May God protect you.

    I have given the keys to Bernabò, and the little knives. I don't know whether he has sent them to you because this morning he went to Arsiccioli. His wife said she didn't know if he had sent them.

    Your Margherita, in Prato.

To Francesco di Marco da Prato, in Florence.
Received from Prato, 15 August 1395. Answered.

---

318. This is Margherita's niece.

Letter 101 (1401779)
13 August 1395
Prato

In the name of God. 13 August 1395.

    This evening we received your letter from Argomento and have understood what you say. We will answer here as necessary. If Lorenzone comes here, we will make him load up as you instruct. I don't think it is right to send someone to see the wood at Figline, and I do not really know whom I could send that understands such things. On market day I will get them to see if there is any flax. If there is good-quality stock, I will buy the amount I think appropriate. I had two pieces of cloth for the cuffs, and the doublet is not finished because the tailor is not there. Niccolaio Martini remains unchanged. We will do for him what you say. Regarding the matter of Lodovico di Ser Iacopo, I will get Fattorino to do what you say. Don't be in a hurry about the prayer book, because Monna Diana di Messer Iacopo Zarini has lent me one until I have one for myself, and she is not worried because she has another one.[319] Don't worry about provisions here because there is no need. We will give Barzalone his letter, and I will tell him about the things you have written to me.

    The verjuice has been made, and we have filled the small barrel that was Lorenzo's, and we have filled a large barrel that Francesca sent me to fill.[320] I have had all the fruit gathered from the garden as well as some from La Chiusura and Il Palco. All the workers are unhappy about the harvest, and they are right, I think, because there are very few grapes. Send me a barrel and if I can fill it, I will. I had asked permission from the *Podestà* to gather along the ditches, but the Eight had already had everything gathered from where we usually send people for the wild fruit. I was told that they are not letting anyone gather there this year. I will see if there is any way of gathering the grass, and if so, I will have it collected. Today we gave six pairs of squabs to Bernardo Checcolini, and there were no more good ones. We will send you the pullets tomorrow with Cristofano di Ser Francia,

---

319. This prayer book is mentioned in letter 96.

320. Verjuice is sour juice pressed from fruit, especially from certain unripe grapes. It was used in cooking much as vinegar is, more extensively in medieval than modern times.

if he is willing to bring them. We will do with the letters as you say. And we have received the flasks. Here we need to send some wheat to the mill. Tell us which one you want us to choose. I think from your letters that you must be very anxious, which I am very sorry about. As for the loss you had at Narli, I would like to know the amount, because sorrow should be in proportion to the loss. I cannot see what remedy there is in this world apart from doing good and remaining content with what happens because, if we were wise and knew ourselves well, we would be pleased that our sweet Lord doesn't punish us according to our sins. I beg you not to torment yourself about every matter in this way. In my opinion you have no reason to do so; rather, you have more reason than other men to thank God, and I urge you to do so, because we bring these woes on ourselves.

Send my regards to everyone. May God protect you always.

From Margherita, in Prato.

Francesco di Marco da Prato, in Florence.
Received from Prato, 15 August 1395.

Letter 102 (1401780)
27 August 1395
Prato

In the name of God. 27 August 1395.

This evening we received a letter from you, and we have understood what you say. We respond here as necessary. Lodovico di Ser Iacopo came to Bernabò and said he needed to go to his country house, and told Bernabò to go to Checco di Monna Lea's house. He went yesterday but could not find Checco, so we will try and find him tomorrow. Cristofano di Ser Francia says he has put the roof on and today he will start work on the rafters. He says to let him know if you want the water to flow outside or inside. He says if you decide not to do the walls this year it would be better for it to go outside. Lorenzone was here this morning and will load the beams. I will let you know if he transports anything else. Cristofano is also here.

Saccente has plowed the green manure in. I did not send the cuttings yesterday because Fattorino was there all day carrying earth, and the work has been completed. We took all the good lime to the warehouse, and we took the soil to the riverbank. We are not sending you the mule because it came back from Florence with sweat running down to its knees. I did not write to you about this so as not to upset you. If you had been here, you would have done what Filippo advised, just as we did. It has improved, and this morning he wants to bleed it because he could not bleed it before. We are not sending the young mule with Niccolò because we received the letter late and the mule is at Il Palco and needs to be shod. I will have it done today, and let us know this evening if you want it to be sent to you. There is nothing to be said for now about Monna Margherita's clothes.[321] You will be told as soon as necessary, but there is no need for anything now and Niccolò is leaving in a hurry. Matterello says he has urgent need of four florins to pay for the donkey, because he borrowed the money and has had a lien put on his property.[322] Because we are supervising the loading of the beams we can say no more. May God protect you.

From Margherita, in Prato.

Francesco di Marco da Prato, in Florence.
Received from Prato, 28 August 1395.

Letter 103 (1401781)
28 August 1395
Prato

In the name of God. 28 August 1395.

This evening we received your two letters: the first at the twenty-fourth hour, and we had the other one from Niccolò di Piero as the town gate was being closed. The reason I did not send Fattorino this evening is because the small mule was shod very late and today the big mule was bled. It had to go four times to Il Palco to assist in the work

321. Fattorino wrote this letter on Margherita's behalf because she was unwell. See letter 104.

322. This meant that Matterello's property was mortgaged until he repaid his debt.

and to bring bread and wine and whatever else was necessary. I don't know how I could have handled the mule without Fattorino, because it needed to be ridden today and to be kept in the water before being bled. So much had to be done that it would have been more than enough for two men as well as Fattorino; and I would not have found either Matterello or Nannino, because Nannino was at work and Matterello was using the oxen.

We told Cristofano about the water. He says he will have it drain on the outside.[323] Bernabò received the money from Lodovico, but the coins are no good; he will get him to replace them.[324] I am sending you Nannino because he has nothing to do tomorrow; and Fattorino is rather tired, with a pain in his shoulder, and wouldn't be able to lead the packhorse. It is necessary to send someone with the mule, which Filippo wants to see often, and I wouldn't entrust it to any youth in case it is treated negligently. I am sending your riding mantle in a cloth, four rounds of cheese in a couple of saddlebags, and two pairs of pullets. They are not in good condition because it is not suitable for poultry up there. They are very wretched; there is so little air that they can't breathe properly. It would be better to send them to Il Palco if you were agreeable. We will attend to this immediately, because it is the fourth hour. This morning we were up an hour before daybreak for the sake of the carter; and we will now get up during the night, at the seventh hour, so as to dispatch the pack animals to you.[325] We have arranged with the *Podestà* for the gate to be opened for us. Master Lorenzo is not here. He went to treat someone beyond Vernio. May God protect you always.

From Margherita, in Prato.

To Francesco di Marco da Prato, in Florence.
Received from Prato, 29 August 1395.

---

323. See letters 99 and 102.

324. This is Lodovico di Ser Iacopo. See letters 30 and 38.

325. This is very early in the morning before sunrise; but "seventh hour" may not be accurately used, and it is often hard in the letters to establish an objective equivalent in clock time. See Appendix 2.

Letter 104 (6101126)
1 September 1395
Prato

In the name of God, 1 September 1395.

 This morning, that is early in the morning, I received your letter and I have understood what you said. I answer here as necessary. The reason I had Fattorino reply to you was that I did not feel well that evening, and I did not believe I had anything urgent to say. If I had thought it necessary, I would not have failed to write even though I felt sick; but I told him to write and tell you what we had received. He says that because he had received a list of everything you sent him, he did not bother to count every single thing. Since your arrival there, I don't think there have been many days that you haven't been sent a letter, and I have never failed to write one with Fattorino whenever I thought it necessary. If you say you stay awake until very late and rise early in the morning, I believe you. But I can't tell you everything I do, and I don't think it is necessary. I simply try as best I can to behave in a manner that pleases you and honors me, and I do not bother about writing all the things I do because I do not think it is necessary. I think you should be satisfied that I am doing what I can. You say that you have no gratitude from the people of this world for what you do. I think you have plenty of company. If I knew how to write, I would do as you say. I have already criticized you because you turn night into day. We receive a letter at the evening bell, and all the while we have to keep two animals here because the mule goes crazy every time it is alone and, as you know, it has been sick and given us as much trouble as body and mind can stand. God has done me a great favor because it is cured. We had to go to see Filippo three thousand times because he is so busy that, unluckily for me, he has been out of town every day. Apart from this there has not been a single day that I have not had to go to Il Palco two or three times, because you know the soil was being tilled and Cristofano worked there too. I had the cooking done here; and as you know, someone who is cooking can't work at anything else. And yesterday I arranged for three pairs of oxen to drag the three beams at the mill to Il Palco. Cristofano went to Il Palco; Fattorino went there today at vespers, and I think the work was finished today.

I sent for him. He refused to come, so I had the letter read at Il Palco. I think Cristofano covered the roof afterward. He will not want to do any more work until you are here, and I think this is for the best. Fattorino will tell you when he sees you about the matter concerning Niccolò di Piero, because he does not know how to explain it in writing in a way you will understand. The wheat of the commune cost twenty-one *soldi*, and the ears of barley twelve *soldi*. We bought two bushels. The spelt was eight *soldi*, and we bought seven bushels. The millet cost fourteen *soldi*, and we bought one bushel. The vetch was fourteen *soldi*, the beans twelve *soldi*, and the lupines eight *soldi*. All sorts of grain were available. It did not cost very much.

We had the shoes made for the mule. Tomorrow we will have it shod and I will send it to you with Fattorino tomorrow evening. Fattorino, as I told you, has been feeling sick since you left, and this evening he told me again that his groin is swollen.[326] So, if he goes to Florence, he does not intend to return until he is better. There are also people in Prato who have it, so it would be better if you came here, because I will not take the risk of getting Meo to come here as I am worried that Antonio di Bonanno might give it to him. Tomorrow I will get Meo to give Fattorino supplies for two days. This morning I sent half the bed to Il Palco. I had arranged to have the other half taken tomorrow, but Cristofano is not going tomorrow morning. I had nine pairs of roosters bought because there weren't any, and they were very cheap. I will add no more because Fattorino is not feeling well. I am not worried about my clothes. If you want to bring them, go ahead. In Florence there is an overgown and a mantle. If you want to bring them, do so; I really don't care. I would rather err in my writing than in my deeds. May God protect you always.

To Francesco di Marco da Prato, Florence.
Received from Prato, 2 September 1395.

---

326. Fattorino's symptom is seen to indicate the plague, which can cause painful swelling in lymph glands.

Letter 105 (1401782)
29 June 1396
Prato

In the name of God. 29 June 1396.

The reason for this letter is that Monna Ave arrived here on Tuesday at nones and said that you had given her permission to leave. I kept her that night and told Niccolò to write to ask you what you wanted me to do: keep her or send her back to you. It seems to me that you would be as happy if I sent her back as if I kept her here, and so I have decided to send her back on Wednesday evening. The reasons that she gave for going are many, and such that I'm not about to write them down; it wouldn't be seemly.[327] She tells me that you want to prepare the house in Florence before you return here. I think you are doing the right thing, but I remind you that on Sunday it will be three weeks since you have gone there. It would be good to finish up as quickly as you can, because you are needed here for many reasons that I don't need to mention. No one knows them better than you. For now Niccolò is attending to the things you gave him to do. I couldn't say if anything remains to be done. There are three things I know that Niccolò and Guido will promptly tell you […]. Tell them from me that I know some very bad things about their affairs.[328] I won't keep them to myself unless I hear from someone […] the woman who told me. People who ridicule others don't like to be on the receiving end. Out of love for Monna Ave I'm prepared to let it be. […] May it please God that he is sound of body and soul. Tell him to greet Monna Mea for me.

Messer Iacopo's wife, Monna Diana, begged me to lend her the mule on Sunday to bring her daughter, who is betrothed, here to Pra-

---

327. Lapo Mazzei refers sympathetically to Monna Ave, Francesco's housekeeper in Florence, in a letter to Francesco of 17 April 1396. He explained that she was unhappy that she had to stay indoors all day when Francesco left her in charge for fear that someone would leave the door open and she would be blamed if something were stolen. Monna Ave found Francesco a difficult and exacting task master. Indeed, Mazzei called her "Saint Ave" because of her patience. See Mazzei, *Lettere di un notaro*, 1:148.

328. Lacunae make the text difficult to reconstruct here.

to.[329] I told her that I think you want to come here on Sunday. Just the same, I don't believe you will come, because I think Stoldo's house will be your ruin. If you decide not to come, I would be glad if you would agree to lend it to her, because she is young and respectable. Answer me, because I promised I would reply on Friday evening or Saturday. I recommend that you get Cristofano di Ser Francia to look after you well, because he needs to be reminded of this although he has always looked after you. You should accept the assistance that people can offer you, and not always insist on wearing yourself out by trying to reform them. It is too hard to make people change their natures. I have nothing further to say for now, except may God protect you always.

I am sending you a set of underlinen, and that's all I can find. Look for things that need washing and send them to me with Argomento or with whoever will bring them, and don't send me any other clothes except for your undershirts. I had three this week; you took away two and I sent you one.

From Monna Margherita, in Prato.

To Francesco di Marco da Prato, in Florence.
Received from Prato, 30 June 1396.

Letter 106 (1401783)
30 July 1396
Prato

In the name of God. 30 July 1396.

We are sending you with Argomento four pairs of squabs that Tantera from Filettole brought. Make sure you get them.

Nanni has brought in all the wheat from La Chiusura. It totals ninety-five bushels, and there are five bushels of vetch. He has done the haystack, and he went to Il Palco. He said that he is going to strip a large quantity of chickpeas tomorrow, and he will put many things in order that need doing. He says to write to him if you need him

329. Messer Iacopo Zarini Guazzalotti. See Fiumi, *Demografia*, 394.

there. He said he can be in Florence on Tuesday morning if you wish. Answer him.

Remind Fattorino to send me my sleeveless jacket.

There is no more to say for now. May God protect you always.

We received some letters, among which there was one for the *Podestà*. I gave it to him and asked if he wanted to send a reply. He said he would do what Manno said, and he asked me if you were here. I told him and he said it didn't matter. He would do whatever Manno told him to do.[330]

Monna Margherita, in Prato.

To Francesco di Marco da Prato, in Florence.
Received from Prato, 31 July 1396. Answered.

Letter 107 (1401784)
16 March 1397
Prato

In the name of God. 16 March 1397.

Today I dictated as long a letter as time permitted to Bencivenni's clerk, so there is not much more to say here. I had some bread made, and it was very good when it went off to the bakery. It did not turn out as well as we would like, but I am sending you twenty-five loaves just the same, although they are not very good. It was the fault of that wretch who came from Florence. He is exactly the sort of assistant you needed! The bread is in a sack, and there is a torn napkin with it. In the pack there is also a jar of grapes, a set of underlinen, a cap and a kerchief—I do not know whether you have any there—and two panniers. One belongs to Stoldo and the other is ours. In each one there are forty oranges with a napkin on top. If there are fewer, I was the one who counted them. It would not be the first time that I have made a mistake.

Our Nanni and Domenico dal Montale measured that *moggio* of wheat. Niccolò and Benedetto were also there, and so they also filled

---

330. This is Manno degli Agli, Francesco's partner in Pisa.

the oil barrels. They took the wheat from the *loggia* as you directed. As for the oil, Niccolò says he knows which one to take, although I cannot see much difference between one and the other. Domenico tells me he got eight loads of wood. He put the other ones in the kitchen garden, and he still has twelve bundles to bring.

We got another four sacks of flour. Since you left here I have not touched it. I don't know what is there or what has to be given back. I gave him that sack we use for vetch, and I did not give him anything else. Until now he has not returned it. I will give him the other one and ask him how many of ours he has. I have understood what you say about guarding the main door properly. Nanni is sleeping beside it. That fellow from Montepulciano, who just arrived from Florence, was infested with lice that he brought to my house. According to Domenico, he said he had not slept in a bed for many months. He has such good company that he need not worry about sleeping alone, because the pests swarm all over him. Fortunately, I remained unaffected.

I will look after the house and the other things properly so that, God willing, I think you will be pleased. I would have liked to send you either mushrooms or frogs, if I had found any, but at the moment there are none to be found. I think that Bellozzo and Stoldo are spoiling you so much that you won't be inclined to come home. I think Bellozzo is probably much more capable than Stoldo. When you go to seek those indulgences and attend those sermons, pray to God for me, because I have not been out of the house since you left and so I am sadder than when you left, and this problem with congestion in my head has greatly troubled me. If you decide to stay there longer and you want us to make you some bread, write and we will do it. But it would be a good thing if you came back here and gave any necessary directions, and then you could return. As it is late, I will stop now. Greet and commend me to everyone. May God protect you always.

From your Margherita, in Prato.

To Francesco di Marco himself, in Florence.
Received from Prato, 17 March 1397.

Letter 108 (1401786)
18 March 1397
Prato

In the name of God. 18 March 1397.

Today I got Ser Baldo's son to reply to the note we had from you.[331]

The reason for this letter is that we are sending you two bottles of oil and a pannier of fresh eggs with Argomento. Inside it there are three reed baskets of frogs with a cloth covering. Send us back the baskets and also the others that we sent on Saturday and the napkins we sent with them.

When the mule came here, she was suffering a little from her old complaint. Filippo applied a linseed poultice, as he did the other times, and she is now as well as one could ever wish. There would be no harm in riding her. I hadn't wanted to write to you about it because there wasn't any need and so as not to worry you. If you had been here, you wouldn't have done any more than we have. You know it is an old complaint, and it is not our fault because she came here from Florence with it.

I will have bread baked tomorrow, and if you decide to stay there longer, I will send you some on Tuesday. If not, I will keep it here. Don't forget to send us some of those panniers that I have sent there.

There is nothing else to say for now. May God protect you always.

From your Margherita, in Prato. Greetings.

To Francesco di Marco da Prato, in Florence.
Received from Prato, 19 March 1397.

---

331. This is the son of the Pratese notary, Ser Baldo di Vestro Nucci.

Letter 109 (1401785)
18 March 1397
Prato

In the name of God. 18 March 1397.

Yesterday evening I received a letter of yours from Argomento. I answer as required.

Antonio Micocchi brought me the thread you sent and told us about the baker. We settled with him and paid. He will leave on Monday morning.

On Monday morning Nanni will stop working at La Chiusura for the present. Afterwards he will go to Il Palco to do what he can and thinks best. When you are speaking to Casino and Nanni Manesco and Nannino, tell them not to start any other job until you decide what you want.[332]

Antonio di Fattalbuio has made an opening in the fireplace and has to build an arch there. Answer me about Schiatta and whether you want him to construct that fence; and tell me whether you want us to give him the walnut stakes for the job, or money to buy some.

I am waiting for an answer to the letter I sent you and for instructions about whatever else I should do.

Casino needs some money and says he is certain he is owed four *lire*. Write and say whether you want us to give it to him. He also asks you to give him two florins and says he will not leave your employment as long as he is paid. Answer me about this.

We will have some bread made. Tell me if you want me to send some on Tuesday morning, although it would be better if you came back and organized what has to be done. It is clearly too much trouble to write, as long as you and Bellozzo and Stoldo are busy chatting with each other and having a good time. Tell them to stop it for a while because it is Lent. Try flattering Monna Mea, who isn't easily convinced and won't believe them. Send her my greetings.

---

332. Casino di Giovanni, Nannino, and Nanni Manesco were agricultural laborers. The nickname "Manesco" implies that he was argumentative, quick with his tongue and hands. See ASPo, D.1105, 1400189 (archival reference supplied by Jérôme Hayez).

We received eight sacks from Argomento. I've no time to say any more because Ser Baldo's boy wants to leave. May God protect you always.

Your Margherita, in Prato.

Argomento has come here with two oil barrels. You say that we should send you a quantity of the oil we have, and you will send him to collect it. We will do so. Let us know if you want to do something other than this.

To Francesco di Marco da Prato himself, in Florence.
Received from Prato, 19 March 1397.

Letter 110 (1401787)
20 March 1397
Prato

In the name of God. 20 March 1397.

The reason for this letter is that I did not send you the chickpeas or the broad beans because Argomento didn't go to Florence this morning. He says that when he returned yesterday evening one of his animals was hurt, and for this reason he did not go. He says he will come tomorrow morning, so if you want anything, let us know about it.

With Bodda the carter I am sending you a basket with a handle, containing twenty loaves of bread, twenty-five oranges, and some chestnuts, so make sure you get them if you haven't done so.

I'll say no more for now. May God protect you always.

From your Margherita, in Prato. Greetings.

Francesco di Marco da Prato, in Florence at Piazza Tornaquinci.
Received from Prato, 21 March 1397. Answered on the same day.

Letter 111 (1401788)
21 March 1397
Prato

In the name of God. 21 March 1397.

     Yesterday evening I answered all that was necessary, so I do not have much to say in this letter. Niccolò took the letter to Niccolaio Brancacci, and he did not want to accept it. Niccolò told you about it, but I am letting you know because sometimes letters are kept back and I know you will get the present one. We have cleared Il Palco and we have only left the doors. We didn't think it necessary to take them now. We will see how things turn out. If we can, and there is time, we will take away some of the hay today.[333] I said to Niccolò this morning that perhaps it would have been a good thing to send some flour to Florence. Tell us if you want any. I am having some bread made today. If you tell us what you want this evening, we will send you some. Here we need some strong, sweet spices like pepper. Send us whatever seems best to you. Here, toward Pistoia and Agliana, many people are packing up, and it seems very probable that people will leave here. May God have mercy on us. I have been told that this evening a message came to the *Podestà* and all the castellans. No one has been able to find out what is happening. May God help us. Guido has looked for that book listing the things left in Florence, but he cannot find it. However, he has found the one listing the things that remained here. I'll say no more for now. May God protect you always.

     The bearer of this will be Ser Baldo's son.

     From Margherita, in Prato.

Francesco di Marco da Prato, in Florence.
Received from Prato, 22 March 1397.

---

333. The Duke of Milan, Giangaleazzo Visconti, was engaged in military operations against Mantua in March 1397, and his soldiers occupied much of Lombardy and Tuscany during his drive to dominate north and central Italy. Mercenaries were roaming the countryside close to Prato, looking for booty and wreaking destruction on crops and property. Margherita was preparing the unprotected villa Il Palco for their arrival. See Brucker, *Civic World*, 144–65.

Letter 112 (1401789)
21 March 1397
Prato

In the name of God. 21 March 1397.

Ungheria delivered a letter from you this evening. I respond now as necessary. Niccolò has told you about the matter regarding Niccolaio Brancacci, and he will tell you more concerning it tomorrow. I showed him your letters to me, and he read them. He has understood your instructions, and he will do what you say. Casino received the two florins.[334] With him there is little risk of losing money; because if we see that we have anything to do at La Chiusura or Il Palco, we will get him to do it if there is no one else, especially at La Chiusura. I will get some of the beans ground and send them to you on Friday morning. I told you what Monna Ave said about the baker. I took her into my room and questioned her without your having told me to, and I behaved in the way I thought best to see if I could drag out of her whether she had ever seen it in Florence or Prato. As far as I can understand, she doesn't know what a seal is, and from her face and the way she talks she must have nothing to do with it, as I pretended to her that I must have lost it if you didn't have it.[335] I can't speak now to Monna Ave because I received your letters at the evening bell, and she is now staying at Messer Niccolò Torelli's house to look after one of his daughters who is very sick. However, I don't think it is necessary because I raised the subject indirectly. I could not have been more subtle than I was to see whether I could drag something out of her, because I am extremely upset about this seal, not so much for its value but because of the anxiety it will create for others. May God and the blessed feast of the Annunciation this Sunday give us the grace to find it so no one will use it to commit a sin.

Eighteen sheaves were brought from the haystack today. If it wasn't for the weather, which held us up, we would have brought it all. We will do what seems necessary about the things at Il Palco. Yesterday Barzalone and Niccolò tasted the wines, and they are the same

---

334. This is the laborer, Casino di Giovanni. See letter 109.

335. Francesco had instructed Margherita to interrogate Monna Ave about a missing seal (FD 79).

as when you left them. I cannot find the towel belonging to Monna Mea.[336] I must have soiled it and left it among the dirty clothes. I will send it to her as soon as I find it. I am sending you a basket wrapped with a piece of torn tablecloth and the large tablecloth that you sent here, and now I have found Monna Mea's towel. Give it to her; it is inside. I am also sending you twenty-five loaves of bread in the same basket. And on top of the basket there is your large cape, in case you need it. It will keep the water off if it rains and stop the bread from getting wet.

Send us back the baskets, this one and the other one that you have there. The bread is a bit darker than it was the last time because it is better cooked, and it seems to me more healthy well cooked than underdone. I treat the peas in the way I will now explain. I leave them to soak in the evening, as you do with chickpeas, and similarly in the morning I put them on the fire, as you do with dry chickpeas. I boil them until they are cooked, and I boil herbs and an onion in a separate saucepan, and then I beat them. When I put the peas in the larger saucepan, I put the herbs and the liquid over them as you usually do with fresh wild peas.

Villana knows how to cook them because she has seen me cook them so many times that she must remember.[337] Monna Mea has also seen me cook them. She and I cooked them; she beat the herbs here in this house and thought they were very good. We ate them in the downstairs room. Bellozzo did not want them because there was too much fish in them. Don't be surprised if Villana can't cook them, because they are a little complicated. Because it is very late at night, I will finish now. May God protect you.

Remind them to add garlic, as you do with chickpeas.

From your Margherita.

Francesco di Marco da Prato, in Florence.
Received from Prato, 22 March 1397.

---

336. This is Bartolomea, or Bellozza. See note 302, above.

337. Stoldo's wife, Villana, and Mea (Bellozza) were often together because their husbands were good friends who worked together in the Florentine branch of the firm.

Letter 113 (1401790)
22 March 1397
Prato

In the name of God. 22 March 1397.

    This evening I received a letter from you. Argomento's boy brought it here as the bell rang, and with it there was a letter to Barzalone, one to Niccolò di Piero, and one to Ser Schiatta. Argomento had been here at the twenty-second hour, and he had told me that you were going to send an answer with Nannino.[338] He brought me the spice and the pepper that you sent me—and gave me several pieces of news that will make me have a bad night, considering the way things are in Florence and that you are there.[339] This is God's will. I got Monna Ghita to put on her mantle and sent her to the sacristan of San Francesco, begging for prayers to be said to God for you, and for all the others, because it seems to me there is urgent need for them. Everyone who loves you is wishing you were here. One must believe that God does everything for the best. Barzalone went to Florence today; Niccolò did not go because he had too much to do. He had to have his house at Gonfienti emptied and see to other matters.[340] I believe he intends to go tomorrow, although I am not very pleased considering that Barzalone is not here. When they, or at least one of them, are here, I worry less about what might occur. If Niccolò comes to Florence and you do not intend to leave there very soon, provided that Barzalone can leave there safely, I beg you not to keep him there, both for the sake of his family and of your own. We have stored all the hay in the house. We will give orders that the bridge be removed after the many rocks that are there have been torn down. If we can, we will have it removed on Saturday evening, although there is not much time for

338. See Appendix 2.

339. Fighting between Florentine and Milanese troops had broken out again in March 1397. Florentine ambassadors had arrived secretly in Paris in February to enlist the aid of the French king, Charles VI, in Florence's struggle against the Duke of Milan. See Brucker, *Civic World*, 159–60.

340. Niccolò di Piero's house was on the road to Florence at Gonfienti, a settlement on the River Bisenzio not far from Prato. He too was concerned to clear his house of valuables for fear of theft by companies of roaming soldiers. See also note 333, above.

them to do anything. It is not my intention to have Il Palco abandoned until the very last moment. Nanni has no intention of leaving until he is just out of range of a crossbow shot and he can flee carrying only his cap. Nanni's father is still there, and he never wanted to take shelter anywhere else. Schiavo went there this morning and took his things. I urged him to look after the place and told him what I thought was necessary. He says he will never leave, neither he nor his brother; and he has no intention of leaving the place unmanned until there is nothing else to be done. Nanni tells me they are looking after it carefully and doing it well. Do not be anxious about these matters, as we will do everything to make you satisfied. I will look at the letter again, and when it rains I will get them to do those things you want done during the rain.

Benedetto was here to see me and says he has no bread or any flour at all. He gave me a worrisome evening. He begged me to write to you on his behalf. His wife is about to have a child and they are in a difficult situation. If you are agreeable, I think he should be helped to some extent, considering that he also clearly loves you and this is something that should never be forgotten. Follow the matter up as you think best. If you thought of saving the cost of Montepulciano, I would agree because he is not very capable; the expense isn't negligible, and the money will be useful in one way or another. There are some expenses that you can't eliminate, as you can in his case, and now there are some good excuses for doing so. Nanni is very upset because no work can be done in the present circumstances. Tell me what you think.

I spoke to Monna Ave today and asked her what you told me to. In short, she tells me she never saw it and never had the key to my chest, nor to the spoon box, except for the time you came to Florence before the fair in that year I came here. Maggio says that you had spoons, knives, and other things put inside there, and claims that you left Ave the key then; and that in this same chest there were spices, ginger, saffron, and rice. From that moment he says she had the key, but not previously; and you did not leave any other things in the chest, and the medicine tin was intact and full. The jar of green ginger was half full, and he says that if she had wanted to steal anything, she could have taken bread and oil and all the other things she had within reach rather than the seal upon which she had never clapped eyes. And he says he would like to know what she has ever done to harm your property. It would be a shameful thing to ask her, as she has never allowed anyone into the house for fear that something could be taken. Fattorino and Bellozzo can be witnesses to this.[341] Because it is already very late, I will add no more. May God protect you always.

From your Margherita, in Prato.

Francesco di Marco da Prato, Florence.
Received from Prato, 23 March 1397. Answered on the same day.

Letter 114 (1401791)
29 March 1397
Prato

In the name of God. 29 March 1397.

Yesterday evening Nanni Manesco delivered a letter from you. I reply here as necessary. Concerning the letter you say you sent me with Andrea di Paolo, I sent someone to his house to find out what had happened to it. His women said that he had left yesterday morning; they did not know where he had gone, and he had not yet returned, so I did not get it. I sent for Nannino and told him I thought he should go to your place immediately. He answered that he had been with you and would not go there unless you sent for him directly. If it had been earlier, he would have gone, but it was compline.[342] He has guard duty every two or three days, and this evening it is his turn. He asked me for four *soldi*. I lent the money to him, because tomorrow he would be so exhausted that he could not come and he has had a pain in his foot.

We will try to send you the *moggio* of wheat tomorrow with Nanni and Nannino. None of your friends in this town has a sack; one cannot be had, even for a thousand florins. I decided that since I had sent a *moggio* of wheat to the mill today and there were still fifteen bushels from the previous lot, I would get it back again. I will send it to

341. For the loss of the seal, see letter 112; and for Monna Ave, see note 327, above.
342. See Appendix 2.

you because it is a precisely measured amount. This evening, because there are no sacks, I will have the curtain unpicked and I will make sure that some are made by tomorrow at three, and I will send you the wheat that I get back from the mill.

I told the baker not to touch the wheat that I had delivered to his house because I did not have your permission for that. If you think that I did the wrong thing, write to me and I will fix it up by taking it to the mill on the first day that is allocated to us. The winnower was here today, and he winnowed all of Messer Guelfo's wheat. The baker has thirty-three bushels, and the vat that Barzalone bought, which holds twenty-nine bushels, has twenty-five and a half bushels in it. I had the husks of the wheat put with what was left previously and I had it all stored away; in all there are five and a half bushels. I will have the wheat taken to the mill and get them to grind it immediately. We have already sent fifteen from this harvest to the mill, and we took the *moggio* that we sent to you in Florence for the monks of Santa Maria degli Angeli from the vat in the *loggia*, as well as the three bushels that I gave to Domenico and the three to Benedetto. I sent nine bushels to the mill, and half a bushel was left. I think that half is missing because of the generous measures they used, because the winnower says he put in forty bushels.

This is all the grain that we found in the *loggia* and in the small vault above the ground-floor kitchen. I am sending you twenty-five loaves of bread. I didn't put the flour I sent you through the sieve because I didn't think I would be sending you any. If you don't like it, it will be fine for the household there. I passed on your message to Niccolò di Piero; but I am not very happy about what you said to me, because if you were here you would say I have authority in everyday matters over both his household and yours. He is in the palace of the commune most of the time, and he hears and knows what is going on there. Events happen that he knows about, and he can inform others about many things that could not be remedied unless he were there. You instruct Barzalone and Niccolò to buy you two cartloads of wood. They will be able to buy it, but they cannot work out how to send it to you because they can't count on having oxen. It would even be difficult for the *Podestà* to get any, as they have hidden them all in various places up in the mountains to prevent them from being found until this wheat is sent to the commune. However, if you had need of them there for yourself, I would do my best to send you some. Let me know and leave it to me to work out how to do it.

Nanni arrived here this evening, and it seems to me that he must have a slight fever. I blame the bad scabies that he has. Have a look at him and you will see what a state he is in. It would be a good idea if Bellozzo, or someone who knows something about medicine, showed him how to treat his arms at least, because he can't bend them. I think it would be best if he took a little cassia.[343] Buy some cheaply and I will give it to him. I am sending you some chestnuts, a jar of raisins, a hand towel, and a basket. Send me back everything that you can, and the sacks, which are often useful. I will ask Monna Simona when Messer Piero is leaving, and I will let you know. Because it is late and because I know that Nanni told you that we passed a bad night, and today we haven't had much rest, I will say no more. May God protect you always.

From your Margherita, in Prato.

To Francesco di Marco, in Florence.
Received from Prato, 30 March 1397.

Letter 115 (1401792)
30 March 1397
Prato

In the name of God. 30 March 1397.

Nanni returned yesterday evening but did not bring a letter from you. I imagine that it is because you have a lot of business on your hands or because you are, as usual, […].[344]

Nanni returned yesterday evening just in time to be admitted into [Prato] […] so when he comes here I beg you to send him off early, as I was very worried and thought they might have confiscated

---

343. Cassia is a variety of cinnamon, used for medicinal purposes.

344. This letter has numerous lacunae due to a large hole in the original.

his wheat and put it in the piazza or that he had encountered some other difficulty.

Ser Naldo came to see me this morning and told me he wants to give you the money and he says Barzalone does too, and he said he wants you to send him a letter so that he can prove that he has given it to you. [...][345] Here they are saying that the *Podestà* will send out the soldiers today, and they are taking whatever they manage to find such as wood or whatever they need. If [Nanni] returns early I will get him to bring four donkey-loads of wood from La Chiusura, because if the soldiers go there it may not be possible any more. I can't bring it back here any other way.

Schiavo brought me another sledge-load of heavy wood this morning and took two bundles of canes and walnut stakes to Tantera. I am making a note of everything. There is no more than one load left. If they had had any animals they would have brought it to me, but they didn't. They have given me a great deal of help.

I have unpicked the curtain, and today I had fourteen strong sacks made. [...][346] This evening I will get Nanni to measure a *moggio* of wheat from the *loggia* to send to the mill, as I have little flour left and the miller still has not brought me the bushels he has. When he has ground this *moggio* I will buy some wheat from Domenico and send it to the mill, as it seems to me the finest. It has been sifted and cleaned and is in good condition.

Monna Simona tells me that Messer Piero is leaving in May.

I am sending you a basket in which I will put some loaves of bread, and there is a small basket with cleaned mushrooms in it. All you have to do is put them in a small saucepan. They were sent to me so I am forwarding them to you.

Regarding the purchase of wood, I asked Schiavo if there were any good-quality cartloads up there. He told me that he believes Niccolò from the oil press has one. I will speak with Ser Schiatta and see if I can be supplied with some.

Send me back the two baskets and keep [...] the cloths if you need them, because they belong there. May God protect you always.

---

345. The next seven lines of the original letter are too fragmentary to reconstruct and have not been translated.

346. The following lines also have many missing words.

I am enclosing a letter from Messer Piero Rinaldeschi.
From your Margherita, in Prato.

To Francesco di Marco da Prato himself, in Florence.

Letter 116 (1401793)
31 March 1397
Prato

In the name of God. 31 March 1397.

This evening Nanni delivered a letter from you. I reply here.

I forwarded the letters addressed to Barcelona that Nanni brought without opening them. No one here touched them. He had a letter addressed to me, and one for Ser Naldo. I told Guido to deliver it and he did so, and before you say that Guido didn't take the letter to him, I saw it in Ser Naldo's hand this morning as he made his way slowly to see me, and that is why I wrote what I did.[347] As for your staying there and enjoying yourself, I don't know what you mean by that. I was not told that you were enjoying yourself. It seems to me you have nothing much to celebrate, unless it be those few words I wrote to you, since I thought the explanation was your usual behavior, but this has nothing to do with enjoying yourself or fine dining.[348]

About that overgown that you claim upset you so because I let you down: I don't want to go into whether it is my fault or not, but I would like to remind you, because I have such a tiny brain, of what really happened with it. Remember that it was you who lent it, and then you got it back; and remember that you removed all the straw from the bed in the room on the ground floor and you told me you had put it there. I remember that you looked for it two or three times under my bed and you actually said, while you were searching for it: "I shouldn't

347. See Mazzei, *Lettere di un notaro*, 2:347.

348. On 31 March 1397 (FD 85), Francesco had written ironically that Margherita had not received a letter from him because he, Stoldo, and Bellozzo had been doing nothing but feasting and enjoying themselves. The real reason, he added, was that he had been working frantically and had not left his premises in Florence for twenty-two days.

be looking here, because I put it under the mattress in the room on the ground floor," and you then said: "I put it on the bed base because I removed the straw and put it on the base." When the overgown was discovered, I was in my room dictating to Guido, and they said to me: "We have found an overgown," and I said, "Where?" They said: "On the boards on Francesco's side of the bed," and I remembered then the time you were looking for it and had said to me, "I have put it on the bed base," so I said "Ah! this is the overgown that Francesco couldn't find," because it fitted the description you had given me. But you had said that it was in the room on the ground floor. I will leave it to you to judge whose fault it is.[349] From now on I refuse to write to you about every trivial matter that happens here; but if I am not mistaken, in one of your letters that I received you told me to write to you about what was going on here, and so I did, thinking I was doing the right thing. About approaching Francesca, or having someone else do so, it is really not necessary, and I neither asked nor sent for her when her need was greater. So I won't ask to see her now, because there is just no need. The Sunday before Carnival she sent Bacofo's wife to me to deliver a backhanded compliment; but I deserve this from her, and from everyone I love, because love is wasted on mortal beings. I have never replied to her, nor will I ever, except face to face. I will do unto others to the best of my judgment as I would like them to do unto me. May God give me the grace, and let people think what they like. I haven't been enjoying a wedding feast here. I don't want to say more. The Lord above knows it, as do the people we mix with. I too have only been outside the house twice, for one reason or another, so in this respect you are no better than I am.

I told Barzalone to talk with Ser Schiatta. He tells me he doesn't want to because he says that he and Ser Schiatta both want to talk to Lodovico. I said to him that, in my opinion, you wanted him to discuss the money owed to you that you need now, as well as the letter that he hasn't given you. Barzalone says he is reluctant to talk to him unless it is about the matter regarding Lodovico. Because I have such a tiny brain, I wouldn't like to make a mistake: I will not mention it to him

---

349. Francesco vowed to resolve this argument face to face (FD 87). He added, however, that although Margherita would never confess her mistake, he knew absolutely that he had told her to look under that bed.

unless you write and tell me again to do so. I have sent a message to the laborer at Arsiccioli to bring us our share of the wood, and I have said the same to the one from Pescia. And so I will do all the other things that must be done without worrying you any more. May God grant me the grace to do them in a way that will satisfy you. Nanni took two baskets for you in which there are two napkins, a small tablecloth, two sets of underlinen, and a coif, and with them a towel belonging to Lucia. This evening I received nine sacks, and yesterday he brought eight. If there are any more, and you want to send them, you can do so. I won't say any more. May God protect you always.

From Margherita, in Prato.

In another letter I asked you whether I was to give anything to the wife of Nannino if she asked me to help her. You haven't answered me yet. She came today to ask for a bushel of flour. I gave it to her.

It seems to me that she has been left miserably poor if she has no bread one day after Nannino's departure. He should have at least said something to you, because after he left here the first time I asked him about how he had provided for his wife. He replied that he had left her hardly anything. I told him to ask you if I was to give her something, but he didn't mention it to you and you haven't answered me. Tell me if you don't want me to give her anything else, because I have given her a bushel of flour, and I won't give her anything more unless you tell me to.

To Francesco di Marco da Prato, in Florence.
Received from Prato, 31 March 1397. Answered 2 April.

Letter 117 (1401794)
1 April 1397
Prato

In the name of God. 1 April 1397.

We sent you a letter this morning with Benedetto's brother-in-law. Fattalbuio was here, and he said that you hadn't received it. Today

I sent Zanobi to Ser Schiatta to find out why he hadn't replied to the letter that you had sent him, and he said that he had replied and sent it to you.

Barzalone wanted to give me twelve bushels of wheat for Stoldo. I didn't want to put it in the baker's house, so I put it in the *loggia* in our wooden vat, as it was empty. They say the wheat is excellent, but in fact it is full of dust. I spoke frankly, joking that he should at least have given it a good shake for the sake of his friend. I talked about it with Niccolò and said that in my view it would be possible to buy some more for Stoldo, if he wished. I will perhaps get about eight bushels bought for him tomorrow, and if he needs it, I would be inclined to give it to him soon. Whenever he has been approached, this *Podestà* has so far never refused any of the requests that I sent him. It would be good when you happen to meet Guido to thank him so he knows it is for you he is doing the favor. If Stoldo needs [some grain], let us know and I will endeavor to send it as quickly as possible, because I believe one can't fail to obtain some for him here in Prato.

Niccolò di Piero says that he believes he will be there in Florence on Tuesday. Let him know if he is to bring anyone with him, or the pack animals, and he will do it.

Fattalbuio told me to tell the laborer from Arsiccioli to load the wood. I spoke to him today, and he says that he will bring it as quickly as he can. I haven't been able to speak to Battagliere. I don't want to delay things. We need to make sure he doesn't work another year there. We took the lengths of timber out of the water today.

I am sending with Argomento a basket covered with a napkin in which there are quite a few mushrooms that were sent to me this evening, and a lot of fresh frogs, gathered today toward evening, but I've had them cooked so you won't have to do it. Send me back the basket because it is not mine, and if you have any others send them back to me.

I am having the bread made on Monday so that if you come you will find some; and if you don't want to come, send me a message whether or not to send you some.

Enclosed with this there is a letter sent to you by Monna Beldì. She sent me a message begging me to tell you to reply to her. Do what you like about it.

I won't say any more. May God protect you always.

From your Margherita, in Prato.

To Francesco di Marco himself, in Florence.

Received from Prato, 2 April. Answered 2 April.

Letter 118 (6300685)
3 April 1397
Prato

[…] La Chiusura because we can't delay any more, and Nanni told Martino and Montepulciano what to do when they hoe the wheat.[350] I will do what you say for Nannino's wife. Send me a little saffron because I have none. This miller is very slow; if you think we should give the wheat to others, tell us and I will do it. I'll say no more. May God protect you always.

Tell me whether or not you received the hooded cape, because I have heard nothing about it.

From Margherita, in Prato.

To Francesco di Marco, in Florence.

Received from Prato, 3 April. Answered 3 April.

Letter 119 (1401795)
3 April 1397
Prato

In the name of God. 3 April 1397.

This evening Argomento delivered your letter, as well as two small baskets and a bigger one. I am replying here. Ser Naldo's money amounted to no more than four and a half *lire*. Monna Caterina visited me this evening and said that if I needed money she would lend

---

350. The first page of this letter is not extant.

me some, and that if I asked for it in writing I could have as much as I wanted, but otherwise I couldn't be given any.[351] I won't do anything until you are here because you must be coming soon and you will do as you see fit.

I will press Michele as much as I can, and I will also get Barzalone to tell him what you say in the way he thinks best.[352]

I have had neither money nor a letter from Pistoia. If nothing arrives, I'll let you know.

I am glad you received the pannier and the things I sent in it. About the hooded cape, there is nothing else to say. I will tell Niccolò di Piero what you told me.

I will send the bran as soon as I can, either with Argomento or with Nanni da Santa Chiara. For now I won't say any more. May God protect you always.

From your Margherita, in Prato.

To Francesco di Marco da Prato himself, in Florence.
Received from Prato, 4 April 1397.

Letter 120 (1401960)
5 April 1397
Prato

In the name of God. 5 April 1397.

Yesterday evening Argomento delivered a letter from you that needs no reply; and then, about eight o'clock, another arrived in which you tell me about the wet nurse for Lodovico Marini.[353] I sent a message to the wife of our worker Ceccarello, who had a child two months ago. I was with Schiavo, who ought to be back here today, and

---

351. See FD 88 and 89.

352. Michele di Falcuccio had borrowed money from Francesco on other occasions and was slow to repay what he owed. See letter 71.

353. Lodovico Marini was related to Francesco's partner, Manno d'Albizo degli Agli, who was married to Bice di Ser Piero Marini. Both Lodovico Marini and Stoldo had houses at Marignolle burnt down by marauding soldiers in March 1397. See FD 83, and letter 111.

I will talk with him and make sure he understands everything very clearly.[354] If she agrees to do what I say, I think Lodovico will be well served. Nevertheless, I will search here in Prato and beyond and see what seems to be best, and I will inform you about everything. In the meantime, I can give you some information. The custom here is to pay wet nurses between four and four and a half *lire* a month. Also, it is usual here to provide other things the women need, and Niccolò can tell you what he provided.

I am sending you the cape with Niccolò. I won't say any more. May God protect you always.

From your Margherita, in Prato.

This morning I sent a sack of bran with Argomento.

To Francesco di Marco [in Florence].
Received from Prato, 5 April 1397.

Letter 121 (1401796)
5 April 1397
Prato

In the name of God. 5 April 1397.

This evening we received a letter from you, as well as one for Ser Schiatta and another for Barzalone. Barzalone read the one addressed to Ser Schiatta, and we have understood everything. I had it sealed by Guido, and we sent it to him with Agnolo, who was here at the time.[355] If Barzalone and I think I should say something to him, I will do so. If I have time to see Messer Piero, I will tell him my opinion, and I will ask Bernabò. Don't be surprised that I haven't written to you for two days because I had the highest fever I ever remember having, with shivering as well. When Guido read me a letter from you, the trem-

---

354. Piero di Lenzo, known as Schiavo, seems to have acted as an intermediary in finding suitable wet nurses in Prato. He lived in Coiano and worked at Filettole and Il Palco. See also letter 171.

355. This is Agnolo di Niccolò di Piero di Giunta.

bling and fever were such that I couldn't understand what you were saying to me. I asked him to reply to you, but not to tell you that I was ill. However, I am not sorry that Niccolò told you. It seems to me you have enough anxieties without me writing to you about being ill, but I don't believe I am sick because of overeating, as I starved myself close to death this Lent. The doctor says that I am unwell more because of weakness than anything else. He tells me to eat minced chicken, and so I have and will until I feel better. So don't worry because I am hoping I won't be unwell long, although anxiety is a big fault of mine, and this evening I am not very cheered by your letter. I am worried that after working so hard you won't be able to bear it.

I sent someone to find the baker as soon as I had the letter, and he was in bed. I told Guido to ask him about that matter. He said it is true that he owes him some money, and that he asked him for two florins; and that if you had been here, he would have asked you for them.[356] Our friend told him that he would be going to Florence and would talk to you about it tomorrow. I will ask on his behalf and find out how things stand. I will say no more since you have enough worries.

This evening Nanni finished hoeing the wheat. The barley is still so short that it can wait for another four or five days. I want him to return to Il Palco tomorrow to tell Montepulciano and Martino what to do, and to get them to move all the rocks that are there. Because Martino can't carry them on his own, Nanni and the others there will have to help, and tomorrow Nanni will do the things that the others don't know how to do.

You sent me a message to send you a *moggio* of the flour stored at the baker's house. I will see on Friday whether I can have the animals. If I can I will get them ready and send the flour with Nanni on Saturday morning.

I haven't baked any white bread because you sent a message not to send more, but I am sending you some of the bread we eat because it is fine for Fattorino and the others there. Of the twenty-three loaves, three are like the ones I sent you that other time. I will have some white bread made for you tomorrow, but I won't send it if you don't tell

356. Domenico dal Montale, who often worked as a laborer on Francesco's building projects, was in debt to a money lender from Pistoia. Francesco was worried that he, rather than Domenico, would have to repay the loan (FD 91).

me by tomorrow evening whether you have to return or not, because if you must return, I want it here.

Schiavo told me that he has not been able to contact the father of the girl he has found. He has already lost a day, and tomorrow he will perhaps lose another. I would advise him not to let this girl go because she is the daughter of a rich and respectable artisan. She won't be worse off financially, as she will be living there with him. As a wet nurse she couldn't be better. She has all the qualities that make an excellent nurse, and she is at the stage where she won't become pregnant for twenty-eight months or more. She has had her milk for only two months. She could feed any baby with no trouble at all.

Today I searched the whole of Prato. Nobody turned up as good as she, but I won't engage her or anyone else until I hear from them whether or not they have a wet nurse. I don't want a repeat of what happened in the case of Domenico di Cambio's son-in-law. He insisted on sending his children here, and he kept us busy looking for at least eight days, and nobody accepted any of the good man's children, and he lost three of the best babies in the land.

For your sake—you don't know what these Florentines are like, and I swore then not to get involved again—but for your sake and Manno's I want to fix this, and so I have promised Schiavo that if she accepts this baby I want it brought straight here at all costs. Both the baby and the wet nurse should stay here, until things settle down and Manno can rest assured that we are looking after the baby at our house. Tell me at once whether or not they have a wet nurse. I will answer you on Saturday. Schiavo will have spoken to the father of this girl. Avoid these involvements as much as you can, because we have more than enough of them.[357] Because it is evening and I don't feel very well, I won't continue. May God protect you always.

From your Margherita, in Prato.

To Francesco di Marco, in Florence.
Received from Prato, 7 April 1397.

---

357. On the wet nursing industry in Tuscany, see Christiane Klapisch-Zuber, "Blood Parents and Milk Parents: Wet Nursing in Florence, 1300–1530," in *Women, Family and Ritual in Renaissance Italy*, trans. Lydia Cochrane (Chicago and London: University of Chicago Press, 1985), 132–64, esp. 132–33.

Letter 122 (1401797)
7 April 1397
Prato

In the name of God. 7 April 1397.

Argomento was here today and gave me a letter addressed to Agnolo. Agnolo told me that Niccolò says that you cannot be here by Monday and also that the child's wet nurse is settled. Today I turned the whole world upside down to find a wet nurse, and to have a good few from whom to choose. And furthermore Schiavo came this evening to spend the night, and tomorrow he is coming to Florence to find out when they would want the woman to come for the child; he decided that, even if he gets nothing out of this, he would do it to please you and me.

I didn't want to tell him this evening that the child is accommodated because it was only two hours after dawn that I found out, and I have four pack animals to bring you grain. I would like him to accompany Nanni, because there are too many animals for one person to handle. You tell him there in whatever way you think best.

Argomento told me that I should send Stoldo's grain to Florence. If Argomento has enough animals he will bring it; if not, he will bring it when he can.

The grain auditors have been here and they looked over everything honestly, and they sent one person to our house rather than many. Guido went with him and took him into the barn, and Guido says that he wrote down five *moggia* of wheat.

We haven't had anything yet from Stefano in Pistoia.[358] Nanni thinks he can bring twenty-seven bushels of wheat. I will send you twenty loaves of bread. It is not as good as usual because today there was the most terrible wind that there has been this year, and it is very cold. It is our fate that when you want something to turn out well, it doesn't; and when you don't care, it turns out well.

I will send the halters for the mules with Nanni. With this letter there will be another for Ballerino sent from Pistoia. Guido says that he found the letter that Bellozzo sent you where he says that he is sending you a pound of incense and says it is dated 30 December

358. This is Stefano Guazzalotti.

1396. And, just as he says that if you don't like it you should number it among life's misfortunes, regard it as one of the things that you know I can't do anything about. You know well that in my state of health nothing makes me suffer more, and if it weren't for love of you, and because I am not free, I would even try to leave behind these tribulations by withdrawing from worldly affairs. I am tied neither to children nor to relatives, money, or commercial dealings; so that nothing prevents me from doing so except the two things I mentioned and the fact that I'm no saint, as God has shown me.

For all the things of this world that I must leave behind, may God grant me the grace to love Him and to do the things that are pleasing to Him.

Nanni is coming to Florence. Ask him about these other things as you like. I won't say any more because it is late, and also because every evening we get the letters very late. May God protect you always. Every day I send you a napkin and you never send any of them back, and you don't tell me if you have received them. This week you will have received three. Keep track of them. I would have done the washing days ago if I hadn't been waiting for you to send the dirty linen.

From your Margherita, in Prato.

To Francesco di Marco himself, in Florence.
Received from Prato, 7 April 1397.

Letter 123 (1401798)
13 April 1397
Prato

In the name of God. 13 April 1397.

Argomento brought us a basket containing Francesco's purple mantle, a towel, and a quilt with a large towel wrapped in the horse blanket.

And then Zanobi brought a lime sack in which there were five sheets, and I have also received a sack of dirty linen, and while you say on the note: "three sets of Francesco's underlinen," there are two shirts and three underdrawers; and where you say nine towels, there are seven; and where you say nine table napkins, there are seven. There are four cloaks you don't mention, and I think you have mistaken them for two towels and two table napkins. According to your list we are missing a shirt and a kerchief.

We will bleed the mules tomorrow, if it is good weather, and this is what Barzalone advises.

We will send you the cask of oil tomorrow.

Niccolò told me that for some reason you told him to bring Caterina here.[359] That is a good idea, and you will be doing me a great favor. I am very anxious about your staying there, for many reasons that I don't want to mention now. I will tell you about them the next time you come here. If you should decide that you want to send anything here, I could send you the pack animals; because Argomento cannot bring them himself, let me know and I will make sure you have some animals. I would have sent Nanni tomorrow, but he has decided to take some medicine.

I will pursue Domenico Scotti and the others as much as necessary. There is nothing else to say here. May God protect you.

From your Margherita, in Prato.

To Francesco di Marco da Prato, at the Piazza Tornaquinci, Florence. Received from Prato, 14 April 1397. Answered 14 April 1397.

Letter 124 (1401799)
16 April 1397
Prato

In the name of God. 16 April 1397.

This morning we sent a letter to you with Ser Giovanni Nerli, and because I haven't received your answer yet, there is not much to say for now.

We are sending you the cask of oil with Argomento, as well as twenty-one loaves of bread. They are not the [best] but they are ad-

---

359. Margherita refers to her niece Tina.

equate. If you should need any bags for anything you want to send here, let me know and I will send you some.

The grain auditors returned and they are searching everywhere because someone told them that there is a great deal of grain hidden here.[360] I am surprised that you didn't return with Niccolò. Please make sure you return here before Easter because I am very worried about a number of things that I have been told. If my own worrying weren't enough, all your friends say nothing else but that you would be better off here for many reasons. And you know yourself what these are. You understand what I am saying. I beg you to please me, and the others who love you, by staying there as little as you can.

We have not recovered any money from Domenico Scotti. He gives us nothing but promises, and so does Giorgio the cobbler. Let us know what you want us to do.

We won't say any more here. May God protect you always.

Ser Lapo's letter is enclosed with this one.

From your Margherita, in Prato.

To Francesco di Marco da Prato, at the Piazza Tornaquinci, Florence. Received from Prato, 17 April 1397.

Letter 125 (1401800)
17 April 1397
Prato

In the name of God. 17 April 1397.

Argomento brought your letter this evening and I have understood what you said in it. I will answer your requests below. I am glad Argomento delivered my letter to you, and the one for Ser Lapo, and the basket of bread and cask of oil.

You said that tomorrow, after eating, I should send you the mules, Barzalone's mare, and his small mule, and that I should send

---

360. The Officials of Abundance ensured that a sufficient stock of grain was available in the city and at a price accessible to the poor. They enforced regulations against holding back grain for speculative purposes.

them with Nanni and Fattorino. And since Nannino has returned and wants to come to Florence tomorrow morning, I intend to send the mare and the small mule with him, and tomorrow evening Fattorino will bring back Barzalone's large mule and his smaller one; in the meantime, Barzalone will have his small mule shod and the large mule shaved. Therefore, I am not sending you Nanni because Nannino is coming; but if you want Nanni to come there with someone else to keep you company, tell us tomorrow evening, and they will be there early on Thursday. Tell us what you want done.

I have found out from Argomento the reason why he didn't bring Francesco Bonsignori's mare, and he says he thinks he is bringing it tomorrow with the documents and the things you want to send us. When you have sent us everything, nothing will be touched until you are here, and we will do what you told us about the mare.

I will tell Niccolò that you have no time to write to him, but you have spoken with Nofri Bischeri, and I will tell him everything that your letter says I should say to him.

We will prepare the beds and the other things, so that all will be well. The grain auditors haven't come here. It seems that they are only looking at houses that weren't previously searched.

Send us a lot of those drinking glasses that are there. I won't say any more here. May God protect you always. Enclosed will be a letter to you from Barzalone.

From your Margherita, in Prato.

To Francesco di Marco da Prato, at the Piazza Tornaquinci, Florence. Received from Prato, 17 April 1397. Answered on the same day.

Letter 126 (1401801)
19 April 1397
Prato

In the name of God. 19 April 1397.

This evening I received a letter from you, as well as a basket, a sack of documents for Argomento, and Francesco Bonsignori's mare and saddle. We sent the mare to the house of Ser Lapo's mother, Monna Bartola. She had it put in the stable and groomed. She doesn't want it to be taken elsewhere. She says that you must have misunderstood because the mare belongs to Ser Lapo, not to Francesco Bonsignori.

We also received a package in which there was a lining of mine, sixteen hides, various pieces of woolen cloth, and some linen and samite, as well as a basket in which there were three of your overgowns, one of mine, a tablecloth, and a piece of fine linen that was also in the package mentioned above.

The Officials of Abundance fined you twenty-five florins.[361] Niccolò went to pay the fine, and they allege that we have kept thirty *moggia* of the wheat we bought. They claimed that we sent it to Florence, not to put it on the market, but to store it in our house. I told him to invite them to come and see how much wheat we have, and to use their discretion to decide, and if they think we have too much for the size of the household as it is now, they should do what they think is appropriate. However, there is just enough wheat for our household as it is now. We told them that we sent five *moggia* to Florence: one to the friars of the Angeli,[362] two to one of your business partners, and two to another partner because they found themselves without any. It seemed to Niccolò that this was the best thing to say. It seems that they have perhaps decided to come and inspect tomorrow, and the official will be someone from the Altoviti family.[363]

As for the animals, we will do as you said in your letter. There is nothing else for now. May God protect you always.

Remember to bring some drinking glasses.

From your Margherita, in Prato.

To Francesco di Marco da Prato himself, at the Piazza Tornaquinci, Florence.
Received from Prato, 20 April 1397.

361. See also letter 124. Francesco Datini instructed Margherita to tell the officials that he had bought less than twenty *moggia* of wheat but had forty employees to feed (FD 98).

362. The convent of Santa Maria degli Angeli in Florence housed friars of the Benedictine (Camaldolite) order.

363. The Altoviti were a prominent Florentine family.

Letter 127 (1401802)
20 April 1397
Prato

In the name of God. 20 April 1397.

This evening Niccolò di Piero delivered a letter from you. I respond here as necessary.

The grain auditors didn't come here to inspect after all, and we don't think they will come.[364] Because we are expecting you here tomorrow or the day after, we won't say much, and also there is little that needs saying. May God protect you always.

From your Margherita, in Prato.

To Francesco di Marco da Prato himself, at the Piazza Tornaquinci, Florence.
Received from Prato, 20 April 1397.

Letter 128 (1401803)
17 May 1397
Prato

In the name of God. 17 May 1397.

This evening I sent Guido to ask Argomento if he could take the bread that I want to send you. He replied that he had to see someone about one of his packhorses and couldn't come to me. He says that he may not be able to carry anything because he has a full load. I sent at once to Nanni da Santa Chiara to find out if he was coming here so that he could take the bread to you, and he said he wasn't. If we can, we will arrange for Argomento to bring you at least some bread, as well as your hooded mantle and the mules' bridles. We will then send you the rest the next morning. If Argomento can't bring you any bread at all, we will at least give him some letters that came this evening, and there are three others enclosed with this one; that is, the two for you and the others are for Bernardo. There was another addressed to Iacopo di

364. See letters 122 and 126.

Visconte and Stefano Guazzalotti in Pistoia.[365] We will have that sent tomorrow morning with Michele del Campana or whoever else is here so it will arrive safely.

And there was another letter addressed to Giorgio di Donato, but because it was very late we couldn't send it to him. I will send it to him tomorrow morning.

We are also sending you your ledger because we think you forgot to take it.

Tarpuccia wanted to see you today; I sent Benedetto to offer your apologies to the *Podestà*, and he did.

Guido says that he went to Ser Simone for those documents. He told Guido that he had done them, but it seemed to him that there were mistakes in them. He wanted to speak with Ser Amelio to see how the thing stood.[366] In order to be clear about it, Guido will go to Ser Amelio tomorrow and tell him what you said he should say, and he will also tell him what Ser Simone says about it, and he will get them to meet and discuss the matter.

I'll say no more here. May God protect you always.

From your Margherita, in Prato.

To Francesco di Marco himself, in Florence.
Brought from Prato by Argomento, 19 May 1397.

Letter 129 (1401804)
21 May 1397
Prato

In the name of God. 21 May 1397.

As your letter arrived late, Monna Margherita asked me to reply to you.[367] We delivered all the letters.

---

365. Iacopo di Visconte and Stefano Guazzalotti were banking partners.

366. Simone di Ser Donato and Amelio Migliorati di Messer Lapo were notaries.

367. This letter seems to have been written on Margherita's behalf by the scribe rather than dictated by her.

There is no need to send any more cherries for now. Filippo the farrier says that it is necessary to stand the mare in the Bisenzio River for a while, so the poultice can soak well, and then we should wash her down with lye and soap, and all will be well, and he says he will then put two new shoes on her because she needs them, so tomorrow she won't be able to come to you. When we can, we will get her ready so she can come.

We are sending you with Argomento twenty-two white loaves and twelve of the other sort, packed in the basket you sent back to us; and in it there are also two large hand cloths, two large napkins, and six table napkins. We are also sending you the small basket that you sent the cherries in, packed with roses and chestnuts as well as the small box.

We received the verjuice safely. May God protect you always.

From Monna Margherita, in Prato.

To Francesco di Marco da Prato, in Florence.
Received from Prato, 22 May 1397.

Letter 130 (1401805)
22 May 1397
Prato

In the name of God. 22 May 1397.

This evening I didn't receive a letter from you. I respond here to what seems necessary, and I enclose some letters for you.

The things that you haven't received we will send tomorrow morning, either with Argomento or with Nanni, depending on who wants to take them. We will look after the mare as Filippo the farrier suggests. I will ask Guido to care for the small mule and all the other animals properly, and Bernardo also reminds him to take her out every evening and morning, for as long as necessary.

There is nothing else to say about Niccolò, except to ask you to speak to Francesca before you leave and write to me if you find out which convent he is in and how he is.[368]

I will do what seems best to me about the bed and the other things. Monna Ghita will look after Bernardo's needs. He is sleeping there with them, and in the evening she brings the syrup and looks after him. When he takes the medicine, I will make sure Monna Ghita does what is necessary.

It is now late and I can't let you know about the wheat. I will speak to Barzalone about it tomorrow and tell him to inform you.

The flour that I sent you was twenty-four full bushels, exactly the amount it was when it came from the mill. Our mare carried nine bushels, the one belonging to our gardener carried six bushels, Tantera's carried another six, and Schiavo's donkey carried three, so add up those amounts.[369] I myself saw it measured out into eight sacks, three bushels to each sack.

On Sunday I sent our Nanni to the dovecote at Filettole to find out if there were any squabs, and he says that there aren't any—apart from very small ones, and many eggs. So there will be some in eight days but not before. I haven't sent you anything else because you are better supplied there.

Nannino da Volterra was splitting a rock and fell to the ground, and he says he is hurt. I don't know if you will have as many doubts about this as I have. I will write to you about how he is when I have more time.

From your Margherita, in Prato.

[Added by the scribe:]
We haven't been able to send the bread or the other things because neither Argomento nor Nanni da Santa Chiara is going to Florence, and no one else can carry it for us. Argomento is not going because he is attending to his packhorse, which was […] and Nanni is no longer transporting goods.

---

368. Niccolò dell'Ammannato Tecchini was ill. See FD 100.

369. Margherita refers here to the farm workers Schiatta di Niccolò, or "Tantera" (see note 139, above), and Piero di Lenzo, or Schiavo (see note 354, above).

Monna Margherita asks you to make sure that she gets her prayer book soon, and to remember to get it bound.[370]

To Francesco di Marco himself, in Florence.
Received from Prato, 23 May 1397.

Letter 131 (1401806)
23 May 1397
Prato

In the name of God. 23 May 1397.

This evening we received your letters, and among them there was one addressed to Niccolò di Piero, one to Giorgio di Donato, and another to Bernardo. We delivered them all. I wanted to send you the basket of bread with Dino del Bodda but he refused to carry it.[371] We have been more upset about this than you, and now the bread is hard because it was made three days ago. I will send you plenty of every kind, tomorrow. So that the castle doesn't surrender for lack of food, make some flat bread if you don't know how to make proper bread. You may lack bread, but I lack money because neither Niccolò nor I have been able to get any from anyone. I borrowed three *lire* from Arrigo di Cafaggio this evening, and he will be in Florence tomorrow and will inform you about the price of wheat.

There is nothing else to say about Francesca. Do as you see fit. I am not happy about sending you vermilion samite for my prayer book. I want black. If you want to fob me off with the nuns' style of cover, there is no need to tell me. I could do that myself. I don't want any sort of white or pink on it because it would dazzle me. I want it black. Please get it done quickly, because it upsets me that I am not reading the hours as I used to.[372]

---

370. See letters 96 and 98.

371. Dino del Bodda became a regular carter for Francesco. He is first mentioned in letters of 1385.

372. See letters 96, 98, and 125.

We will get all the pack animals ready tomorrow so that when you send for them you will be able to have them.

I haven't said anything to the baker. I will tell him tomorrow morning. Remember to send me the kerchiefs or at least those that Bellozzo bought for you.[373] I enclose a letter that came from Pistoia.

If Dino agrees to take them tomorrow morning, I will send you twelve loaves of bread of one kind and twelve of the other, as well as the napkins and the other things we wrote to you about, but not the pannier of chestnuts,

Tomorrow I will have plenty of bread made, and I will send you some on Friday unless you come here in the meantime. I'll say no more for now. May God protect you always.

From your Margherita, in Prato.

To Francesco di Marco da Prato himself, in Florence.
Received from Prato, 24 May 1397.

Letter 132 (1401807)
24 May 1397
Prato

In the name of God. 24 May 1397.

This morning we received your letters concerning the mare, so we were thinking of sending her tomorrow morning. She doesn't seem to have been washed properly, although they followed the farrier's instructions. Have her looked at thoroughly there, because the farrier hasn't yet made the horse shoes and Marchetto says she needs them immediately, so see she is attended to.[374]

This morning we sent you a letter with Meo, the nephew of Ser Schiatta, about a matter that seemed important to us. It concerned a

---

373. Bellozzo Bartoli was a Florentine spice merchant and friend of Francesco.

374. Marchetto, or Marco di Feo Ridolfi, was recruited by Francesco for his warehouse in Avignon.

loan agreement drawn up by the officials in charge of notarial deeds.[375]
If you haven't received the letters, make sure you get them.

There is nothing else to say for now. May Christ protect you.

Greetings from your Margherita, in Prato.

To Francesco di Marco himself, in Florence.
Received from Prato, 25 May 1397.

Letter 133 (1401808)
24 May 1397
Prato

In the name of God. 24 May 1397.

We are sending you twelve loaves of bread with Schiavo, our worker from Filettole. We are not sending you any more for now because Dino del Bodda is not going to Florence, and neither is Argomento nor anyone else who could bring you some.

The baker's assistant has left the bakery because of a dispute about his salary. He wants thirty *soldi* a month, and the baker refuses to pay him more than twenty-five. They also fell out over the assistant not wanting to remain with the baker during the time of reaping and threshing. That is when the baker wants him most, so he himself can go and earn money at the harvest. There is nothing else to say here.

May Christ protect you.

The baker cannot go to work at Il Palco.

Greetings from your Margherita, in Prato.

To Francesco di Marco da Prato, in Florence.
Received from Prato, 25 May 1397.

---

375. Legal contracts between individuals or parties were taxed on a proportionate basis. A magistrate and officials, the Maestri della Gabella dei Contratti, enforced the tax. See also letter 134.

Letter 134 (1401809)
24 May 1397
Prato

In the name of God, 24 May 1397.

Today we were fined by the office for tax on contracts.[376] Ser Chimenti says that you paid and have the receipt regarding the tax. So go to the tax office and see what has to be done to recover the money.

In this package we are sending you the receipt that the messengers gave us.

I have no more to add for now. May Christ protect you.

From your Margherita, greetings.

To Francesco di Marco himself, in Florence.
Received from Prato, 26 May 1397.

Letter 135 (1401810)
6 June 1397
Prato

In the name of God. 6 June 1397.

This evening I received a letter from you, as well as one addressed to Barzalone, one to Ser Schiatta, one to Ser Nicola, and one to Stefano di Ser Piero.[377] I had Paolo di Bertino deliver all of them.[378]

The reason I didn't send you the bread was because neither Argomento nor Dino del Bodda went to Florence. Argomento will come tomorrow morning, and I will get him to bring a basket containing sixteen white loaves and six of the kind we use for the household. I am not sending you the squabs because they have been kept here too long. I will keep them here for the household. I am also sending you two napkins with the pannier, so make sure you get everything.

376. See letter 132.

377. Margherita refers to the communal notary, Ser Nicola di Iacopo da Montecatini, and to Stefano Cepperelli.

378. This is Paolo di Bertino Verzoni. See note 127, above.

We will give your message to Messer Guelfo's wife, Monna Piera, tomorrow morning; this evening it is too late.[379]

I'll say no more for now. May God protect you always.

From your Margherita, in Prato.

To Francesco di Marco da Prato, in Florence.
Received from Prato, 7 [June] 1397.[380]

Letter 136 (1401811)
8 June 1397
Prato

In the name of God. 8 June 1397.

This evening I received a letter from you. I respond here.

What Barzalone told you about my being unwell is true. I have the usual pains that I suffer from. We are very puzzled about a letter from you to Niccolò that he is asking about. It wasn't among ours. There was a letter addressed to Barzalone, one to Bernabò, one to Stefano di Messer Piero, one to Ser Nicola, and one to Ser Schiatta. Look for the one to Niccolò di Piero. It is probably still there on the table.

I am sending you a small basket of morello cherries because I think that for various reasons you have many types of choleric humors, and the cherries are acidic and will reduce them. Please remember my saying: we reap what we sow in life. I am very pleased that Francesca, Niccolò, and the others are well. Tell Francesca to give Argomento the cage in which I sent her the squabs, and give her a few chemises for Caterina.

We will stop now because we are expecting you tomorrow evening. May God protect you.

We will give your message to Messer Guelfo's wife. She said she would stay until the feast days, as we invited her to do. I enclose a letter from Bernabò.

379. Monna Piera de' Cavalcanti, the wife of Guelfo di Simone Pugliesi, was from a prominent Florentine family.

380. The scribe mistakenly wrote July here.

From your Margherita, in Prato.

To Francesco di Marco da Prato, in Florence.
Received from Prato, 9 June 1397.

Letter 137 (1401812)
18 June 1397
Prato

In the name of God. 18 June 1397.

I am writing to remind you: tell Domenico di Cambio to get enough worsted cloth for two hoods. Tell him not to buy it unless it is fine and beautiful, because I want it to be of the best quality. Get him also to buy an ounce of light-colored thread suitable for embroidering silk hangings for Messer Piero's wife, Monna Simona; and tell him to make sure it is as thin as possible.

I would have sent you some bread except that Barzalone tells me you will be here tomorrow.

Remind Francesca about my black thread.

Barzalone told me that you now regret the loan you made. He meant well, but I am very worried about it because I think these are wearisome matters and they also worry you. May God make things turn out for the best. May God protect you always.

From your Margherita, in Prato.

To Francesco di Marco da Prato, in Florence.
Received from Prato, 19 June 1397.

Letter 138 (1401813)
11 July 1397
Prato

In the name of God. 11 July 1397.

I am writing to remind you to bring my veils when you come here, and to tell Francesca I am still searching for a serving girl for her. If she has found someone in Florence, tell her to let me know so that I don't send her another from here.

With this letter I enclose one that came today from Pistoia and two letters from Barzalone; one is for you and the other is for Giovanni di Giovanni Aldobrandini.[381]

There is nothing else to say for now. May God protect you always.

Nanni says that Antonio Micocchi says he can't fix the carts tomorrow, but will do them on Saturday without fail.

From your Margherita, in Prato.

To Francesco di Marco da Prato, in Florence.
Received from Prato, 15 July 1397.

Letter 139 (1401815)
28 August 1397
Prato

In the name of God. 28 August 1397.

Yesterday evening Argomento delivered your letter, and we received all the things you sent with it, so all is well.

I received the text of the statutes. I will have it copied and take good care of it. There is no more to say about Bindo's return from Venice.[382] Give him and Nanna my greetings, as you see fit.

---

381. Giovanni, or Nanni Aldobrandini, had been *Podestà* in Prato in 1386. Francesco cultivated good relations with him because of his political influence. See Hayez, "Le rire du marchand," 455, and Mazzei, *Lettere di un notaro*, 1:4.

382. This is Bindo Piaciti.

Today I will send Guido to the kitchen garden at La Chiusura to collect figs for drying. I think they will be good. Zaccheria says to give Goro the money for which he is asking.[383] It should come to three *lire* and […] *soldi*. He came and worked here for a while yesterday evening and will do the same this evening; he will finish using that lime that was left over.

Monna Simona di Messer Piero was waiting for the horses yesterday evening so she could go to Florence today. As soon as they arrive, she will leave immediately.

Biagio, the carter, has not come. I sent him a message, but he was not at home. If he comes here, I will pass on the orders you gave me.

We are sending you a pannier of walnuts, peaches, and grapes with Argomento. If we had been able to obtain larger quantities, we would have sent them to you. However, I think there must be some fine ones in Florence.

There is no more to say for now. May God protect you always.

From Monna Margherita, in Prato.

To Francesco di Marco da Prato, Florence.
Received from Prato, 28 August 1397.

Letter 140 (1401814)
28 August 1397
Prato

In the name of God. 28 August 1397.

Argomento delivered your letter as well as what you sent with it. I answer it here, though briefly.

I am pleased you received the pannier of walnuts and peaches that I sent with Argomento. Send me back that pannier, because it is

---

383. Iacopo d'Agostino, or Zaccheria, was a stonemason who worked on Francesco's building projects, and Goro di Niccolò was a Florentine stone carver who supplied more specialized stonework such as doors, window frames, and mantelpieces. See Cavaciocchi, "The Merchant and Building," 138–63.

not ours; if there are any other baskets there, send them back to us as well because there are hardly any left here and we need them to gather the figs. So send them back as soon as you can.

Monna Simona di Messer Piero has hired horses so as not to delay her departure, because she thinks she has been here too long. I told her that you were planning to come today but for some reason you could not. I said you would be here tomorrow, and that she would have the horses on Thursday. She does not wish to wait so long, so she is coming to Florence tomorrow. This evening Zaccheria will finish using that small quantity of lime.

Niccolaio Martini came to see Monna Margherita this evening and says that Biagio di Bartolo Tanfuro is very ill; he needs a pound of cassia pods, the best to be found. So make sure he is well looked after: whatever the price, as long as the cassia is good.[384]

I have no more to add. May God protect you always.

From Monna Margherita, in Prato.

List of things Francesco leaves us to do today, 24 August, as he goes to Florence.[385]

To Francesco di Marco da Prato, in Florence.
Received from Prato, 28 August 1397.

---

384. Biagio di Bartolo Tanfuro's son Domenico had been Francesco's partner in collecting the wine tax for the commune of Prato from 1389 to 1390, and apparently owed him money. In April 1398 the Magistracy of the Eight Defenders investigated the matter. In 1400 he owed Francesco 500 *lire* and was jailed for debt. See Brambilla and Hayez, "La maison des fantômes," 175–76.

385. This list does not survive.

Letter 141 (1401816)
23 October 1397
Prato

In the name of God. 23 October 1397.

This morning we received a letter from you that Carlo sent on to us. As it was too late, I could not reply—nor send you what you wanted, apart from two caps rolled up in a large cloth that I sent with Argomento, as well as a letter saying I will bring everything else with me.

Today I sent Guido to tell Ser Schiatta to let Tommaso know that you were expecting him.[386] He says that since it didn't stop raining yesterday he could not get any message to him at all, but he would do so today if he could. He told Biagio di Bartolo to come to an agreement with Matteo the miller.[387] He said that they should go to the *Podestà* and formalize it and that Biagio should ask either Ser Schiatta or Niccolaio Martini to go to the commune on his behalf, and Matteo should call on whomsoever he liked and should do so as quickly as possible. Biagio said he would be in the piazza and would do so. Biagio went to Iacopo da San Donnino's place twice and could not find him. He left a message with his son to tell him to cut the beams. Tomorrow Biagio will return and tell Iacopo personally what he did about Matteo.

We heard from Besso about the wood supplier. He says he has not come yet, but when he does he will tell him to bring a load, as you require.[388] Guarnachetta and Nanni di Senso say that when they are able to get the donkey drivers, they will bring the earth to the threshing floor. We will keep the door open so the donkeys can get through. Bartolomeo the apothecary was not there because […] had come. He left a message to pass on when he came back.

They put [the wine barrels] one on top of the other, and cut the hemp that was soaking in the vats. We milled the flour, and I had the small wine barrel emptied and the barrels in the *loggia* repaired.

---

386. Tommaso del Bianco, a Florentine merchant and Ser Schiatta's father-in-law, had known Francesco in Avignon. He had retired to the small hamlet of Leccio.

387. Biagio di Bartolo was to negotiate with Matteo about trees that Francesco wanted to buy for his building works. See FD 110.

388. The wood merchant was a friend of Besso (a builder). See FD 109.

Because the weather is humid, we didn't wash the barrels. We will see to them properly. The rafters that were to be brought have been delivered; that is, thirty to Bartolo's house, thirty to the garden near the house, and thirty to the kitchen garden. The lime has been prepared, and the sand and rocks will be brought when possible. Because the Bisenzio River is very high, it was not possible to collect anything; if it had been possible to bring some sand, they would have prepared the mortar that still remained to be done for lack of sand. As soon as we can get some, we will do it, as there isn't much to be done.

Nanni says that Monna Mellina's Piero has baked some lime. Tell us what you want done. Do you want it to be slaked, or would you prefer us to wait until you come back?

[…] we have not decided when Nanni will come there. If the weather is fine, we will keep him here; if it is not, we will send him to you, although he is always busy whatever the weather. Nonetheless, if the weather is bad, we will send him. We had some bread made to send you, but we won't send any because the baker ruined it and also because Argomento can't tell us for certain if he is going; but if he does, we will send you a pannier with plenty of the finest loaves and oranges.

I will say no more. May God protect you always.

From your Margherita, in Prato.

To Francesco di Marco da Prato, in the Piazza Tornaquinci, Florence.

Letter 142 (1401817)
23 October 1397
Prato

In the name of God. 23 October 1397.

The reason for this letter is that on Sunday evening Ballerino sent us a quarter of a boar, weighing eleven pounds.[389] On Monday morning we gave it to Argomento to bring to you, but because of the

---

389. Giovanni di Bartolo da Carmignano, or Ballerino, was a textile manufacturer based in Pistoia and a long-time associate of Francesco's.

weather, he did not go to Florence because it did not stop raining all day. For this reason I decided it would have been too stale to bring on Tuesday, so I divided it into three portions. I sent one to Barzalone and the other to Niccolò, and we kept the other for ourselves. I had Guido write to Ballerino to tell him that we had received it, that you were in Florence, and that we had sent it to you. So if you write to Ballerino, thank him and tell him that you got it.

Marco's wife, Monna Agnola, came to see me today.[390] It seems that Ser Schiatta sent for Marco. They exchanged words, and among other things, Ser Schiatta told him that, come what may, on Tuesday he will put into effect the legal proceedings he has in hand. Marco and Monna Agnola were distressed, and begged me for the love of God to ask him to delay the matter for a few days. I contacted him, and he promised me he would not take any further steps before you arrived. I don't think he would have gone ahead unless he had some good reason. If you wish to write to him, do so.

It has not stopped raining here. Besso and Allodola were here today and prepared that lime. They brought the thirty rafters to the garden and another thirty to Bartolo, who is getting them ready, and they took another eight to the kitchen garden. Nanni was working with them. They could not bring either sand or rocks because the Bisenzio River has been very high.

Remember to send us some candles—and to get my mantle if you can. May God protect you always.

From your Margherita, in Prato.

To Francesco di Marco da Prato in Piazza Tornaquinci, Florence.
Received from Prato, 23 October 1397.

---

390. Monna Agnola was the wife of Marco di Tano, the apothecary.

Letter 143 (1401818)
24 October 1397
Prato

In the name of God. 24 October 1397.

We received a letter from you today, and the boy who delivered it said that Bartolomeo the apothecary had brought it from Florence. You said in the letter we received yesterday evening that Foffo would bring it.[391]

I received mine at terce, and Ser Schiatta received his at vespers, and he seems to know who brought it and what happened. I sent to Bartolomeo the apothecary to ask why he had forwarded one letter when there should have been two. He answered that he had not dispatched any letters. Ser Schiatta knows perfectly well who brought him his and what happened, and he will be able to tell you.

Because night has fallen and it is raining, I don't want to send anyone to Ser Schiatta's house to find out the reason, and perhaps he would not tell me anyway.

I made a mistake in saying they had worked that day, but they did work the previous day. Yesterday morning they stayed there until terce. They brought twenty-three rafters and carried many barrowloads of stones. They then left because the weather didn't permit them to do anything else.

Today the miller did not do any building because of the unsettled weather, and it also rained today. Today Allodola and Besso were there and they carried stones all day, as they claim.

I am pleased about what you did with my mantle. We received Carlo's letter in the morning, not the evening.[392] Because the letter was sealed and Guido was about to take it to Argomento, we gave him the caps in a hurry, and I decided to give him the oranges because we knew you needed them. We did not write another letter because it was late, and that is why we did not answer you item by item.

---

391. Foffo is introduced by Francesco as a young lad (FD 109).

392. This is Carlo di Francesco Mainardi Guazzalotti.

I sent your message to Nardo, and he came here.[393] I will send you some bread and chestnuts if the carters can bring them. I will send you some bread every day, because they frequently have large loads and cannot bring all of it at once. The bread is not very white. Regarding the flour that has come back from the mill, if you want us to send some sacks of any other grain, write and we will do it. We will send you the cheeses and do what you say with the rest.

Nanni di Guiduccio was here yesterday evening and says that tomorrow, if the weather is fine, he will work in the kitchen garden together with the miller; but the weather does not look promising.

Nanni will see whether the lime is good enough, and will slake it when he can get some sand. Niccolò di Piero received the textile combs.

I cannot tell you about the wall at Il Palco with any certainty, but Schiavo was there today and he did not speak about any damage. Guido was there yesterday and did not see anything.

Nanni di Guiduccio and our Nanni will go there tomorrow at the morning bell. I will tell you more in another letter. Nanni says he does not recall that you said anything to him about the four *moggia* of lime, but I reminded him that you wanted to tell him something but could not remember what. Was it this perhaps? We do not know what work Biagio has done, but in our next letter we will tell you.

We have checked all the things you sent with Argomento against your letter, and we received everything; so all is in order.

We will buy the lime from Bartolo da Mangone. We have done the pickles.

Goro the stonecarver came here with Iacopo da San Donnino. They asked me to show them the space where I wanted to make a small kitchen garden. They are convinced that the garden could not be put on the side facing Messer Piero.[394] They think that the area near the well in Via Porcellatico would be suitable. Goro will consult you when he gets to Florence.

I will say no more for now. May God protect you.

Nanni di Guiduccio asks you to remember his lining.

393. Francesco had sent a message to the cobbler Lionardo di Calendino, instructing him to bring papers regarding a legal matter to Ser Niccolò, the Florentine notary (FD 107).

394. Margherita refers here to her neighbor, Piero Rinaldeschi.

Our Nanni says that Bencino begs you to assist him with the *prestanza* tax, if you can.

We are sending you three dozen loaves of bread with Argomento. Send us back the bags and the things we have sent you. The bread is in two bags because the carters do not want such large bundles.

Your Margherita, in Prato.

To Francesco di Marco da Prato, in Piazza Tornaquinci, Florence. Received from Prato, 25 October 1397.

Letter 144 (1401819)
25 October 1397
Prato

In the name of God. Amen. 25 October 1397.

Nardo di Calendino delivered your letter today, as well as one for Barzalone, one for Niccolò di Piero, and one for Francesco di Matteo.[395] We had them all delivered safely. We wrote to you in a separate message about the letter for Ser Schiatta.

The builders were not at the kitchen garden yesterday. Even if they had been, they would not have been able to do anything because of the rain. They were there today and had good weather. Nanni di Guiduccio, Nanni the miller, Manesco, Besso, and Allodola came and built the foundations up above the ground level, and built the arch that faces Biagio's place. I think they will also be at the small garden tomorrow to use the lime that is there, and on Saturday they will finish the threshing floor. Tomorrow Nanni will slake four *moggia* of lime at the small garden, and if he can, he will slake a bushel at the kitchen garden on Saturday or Monday. I would buy some lime from Bartolo da Mangone for making the oven. As for keeping records, I leave it to Guido and Nanni. I remind them every evening before they have supper, and they say they will do it. I can't do much about the bread because I have none to send you, as the household here needs it. I also

---

395. This is Francesco di Matteo Bellandi di Prato. See letter 38.

wrote asking you which wheat you wanted us to get, so we could send a sack of good-quality grain to the mill here.

I would have sent you the chestnuts tomorrow morning, but Argomento says he has such heavy loads that he cannot bring them. I will give him a round of cheese instead because it slipped my mind this morning. If you have to stay there after Sunday, write to me and I will buy some flour from Barzalone, make some fine loaves, and send them to you.

We will put the tiles where you say. I told Iacopo about the wood, and he said he would go to see Paoletto and get him to cut it. Because Paoletto has had some difficulty and did not do it, I will ask Iacopo to get him to cut it.

Barzalone came here and I told him about Matteo the miller, and he told me that I should not get involved because Niccolò would tell you all the details.[396]

We told Nanni about the lining. We will tell you in the next letter whether Piero will bake the lime or not, and likewise about the bricks and all the rest.[397] Concerning Simone's mother, I went to Monna Gaia's place and found her there. I asked her to come here to see me because I wanted to tell her many things. I also begged Monna Gaia to persuade her to come to me because you had asked me to discuss things with her. She is very deaf, and I did not want to stand there shouting so that everyone could hear. She has not come yet. I will send for her and give her your message.[398]

We received twenty-five *lire* from Stefano the cobbler. We needed some money, so we took this amount. We will see if we can get any more of the money owed to us.

Regarding the chestnuts, we will send for Bartolo and tell him what you say.

Perhaps we will eat the turtledoves. What does it mean, that you have to remind us about every little thing? The horse that you put in

---

396. See letters 141 and 147.

397. Piero di Monna Mellina, the brick maker and kiln owner from Filettole.

398. In FD 110, Francesco had instructed Margherita to send for the widow of his partner Andrea Bellandi, to reassure her that he would help her financially. Bellandi had died in January 1393, and his sons, Simone and Matteo, were under Francesco's guardianship. See also letter 146.

the stable here is worthless, although he would be fine for a gentleman because he knows how to bow. These are some of the never-ending problems we have to deal with. As for his other qualities, he eats well and carries little.

There has not been any damage to the Saracens' wall.[399] We will ensure that the barrels and the door are looked after.

That is all I have to say now. May God protect you always.

Return the sack and the pannier that I sent you as soon as you can.

Enclosed with this there is a letter from Ser Schiatta and one from Barzalone.

Your Margherita, in Prato.

To Francesco di Marco da Prato, in Piazza Tornaquinci, Florence. Received from Prato, 26 October 1397.

Letter 145 (1401820)
26 October 1397
Prato

In the name of God. 26 October 1397.

I sent you a letter with Dino del Bodda this morning telling you what was necessary then, so I have less to say in this. I sent you twelve loaves of bread with him and a round of marzolino cheese.[400] We have not heard back from you.

The reason for this letter is to inform you of what has been done today, which I know will please you. The lime from the kitchen garden has been used up, and tomorrow they will work on the threshing floor. The weather has been good. They slaked four *moggia* of lime in the kitchen garden, and in the garden they slaked one *moggio* for the oven. They brought stones, bricks, sand, lime, and the things they needed.

---

399. The Bisenzio River was so high that Francesco was worried that the retaining wall at Il Palco had been damaged (FD 110).

400. Marzolino is a cheese made from sheep's milk or buffalo milk.

Piero di Monna Mellina says that he will not be baking any more lime after this. He has plenty of lime that he says is good and easily worked and well baked; so just tell us what you want done.

We think you will be here tomorrow or the next day, so we will not say any more. May God protect you always.

Your Margherita, in Prato.

To Francesco di Marco da Prato himself, in Piazza Tornaquinci, Florence.
Received from Prato, 27 October 1397.

Letter 146 (1401821)
27 October 1397
Prato

In the name of God. 27 October 1397.

Ridolfo Lanfranco's son delivered one of your letters, as well as one for Niccolò di Piero, one for Barzalone, one for Ser Schiatta, one for Biagio di Bartolo, and one for Iacopo di San Donnino. I had them all delivered this evening, so everything has been attended to. This is my reply.

We spoke to Nanni di Guiduccio about the lining for his wife and he says she wants it to fit over her gown, and it should be loose and have sleeves, and not be cut away in front.[401] Now, since she is a very big woman, I will send for Nanni tomorrow and tell him to make her try one of mine that I will give him. If it fits her well then I will send it to you so you can use it as a model.

Tomorrow Ser Schiatta is coming and I will find out about everything. Because you are not coming back, I have decided to send Nanni to you, and he is glad to come and will tell you in person how much work has been done, and if you want to advise him of anything, you will be able to, and if you have anything to send, you will be able to do that too.[402] I am glad you ate the tench. Nanni says, "I don't

401. See FD 111.

402. This is the stonemason Giovanni di Guiduccio.

have any idea what happened to the wheat that was winnowed for the household. The other flour has been used."

I sent for Simone's mother.[403] I spoke to her, and offered what I thought was appropriate. She answered that she had urgent need of fourteen or fifteen florins, not for food or expenses but so she could get back her dowry. She says she does not know what to do because she has nothing to pawn, and she begged me to write and tell you. This is something she cannot do without.

I am sending a large quantity of figs and broad beans for Cilia and for that girl. I am also sending some figs, broad beans, and chick-peas to my aunt, Monna Giovanna. Send them on to her.

Tell us where we should buy the downspouts for the cistern and for the storehouse that is being made at the small kitchen garden, because there aren't any.

I have no more to add. May God protect you always.

Your Margherita, in Prato.

To Francesco di Marco da Prato himself, in Florence.
Received 28 October 1397.

Letter 147 (1401822)
28 October 1397
Prato

In the name of God. 28 October 1397.

We received your letter from Nanni, and this is my reply.

I reminded Barzalone and Niccolò about the matter concerning Matteo the miller. Ser Schiatta did not come to see me today. It has not stopped raining all day.

As regards the wheat to send to the mill, we will do it. I will reply to Simone's mother as seems best.

I am pleased that you did as I suggested with the things I sent.

---

403. Simone's mother, Piera, was the widow of Francesco's relative and partner Andrea di Matteo Bellandi.

As for the lining for Nanni's wife, they seem unable to say what they want, and they do not know the difference between a coarse material and a smooth one. But I can't see why she would want a high-quality lining when she will not be wearing it against the body, so it would be better if you bought a coarse one. He wants to spend up to three florins, and even more if you think it appropriate. I will send one of her gowns. Make it on that model, and make it hang more broadly at the front—not tight. And make it longer. This way she will be properly covered. She wants the sleeves wide and a little open at the ends. Have it made broad enough for her to put on easily.

I will send to Il Palco to find out if there are any downspouts, and we will do as you say.

Regarding the smocks, you say you will send me the length and the width that is required.

If I were not going to take medicine tomorrow morning and the builders were not going to be working here as well, you would have seen me tomorrow with the entire household, weather permitting. I would have brought my young ducks; we would have celebrated All Saints' Day with Villana, Bellozza, and everyone; and I would have fulfilled my vow.[404] I am expecting you here on the evening of All Saints' Day. Remember the candles. Send my greetings to everyone. May God protect you always.

Your Margherita in Prato.

To Francesco di Marco da Prato, in Piazza Tornaquinci, Florence. Received from Prato, 30 October 1397.

404. Margherita refers here to Stoldo's wife, Villana, and to Bartolomea, the wife of Bellozzo Bartoli.

Letter 148 (1401823)
29 October 1397
Prato

In the name of God. 29 October 1397.

This evening we received a letter from you and also one for Barzalone. I had it delivered to him. I will answer briefly because the letter arrived late, and also because we believe that you are coming here on the eve of All Saints' Day. Nanni di Guiduccio's wife came to see me today with one of her gowns, and told me that it is too small for her. I marked on the shoulder how much wider she wants the new lining, and I marked it at the waist, as she wants the same width from the top down to there. From the waist down, if they think it is too broad, they should make it the size they think best. I tacked on a piece of cloth to show how much longer it should be. I put another piece of cloth to mark how far down the split in the front should be. Don't broaden the split in the middle. Don't take any notice of the fact that the gown is cut away at the front. Make sure that the lining is comfortable enough for her to put it on easily. She wants it to be black and warm, and she wants the sleeves broader and longer than these ones.[405]

I will pass on your message to Niccolò tomorrow. Today Nanni slaked two *moggia* of lime at Il Palco. He says that after he did it he saw the assessors of the commune with some other men from Prato. It was late when he left. We do not know what happened afterward. Niccolò or Barzalone will probably tell you.

The builders were at the kitchen garden today. The weather did not give them any problems.

If you are not coming back tomorrow, tell us if you want us to buy anything at the market on the eve of All Saints' Day, and we will do so.

Besso says he wants you to get a lining for his wife, either white or black and costing up to eight *lire*. May God protect you always.

From your Margherita in Prato.

To Francesco di Marco da Prato in Piazza Tornaquinci, Florence. Received from Prato, 30 October 1397.

405. See letters 146 and 147.

Letter 149 (1401824)
20 November 1397
Prato

In the name of God. [...] November 1397.

The reason for this letter is that on Sunday morning, upon opening the strongbox where I keep my rings, I didn't find the one given to
me by Niccolaio di Bonaccorso.[406] You can imagine the upset and pain
that I felt for all sorts of reasons. All Sunday I did nothing but search,
and today I did the same, and I got Niccolò di Piero and Stefano di
Ser Piero to search the stalls of all the pawnbrokers. I have left no
stone unturned, but up to now nothing has been found. I cannot give
you any explanation as to when it was lost, because I never wore it; it
didn't fit properly. I can't imagine how it got lost, unless it happened
this way. It might have fallen in among the clothes, and when someone
shook them out it fell onto the ground from the windows. Or else it
was taken from the box because, if it were one of those I wear, I would
not be so surprised. I would say to myself that I could have dropped it
or left it somewhere. I am more at a loss to explain this than if it had
been one of the really good ones. I had the street swept, and I carefully
sieved what was collected. Some people have told me one thing, some
another, but for a number of reasons I decided that you should know
everything. I would have waited until your arrival to give you the bad
news, but then I thought you could search there or get others to search
for it, so I am telling you before you get here. You should recognize it
because the other day, when you were doing the inventory, you noted
it and you must have picked it up. It is a sapphire.[407] I had a letter
written to Stefano in Pistoia telling him about it.[408] I can't say anything
else to you because I am so upset, I don't know where I am. May God
protect you.

406. The lost ring may have been given to Margherita in 1387, because Francesco's friend
from Avignon, the spice dealer Niccolaio Bonaccorso, visited Prato between July and November of that year. See Hayez, "Tucte sono patrie," 90.

407. The inventory was made in July 1397 and lists the ring as "1 blue sapphire with a gold
ring, given by Niccolaio di Bonaccorso, cost 10 florins." See Origo, *The Merchant of Prato*,
303.

408. This is Stefano Guazzalotti.

From your Margherita, in Prato.

To Francesco di Marco da Prato, in Piazza Tornaquinci, Florence. Received from Prato, 20 November 1397.

Letter 150 (1401825)
25 November 1397
Prato

In the name of God. 25 November 1397.

Fattorino showed me the passage, which you told him to bring to my attention, where you say that it is bad for you and for me that this ring has been lost. It is certainly true that it is bad for me, and I don't believe that there is anyone so upset about it as I am—for many reasons, and especially for your sake—because from the moment I lost it I have never felt well, neither day nor night. I thought you would console me, realizing how much pain I felt, and would feel sorry for me. If you are tempted to say that it will do my soul good, I will answer that it is not so at all. I have never been so ill that I wanted to resort to charms or spells, but now, I tell you, I would pray to the devils in hell if I thought that I would find it. I would do this for your sake, not for mine, because if it were up to me, I wouldn't dream of it, even if I lost three rings worth as much as this one. Such things occur every day, and I am not the first to whom this has happened.

I gather you are surprised that Niccolò didn't write to you about it.[409] The reason is that I told him I wanted to tell you about it myself, so he didn't write. I received the pelts from Nardo di Calendino, and tomorrow I will order the overgown.[410] I haven't had the doublet. When will you send the lining?

Guido came this morning at terce with the large mule, and said that he had to return at once to Grignano. I said that he was welcome to go; and if Ser Lapo agreed, he should bring both mules here and

---

409. Margherita refers to Niccolò di Piero di Giunta del Rosso.

410. This is Lionardo di Calendino. See note 393, above.

take them back tomorrow. After that it didn't stop raining, so I think he is probably still at Grignano or has gone to Florence.

We would have sent you some bread—but there are only about ten loaves, and we don't have any panniers. Because we are expecting you tomorrow anyway, we won't send it.

Barzalone says the nephews of Matteo the miller have begun to dig a ditch in that field where the trees are, and it is their intention to extend it to the new wall that you have had built. If you want to give them any instructions, let us know.

That's all I will say in this. May God protect you.

From your Margherita, in Prato.

To Francesco di Marco, in Florence.
Received from Prato, 26 November 1397.

Letter 151 (1401915)
12 March 1398
Florence

In the name of God. 12 March 1398.

Today I received a letter from you; because Fattorino was dining here, I got him to open it, and I have understood what you say. I respond here as necessary.

It's true, what Benedetto told you and Fattorino wrote: about the return of Niccolò's hiccups.[411] I delayed sending a message telling you about it because I heard that you were busy overseeing the planting of the vines; but if it had been necessary, I would have sent Fattorino immediately. Now, because of the medicine he took yesterday, the hiccups have stopped and the fever has passed. Nevertheless, I have decided to come to Prato—because I see it will be a long business; but it would be good if you could come here before I leave. Monna Taddea would really like to speak to you, and so would Monna Giovanna

---

411. Niccolò dell'Ammannato Tecchini.

di Paolo Mattei.[412] Nevertheless, I am ready to come whenever you like.[413]

Concerning the mantle, I came to no prior agreement because she didn't send me details of how to pay for it, nor I to her, and therefore I will pay her in the florins they use here; that is, in sealed florins.[414]

I got Stoldo to deliver the letter addressed to Ser Giovanni Baronetti.[415] I believe he will have trouble paying. I will wait to see how he answers, and if the answer is not to my satisfaction, I will write a letter to Monna Simona, as I see fit.

Fattorino will go to Niccolò Piaciti and give him your message.

Schiavo's barrel of oil is empty. I will send it to you at the first opportunity, and also the oil barrel that you sent to Manno.[416]

We have divided the sturgeon in two and I will send it to you as soon as possible; and I will also send you some tallow candles.

I gave Stoldo the note that Barzalone sent to Fattorino; but as soon as Fattorino has finished this letter, he will go to the warehouse and find out from Stoldo what the note says and will act on it.

Commend me to Monna Ghita and tell her that I will be there soon.[417] I'll say no more. May God protect you.

From Your Margherita, in Florence.

---

412. Monna Giovanna was the widow of Paolo Mattei, a Florentine merchant who operated in Avignon from at least the 1330s until his death in 1380. Mattei may have been instrumental in Dianora Gherardini's move to Avignon, and appears to have been her relative. When Giovanna returned to Tuscany with her son Talaranno, Margherita and Francesco often invited her to family gatherings.

413. Just over a week later Francesco was in Florence, and Margherita was obliged to return to Prato to keep an eye on the household there.

414. Sealed florins (*fiorini di suggello*) were issued by the Florentine government in purses sealed with red wax and stamped with an official value. These gold coins were chipped or worn down, and had therefore lost some of their integrity. Although they circulated at a slightly lower price than freshly minted florins, the sealed purses were used when large transactions were made because they eliminated the need to count large numbers of coins. See Richard Goldthwaite, *The Economy of Renaissance Florence* (Baltimore, MD: The Johns Hopkins University Press, 2009), 52–54.

415. Ser Giovanni di Barnetto owed Francesco four florins (FD 115).

416. This is Manno d'Albizo degli Agli.

417. Monna Ghita, Ghetto Guizzelmi's wife, was Francesco's housekeeper.

[Added by the scribe Fattorino:]

[The letters were] delayed until today because there was no one to take them. Then we received a letter from you. Because Argomento wants to leave, there is no time to reply to it properly. Niccolò is now fine although he still has a little fever, and Monna Margherita thinks there is no need to bring Barzalone with you because she wouldn't want to leave on the same day that you arrive. As you know, there is nowhere for him to sleep here. Once you are here, you can send for him.

I will have the letter copied as you ask, and I will also do everything else and reply to you about everything.

We are sending you ten pounds of tallow candles and four and a half pounds of sturgeon, and the barrel.

To Francesco di Marco, in Prato.
Received from Florence, 13 March 1398.

Letter 152 (1401826)
20 March 1398
Prato

In the name of God. 20 March 1398.

I received your letter that Niccolò di Piero forwarded to me. Here is my answer.

Regarding sending Caterina's house gown, I will send one as you wish, but in my view, it is unnecessary for many reasons. It seems to me that she has a perfectly good house gown, considering her father's situation and the difficulties ahead. I think you should put a bridle on the mule by ensuring that her house gown is not made of too fine a cloth and the [...] has about ten ounces of silver and the belt no more than six.[418] I noticed that Strozza di Carlo's daughter, who is your neighbor in Florence, has a plain woolen house gown no better

---

418. Francesco's brother-in-law Niccolò dell'Ammannato Tecchini was in severe financial difficulties at this time, and was declared bankrupt. Although Francesco had taken on financial responsibility for his niece Tina, Margherita was concerned that the girl should not be dressed so finely as to forget her family's circumstances.

than Caterina's, and her belt is no finer than the one that Domenico is having made.[419] I believe that if I had a neighbor whose social standing merited that his daughter should always dress better than me, I would be very embarrassed to wear a house gown that was finer than hers. Nevertheless, if you decide that is what you want, I will send it to you.

I will tell Monna Simona my opinion tomorrow and reply to you.

I will see to the household in a way that will satisfy you. We have put the willow under water to soak.

We will delay sending the wheat until Nanni is here.

Nanni left for Florence, and he has probably told you everything we need. I will have the white wine tapped as you instruct.

The small mule is being looked after according to Filippo's instructions. Barzalone will then take her to Cafaggio very slowly.

I will look after the barrels as necessary.

We have received nothing apart from those sheets that you sent us the first day because Argomento did not bring us anything this evening. He says he didn't contact you because he thought you were here in Prato.

We have given Niccolò your message and Manno his letter.

We are sending you a pannier with Argomento. In it there are walnuts, eight loaves of bread, some herbs for omelets, and a hemp cloth with various things in it. Write to me about how Niccolò is, and pass on my greetings to everyone.

That is all for now. May God protect you.

From your Margherita, in Prato.

To Francesco di Marco da Prato, in Florence.
Received from Prato, 21 March 1398. Answered.

---

419. Strozza di Carlo degli Strozzi was a member of a prominent and very wealthy Florentine family.

Letter 153 (1401827)
21 March 1398
Prato

In the name of God. 21 March 1398.

I received your letter for Niccolò di Piero. In the package there was the one to Niccolò di Piero and another to Lorenzo the goldsmith. We gave them their letters.

Send me my gray woolen overgown with Argomento, and the large mantle Guido usually wears that is hanging on the post there. Tell Francesca to return to Monna Mea the gown I borrowed from her, if she hasn't already done so. She'll find it under the daybed. Tell Caterina to search in the room upstairs for that headdress I used to wear—in every place where I might have left it—and send it to me. Remember to bring Monna Lapa's thread.

Barzalone has given four florins to Schiavo. He doesn't want Guido to write it down until you are here. He says that once he has explained the matter to you, he will write it down.

I discussed the money for the mantle with Monna Simona. She told me that Stefano had gone to Florence and would pay you in full.[420]

Search for small and large panniers there, and tell Francesca to send me back the ones she has when someone is coming this way. If I want to send her something, I will then be able to do so; but I don't have any now.

Tell Francesca to send me the black thread that she doesn't want to use, because I will use it in this household.

Because you say you are coming on Saturday, I will stop here. May God protect you always.

From your Margherita, in Prato.

To Francesco di Marco da Prato, in Florence.
Received from Prato, 22 March 1398. Answered.

---

420. Stefano Cepperelli was Monna Simona's son-in-law.

Letter 154 (1401828)
22 March 1398
Prato

In the name of God. 22 March 1398.

Argomento delivered your letter to me. With it was one addressed to Niccolò di Piero and two sacks of dirty clothes that we checked against the list; everything was there.

I received Stefano di Ser Piero's letter so late that I wasn't able to say anything to Monna Simona. I will tell her tomorrow.

Here there is a rumor that Toringo has been arrested.[421]

I don't think I need to say anything else because I'm expecting you on Saturday.

I enclose a letter to you from Barzalone. May God protect you always.

From your Margherita, in Prato.

To Francesco di Marco, in Piazza Tornaquinci, Florence.
Received from Prato, 23 March 1398. Answered.

Letter 155 (1401829)
12 April 1398
Prato

In the name of God. 12 April 1398.

Ridolfo di Lanfranco's servant delivered a letter from you that requires only a brief reply and another addressed to Barzalone that I sent immediately to Cafaggio. I gave the note that was enclosed in it to Guido, who took it to Monna Bartola.[422]

We received your letter delivered by Niccolaio Martini's servant this evening, and I reply here. We sent you the small knives this morning with Ser Lapo Mazzei. You will have them by now. We will

---

421. Toringo di Tegghia Pugliesi was Lapo di Toringo's father. See Brambilla and Hayez, "La maison des fantômes," 117–18.

422. Margherita refers to Ser Lapo Mazzei's mother.

tell Barzalone about Ser Lapo's wheat, and I will have Guido examine the account; he is sometimes a little forgetful. If it were up to me and I had to deal with the likes of Ser Lapo or Monna Bartola, I wouldn't quibble about a bushel, and I would try to avoid such annoyances next time.[423]

I will have your message sent to Zaccheria. We told Nanni to tell Piero di Monna Mellina to pass on your message. Nanni has slaked three and a half *moggia* of lime. Piero says that he had promised six *moggia*, but he doesn't think that he can provide more than five. And we told him to be careful not to mix in any soil. He says he will make it properly. Niccolò says he can't come to Florence tomorrow. We have sent the letter addressed to Tommaso del Bianco to Ser Schiatta.[424] We will speak to Messer Piero and Ser Schiatta tomorrow and tell them what Niccolò di Piero says.

I have had the wine tasted, and it seems to them that it is good wine, although a little light.

I am sending you a basket with three towels and three napkins, both small and big, a small towel, a tablecloth, and a set of underlinen for you. I am not going to write to Maso this evening because that tooth of mine is too painful. I'll say no more for now. May God protect you.

From your Margherita, in Prato.

To Francesco di Marco da Prato, in Florence.
Received from Prato, 13 April 1398. Answered.

Letter 156 (1401830)
14 April 1398
Prato

In the name of God. 14 April 1398.

Argomento delivered your letter yesterday evening. With it there was another addressed to Barzalone, one to Niccolò di Piero, and a basket with three pieces of veal, the best piece of which we sent

---

423. See letter 156, and FD 118, for details of this dispute.

424. Ser Schiatta was Tommaso del Bianco's son-in-law. See note 386, above.

to the wife of the *Podestà*, the breast to the friars, and we kept the other piece for ourselves.[425] I had such a bad stomach attack that I thought I would die three times over from it, like the time I was ill in the country on All Saints' Day; so I decided to send half our veal to Messer Piero, and I kept the other half for us and invited Niccolò and Lapa. They wouldn't come because they were expecting Salvestro for dinner, so I sent them their share when I had cooked it.[426]

I examined the account of Ser Lapo Mazzei again and discovered that he had received seventeen bushels, counting both wheat and flour; that is, eight of flour and nine of wheat. His mother, that is, Monna Bartola, sent us her miller, who said she claims she should have received seven bushels of wheat; and in my opinion, she did not want it sifted at her expense. I answered that I would not be giving her more than six bushels, because I knew it had been sifted twice and not just one bushel but more than two had been lost—but that I was acting according to my own judgment, not on your orders. I was doing this, I explained, so you would not think I mistook how much wheat had been lost in the sifting, but if I was mistaken you would be able to put things right when you arrived.[427]

Seeing that you were staying there so long, I had my mantle and overgown cut out, but when I had the cloth remeasured I discovered that there were twenty yards, so it must have shrunk by four yards when it was dyed. Once the mantle and the overgown were done, I had half a yard of worsted cloth left and not enough for me to have a hood; so see if you can manage to obtain a little more for a hood, because I wouldn't like to wear a new mantle and an old hood.

You will find a letter from the friars of San Francesco enclosed; this morning the preacher who used to preach at Santa Reparata preached to us, and it seems they are requesting that their chapter house be finished earlier than agreed. For this reason, it would be good if you were here, so try to come soon.[428]

425. The *Podestà* between November 1397 and April 1398 was Agnolo d'Ugo Spini.

426. Lapa's father, Salvestro, was a tavern keeper.

427. Francesco had instructed Margherita to give Monna Bartola no more than 23 bushels. Mazzei's mother claimed she was owed 24 bushels. See FD 118.

428. Santa Reparata was the old name of the Florentine cathedral, Santa Maria del Fiore. For Francesco's patronage at San Francesco, see Origo, *The Merchant of Prato*, 258–63.

Nanni went today to see the timber and says it is all there, and Zaccheria says that he will go tomorrow to inspect Piero's bricks. May God protect you.

From your Margherita, in Prato.

To Francesco di Marco da Prato, in Florence.
Received from Prato, 15 April 1398. Answered.

Letter 157 (1401831)
15 April 1398
Prato

In the name of God. 15 April 1398.

We received your letter this evening. I am answering it here. With it there were two letters, one to the friars and the other to Tommaso del Bianco. We will forward them.

We received your letter very late, so we can't talk to Zaccheria or anyone else; but I asked Nanni and Guido, and they told me Zaccheria has promised those furriers that he will stay there until Wednesday. He also promised Barzalone to go to Cafaggio on Wednesday, so I don't think he is available this week.

I would be inclined to wait until you are here because the builders are not available and Nanni and Manesco are busy bringing down the logs of wood on the Bisenzio River. They say that they have brought thirty-four of them down as far as beneath Cervello's dovecote, and some as far as Pietra Cava.[429] They will continue tomorrow until they have brought them to where they are needed. Four of the biggest and some others are still up there, because there was not enough water to carry them.

We sent for Monna Lorita and for Ser Chimenti and we read him the passage.[430] He said that it is true that he paid, exactly as you say. Monna Lorita says don't worry about paying on her behalf be-

429. Cervello was a miller who lived by the Bisenzio River. See note 208, above.

430. Monna Lorita di Aldobrandino Bovattieri, the widow of Francesco's partner Monte, wanted to redeem a pawned gown and pay the tax on the contract.

cause when you are here she will give the money to you, and she said that you would be doing her a favor by settling everything.[431]

We will get the flour from the miller. It still has to be sifted and bagged so everything will be ready soon.

I will tell Niccolò di Piero and Benedetto tomorrow, which is market day, and we will see whether baby goats can be bought, and they will let you know whether or not we can have them.

I am sending you twelve loaves of bread in Francesca's basket, and also a small amount of my worsted cloth so she can have the buttons made for my overgown and mantle; she should make sure they are done properly, by someone who knows how. Give her the money for the silk and for whatever else is necessary.

We will tell Niccolò di Piero what you told us.

For lack of time, I'll say no more. May God protect you always.

From your Margherita, in Prato.

To Francesco di Marco da Prato, in Florence.
Received from Prato, 17 April 1398. Answered.

Letter 158 (1401832)
3 June 1398
Prato

In the name of God. 3 June 1398.

I received your letter, and with it there were other letters that I had delivered at once, except for one addressed to Francesco di Ser Niccolaio, who must be on his way to Florence because he is not here. We were told he is studying there, but I leave it to you to take care of it.

I will have your note read to Nanni and see to those things that are most urgent. We will tell Benedetto what you say.

We will find out if we can send you the dog, and we will take care of him and feed him well.

431. See FD 119.

We can't send you any bread until Wednesday because none has been baked. I will have some made and see that you have it on Wednesday. The baker will supply what we need.

Get Domenico di Cambio to buy me two ounces of silver buttons, suitable for a doublet or overgown, for Ginevra's bodice.[432] Get used ones if there are any.

Today Nanni and Rosso carried home on a hand barrow those rocks that were in the vineyard, and took the wheat to the mill.[433]

It is late, so I won't say any more. May God protect you.

From your Margherita, in Prato.

To Francesco di Marco da Prato, in Florence.
Received from Prato, 4 June 1398. Answered.

Letter 159 (1401833)
4 June 1398
Prato

In the name of God. 4 June 1398.

I wrote to you this morning and sent the letter with Ser Stefano's son. I have had no reply from you, so there's little to say in this.

Nanni, Rosso, and Ceccarello were at Master Andrea's place today, and they excavated that vein of limestone there; they say that tomorrow they will slake the lime at Il Palco.

Provided we can find someone to take them, I am sending you thirty loaves of bread in a basket covered by a napkin with embroidered edges. Return all the things in which they are packed.

For lack of time, I'll say no more. May God protect you always.

From your Margherita, in Prato.

---

432. This is the first mention of Francesco's child, Ginevra. She was in the Datini household by April 1397, when a record of Margherita buying her two chemises appeared in Francesco's account book. See Joseph Byrne and Eleanor Congdon, "Mothering in the Casa Datini," *Journal of Medieval History* 25, no. 1 (1999): 51.

433. For Margherita's poor opinion of the laborer Rosso, see letter 163.

To Francesco di Marco da Prato, in Florence.
Received from Prato, 5 June 1398. Answered. One basket.

Letter 160 (1401834)
5 June 1398
Prato

In the name of God. 5 June 1398.

I received your letter this evening, and with it one addressed to Barzalone and one to Niccolò di Piero. I had them delivered. Paolo di Lioncino's letters arrived this morning at terce.[434] I immediately gave Ser Nicola's to him and one to Barzalone. I did not send a reply to you because we couldn't find anyone to deliver it. We got back the bags, the basket, and the napkin. I have seen Ginevra's buttons and I have decided that I don't want that type. I want them round and white like those on Caterina's gray overgown, because the mantle is yellow and these small ones don't match it well at all and can hardly be seen. The girl needs ones that people can see. Have them bought for me on Friday morning so that I can have them by Friday evening; buy me three ounces.

Nanni slaked four *moggia* of lime at Il Palco, and here at the kitchen garden beside the canal he slaked one *moggio* during the night. I will send you back the buttons with Argomento on Friday morning.

Since he needs to see to the lime, I will not send Nanni unless you tell me on Friday that he should come with the flour, or whatever you decide you need. Because of [the time spent slaking] the lime, it is now very late, so I'll say no more. If we have left anything out, we will answer tomorrow. May God protect you always.

Piero di Monna Mellina says that if you want bricks, there are some well-fired ones, so let us know if you do.

From your Margherita, in Prato.

---

434. Paolo di Leoncino was an apothecary (Mazzei, *Lettere di un notaro*, 1:250–51). He died in poverty in 1410 (Fiumi, *Demografia*, 406).

To Francesco di Marco da Prato, in Florence.
Received from Prato, 6 June 1398. Answered.

Letter 161 (1401835)
5 June 1398
Prato

We wrote to you this morning and sent the letter with Ser Simone di Ser Donato. We told you about everything up to that point.

Today Nanni brought the lime from Il Palco and from Prato.

We won't send you Nanni on Saturday unless we hear from you to the contrary. I am returning the buttons to you, as I said to you in another letter, because I don't want that type. I want three ounces of white buttons, like those on Caterina's gray overgown, and I would like sixteen of those little buttons of any shape available, suitable to make her a pair of cuffs.[435]

Lucia would like you to buy her a piece of cloth for a striped overgown, not in the Sicilian style but another sort, as long as it is strong and of good quality. I need one too, but I want it in the Sicilian style. Ask Francesca how much she needs for one of hers, and buy two lengths. Master Andrea's daughter has had a baby girl, and she asks you to send him here.[436]

We include a letter that has come from Vernio. For lack of time, I won't say any more. May God protect you always.

From your Margherita, in Prato.

To Francesco di Marco da Prato himself, in Florence.

---

435. See letter 160.

436. Andrea seems to have been a master stonemason. He had supplied limestone to Francesco two days before this. See letter 159.

Letter 162 (1401836)
6 June 1398
Prato

In the name of God. 6 June 1398.

The reason for this is to let you know that yesterday evening at the twenty-second hour, Ubaldo di Fatto sent me a message to say that he, the *Podestà*, and all their people wanted to go to Il Palco this morning; so I sent Niccolò di Piero to enquire whether they were in fact going. Ubaldo replied that they had decided to, but that we shouldn't send anything, because if they knew we were doing so, they wouldn't go. Niccolò and I thought it right to buy some candied pine nuts, and to give them what we had left over.[437] We took the box of sweets, and we sent a lot of oranges and beautiful cherries and some of the white wine you bought from Nanni, as well as our own house wine, and bread, napkins, and everything else that was necessary. Niccolò, Barzalone, Benedetto, Bretone, and Angelo have gone there. Niccolò also offered them the mules. They accepted and were very grateful because they had left their own mounts in Florence. Ubaldo and Arriguccio and our Nanni went with them.

Because it is very hot here today—and as you know, I cut down my cotton gowns for Ginevra—so I don't have any; tell Domenico di Cambio to see if he can find some pretty ones in the Sicilian style. I don't want real Sicilian ones because I don't want to spend much. And remember one for Lucia also, but not the same as mine. Get one with three stripes, or whatever he thinks, as long as it is not like mine, and it should be a strong material because she wants a serviceable one. I will sort through the old water pitchers here and send them to you. Tell Domenico to find a way to exchange them for two smaller ones so that when we need them, we don't have to borrow them. I want them neither too small nor too big, but medium-sized, as long as they are fine and attractive. We told Niccolò about the barrels and he said to leave it to him. We read the message to Nanni and he and Rosso will do what they can and what they think is best.

---

437. The text refers to *pinocchiati*, which were sweets made of pine nuts, sugar, and beaten egg whites.

I received your letter just now, and with it were the white buttons and the gold ones, and Lucia's cloth, as well as mine. I can't work out this evening whether or not I will have enough [cloth]. I will tell Domenico in a later letter to buy some more if I need it.

Niccolò di Piero says that he can't come tomorrow because of all his commitments.

As for the veal that is to be divided here, we will try to get the best piece possible. I will make every effort to see about the bed and the other things.

Monna Simona and Stefano di Ser Piero will bring our mule and Barzalone's, because Monna Simona is going to Florence.

Nanni will also be coming to you with the flour.

Up until now Benedetto hasn't received any money from the miller. I have a little cotton wadding and I will send it to him, but in my opinion it is not as perfect as I would like. The dog hasn't been found, but Barzalone and the others have done everything one can do to find a dog. Barzalone and the others saw him here at home until mid-terce. We think someone saw him and led him away.

It is true that Lapa wasn't well on Tuesday and Wednesday, but she was still able to spin and sew.[438] I kept Papera there on Tuesday and Wednesday, and when I sent Guido on Wednesday evening he found Papera spinning and Lapa sewing. Then Papera returned here, and it seems that soon after Papera's departure the pain in Lapa's side returned so badly that they thought she was going to die. They gave me no word of this at all, but the wife of the *Podestà* sent for me on Easter Sunday, and I found out while passing by. You have tied me to that wife of the *Podestà* to such an extent that she wouldn't step outside if I weren't with her.[439] You know very well how willingly I do this because if it weren't for your sake, I would not set foot in that building. Faced with the choice of being with her or looking after those government officials who had decided to go to Il Palco, for a long time I didn't go to see her; but today I went there twice. She had a miscarriage, so I remained there for lunch, and I would have stayed until evening if I hadn't had the washing to do (you know what gets done in our house

---

438. Margherita refers here to Lapa, Niccolò di Piero di Giunta del Rosso's wife.

439. The *Podestà* at this time was Vieri Guadagni. Despite Margherita's dislike of Vieri's wife Ghita, Francesco continued to insist that she should be friendly to her. See note 500, below.

if you or I aren't here); then I returned this evening at dinnertime and stayed there a little longer.

As it is late and you will be here on Sunday, we won't add anything more. We will discuss in person anything that comes up. May God protect you always.

From your Margherita, in Prato.

To Francesco di Marco da Prato, in Florence.
Received from Prato, 8 June 1398.

Letter 163 (1401837)
22 June 1398
Prato

In the name of God. 22 June 1398.

Argomento delivered your letter this evening as well as a bundle of letters for Niccolò di Piero, and enclosed in mine there was one for the captain of Pistoia.[440] I will find Guido and we will write the note and send it on as soon as we can.

The reason I didn't write to you is that Rosso didn't tell me anything, and he didn't say in the evening that he had to come here. I told Guido that he should go to help Cristofano as soon as he got up in the morning, because I think he is needed. Rosso has only just come, but he is already failing; and in my opinion he doesn't even know where he is. I don't know if he owes you money, but it would be worth paying him some to get rid of him because if he stays here another month, all his brain will allow him to say will be: "What a good donkey! What a good donkey! What a good donkey!"

---

440. The holders of the office of captain of Pistoia were important Florentines from the political elite who were elected to govern nearby Pistoia. Francesco was always keen to cultivate such men, and his note was probably an offer of hospitality to a newly appointed official. This letter reveals that when the captain's wife made a brief visit to the convent of San Niccolò in Prato, Margherita tried to persuade the woman to stay as her guest at the Datini residence.

We will tell Cristofano that you will be here on Monday and let him know what you are planning to do.

We will give Barzalone your message. We will do as you instruct concerning Monna Giovanna.

I will send Martino a message telling him to throw water on the walls every evening.

Your letter has been read so many times that we have understood it very well and we will carry out your instructions.

The wife of the captain of Pistoia dined at the convent of San Niccolò yesterday. She was accompanied by her brother and other young people from Pistoia. I went to visit her at the convent and tried very hard to persuade her to stay with me for a few days. I couldn't get her to accept, and she returned the same day to Pistoia. I presented her with wine and fruit and paid her many compliments.

For lack of time I cannot say any more. May God protect you always.

From your Margherita, in Prato.

To Francesco di Marco da Prato, in Piazza Tornaquinci, Florence. Received from Prato, 22 June 1398.

Letter 164 (1401838)
3 July 1398
Prato

In the name of God. 3 July 1398.

This evening we received your letter and with it one for Barzalone and one for Agnolo.[441] I gave Agnolo his, and Barzalone is at Cafaggio, so I will give it to him tomorrow. I gave the receipt for the florins to Bernabò and told him what you wrote to me. He says not to change them until he writes to you because tomorrow he wants to meet the person who gave them to him and come to an agreement with him, and then he will answer you.

---

441. This is Agnolo di Niccolò di Piero di Giunta. He had entered into partnership with Francesco in January 1396, the third generation of his family to do so.

We are having the buttons made with black silk, but I want bright red silk to make the buttonholes and to attach the buttons.

Our workman is threshing at Arsiccioli, and Nanni is with him.

I am sending you twenty loaves of bread in a basket with Argomento, and a towel. Tell Francesca to keep it, and I will also send a tablecloth of hers that I have. Send us back all the baskets that are there in Florence.

As it is late, I cannot add any more. May God protect you always.

With this letter there are two others that Ser Baldo gave us yesterday evening.[442] We gave them to Argomento this morning to bring to you, but he didn't take them because he couldn't go to Florence.

From your Margherita, in Prato.

To Francesco di Marco da Prato, in Florence.
Received from Prato, 4 July 1398.

Letter 165 (1401839)
4 July 1398
Prato

In the name of God. 4 July 1398.

Argomento delivered your letter, as well as the new basket, the cassia, and Monna Ghita's gown. We then gave the letter to Barzalone, and we sent you his reply with Ser Baldo. You will have received it. We haven't had anything else from Ser Baldo except the letters we sent back to you. I imagine he saw you today and you have discovered what he has done about that money.

I also got the silk. If I run short, I will let you know.

I will send a message to Cristofano tomorrow morning to tell him what you said, and if he comes here I will supervise him and do what you say.

I will send you the basin as soon as I can. Argomento is not going to Florence tomorrow because he wants to do the threshing.

---

442. This is the notary Baldo di Mannuccio.

The planks are not cut yet because the sawmiller says that he can't find anyone to help him; his assistant is threshing, so he can't help. Guido goes there every day to remind them, and he promised that he is likely to come here tomorrow.

We will send you the slippers if we find someone to take them to you. I reminded Guido about what you said. We have no more red wine because there is none in the barrel, which is completely moldy, so write to tell us which one we should open.

I had someone call out to Bernabò for a good while, but he didn't answer because he had already gone to bed. I will tell him tomorrow morning. Because it is late I won't say any more. May God protect you always.

From your Margherita, in Prato.

To Francesco di Marco da Prato, in Piazza Tornaquinci, Florence. Received from Prato, 5 July 1398. Answered.

Letter 166 (1401840)
5 July 1398
Prato

In the name of God. 5 July 1398.

I received your letter and also one for Agnolo di Niccolò, which I had delivered. I will respond to mine here. I gave Bernabò his letter, and I will give Barzalone his tomorrow morning.

I sent someone to the mill to find out about the wheat, and he tells me it will be milled and ready tomorrow morning. I will send for it, and you will have some bread on Monday if I find a carrier.

I sent someone to Cristofano to find out if he is coming here. He says he has to be at the parish church tomorrow because the person who is fixing the bell will be there, and he has to be at the church all next week so he says he can't come; but afterwards, during the following week, he says he will be able to help you, and today he was at his vineyard.

I have been asking about the planks as often as possible, but they are not yet ready. He says that he will do them tomorrow, if he can.

We will open the barrel that you mentioned. We will see to it that the pack animals are shod and groomed to your satisfaction.

I spoke to Monna Lorita and this evening I also sent Papera to her. Guido has also spoken to her, and he says she is trying hard to make sure you have the money. He says there is no need to pursue her because as soon as she has [the money] she will give it to me.

The market gardener says that he will bring twenty-five *lire* on Sunday, the day after tomorrow.

Neither Marco delle Tovaglie nor Iacopo has started threshing. As soon as they have finished, they will deliver the wheat to us. I am asking Guido to read the memorandum and record [the amount], and we will spread the wheat out well so it will be fine.

We have received the wheat from Arsiccioli, and they are preparing to thresh down at La Chiusura.

Schiatta has threshed all his wheat; but he says it is under cover because he was unable to deliver it, with his other commitments. He says he will bring it as soon as he can.

I don't want any more silk because I have plenty. We told Messer Piero what you said to me. Domenico del Pace says he received those twelve *lire*.

If we find someone going to Florence, we will send you a pannier of hazelnuts covered with a napkin.

For now I'll say no more. May God protect you.

From your Margherita, in Prato.

To Francesco di Marco da Prato, in Florence.
Received from Prato, 6 July 1398.

Letter 167 (1401841)
6 July 1398
Prato

In the name of God. 6 July 1398.

Rosso and Pellegrino delivered your letter. I will reply to it here as necessary.

I received the letter you sent me with Roberto da Vernio yesterday evening, and this morning I sent a reply with Dino del Bodda explaining the matter concerning Monna Lorita.[443]

I will tell Nanni to stay here this evening and then go to Barzalone tomorrow so that they can do what you say.

As for the instructions you left me, I am doing everything I can. I go every day to see about getting those planks sawed; and because he has no assistant, he says he cannot do them. As we mentioned in this morning's letter, tomorrow we will receive twenty-five *lire* from the market gardener; and as for whether the others are here, some are and some are away. Zaccheria is not here. Tomorrow Benedetto and I will visit all of them; as it is a holiday, we will find them home and we will see what they say; and whether we can get something out of them. Benedetto says he will call on them all again on Monday morning.

I went to visit Nanni di Messer Arrigo to collect the two *lire*, ten *soldi*, and eight *denari* that he owes for that Perpignan cloth he bought to make hose. He says that he spoke with you and told you that Cecco owes him twenty *soldi*—and that you told him you would meet him, consult the account book, and sort it out.

And Bolco says that he has given oranges and other things and doesn't owe three *lire*, thirteen *soldi*, and ten *denari* as we say. Tell us if you know what we have received from him, so it can be deducted from his account.

We haven't been able to sell Niccolaio's cloth and the head veils.

We will send the message to Giovannetto da Mangone if we can, and if he is coming here, we will ask him about the matter; if he doesn't want to come, we will send someone to him up there.

We answered about Cristofano this morning, and told you the amount of wheat we have already received.

443. See note 430, above.

We are sending you the mules with Rosso and Pellegrino and a pannier of hazelnuts that we couldn't send this morning because Dino had too great a load and couldn't carry them. Argomento is not coming to you because he has to do the threshing.

He says that your overgown can't be finished by Monday.

I'll say no more for now. May God protect you always.

From your Margherita, in Prato.

To Francesco di Marco da Prato, in Florence.
Received from Prato, 6 July 1398. Answered on the same day.

Letter 168 (1401842)
7 July 1398
Prato

In the name of God. 7 July 1398.

I received your letter this morning and also one addressed to Agnolo di Niccolò di Piero, which I had given to him. I am responding to yours, although only a brief reply is required.

We have had thirty-eight bushels of wheat from Arsiccioli; we put it in the granary in a loose pile, and above it we carefully wrote the amount. And the laborer—that is, Andrea—took away thirty-six bushels because Nanni says that in this way, when they thresh at La Chiusura, we will have another two bushels that we'll thresh on Tuesday, because tomorrow they want to prepare the threshing floor.

Today I received twenty-five *lire* from the market gardener. We have had nothing from the others. I don't know whether Benedetto will visit them again tomorrow. I will call on him tomorrow and find out what he wants to do, and I will let you know.

This morning Nanni went to Barzalone's house at Cafaggio to buy the hay. Barzalone couldn't wait there for him to arrive; he had to go to Prato in the morning because of his friendship with a young priest who had been at the church of Santo Stefano in Cafaggio. He went later today, and he says they went to Castello Nuovo, to Tavola, and to Iolo and found some hay. It's all expensive. Among what was available they found two stacks at Iolo belonging to Matteo Verzoni; but because Matteo was not there, they weren't able to discover how much he wanted per cartload. Barzalone said he would find him and ask, and let us know; then we will tell you. At Tavola the price is three and a half florins a cartload.

If we can find a carrier, we will send you twelve loaves of bread in a basket and some muscatel pears given to us by Bartolo da Barberino, Tantera's brother-in-law—along with some hazelnuts from the orchard. I have kept some of the pears, and you will have the rest. He says he had come to apologize for not bringing the cherries, which he says had all been picked and sold. Argomento is not coming to you tomorrow. If Dino is willing to bring a load, we will send it to you.

I'll say no more for now. May God protect you always.

From your Margherita, in Prato.

To Francesco di Marco da Prato, in Piazza Tornaquinci, Florence. Received from Prato, 8 July 1398.

Letter 169 (1401843)
17 August 1398
Prato

In the name of God. 17 August 1398.

Today at the twenty-first hour Master Andrea brought us your letter, and I have understood what you say and will reply here.

I have not yet found a wet nurse for Manno because it was late.[444] Tomorrow I will see whether I can find a good one, and I will do so as if I were looking on my own account.

We told the furriers from Florence what you said about the fleeces, and they say they will be there on Wednesday to see them; I told Marco di Ceo as well.[445]

---

444. Manno d'Albizo degli Agli, Francesco's partner in Pisa, had fathered a baby boy. Manno's mother, Monna Bice Marini, involved herself in the search for a wet nurse. See letter 170. Manno died in the plague of 1400.

445. Marco di Ceo was a weaver. Francesco refers to the fleeces in FD 137.

We told the shoemaker Niccolaio Mastriscia about the squirrel pelts; he says that he will come to Florence on Tuesday or Wednesday to inspect them, and he thanks you. I have not yet received the florin from him. He says he will give it to me before he comes to see you, but that the matter needs to be discussed. Sixteen *lire* is better than four florins, and he gave you a newly minted florin and the shoes; so the matter needs to be sorted out.

This morning, with Argomento, we sent you some bread and eggs, and a number of letters that came yesterday. You will have received them and already written to me about what to do.

We will tell the broker Zaffo about the wool tomorrow because this evening he couldn't be found.[446] We gave the message to Niccolò, and he read the letter. He says he told you everything about the price of wheat this morning.

This evening we received from Argomento six lead weights, a curtain, and the red linen to make the bedcover; he had no letter apart from one addressed to you, and he says he doesn't know who gave it to him.

Argomento brought back the bag for the linen from Florence this evening.

Tommaso's brother-in-law came here and arrived at the twenty-second hour, believing he would find you here. He arrived very tired and wanted to return there, but I wouldn't allow it. He says he will come there tomorrow morning and will bring you this letter.

We dismissed that errand boy because we did not like him.

The sawmillers did the timber on Wednesday, and it is safely under cover. Matteo made the door of the threshing-floor barn, and a new window facing the threshing floor. The sawmillers have finished sawing the beam. They cut that timber in two as you told them to, and it is rotten inside. They are beginning to saw the timber they prepared on Wednesday, which you say is to be put under cover, and they are making three planks from it.

Nanni took Messer Piero's stones to the warehouse. There are twenty loads altogether, and the sum is credited to his account in the account book.

446. Zaffo was a dyer and wool broker.

Ser Schiatta's barley has been delivered, and it amounts to twenty-seven bushels. The meadow produced twenty-one bushels of vetch. Tell me if you want me to write it as a credit in the account book.

Piero says that they will be here to work on Monday. Tell us what you want them to do.

We gave Monna Giovanna your message.

As it is very late, I'll say no more. May God protect you always. From your Margherita, in Prato.

To Francesco di Marco da Prato, in Florence.
Received from Prato, 18 August 1398.

Letter 170 (1401844)
19 August 1398
Prato

In the name of God. 19 August 1398.

Argomento delivered your letter this evening. I reply here. He also delivered the box, the pannier with the circle on it, and the small basket. Argomento didn't give us the buttons; we think he forgot. We will get them from him tomorrow.

I have looked, and am still looking, for wet nurses. I still haven't found one I like. It is true that Lapa says she has placed her baby with a wet nurse who has a child of her own that she wants to wean; but if it were my baby, I would only give it to her with the intention of taking it away as soon as a wet nurse with fresh milk came along, because I could never believe that when a wet nurse had her own one-year-old child she wouldn't be feeding it as well. One hears such things all the time. A wet nurse might turn up from one moment to the next, and if no one appears, I won't wait for the carter to come but send someone from here to let you know the situation. Because you are in urgent need, one solution might be to engage one of these wet nurses for a month or two weeks until the perfect person comes our way. I see no other way if we can't find someone else. Tell Manno and Monna

Bice that if this child comes to us, I will treat it as if it were mine.[447] I wouldn't have the heart to do anything else. I will never agree, as Barzalone and Niccolò have, to give it to someone with little milk; and if I do, I will take it back again. I will act in this matter as if he were my son or yours. And, for the sake of Zanobi, I will take greater care than I did before because I understand his needs.[448]

We haven't received the letter from the barber. We will try to get it, and I will reply.

The builders will be told to do as you say.

We are sending you with Argomento twelve loaves of bread suitable for the household. It has turned out very well. I am also sending three caps and a pair of slippers.

We will do the other things without reporting back to you. If you have dirty washing, send it to us. We couldn't get any green sendal silk.

Today Niccolaio from Tavola sent us five hundred lengths of terra-cotta guttering of better quality than the others.

As it is very late, we will say no more. May God protect you always.

From your Margherita, in Prato.

To Francesco di Marco da Prato, in Florence.
Received from Prato, 20 August 1398.

447. See letter 169.

448. Zanobi di Taddeo Gaddi, brother of the painter Agnolo Gaddi, was unhappy with his wet nurse and wanted another one. It seems, therefore, that Margherita was to look for two wet nurses. See FD 137 and 138.

Letter 171 (1401845)
20 August 1398
Prato

In the name of God. 20 August 1398.

This morning I sent you a letter with Dino del Bodda about what needed to be done up until then. We also sent you the bread, slippers, and caps with him.

Schiavo wants Domenico to buy the following items for him: two inexpensive but decent-looking imitation rings, a silver belt worth about four *lire*, and if possible, one of those garlands that are a little showy. Even if it is second hand, as long as it is pretty, he would be happy. He would also like an imitation belt to give to his sister, who is fourteen years old. The cost of all these things, that is, what he would like to spend, should be ten *lire* and no more. It would seem better to me to buy the brass items first and to spend what remains on the belt. He wants to give her the ring on Saturday, so it would be best if the things were here by Thursday evening without fail.[449]

Remind Stoldo about Barzalone's hose.

Argomento says that he didn't bring Barzalone's buttons because you didn't give them to him.

As for the wet nurses, we haven't found anyone yet. Today we will search high and low, in Prato and beyond, leaving no stone unturned, and this evening I will answer you. Tell us if you find someone so we don't waste time.[450]

The builders Piero and Matteo are at the kitchen garden and doing as they were ordered to do.

Piero di Guiduccio has a bad pain in his side and would like some medicinal cachets; and what's more, he has asked me if I have some Malvasia wine. I said no. You would do well, if you find some there, to send him a flask because he deserves to be treated well, and I would send it to him in your name.

You will find enclosed some green sendal silk for your riding overgown.

---

449. The laborer Schiavo was preparing to marry.

450. See letter 169.

The carrier of this letter will be Niccolaio Mastriscia, the shoe-maker. He still hasn't paid those florins. He says he is short of money to buy things. Now that he is with you there, say what you please to him. May God protect you always.

From your Margherita, in Prato.

To Francesco di Marco da Prato in Piazza Tornaquinci, Florence. Received from Prato, 21 August 1398.

Letter 172 (1401846)
21 August 1398
Prato

In the name of God. 21 August 1398.

This morning I received a letter from you to which I respond here as necessary. With it came a letter addressed to Ser Piero, and a bundle of letters to go to Pistoia that I gave to Niccolò because he had some to send there himself.

Yesterday we sent you a letter with Niccolaio Mastriscia. After a good deal of searching, we found the letter that Mariola had in his possession. There is no need to reply to it because I reported the things we had received in a previous letter. We gave Niccolò di Piero his letters because there were no others with them and he—that is, Mariola—had no others. There weren't any letters for Pistoia.

We sent you a letter yesterday with Niccolaio Mastriscia, and we think that you received it early. We told him to tell you that we hadn't found a wet nurse except for one who was weaning, but that I had found one who, if necessary, could take the baby for a month or two until we found a really good one. She doesn't want to come to Florence to get the baby. Rather, I need to find a woman to collect it, if you decide you want to send me the baby in this way. Yesterday I sent Monna Bartolomea d'Alesso as far as Iolo to find out about the one that Lapa and Niccolò had told me about, and I discovered that she had been dying of hunger all year. I also sent Monna Caterina d'Andrea to San Giusto and to all those villages nearby to see if someone could be found there, but she found no one suitable. The situation could change from one moment to the next, but there's not one of our friends or any other person that I have neglected to ask.

We have answered your letter that the barber brought.

We didn't send you the sendal silk any earlier because we couldn't. We sent it yesterday after we obtained it.

Niccolò sent us the letter that the barber brought. If we depended on Argomento, we would never get any letters unless Niccolò himself sent them on to us. He, I mean Niccolò, is in Prato, and I haven't heard that he has gone anywhere else.

They are hurrying the builders on, and Nanni says they are working well but complain that they want you to see them work—because you won't believe afterward how careful they are. They have built the wall up to the kitchen ceiling. There was plenty of lime, and there is some left over.

You complain that we don't answer half your questions, but I don't think this is true. We are rushing because the carrier wants to leave, so we will say no more here; but if anything has been left out, we will answer fully in the next letter. May God protect you always.

From your Margherita, in Prato.

To Francesco di Marco da Prato, in Florence.
Received from Prato, 21 August 1398.

Letter 173 (1401847)
21 August 1398
Prato

In the name of God. 21 August 1398.

We sent you a letter today with someone Niccolò told us was from Florence. We have had no reply from you, either to that one or to the one we sent with Niccolaio Mastriscia.

Niccolaio returned and brought us a basket. Inside there were twelve cachets, a flask of Malvasia wine, a napkin, and the taffeta; but he did not give us a letter. We sent the cachets and the Malvasia wine to Piero di Guiduccio, who was very grateful and thanks you very much for them.[451]

We have found a wet nurse at Montemurlo, and she is a definite possibility. She has fresh milk and would suit very well—except, it seems to me, she is a little too far away. I found another above the piazza of the parish church who has had fresh milk for two months. I am told she is a good wet nurse; and she promised that if her dying baby succumbs tonight, she will come as soon as it is buried. I thought about it, and I have found a woman who is our neighbor on the Porcellatico side. She is a good woman, and her husband has given his word that she will do as I wish. She has milk. She will come to Florence for the baby accompanied by someone I send with her. This will not be the woman who is to keep the baby. It seems to me best that you should send the baby to me. When he is here, I will find the best way of looking after him well, and I won't spare any expense. They shouldn't think, just because he is illegitimate, that I won't act as if he were mine.

I asked Stefano d'Arrigo's daughter-in-law about the wet nurse that Niccolò tells you he thinks he has found, because it was she that nursed her daughter. I asked her why she had taken her daughter away from the woman. She says that the longer the baby stayed in her care, the unhealthier she became. She also says she only has one eye. She—that is, Stefano's daughter-in-law—says also that she had made an agreement with the castellan. Benedetto went there this evening, and he says she is in the Cassero.[452] I didn't like her. My plan, that you send me this child and let me deal with it, seems to me to be the best one, as I will easily find someone to look after it until we find a good wet nurse who is suitable for us.

I had just written this when Saccente delivered your letter. I will reply here briefly because it is very late. As for the mother, you have done right not to send her. Saccente's wife, Domenica, has inadequate milk and is unwell, so would be useless.

I am sorry to hear that Domenico is unwell. I pray that God will heal him.

We will pass on to Piero di Guiduccio what you have written.

451. Piero di Guiduccio was ill. See letter 171.

452. The Cassero was a fortified corridor leading from the city wall to the castle in the center of Prato.

We have had the kitchen garden watered twice. It rained heavily today, so now it is not necessary.

Ser Nicola says that he hasn't yet had a reply from that relative of his, and he doesn't know if he will agree. He says he is very grateful that you went to see his place, and he will look after both matters quickly.

Guido told Nanni di Zarino about the wheat and he says that the only reason it is still there is because his worker's beasts of burden have been unwell, so he didn't send him but will do so soon.

We are not replying to every item, but write what you want and we will try the best we can, and if we don't answer you, don't distress yourself. If you only knew the effort that it has cost me, as well as my friends, to search for these blessed wet nurses. When they bring them to see me, I have to find out about their health and circumstances, and the more you look the more problems you find. It is not as easy to find them as people think, if you want someone really good.

With Argomento I am sending you three dozen loaves of bread in the box with a napkin over it. There are two dozen loaves of white bread, one dozen of brown, and your brown mantle. May God protect you always.

Tomorrow, without fail, we will send for the child, so all will be well.

From your Margherita, in Prato.

To Francesco di Marco da Prato, in Piazza Tornaquinci, Florence. Received from Prato, 22 August 1398. Answered.

Letter 174 (1401848)
22 August 1398
Prato

In the name of God. 22 August 1398.

We sent you a letter this morning with Argomento about the most pressing matters, so there is less to say in this one.

The reason for this letter is that I am sending you the woman whom I wrote about in the letter delivered by Argomento. As I explained, this is not the woman who is to breastfeed the baby, but I am sending her to collect him because she has milk. I am also sending Colomba to carry the baby back here because otherwise the nurse would not travel comfortably. I have made an agreement with Colomba like the one she had when she carried the children of the *Podestà*. She is strong and suited to the role as no other in this town. At this point there is no need to look further afield.

I am also sending you Pellegrino so that he can show them the house to go to. I am not sending a donkey because I haven't found one available, and it doesn't seem to me to be necessary. Give them the cloths and other things that they will need immediately, and give the other things to Argomento either today or tomorrow. Nanni needs the mare, and it would be a pity to leave her idle when there is no need to do so. I don't want to give them any other task apart from bringing back the baby.

I have engaged the woman who will care for the baby until I can provide someone really suitable. Send him early this evening so that it is not too hot and they can rest on the way and carry him in comfort. You can send him at a good hour, as soon as the heat has passed. If you agree, you can keep Pellegrino and send him back tomorrow, because twenty miles in a day is perhaps too tiring a walk for him. Do as you think best. Don't give them anything, because I will look after them here myself.

Send them back as soon as you can because I have the child of this woman here with me. She would fret if her mother didn't return, and I will have to look after Colomba's child as well.

Tell Bellozzo that I gave the letter to the prior, who says he has to be in Florence the week after next and that he will give him that money. May God protect you always.

From your Margherita, in Prato.

To Francesco di Marco da Prato, in Florence.
Received from Prato, 22 August 1398. Answered.

Letter 175 (1401849)
22 August 1398
Prato

In the name of God. 22 August 1398.

Rosso delivered your letter as well as the box with the things you listed.[453] You know that Schiavo is not in Prato. Tomorrow morning we will send for him and show him the things, and he can choose what he likes. We will send back the remainder to you as soon as possible.

I don't know why you ask me about the verjuice because if I were to tell you the truth, you wouldn't believe me. If the verjuice has gone off, blame the poor-quality barrel, not me; and Francesca knows perfectly well that not one drop of the lot we sent to Florence three years ago went bad. If it has leaked, it's no fault of mine because this very year I told you many times to plug it up well, and you plugged it so expertly that half of it leaked out (but you didn't say a word about it that morning because it was your doing)![454]

Tell Pellegrino that he is not telling the truth.[455] He didn't see the rain, there wasn't any in the house, and there was not enough rain for it even to reach the drain. Nanni was at table, Monna Giovanna was in the *loggia*, as were all these women here, and Guido and I were answering your letter. If I told you the truth you wouldn't believe me, so ask Nanni and Monna Giovanna.

You tell me Guido says that his wife has never given him any sorrow.[456] I think he is telling the truth, but I believe he has given her even less sorrow than she gave him. And it is not that Guido doesn't know how to exert authority over a woman, because he has authority over an entire city. I found out from Ser Lapo and his daughter-in-

---

453. Francesco had sent one hair garland, four rings, and two belts for Schiavo to choose from to purchase for his bride. See FD 140, and letter 171.

454. For verjuice, see note 320, above.

455. Pellegrino had reported that rainwater had run into the cellar. Francesco ironically accused Margherita of finding a good way to keep the cellar cool. In his view, she ought to have put sand in front of the entrance to stop the water, as he would have done (FD 140).

456. Guido del Palagio's wife was Niccolosa di Bartolomeo degli Albizzi, whom Lapo Mazzei also regarded as a paragon of female virtue. See his letter to Francesco of 5 September 1392 in Mazzei, *Lettere di un notaro*, 1:33–34.

law, who were here, just how Guido behaves in his own home. Guido cannot be compared to other men. He treats his wife as a lady, not like an innkeeper's wife. It is fifteen blessed years since I came here, and I have lived as if at an inn. I don't think there is a single innkeeper who runs the inn while organizing building works at the same time! And furthermore, you have always had me do your dirty work. As if Florentine visitors weren't enough, you even recruited one in Castiglione Aretino![457]

About the two women I sent you today, you say there is no need to say any more. But there is a need to say more as far as I am concerned because we, Monna Giovanna and I, kept two little girls here who poisoned the day for both of us. I am also expecting that we, Monna Giovanna and I, will be doing more penance tonight. These are the favors you seek out for me! Keep on seeking them often, because they're all I'm good for—and make me do those things that you think I'm capable of because I'm only fit for cleaning filth and you should have seen us, Monna Giovanna and me, holding those little girls in our arms and Caterina and all the others, because the children were screaming so loudly the whole neighborhood came to see them. You have such foresight that you didn't tell me the baby was not in Florence. Otherwise I would never have sent the women at that hour. On top of all this, the mule arrived this evening, and you have given her so much to eat and kept her in such comfort that she is about to burst, and at terce it was decided to bleed her because Filippo said she needed it because she had been idle too long and was given too much to eat. Would to God you kept me at rest this way!

The lime was slaked last night at the warehouse.

We don't know whether we'll send the mare or not. The overgown isn't finished yet.

We'll give back the basin to Bonaccorso di Chello.[458]

457. Castiglione Aretino was a sizable town and castle in the territory of Arezzo.

458. Bonaccorso di Chello Bonaccorsi, brother to Andrea Bellandi's wife, Piera, seems to have migrated from Carmignano to Prato some years earlier. See Brambilla and Hayez, "La maison des fantômes," 110; FD 140; and Vestri, "Istituzioni e vita sociale a Prato," 33–34.

I will tell Niccolò di Piero what you said about the affairs of that fellow from Pistoia.[459]

The timber hasn't been brought down because Nanni says there wasn't much water [in the river].

I sent your message to Messer Piero.

As it is late, and so as not to impose further on Monna Giovanna, and to allow Guido to get to bed (and also because I'm so busy I don't know where I am), and your letters comfort me so because, you know, when you are here you do as you like, whereas I have your and my own tasks to attend to, and you know very well how little I can rely on others to do the things I can't get done, and I am no longer as well as I would like, but I would resign myself to everything if only half of what I do were acknowledged![460] May God protect you.

From your Margherita, in Prato.

To Francesco di Marco da Prato, in Florence.
Received from Prato, 23 August 1398.

Letter 176 (1401850)
23 August 1398
Prato

In the name of God. 23 August 1398.

I am writing this to tell you that the baby arrived, and they looked after him very well during the journey. We sent him to the wet nurse, who will keep him until we find a better one. May God allow me to gain honor from this matter, which I wish I had never taken

459. Francesco had complained to Margherita in his letter of 22 August that his partner, Manno d'Albizo degli Agli, had settled too hastily and on unsatisfactory terms with a debtor imprisoned in Pistoia. This had compromised Francesco's own negotiations to collect the full amount he was owed (FD 140).

460. The initial "as it is late" anticipates a concluding principal clause, "I will say no more"; but that does not eventuate. The sentence reflects the oral composition of the letter: as Margherita added clause to clause she was distracted by the overwhelming difficulties she confronted and forgot to complete the sentence.

on because one could come out of this business covered with shame rather than honor considering all the things that could go wrong, but I will do my part and may God do the rest.

The tailor promised me that the overgown will be ready this evening. I will send it to you as soon as I can.

We are not sending you Schiavo's things, as he cannot be found and appears to have gone fishing. I sent for him twice today.

I searched for the mule's cover, but it could not be found. I was upset thinking that it was here, and now they tell me it is in Florence. Send it to me if you want me to make one, because I don't want to do it unless I can copy that one.

Filippo, the farrier, says he will look after the mule better than if you were here. He applied a poultice of dry brick clay, crushed and mixed with vinegar.

There is no time to write any more as the messenger wants to leave. May God protect you.

Your Margherita, in Prato.

To Francesco di Marco da Prato, in Florence.
Received from Prato, 24 August 1398.

Letter 177 (1401851)
24 August 1398
Prato

In the name of God. 24 August 1398.

I decided to send Nanni to you so I could let you know about the work that has been done here and so you could tell him what has still to be done.

We are sending with him the box that has eighteen loaves in it, twelve eggs, a napkin, your overgown, a set of underlinen, a pair of slippers, and a large wrapping cloth. Where I just said "box," I meant "basket." There is also a cage with three pairs of pigeons, a pannier of peaches and grapes covered with a table napkin, a small basket of figs covered with a napkin, two half-quart flasks, Schiavo's belt, two of those rings that you sent, and one sack.

Send back the small and large baskets and whatever else you can send. Tell Francesca to give Nanni the dirty clothes to bring us tomorrow evening.

I have no more to add. Nanni will tell you about everything. May God protect you always.

I enclose a letter that came from Pistoia.

Your Margherita, in Prato.

To Francesco di Marco da Prato, in Florence.
Received from Prato, 25 August 1398.

Letter 178 (1401852)
25 August 1398
Prato

In the name of God. 25 August 1398.

The reason I am writing is because I gathered from your letter to Niccolò that you would be glad for us to come to Florence to have a break from things here. I would be happier to do so than you, and I will if I can. But I could not leave this week for anything in the world because I have to do the washing and hang it out to dry, as well as leave the house in a proper state. In the meantime, I would be happy if I could find a wet nurse with fresh milk for Manno's baby because the woman he has is not the one I would prefer. Although for the time being the baby is fine, he would not be so in the future. It seems that the world has come to an end because I can't find anyone. I had some women available whose children were about to die, but they recovered. You said that you would come tomorrow if you could get Guido's animals, so I will not prolong this letter. May God protect you always.

We are sending you the mare with Argomento.

From your Margherita, in Prato.

To Francesco di Marco da Prato, in Florence.
Received from Prato, 26 August 1398.

Letter 179 (1401853)
15 October 1398
Prato

In the name of God. 15 October 1398.

Cristofano, the laborer, brought me your reply to my two letters. In this one I am writing just a short answer, as that is all that is needed.

There is no more to say about the leather for Monna Giovanna's hat and my gray cloth and the threads.

Do not send me any more cotton wadding until I tell you. The child is being looked after properly.[461]

Regarding the money that you will send or bring, I have nothing more to add. Tomorrow we will find out if it is possible to buy panic, sorghum, millet, or spelt at a good price.[462] You will be told if we get anything, and if there are any tax officials, we will tell them what you say.

Today Piero almost finished that wall, and during their break he and Nanni went to see that timber cut from the trees, so I won't lose any time on this.

Tomorrow Piero will be at the kitchen garden; he will put in those bed heads and start to put in some planks. He is not going to Il Palco because he says the lime is not suitable for rendering. Nevertheless, he says that if you want him to go, you should say so and he will do what you say. He will work on the lime to make it usable, but it will be harder to do the job.

Piero di Monna Mellina will bake some more lime next week.

We told Niccolaio di Biagio about the bundle. He says that if tax has to be paid, he wants the bundle to stay there and not be brought here.

I will say no more for now. May God protect you always.

461. The child is Manno's newborn baby. See letter 169.

462. Panic is a grain related to millet.

Enclosed with this is a letter for Meo Cambioni from Messer Antonio.

From your Margherita, in Prato.

To Francesco di Marco da Prato, in Piazza Tornaquinci, Florence. Received from Prato, 16 October 1398. Answered.

Letter 180 (1401854)
16 October 1398
Prato

In the name of God. 16 October 1398.

This morning we sent you a letter with a priest from the parish church. In the letter we received from you this evening you do not mention it. You must have received it later and so we will only answer your first one.

First of all, this evening at the Angelus, I received thirty *lire* from Mastriscia. I did not make any entry in the register, except that I wrote in his book, underneath the accounts as one usually does, that I received the aforementioned money, and I noted it in the small notebook I keep for expenses. Therefore, tell me in your next letter whether you want me to adjust the entry where it is written in the register "Francesco and Stoldo are owed thirty *lire*," as was done in the past, and if not, what you want done instead.

I also received twenty *lire* from Barzalone di Spedaliere and did not make any record, apart from noting on a piece of paper that I gave twelve of them to Schiavo, which Nanni told me you had said to do. I also gave twenty-seven *soldi* to the carrier, and we spent three *lire* and four *soldi* today on poultry. We still have the rest of the money. Regarding the money that I gave to Schiavo, tell me if you want me to write him down as a debtor in the register or what you want me to do, since there is no other record. Answer me without fail so I won't forget, as I have not made any entry.

Mastriscia says to remember his buffalo hides and to make sure he gets them at a good price.

Tomorrow morning Nanni and Argomento will go to Florence and bring the wines: six barrels from Il Palco and six barrels of wine from La Chiusura. Nanni will tell you what Piero did today and what he will do tomorrow. He did not go to Il Palco because Nanni did not want him to go, as you will have found out in the letter that I sent you this morning. I enclosed a letter for Meo Cambioni and one for you from Niccolò di Piero. In my letter I told you not to send any more cotton wadding until we asked for it.

Barzalone says that the carter will not come down here and he tells you why in a letter enclosed here.

Tell Nanni what you want done with the wine that is left over in the large barrel from La Chiusura, which must be the equivalent of two small barrels, and what you want done with the small barrel left over from Il Palco, which is about half full. We will leave it here until Nanni comes back and we find out what you want done with it. You can also tell Argomento what barrels you want him to bring because he won't refuse you as he would us.

We are sending you the cask of verjuice with the above mentioned items.

For lack of time, we will say no more. May God protect you always.

From Monna Margherita, in Prato

Francesco di Marco da Prato, in Florence.
Received from Prato, 17 October 1398.

Letter 181 (1401855)
17 October 1398
Prato

In the name of God. 17 October 1398.

Nanni brought your letter this evening, as well as one for Niccolò and another for Barzalone. We delivered them.

Nanni arrived here very late yesterday and because of this he decided to bring the small barrel of wine and the wood, as he told you, and then on Saturday he will bring the large barrel, as you say.

I am sending you back Monna Giovanna's leather because she does not know what she wants. When she is in Florence she will buy it herself.[463]

I will show my cloth to Niccolò tomorrow and will let you know what he advises me.

Nanni did not bring the money. I received the black thread.

The priest you sent to me arrived safely but it was too late to send him to the hospital. In my view, they would not have taken him in anyway because, as Monna Filippa has told you, they don't want to take in needy people from Florence. Just the same, I did not want to make a decision by myself, so I sent for Niccolò, and we were both of the same opinion. When these things happen, I think it would be best if you gave such people some money so that they could be taken straight there rather than be taken by your household. Tomorrow, at the proper time, I will tell him to go to the hospital by himself. We had Nanni take him down to the kitchen garden, where he will sleep.[464] We brought him food and drink and whatever else he needed.

Mastriscia and Schiavo will be attended to as you say.

Today Piero fitted the bed heads into the wall, and he put the shelves on the beams and began to put in the planks, three on each side. He has prepared it beneath so that he only has to fix in the planks and fill in the holes around the beams.

We will say no more in this letter. If we have left out anything we will write it tomorrow. May God protect you always.

From your Margherita, in Prato.

To Francesco di Marco da Prato, in Florence.
Received from Prato, 18 October 1398.

463. See letter 179.

464. Margherita is referring to accommodation beside the kitchen garden, adjacent to the Datini palace.

Letter 182 (1401856)
19 November 1398
Prato

In the name of God. 19 November 1398.

This morning we sent you a letter with Argomento. We also sent eight loaves of bread, as well as some grapes and apples in a basket covered with a napkin, and this evening we have still not received an answer from you. We think he must have stayed in Florence because of the weather, as there was a storm with rain and wind today, the like of which we haven't seen for a year. Nanni came back from Pistoia this evening and he brought the ash to Niccolò. Nanni thought it would be better if he went himself because he did not think that the animals would go readily with that boy of his, and he has decided to go to Florence tomorrow because he can't do anything here due to the weather, which is rainy and windy all the time, and he wants to speak to you anyway.

He will bring some bread and oil. We are not sending you any meat because we have not bought a pig that would be suitable. You will have some oranges instead.

I am really wondering what you are doing there since you have no one to serve you or help you in any way. Please tell me how you are managing or what you are doing, as perhaps I am worrying unnecessarily.

Francesco, I remind you that times seem to be going badly, and we are heading for a plague; Master Antonio also believes that one is on the way, though others think it will never happen. Francesco, I will never tire of telling you, and you know I have been saying nothing apart from this for an entire year—but I am not about to stop, even if it has had no effect. There are no more than three months left for those who want to flee. When it is time to flee, one should do so.

I remind you of the vow I made for you to Saint Biagio and which I would like to keep: it is to buy that chalice for the Eucharist and the veil to cover it. Please help me to fulfill this vow that was made for you as long ago as the last plague.

Master Antonio Spedalieri was here today and I asked him whether it is true that he was poisoned, and he said yes: he and his servant and a notary who dined with him.[465] It was a man, not a woman [who did it]. It seems extraordinary to me that a man should show so little love, because you say that no man would ever have the heart to commit such a great evil. I think that in trying to explain it, you will find an excuse for him by claiming he is mad. Master Antonio seems happier than ever, and it seems to me that he bears no grudge against the person who poisoned him; he says that it is certain now that he will not die of the present plague, as the friend who poisoned him purged him far better than Porretta could ever have done.[466] As a result, he has no need to worry about the plague now.

Send me back my hose so I can whiten them, and send me back all the baskets and some cumin, if you can.

We will not list what we are sending you, because Nanni will be bringing it.

I went to see Mastriscia today with Guido, and he had gone to Florence. I imagine he will be there with you and will have made an agreement with you.

Niccolò wanted to tell Ser Nicola everything himself. You will be informed of his reply.

I told Barzalone what you said. He and Niccolò were with Antonio di Zarino, and they will tell you what they did.[467] May God protect you always.

The reply from Pistoia will be enclosed with this letter.

Send us some pomegranates, as there are none to be found here.

From your Margherita, in Prato.

To Francesco di Marco da Prato, in Florence.
Received from Prato, 20 November 1398.

---

465. Antonio Spedalieri was a Dominican friar from a prominent family in Pistoia. His letters to Francesco and others will be published by Simona Brambilla.

466. Margherita refers to the thermal baths at Porretta, near Bologna.

467. On 17 October Francesco had instructed Margherita to tell Antonio di Zarino to keep his word, if he ever wanted help again (FD 143.)

Letter 183 (1401857)
20 November 1398
Prato

In the name of God. 20 November 1398.

Paolo delivered your letter to us. I reply here. We don't have the letter addressed to the prior of San Fabiano to which you refer, only one addressed to Ser Conte, and we delivered that. I will send you the fruit as soon as possible.

We sent you the bishop's letter with Nanni. Guido says that Antonio Micocchi never asked for him and never saw him since you left, so you can see that he is telling the truth.

Niccolò will be reminded about the things that have to be done and will do his best. Please tell Nanni what you need when you see him.

The very mature oranges have been picked, and I sent a lot to San Niccolò. They were picked before Sunday.

All the barrels are sealed with chalk and soft hemp, as you instructed Niccolò, and we advised you of this in a letter sent to you with Argomento yesterday.

We got the chalk and the sacks, and we told Niccolò that he can have some if he needs them. I will have the wheat done on the first day the wind is not so strong.

I sent word to Monna Luca about the flax. She says she doesn't have any more, but I asked Domenica and she says they processed some this year. She says the worker to whom they gave half of the flax to ret produced fourteen measures, while hers produced twelve.[468] She says it very much depends on whether you soak it in a little water or a lot. It weighs more when it has less water. Ours has been well retted.

We told Niccolò what you said about Bindo Piaciti.

Guido gave your instructions to Guiduccio di Duti, and he says that however matters turn out he will ensure you are satisfied.[469] May God protect you.

From your Margherita, in Prato.

---

468. Retting is the process of soaking flax or hemp in water to loosen the fibers; for hemp, see letter 141.

469. See letters 183, 186, and 190.

Later, this evening, Niccolò showed us a note in which you tell us that you have kept Nanni and you will send us an answer with him as well as those things mentioned in the letter.

Piero da Donnino was here yesterday evening and he says that on Friday and Saturday he will be working at the threshing barn and will finish the fireplace and construct the drain. He would like Nanni to prepare everything beforehand.[470]

Tomorrow Guido will go to La Chiusura, and he will see Pagliaio.

We gave Mastriscia the cheeses and two buffalo hides and noted them on his and Domenico's account. You do not specify whether it is to be paid in cash or the date by which payment should be made. Tell us in the next letter, but it is certainly true that Mastriscia says it is to be paid within four months. Tell me whether this is correct.

Regarding the wheat you mention, I made an entry about Antonio di Zarino's wheat. The entry reads that Francesco and Domenico should be registered as receiving five *moggia* of wheat that we accepted on their behalf from Antonio, to defray the forty florins that he borrowed in Florence to pay his *prestanza* taxes. There is no other record in the register, and this is what I said to Niccolò di Piero and Barzalone. They said that there were seven *moggia*, and I said, "I find five. Perhaps he gave us another two later and no record was made. But I do not remember this and I can't find more than five." They said that you would know, and they wanted to inform you about it. So if a record was not made, it is not my fault, because perhaps I was not there when the two *moggia* came. I do not remember seeing them come, although I certainly knew that there were two remaining to be delivered, since I asked him for them several times, and for this reason I think he did give them as he says. May God protect you always.

To Francesco di Marco da Prato, in Piazza Tornaquinci, Florence. Received from Prato, 21 November 1398. Answered.

---

470. See letters 169, 171, 179, and 180.

Letter 184 (1401858)
23 November 1398
Prato

In the name of God. 23 November 1398.

This evening we received a letter from you. I reply here.

We have not received the letters that you say you sent with Dino. This evening I went to his house to find out what he did with them, but he was not yet home. Tomorrow, when he has come back, I will go and see him. This explains the short letter we wrote. It was because we had not received a letter from you and I was expecting you this evening. For this reason we did not write very much.

Piero worked yesterday. He constructed the drain and rebuilt the doorway. Today he cemented the drain and the fireplace and built a threshold for the middle doorway and laid a row of raised bricks to separate the threshold from the street.[471]

Meo di Bartolomeo, the dyer, brought the letter from Pistoia. Tomorrow I will write to the man about it, and I will keep doing so until he sends us a reply.

I did not ask Niccolò di Piero about the wool because it had been there such a long time and because there had been so much wind that it was bone dry. Just the same, if it had seemed damp, I would not have had it baled. I would have told Niccolò and written to you and asked if you wanted me to have it baled.

I went to see Matteo di Fattalbuio. He said he wishes you had written to him a couple of days earlier, and then he could have come. Now he has made a promise to those Jews and he says that although he would prefer to be with you rather than with them, he has given his word and he begs you to excuse him because he does not want to break his promise.

Piero is not working here this week but doing some work of his own. Nanni will keep you informed.

I told Niccolò di Piero everything you wrote to me, and he says he will explain it all to you tomorrow.

---

471. This work was to stop water flowing into the cellar. See letter 175.

[Added by the scribe:]

Monna Margherita says she is very pleased that you have bought the altar cloth to fulfill her vow to Saint Biagio.[472]

If the messenger comes here, we will give him a warm welcome.

Monna Margherita says she looks after the house and the household far better than you would have, because she has worked harder at it than you.

We will send you the mantle and eight loaves of bread with Nanni tomorrow.

We gave the buckskin back to Stefano Baldinucci today.

[Dictated by Margherita:]

I, Margherita, decided to send Nanni there tomorrow, and he is bringing your mantle and eight loaves of bread. Tell him about the bed and what is to be done here. May God protect you always.

Your Margherita, in Prato.

To Francesco di Marco da Prato, in Florence.
Received from Prato, 24 November 1398. Answered.

Letter 185 (1401859)
24 November 1398
Prato

In the name of God. 24 November 1398.

This evening we received your letter from Nanni. I reply here.

I am astonished that you are so amazed that Nanni went to Florence today. You apparently do not remember what you wrote to us, and now he has wasted a good day's labor. I don't know if it's Sunday there in Florence. It's Sunday here! Our friar preached a week ago that Saint Catherine was absentminded, and today he repeated that she was absentminded! Your letter says that upon receiving it we should pass on this message to Niccolò di Piero: "If possible I want him to come and stay with me for the next two days, and if he can, he should

---

472. See letter 182.

come tomorrow and bring the white mare." It also says: "I will send it back tomorrow evening so Nanni can come here if Matteo can't. Let me know in one of tomorrow's letters and have Nanni come here, as well as Niccolò with the other mare. In the event that neither Niccolò nor Matteo can come, send Nanni tomorrow on any saddle horse he pleases and give me a proper answer."[473] I reflected on this, seeing you wanted to know whether Niccolò or Matteo could come. You also said that Nanni should come to you in Florence and that we should tell you everything through him, and that he should come to Florence with the riding saddle. Two explanations came to mind: the first was that you wanted to come here, and the second that you wanted to discuss something with one of the builders. I would never have sent him except for the fact that in your letter you insisted that we should send Nanni, if Niccolò and Fattalbuio were not able to come, and that we should keep you fully informed. If you wish to contradict me, the letter is right here. I will keep it. It is in your handwriting.

To keep you happy the lock was put on Il Palco today even though it's Sunday. The barrels were opened this evening and they were cleaned out, refilled, and replugged properly.

The grain has not been put in sacks. No one is to blame because the miller has not yet brought us back what he has at the mill. I reminded him, but he still hasn't brought it to us. I had six bushels put in sacks, so if he brought the flour to us, I could give him the rest.

In my opinion, it is better off in the vat because when it is in sacks the mice eat it. On Monday evening it will all be in bags and he will be told that Rosso is coming to collect it.

We received a letter of yours from Dino del Bodda today. I reply to it here.

Messer Piero has been told what you wrote to us.[474] You were told about the sack of wool.

The measurements of the bed in the ground-floor kitchen are five and a quarter yards in length and seven and three-eighths in width. The higher bed end is two and three-quarter yards high, and the other end is one inch short of two and a half yards.

473. Francesco's letter is not extant.

474. This is Piero Rinaldeschi.

Tell Monna Bice that the cloths she sent him are very good, and all he needs are a few good swaddling bands. The baby was here today and he is very well; he is such a good boy that he could not be any better.[475]

We will find a way of sending you the brazier, and today Niccolaio from Tavola was told what you said.

Michele del Campana's sieve is here, and Nanni says we need it here. Why don't you buy one there in Florence? Just the same, we will send it to you, if you want it.

We have not picked the oranges yet because there has not been a cold snap yet. Still, I will make enquiries; if it is advisable, we will pick them.

It is true that Domenica was arrested for some debt that Saccente incurred.[476] I sent for Niccolò and he said that it was best for me to pay it. You were not involved. Domenica was locked up for one day and then went home to her place. It all happened because of Saccente's usual evil nature.

I told Monna Giovanna what you said. Monna Giovanna said she has no doubt you will do all and more than you promised, but that she has other worries you know about.[477]

Nanni came back here this evening and says he refuses to return unless you write a letter directly to him in your own hand. Otherwise he will not come. He partly blames Niccolò di Giovanni di Ser Dato for the wasted time, although he is used to this sort of thing happening.

The quilt that is there in Florence belonged to Monna Dianora. I won't send a quilt there until you decide which bed is to remain. Then I will decide and look after whatever else I see needs to be done.

I will say no more since it is late. May God protect you always.

From your Margherita, in Prato.

To Francesco di Marco da Prato, in Piazza Tornaquinci, Florence. Received from Prato, 27 November. Answered.

---

475. Manno d'Albizo degli Agli's baby was born in August 1398. See letter 169. Monna Bice Marini, Manno's mother, had sent the necessary supplies to the wet nurse in Prato.

476. Margherita's servant Domenica was Saccente's wife.

477. Margherita refers here to the widow of Paolo Mattei.

Letter 186 (1401860)
28 November 1398
Prato

In the name of God. 28 November 1398.

The reason for this letter is that Nanni arrived here this evening, but I did not receive a reply from you. It doesn't matter very much.

Tomorrow I will send you the quilt, the two feather pillows from the warehouse, and the curtains. I will send you lots of broad beans and dried chickpeas in the pod for the household. I will send you some figs that [you can give to] Francesca if you like. Otherwise keep them there […].

I had a very bad stomach ache this week, so I need some Malvasia wine and some […]. I did not want to write so as not to upset you.

I am sending neither eggs nor bread because Nanni says that […] and it seems to be true. We bought some veal on Saturday […]. We ate it on Monday morning because we thought you were coming back on Sunday with Nanni. If you are not coming next Saturday, I won't buy any, although I could; or you could buy some there if you have to offer hospitality to Niccolò before Sunday. Niccolò was here yesterday evening and looked for that document, but he didn't find it. Tell us where you left it.

Today Guido was at Monna Luca's place and told her what you said. He says that she doesn't have the money to pay, but there is no need to worry about it because if you were to lose anything she would keep the agreement by forfeiting her property. If it comes to this you can have everything except the barrel that is full of wine. She says she is owed ten *lire* by you for slippers. Guiduccio has been at Prato since Tuesday. I gave Ser Schiatta your message. He says he will do it. […][478]

May God protect you always.

From your Margherita, in Prato.

To Francesco di Marco da Prato, in Florence.
Received from Prato, 29 November 1398.

---

478. This letter has a number of holes, as indicated. At this point there are three lines where lacunae make it impossible to reconstruct the meaning.

[Added by the scribe:]

We are not sending you the pills because Monna Margherita says that she does not wish to send you medicine that has to be swallowed unless she can trust the person who brings it. If Nanni returns to Florence, we will send the pills with him or some other trusted person.

Letter 187 (1401861)
29 November 1398
Prato

In the name of God. 29 November 1398.

We received your letter from Nanni. We answer here.

Because Nanni arrived tonight at the fourth hour after sunset, I will reply briefly because there is nothing of any urgency. There is no need for you to remind me of the fact that you have been there for two weeks and are getting little sleep, because I am more than certain that you are staying awake and taking little care of your health. I am very upset about this and I cannot help it. Niccolò said that he did not pay tax for that coarse wool, but that Guido will see him again tomorrow anyway and ask him about it.

We will send you the quilt that was in the bedroom at the kitchen garden, as well as a mattress of the same size. You do not mention a mattress. I think one is needed for the quilt that Nanni took there. According to me you have enough quilts, but if you want one for Nanni, it occurred to me, if you agree, that there is already a cover there that Domenico was supposed to fill. It could be filled with the stuffing from the household quilt that was made for Lucia and that is up there where Cilia used to sleep. I know that I overfilled it because the feathers were bad. I always planned to take some feathers out. If you wait until I arrive, I would like to fix it so one would be good enough and the other better, because you certainly don't want too many bad feathers in a quilt. Two things have kept me here: one is that I have not been well, and the other is that I know that these goods have to go to Florence. No one knows better than I that I would have come there myself with Lucia. I would have fulfilled my vow, and we would have cooked and prepared the things that you need. You would have spent your time on more important matters, and in my opinion you would have been more comfortable and in a better state, and I would have been happier. I beg you, if you have to remain any longer, to send me a message and I will come with Lucia. It will be for the best and you will finish off your business more quickly.

I received the Malvasia wine and the theriac.[479] I drank a little this evening and it did me a lot of good and almost cured me.

I will send you as much bread as I think will last you until Monday, but I think it would be a good thing if you returned here for a few days. Monna Giovanna was present when the letter was read, and heard what you say. She says may God give you a good life, and she commends herself to you and asks you to commend her to Tommaso.[480]

Monna Margherita della Maglia's feather quilt doesn't properly fit the bed that I sent you, so I am sending you one that does.

We can decide what we want to do about Baldetto's affairs when I arrive.[481]

Regarding the bedding mentioned above, I will not send it to Zezo now because I am using it and he doesn't need it now.

Guido will pass on your message to everyone and will do as you instruct.

I am pleased to hear what you say about Monna Margherita's affairs. If you see her again, send her a hundred thousand thanks from me.[482]

---

479. Theriac was a cure-all medicine, the essential ingredient of which was viper's blood. (In its original meaning the word "treacle," or "theriacle," is closely related.)

480. This is Tommaso del Bianco.

481. Baldo, or Baldetto di Giovanni Villanuzzi, had left for Barcelona in October 1397. See FD 111. On Baldetto's services to Francesco's companies in Spain, see Melis, *Aspetti della vita economica medievale*, 272, 276.

482. Margherita della Maglia was the widow of Michele Barducci, a Florentine merchant who operated in Avignon from the late 1350s. In 1381, Margherita sold a draper's shop in Avignon to Francesco, and after this she and her family moved between Tuscany and Provence. Her nickname, Della Maglia, came from the activities of her son-in-law Bartolomeo di Lapo da Pistoia, who was a dealer in armor (*maglia*; compare "mail"). See Luciana Frangioni, "Avignon: The Beginnings," in Nigro, ed., *Francesco di Marco Datini*, 256.

I am sending you a bag containing two pairs of sheets and two shirts that are tied together with a length of thread. I think one belongs to Rosso and the other to Stoldo. Give them the shirts, and there are seven small napkins, both good quality and bad. There are also knives that need to be sharpened; and four napkins (two white and two embroidered); four tablecloths; four small towels and two large ones, as well as another wrapped in a thin kerchief; three caps; two head veils and one gown; a shirt for you and one for Pellegrino, with a hood and his overgown; and a pair of white hose for you if you want to change them. Change the sheets of the young boys, and your own as well, and send me all the dirty clothes. Everything I am sending you is old. This is because it is hard to dry new things in winter. There are two baskets, one with bread and the other with fruit in it. I will send you a quilt, a cover, and some stuffing for Guido's bed. I can't send you any more because, as you know, it is winter. We are still here. You have to come back, and we will all need to be warmly dressed when we leave for Florence. We will bring everything then. We are sending you the worst daybed mattress that we have. It is five yards long. In this room, where there is poor light, it looks fine. There are also two napkins covering the baskets. Put them away so they don't get any dirtier than necessary.

Today we received five sacks of washed wool from Pietrasanta; we paid the carter, and he received nine florins and one *lira*, one *soldo*, and four *denari*. Niccolò lent me the florins because I did not have any. Tell me if you want me to record a credit against Niccolò's name, and I will do so. I only made a note about the wool on a piece of paper. Niccolò thinks the wool is rather wet. I think we will hang it out somewhere tomorrow, as Niccolò thinks best. He will report to you about its condition. Today I received seven *lire* and two *soldi* from Agostino Buonfiglioli. I will write down "he is owed" in the place of "he owes."

On two occasions I lent Niccolò twenty-two *lire* and twelve *soldi*. He said he would pay me back. I made a note on a piece of paper. There is no other record.

Since it is the seventh hour at night, and we need to prepare the things to send you, we will say no more. May God protect you always.

From your Margherita, in Prato.

To Francesco di Marco da Prato himself, in Florence.
Received from Prato, 30 November. Answered.

Letter 188 (1401862)
1 December 1398
Prato

In the name of God. 1 December 1398.

    I am writing this because Nanni arrived here yesterday evening at the fourth hour and said that for some reason you had not been able to write to us.[483] He said that you would write everything you wanted to say this evening. No letter has come yet. Nanni told Monna Giovanna that he met Tommaso on the Leccio road.[484] She was very worried. I told her that in my opinion she had no reason to be because I believe Tommaso must have finished what he had to do in Leccio and have gone away for a good reason, and he has probably done more than she realizes. I said that men do not want to tell us their secrets because they realize we have little strength of character. Please, if you have something to say that you don't think should be spread around, tell me if you like; but if you don't want it to be known, perhaps it is better that you don't tell me. You know what an unhappy and grief-stricken state she was in when you left. I tried to comfort her as best I could. I can't tell you much except that when she knew Tommaso was in Florence, she was always happy; but now that she has discovered he has gone, she is the opposite. Nanni, who saw her, can testify to this. Francesco, if you need any advice about how you should treat her, please let me know so you can do what you promised for her. If you are willing to reveal that the help comes from you, I would be pleased, and if you agree to say that I wrote this to you, I would also be pleased, because I will say it to her directly anyway, no matter how much she wants to deny it out of fear of you. Nanni told me last night

483. This was around ten in the evening.

484. This is the Florentine merchant Tommaso del Bianco. See letter 141. Monna Giovanna, the widow of Paolo Mattei, was anxious about investments Francesco had made on her behalf. See also letter 191.

how pleased you were that I was coming there, and Monna Giovanna seems very unhappy that I am leaving her here. Ginevra had a swollen throat for which I had to make a potion every day according to Master Matteo's instructions.[485] You know that the girl is not afraid of anyone except me, and now she has fallen again and injured her forehead a little. I hope that with good treatment she will recover. In my presence she is the best girl there ever was, and if I am not here, they say she will not do what they want, although I don't believe it. I was coming just for you because I don't think you are as well as I would like; and if I were there, you and those with you could look after your affairs better. This was the reason I was going to come, rather than the vow I made.

Matteo di Fattalbuio says he is ready whenever you like, although he hasn't finished that job yet and it is paying him well. Just the same, he puts himself in your hands; you only need to tell him to come and he will. Tomorrow is market day, and I would rather not leave then as I would run into too many people. Write and tell me what you want me to do. I will not leave unless I receive another letter from you. May God protect you always,

From your Margherita, in Prato.

To Francesco di Marco da Prato, in Florence.
Received from Prato, 2 December 1398. Answered.

Letter 189 (1401863)
1 December 1398
Prato

In the name of God. 1 December 1398.

The reason for my letter is that Agnolo arrived here this evening without any letters, and he says that he came into Prato from the high road, as you had instructed, but found no letters at the gate because they said they hadn't received any. Niccolò told us the name of the person to whom he gave them. It is the fourth hour after sunset now, and we still haven't received them.

---

485. This is the doctor Matteo di Giovanni Giuntini.

Nanni won't be coming to Florence tomorrow because we are not sure what he is supposed to bring. The market is being held here, so Niccolò can't see to the wool either, though he thinks it should be washed now while the weather is good. If you suggest we employ someone else, Francesco, you should realize it isn't easy finding people who do this kind of work and deliver it as well. If it is good weather tomorrow, the wool will be washed and brought to our house. While the wool is drying, he will carry the firewood inside, pile up the lime, and do whatever there is to do so that he doesn't waste time while the wool is drying. On Tuesday Nanni will go to Florence, whether we receive letters from you or not, and he will bring the things that we want. By tomorrow we may well have the letters you sent us, and we will follow your instructions. Agnolo has hired a packhorse, and tomorrow he is going to Pietrasanta. We will have the mule well looked after. Tell us when you want it and whether we should send it to you or keep it here.

Today we sent you a letter with Meo di Goro, and I told you what we needed. I am not leaving if you don't let me know whether or not I should. Thinking about the things that have to be taken to Florence, it occurred to me that it is best for me to stay here, because I know better than the others what has to be sent there to Florence. Nevertheless, I will come whenever you say. Agnolo tells me that you are well, and have been except for the day when you took the pills that upset you. Saccente has been sending me desperate messages. Because he is such a great liar, I didn't take much notice, because Nanni doesn't tell me these things in case I worry. Saccente has been imprisoned, and he has sent me many messages imploring me to lend him forty *soldi*, and then he drops it to twenty. If I were to see that liar on the gallows, I wouldn't spend a farthing to save him, because he is nothing but lies and deceit.[486]

I wrote to you today about that business concerning Monna Giovanna.[487] She has no doubt that as long as you live, you will not take the legal action you should, but she is worried about the future and has told me so. As I wrote to you today, if you can get any information there that you need to present to her, please obtain it so that

486. The servant Saccente had aroused Margherita's wrath several days before because his wife, Domenica, had been imprisoned for a day because of his debts. See letter 185.
487. See letter 188.

when you get here, you can help her as you should. And if you want to say it was your idea to do what you must for her, I will be pleased. On the other hand, if you want to reveal that I spoke to you about it, I will still be pleased. She thinks that Tommaso is leading her by the nose to the slaughter, and perhaps she thinks that you are not just twiddling your thumbs either. Francesco, you know I told you to be careful not to get so involved that you could end up regretting it, and it seems to me that you forget about a lot of the money that other people owe you. I think this is very sensible, but there are plenty of people who wouldn't think twice about ruining a friendship to get back five *soldi*, and these are not good friendships; but it's no use taking it to heart because everyone has this fault and when people are foolish, it takes a good deal of wisdom to know how to tolerate them. And consider that she is a woman, and women have little judgement—so wiser people should be tolerant of them. When you are here, you can quietly question her, see what she wants, and afterward you can say what you like.

Don't worry about Ginevra because fortunately I don't think her sore throat will get any worse. I don't need to tell you this because I know you are convinced that I treat her better than if she were my own daughter, and I do indeed think of her as mine. I didn't want to say anything about it because I know that you have other worries and it just wasn't necessary. The bump on her head is nothing, but I was worried about her sore throat. The doctor told me he didn't think there would be any complications. We are doing what he says; she has not had a fever or anything else and she has kept on eating and drinking. May God protect you always.

From your Margherita, in Prato.

To Francesco di Marco, in Piazza Tornaquinci, Florence.
Received from Prato, 4 December 1398. Answered.

Letter 190 (1401864)
2 December 1398
Prato

In the name of God. 2 December 1398.

This evening we received your letter of 30 [December], delivered by Lorenzo Cosi, and also one for Bernabò and one for Niccolò that we gave to them immediately.[488]

As for Monna Margherita della Maglia's feather quilt, I knew it wouldn't be right for that bed because I know what it is like. It seems to me that there is no need now for any more feather quilts. I am sending you the mattress that was on Monna Giovanna's bed, as well as the good red cover, the cover for the sides, the blue curtain, the black one, as well as the Romagnol one that was at Il Palco, a blue bench cover, the carpet from beside my daybed, and a small pillow and a big one of Nanni's. […] nice gestures and kind words are a waste of time.[489] He does well who knows what to do and when to stop.

I have searched here for the quilt cover and I can't find it, but I will look again more carefully. I think it was sent to Florence for Domenico di Cambio to fill, and he replied that feathers were too expensive or that the ones we had put away there had been sold. I can't really remember. I think perhaps it was taken there when we were at Il Palco. I am sure it is not in the big wooden chest next to the wardrobe because it was full of feathers, and the only place I put it was under the bed or somewhere out of the way to keep the house tidy.

As for coming there, I think it best that I don't come for quite a few days. I really must find the things that have to be taken there and prepare for the journey, because there is no one here I can trust to do these things properly, nor could I leave them and be satisfied. What I did, I did for love, because I don't think you are as well as I would like, and you never have been. I'm here taking care of people I ought not to be, and I'm not taking care of those I should be; but I will happily do whatever you wish.

---

488. The scribe made an error here. He ought to have written 30 November. Lorenzo Cosi was a butcher and friend of Naddino d'Aldobrandino Bovattieri.

489. The manuscript is damaged at this point, and the meaning of the sentence is unclear.

In my opinion, Francesco, you should return here on Sunday and stay for a few days, as you keep promising. You could organize things here as if you were staying; and if you have business to attend to, you could do it for a few days, and in the meantime, I will get everything prepared and I won't rest for a moment, so that when you arrive here you will have less to do, and you can tell me what needs to be sent to Florence and I will look after it.

I told Monna Giovanna what you said about Tommaso and she was very happy. Don't be too worried about her affairs, Francesco.

I have [...] women to the men from Prato who are trading at the market. They are not very experienced, and you know how they always assume they are being duped. If I were a man, unless I had experience, I would not get involved in women's chores, or even men's. It is very tiring work and they are convinced they will be deceived, and you have had this experience dealing with people from Prato.

I am sending you the bedclothes, but if you don't need them, don't lay them out there.

We will send you the dried vine shoots as soon as we can, but it needs to be a fair time after they are crushed, given that they are for the bed filling. If we don't send you things exactly as you require, don't be angry because I am only a woman. I am here alone with a gaggle of girls and I have had no one here to help me. I am sending you things as I think best.

I will send you bread, and now that Nanni is to come to you every day, he will bring what you need from day to day.

Stefano Guazzalotti's servant came here and asked me for your surcoat for Papero. He said that you were supposed to tell me about it, but I informed him repeatedly that I hadn't yet received your letters. He gave many convincing signs that he had indeed been to see you, but all the same I told him that you had once told me never to lend any of your clothing to anyone, and I intended to abide by that. I added that it was no fault of yours, but of those who hadn't delivered your letters. He and Niccolò left. After turning over in my mind why he wanted the surcoat and considering what a fine young man he is, I sent for Niccolò and asked him if he knew why he had asked for this surcoat. He replied: "Don't you know what happened to Papero?" I knew nothing or I wouldn't have responded as I did. I told Niccolò to tell him that, given the situation, I had decided to ignore your order since I was sure you would be happy about it. It seemed the right thing to say in the circumstances.

I have discovered two surcoats here, one of which I think doesn't belong to us because I remember that I put two buttons on the front of yours and sewed the border of the collar. There isn't one like that here. I asked Lucia and she said that once you lent it to Manno, and he left us his. I know nothing about this. Tell me: is it true? I will show him both and he can take the one he prefers, and we will make a note of it and then let Papero know. I have had both weighed, and each weighs thirty-one pounds and nine ounces. They are exactly the same weight.

Guido will look at the account book—that is, Monna Giovanna's account book—and let you know what you asked about.

I like that wine from the Strait of Messina, and it seems to me nothing needs to be done to it.

I will pass on your message to Niccolò.

I will remind Guido about his mule. You would be better off sending the small mule here. I was amazed that you took on that inconvenience in Florence, because it seems to me you have enough worries.

Guido will tell Niccolò what you say about Matteo.

The key to the kitchen garden is being cut. It will be ready tomorrow.

I will have the latch removed tomorrow, because this evening it is already late, and Nanni will bring it to you the following day. Pellegrino's doublet has not been made because the tailor is the worst liar there ever was. I have never been able to get my overgown back from him. Not only have I not had it back, I have never even seen him. On Sunday I told his wife that I would never send him anything else, and I won't. He received the cotton wadding, and I made the sleeves. I told Guido to press him about it.

Yesterday we dried some of the wool, but today there was not enough sun to dry the rest, and it seems to me that it is still damp.

Niccolò will keep you informed about the matter.

We gave the letter to Bernabò, and tomorrow he will come to Florence. As for your not wanting Nanni and the two animals to be wasting time here, I think you are right, and there is not a hair on my body that isn't sorry that he didn't go there today, especially when I saw there was no sun. However, he was not idle; during the day he piled up the lime, brought in the sand that was outside, stacked up the wood on the threshing floor, and brought the wool home: in all, hardly anything!

Because it is late, don't be surprised that we cannot answer you point by point. I am not worried about staying up late on my own account, but rather out of concern for the rest of the household and for Nanni, who is going to Florence. Send him back as early in the evening as you can, for his sake and that of the animals, because he has returned twice at the fourth hour after sunset. It is not that Nanni complains. I am saying this of my own accord. I think that sometimes you get him to bring things, not for your own profit, but as a favor to others. The days are so short that he can hardly manage, even if he throws the loads in the middle of the road and turns around immediately for the return journey. Just think, Francesco, if these animals get sick or Nanni falls ill, it would be a disaster for us. These last few nights there has been such a heavy fog that in the morning it seemed as if it had snowed. Stop serving others, and let's concentrate on our own affairs.

I am sending you the walnut table, the old table, and your old lined doublet. Send me all the dirty washing with Nanni and the large and small baskets, and I will send them back gradually. If you can't send them tomorrow, get them ready tomorrow evening so that the day after tomorrow they can be brought here.

Schiavo is here and says he needs ten florins. Today Guido gave him four *lire* to buy barley, beans, and other things to sow. Let me know about what should be given to him. In this letter I will say no more. May God protect you always.

From your Margherita [in Prato].

Today seven sacks of Barbary wool arrived here from Bologna. The total weight is 2,361. We paid the carter for transport and the toll but not for the duty. The toll gatherer has written […] we have kept the letter. Niccolò said that he thought the toll gatherer had made a mistake in calculating the duty. We gave the carters forty-six *lire* and four *soldi* for transporting it; that is, ten heavy florins that Niccolò lent me, six *lire*, and four *soldi*. I will see that everything is in order, as I did last time, following your instructions. If you want to pay Niccolò back there, do so. Tomorrow I will get Niccolò to write down for me the money he spent for that sack of coarse wool, and I will forward it to you.

Today I received twenty-five *lire* from Niccolaio Mastriscia, and I recorded it properly.

I had the remainder of the money from Antonio di Zarino, that is, eight *lire*. Tell me how you want me to record it. I only have it as an entry in my little notebook, and I also made a note of it on a piece of paper. Tell me how you want it recorded.

I couldn't get any money from anyone else. I will tell Niccolaio Brancacci what you say. I will wait to see what he says.

Guiduccio di Duti says the wool should be paid for by the 14th of this month, but tomorrow he has to send some gray cloth to Florence that is as good as sold. The day after he will come to see you and he will find out whether Stoldo agrees it is worth the market price he says he could get, but he doesn't say whether he will give him the full amount, which is approximately forty or forty-five florins.

Nanni says that Matteo di Barberino came to see him today and told him that Cristoforo's laborers have been engaged again.

I will make a note of the wool, as you instruct, and likewise of the wool that arrived today from Bologna.

We are looking after the wheat, the barrels, and the other things properly.

To Francesco di Marco da Prato, in Florence.
Received from Prato, 3 December 1398. Answered.

Letter 191 (1401865)
3 December 1398
Prato

In the name of God. 3 December 1398.

I received one of your letters, delivered by Nanni, to which I will reply briefly because it is almost the same as the one we received yesterday.

I am absolutely certain you are staying up all night because you say that the days are so short that one can't get anything done unless one works all night. Don't think that way about Monna Giovanna. You can be sure that she is concerned about her own affairs. If I hadn't advised her against it, she would have gone to Leccio to find out about her situation, and she had asked Nanni how far it was. I told Nanni to tell her the road was so long she wouldn't arrive this year, but perhaps it would have been kinder to let her go and see what happened.[490] Francesco, don't be upset, because this is the way everyone behaves, and even Ginevra, who is six years old, knows how to get what she wants; but this doesn't happen to me, and there is no need to be grateful to me because I carry on as always. The donkey's owner always gets the best deal. Don't write any more about your way of living and your constant late nights, because I am already worried enough about them; and if you had seen me on Sunday, perhaps you might have felt sorry for me, because I imagined and was told about the sort of life and discomforts that you suffer there. I decided not to depart because I didn't think I would be able to leave the household in a proper state. You can't just hope things will be done properly, given how young the servants and employees I have here are; it could end in disaster. Francesco, from now until Sunday, I will get on with what I have to do and wait for you until then. But I have decided that if you are not here by Sunday, I will be there in Florence with the whole household in tow on Monday or Tuesday. However, I should dearly have liked it if you could have first come with me to San Biagio; although not on foot, because the vow is mine and I don't want to do myself harm, given how things are these days, and my health isn't what it might

---

490. See letter 188.

be.[491] Francesco, I gather from your letter that you are very anxious. I want to remind you about what I said to you on another occasion: that the blessings and pain that we have in this world are of our own making. Now I've also thought of something else: that if I am to be at peace with myself, then I must only desire to do the will of God and so be at peace within myself; it does not seem to me that expecting recognition from others leads to good, or to good spirits, and if you don't expect recognition, you will have more peace of mind than if you do the contrary. And if you wish to say "I am doing this for their own good, you shouldn't worry about this," I am convinced, Francesco, that I am right to try to the best of my ability to remember those two things every day. If you say "You won't succeed," events will prove you wrong, and I cannot see another way of attaining peace in this world.

You can see what sort of weather we are having at the moment, so I can't tell you what I will be sending you. We will act according to the dictates of the weather.

I searched here for the cover of the feather quilt but I cannot find it, Francesco. You are mistaken in saying that it is in the chest at the foot of the wardrobe, because it has never been there, although I keep the pillows for the gold coverlet and all the finest things that we don't use there. I wouldn't have put the cover where the feathers had been. Look there in Florence, instead, either above where the hats are kept or where you used to keep the fruit, in case you ever put them away there. Ask Domenico di Cambio about it because I believe that it was taken to Florence.

I have given the surcoat to Giovanni, and I have already told you about the one that came this morning. We will do it without any further discussion because in the letter that we sent you this morning I answered all the queries raised in yours of this evening. Don't sit up all night writing replies to us. You have enough letters to write to others. Even if we write long letters to you, don't worry. Just respond to the most urgent matters.

On the 3rd of June 1398 there are eight sealed florins, six *lire*, eleven *soldi*, and two *denari* in Monna Giovanna's account. Two *de-*

---

491. See letter 182, where Margherita refers to the vow she had made to Saint Biagio, to whom she had prayed for protection against the plague. She may be referring to a church attached to the monastery of San Biagio at Carmignano, not far from Prato.

nari were paid out for her to the Monte for the tax on the 800 florins of communal debt you bought from her.[492]

If you haven't already received them, get Domenico to give you the twenty *lire* and eight *soldi* for the duty and the transportation costs of the three bales of black buffalo skins and the cheeses that Mastriscia received.[493]

Niccolò was in the commune a good deal today. He wasn't able to tell me what he paid for that coarse wool. Tomorrow I will get him to give me the account, and I will send it to you. He says to take note that because the toll gatherer was not in Pescia, he didn't pay down there and so must pay the duty here.

We are sending you the latch for the main door tomorrow. May God protect you always.

From your Margherita, in Prato.

To Francesco di Marco da Prato, in Florence.
Received from Prato, 4 December 1398. Answered.

Letter 192 (1401866)
4 December 1398
Prato

In the name of God. 4 December 1398.

[…] I received a letter from you and there are many items that require an answer. We reply to those that seem most urgent to me.

Regarding Bernabò, you did well to be courteous to him about the matter. I will tell Niccolaio […] what you say if he comes to Prato. With regard to Margherita della Maglia's quilt, it is not needed here now because we have my big bed, Monna Giovanna's, Lucia's, the two beds on the ground floor, and the two in the house next door. There is also an additional large quilt on Monna Giovanna's bed. No more are needed.

---

492. For sealed florins, see note 414, above. The *Monte Comune* was the public debt fund for Florence.

493. See letter 183.

I really cannot find the quilt I have been looking for, but I will look more carefully just the same. Find out from Domenico if the quilt ever went to Florence. If it did and was not filled, it did not come back here. In my opinion the quilt went there more than two years ago, before we returned to this house, in the year we had so many people at Il Palco.

You say you are sending us the dirty clothes and the rooster, but I think you thought that Nanni was coming to you this morning.

Guido went to Ser Conte, who says he will give him the money tomorrow, and afterward Nanni will pass it on to Schiavo.

We will send you some broad beans from the sack whenever you want them.

I told Guido to supply the wheat as you say. He says there is no problem.

The letter for Barzalone was not among our letters; only one addressed to Niccolò di Piero.

You were right to be surprised that Nanni did not come. Guido was wrong not to tell you why, because I did tell him what we intended. Yesterday evening at the third hour, Nanni arrived here soaking wet and in the condition you predicted. Just the same, we decided he would return to Florence if the weather was good. We put twelve bushels of sifted flour into sacks and he said, "If it doesn't rain I will go." It didn't stop raining all night and continued until halfway through the morning. I got up and found that Guido had gone to take the letters, and he did not remember to put in the one explaining why Nanni was not coming. I was very upset because I could well imagine what you were thinking. Later, when it got to terce and I saw that the weather had improved a little, I had a good reason for not sending him because if he went there today he would lose a day's work tomorrow. It was too late for him to be able to return today, and he would have wasted tomorrow traveling back. Today he spread out a sack of wool at the dyeing vat where Niccolò told him to, and afterward he went to his uncle's house and brought his uncle and his nephew with the oxen. They dragged that great beam that was at San Salvatore here, and put it on the wall under the roof of the garden opposite the house. They brought the other pieces of wood that were to be placed […] and put them under the portico of the kitchen garden. And I had those two vats filled with wheat [...] and this evening Nanni [...] and he also brought those grape skins and those old [barrels] and that vat to Il Palco. Today I re-covered that quilt that was above the stable because it did not have a cover; and I filled a small mattress, because as you know there was a bed in the main room that did not have a mattress, and a bed without a mattress does not look good. I took one of the beds, the best there was, and I put it on the platform in the kitchen, as it would be a good thing for Nanni to sleep here in the house when we go to Florence. That bed did not look good in the main room, although it had to be put there. As you know, it was at the top of the stairs, and no one sleeping in it could keep warm.

Yesterday evening Niccolò came here, and he told me that Agnolo is going to Florence for some reason. I am very pleased that this is so, and several times I had thought of writing to you to ask why you did not send for him; but then I considered Niccolò, who was so alone that he had great need of him. Now he has been elected as one of the Eight, he loses a lot of time and has no one in his shop. For this reason I did not dare to write anything to you, but I truly think that it would have been much better for you to have him with you than staying alone as you were.

I had two hoods made, but I did not have them lined. Tell me if you want linings out of that same material. It would seem better to me to keep that cloth to make a hood for summer. However, if you wish, I will line them with it; but send me your old summer hoods, and if there are any that I think should be unpicked, I will do so and make linings from them.

If you need them, I will send you two large sheets for the bed I sent. I am also sending you some chickpeas because I imagine you don't have any. I sent half a quart of chickpeas the day before yesterday and a quart of broad beans to Francesca when she was in that house, so I think she probably took them with her. If she didn't, please send some of them to her, as well as a good supply of broad beans. Even a small amount will do.

I am sending you four loaves that Monna Caterina di Niccolozzo sent me.[494] They are very good. I am sending you thirteen fresh eggs for the Vigil of Saint Nicholas when you won't be eating meat.

494. This is Niccolozzo Binducchi. See Mazzei, *Lettere di un notaro*, 2:347.

Tell Manno's mother that the cloths she sent were all very fine but that the child needs swaddling bands. I think that the person who took the message to her didn't know how to explain, so make her read this paragraph and tell her to send the right ones.

I will get Guido to help Niccolò when he is not needed here.

With this letter is an account of the money I am owed by the warehouse, for cartage and tax on various items from Bologna, Pietrasanta, and Pisa received on their behalf in Prato.

To Francesco di Marco da Prato, in Florence.
Received from Prato, 5 December 1398. Delivered by Nanni.

Letter 193 (9290932)
5 December 1398
Prato

I am sending you the letters that Bonaccorso needed in Rome. I decided not to send on a large one addressed to Ser Stefano. Write and explain to him that at the moment it doesn't seem very urgent, and also it seemed best not to send such a large bundle of letters to Rome.

I have waited for you the whole day. I suppose you weren't able to come because of the many things you have to do, and that will never end until you are no longer able to do them. Lent will be here soon, a time to devote to the health of soul and body.[495]

To Francesco di Marco da Prato, in Florence.
Received from Prato, 5 December 1398. Delivered by Nanni.

495. Although this letter is unsigned, the tone of the second paragraph suggests that it is from Margherita.

Letter 194 (1401867)
5 December 1398
Prato

In the name of God. 5 December 1398.

Nanni delivered a letter from you. I reply here as necessary. I will let Guido reply regarding Mastriscia's work, but I will answer about the quilt.

I am searching here thoroughly. I cannot find it, but in my opinion it was never on the bed in the room by the kitchen garden. It was taken to you in Florence. The bed in the kitchen has been completely dismantled, and I replaced it with the one that was in the bedroom over the stable. I put the one that was in the main room in the bedroom. I know very well that it is not in the twin bedroom, and I have also looked there. This is not a little piece of cloth that can't be seen. I have looked on my bed, and it is not there. It never went into any of my chests. This is because, when I emptied it, I took out the feathers but I didn't turn it upside down; and so some feathers remained in it, as you know happens to quilts if you don't shake them well. I tied it tightly with a cord so it wouldn't make a mess everywhere. Why ever would I have put it in one of my chests? You say you have seen it, but that was a linen cover that I put on the quilt. The quilt was where Nanni slept, and you know it had no cover. You saw all this. I kept the red cloths in the chest, and afterward, when I returned, I put the quilt in the locked chest beside the wardrobe. This is the covering that you remember. I also think that when you and Fattorino did the inventory of those things, you found it inside the chest for the sheets. It had been there for more than three years. I think you will find it noted in your book when you turn your attention to the matter. Then you will understand which one it was. I asked Lucia, and she says that at the time, when it was in the chest, it was noted down.

In my opinion that quilt went to Florence three years ago this winter. Nanni remembers that when we were at Il Palco he heard it said that there were no feathers for this quilt in the warehouse. He says it had not been there for a month. Francesco, look for the letters from Domenico di Cambio. I think that during the three years there can't have been more than about fifteen. If you discover the quilt was sent there, at least you will be certain that there is no thief here. I can't stress enough how upset I am. I am really very upset. God knows how much I am suffering. I think Monna Ave was in Florence at that time. I will send for her tomorrow and find out if she ever heard about it, and Fattorino could come as well. This happened when they were joking so much and doing such crazy things, at the time Monna Ave came to Il Palco because her daughter was sick. Send for Fattorino and find out if he remembers that she came. He will remember and will tell the truth.

Nanni will bring the wool to you tomorrow if the weather is fine. We received the dirty clothes from him and the letter for Niccolaio Martini. We received Monna Ghita's rooster.[496]

If you decide to come back on Sunday and might feel like eating veal, which is rarely slaughtered here, bring some. If you want anything else that you can get there, bring it as well and tell me what you want me to prepare, rice or something else.

Get someone to buy me a pair of clogs and a pair of slippers. I want the slippers for Domina because I got the ones that Ginevra has from Monna Simona, who bought them in Florence. I can't buy them here, and I want to give them back to her. The measure for the clogs is the broader one and for the slippers the narrower one. They are together with this letter, which Guido is delivering.

I will tell Mastriscia what you say tomorrow morning. I said the right thing when he returned from Florence and brought the letter where he had agreed to pay you the sum of forty [...] florins, and I said, "As for Francesco, in my view he is losing three florins [...]."[497] He asked why and I explained that you and Stoldo would have managed to make a profit of two florins [...]. Tomorrow I will speak to him about everything and read to him the paragraph you have written. [...][498] We will let you know what happens.

I sent you the list of expenses for the wool and everything else with Nanni this morning.

Bachele will be told what you say.

496. See letter 192.

497. See letters 166, 174, 183, and 184.

498. The precise situation regarding this financial transaction is unclear because the manuscript has several lacunae.

If Agnolo returns before you, we will tell him to wait here for you to attend to the wool, as you say.

Concerning the things that I have to do, I have replied as you instructed and we will do what we can.

I will give Niccolaio Brancacci your message.

I will find out about the panic seed from Morello. May God protect you always.

From your Margherita, in Prato.

To Francesco di Marco da Prato, in Florence.
Received from Prato, 6 December 1398.

Letter 195 (1401916)
17 February 1399
Florence

In the name of God. 17 February 1399.[499]

I just received a letter from you and have understood what you say. I will now answer your queries briefly because there is no time, as Nanni wants to leave.

As for excusing myself to the *Podestà*'s wife and the other women, I will not make any excuses by letter. I will leave it up to you to do what you like about the *Podestà*'s wife and the other women.[500]

499. In early 1399, Margherita had moved rather suddenly to Florence and remained there for most of the year. The plague was spreading in Italy, and she was convinced that Florence had better doctors (letter 216). When plague threatened Florence and Prato in mid-1400, Francesco moved his household to Bologna, a decision that proved to be very sound, because the death toll in Florence and Prato was particularly devastating.

500. The wife of Benozzo d'Andrea Benozzi, who was *Podestà* in Prato from November 1398 to April 1399, is not mentioned by name. In 1414 Benozzo's wife was Agnola, daughter of Giovanni Baroncelli, but it is not known whether this was a second wife. Margherita Datini had left Prato for Florence without calling on either Benozzo d'Andrea Benozzi's wife, with whom she does not seem to have been particularly intimate, or on Margherita, the wife of Vieri Guadagni, who had been *Podestà* earlier in 1398. Francesco continued to press Margherita to write to the *Podestà*'s wife and to call on Margherita Guadagni in Florence. See FD 144, 145, 146, and 147. Margherita Datini had an antipathy for Margherita

I told Stoldo to tell Ser Lapo that I have arrived and for him to send his boy whenever he likes.[501] I have not yet heard back from Stoldo.

When you receive this, send the padded hair roll. It belongs to Caterina and is in the chest where the sheets are kept.

Take care of the bedroom key, because I left everything at Prato. Make sure you don't give the key to anyone until every item has been noted down.

Try to send me that strongly flavored fennel, and I will send you the mild one.

As time is short I cannot say any more. May Christ protect you.

From Monna Margherita, in Florence.

Francesco di Marco himself, in Prato.
Received from Florence, 17 February 1399.

Guadagni and resisted her husband's attempts to persuade her in this matter (letter 201). On 8 April Francesco wrote a letter of recommendation in Margherita's name to the wife of the *Podestà*, apologizing for not calling on her before moving to Florence. In May he also wrote to Margherita Guadagni and sent some Malvasia wine as a gift. It may be that he felt more confident of his epistolary abilities than Margherita did of hers, because these letters to important women required a rhetorical tone that did not come easily to her. On the other hand, Margherita's intransigence may explain why Francesco was forced to write the letters himself. Francesco explained to Margherita Guadagni that the wine had been sent from Venice by Margherita's cousin, Bindo Piaciti, and was reputed to encourage the birth of male children. Margherita Guadagni had suffered a miscarriage in June 1398 (letter 162). See Hayez, "Le rire du marchand," 443–44 and 453–54.

501. Piero Mazzei arrived the next day, and Margherita set the young boy to work immediately, overseeing the first stage of his apprenticeship, which consisted of practicing handwriting and improving his ability to read. See letters 196 and 197. He became her scribe once his skills improved. On 4 February 1399 Ser Lapo Mazzei informed Francesco that Piero had written his first letter. See Mazzei, *Lettere di un notaro*, 1:215–16. Piero Mazzei was transferred to the Catalonian branch of the company in 1403 and was still there when Francesco died in 1410. See Melis, *Aspetti della vita economica medievale*, 250–53.

Letter 196 (9281478)
18 February 1399
Florence

In the name of God. Amen. 18 February 1399.

The reason for this letter is that I have a new errand boy. He is Ser Lapo's son, and today I set him writing, as he would have to do to work as a secretary. We need that pannier to take bread to the bakery. We also need some knives for the table, a copper jug—not that big one but one of the medium ones—and one of those tin dishes for washing feet. Send us the raisins, send me Caterina's padded hair-roll, and two caps for drying hair that are in Monna Giovanna's bedroom. Put it all in a container. If it is not full, add a couple of footstools and some of the dried figs that are in Monna Giovanna's room. If you have not bought any peas or beans at the market, send us some olives and some fennel stalks to preserve. Send us some oats. Send me that book on the Passion that is in Monna Margherita's room and has an "M" at the beginning. Send me also that small book on the desk. Send me at least some of these things. For lack of time I have written no more.

To Francesco di Marco, in Prato.
Received from Florence, 19 February 1399.

Letter 197 (1401917)
19 February 1399
Florence

In the name of God. Amen. 19 February 1399.

Yesterday I sent you a letter with Argomento. I have just received a letter from you, and with it there were various others that I sent on to the warehouse with Fattorino, as I always do as soon as they arrive. I am very surprised about the account for Niccolaio di Bernardo, because if it had been with those letters, Stoldo would have had it; but he gave me nothing else. As for your saying that you aren't happy if you don't have to appear so—don't be offended if I remind you, and if it weren't for Lent, I wouldn't venture to say so—you have been unhappier than you used to be for quite some time now. Lenten food tastes terrible, especially when there's no one there to prepare it, but I restrained myself as much as I could simply for the sake of Ser Lapo's son.[502] I send him home every evening to eat because that seems best to me when you aren't here. In my view he is fine as an errand boy, but we will take each day as it comes. The thing you will like about him is that he is a quick reader. As for his not writing to you directly, don't be surprised about that, because he doesn't know how to write yet because he is concentrating on his abacus. He seems to me, however, to have the ability to learn quickly, if he is taught, and this will happen when you are here. As for remembering if I need anything, remember to bring me the chest with the veils in it. As Argomento wants to leave, I will add no more. May God protect you.

From your Margherita, in Florence.

To Francesco di Marco himself, in Prato.
Received from Florence, 21 February 1399. Answered.

Letter 198 (1401918)
20 February 1399
Florence

In the name of God. Amen. 20 February 1399.

I sent you a letter with Nanni yesterday, and I have not had a reply from you. I am writing this to inform you that Argomento has brought us three footstools, four books, a lamp holder, two small knives, one large basin, a small sack of lupines, two burdock roots, five jars of raisins, one copper jug, two small baskets, and there were also several letters that we sent on to the warehouse. We need one of those big knives and some of those smaller ones that are in the kitchen, and one of those cushions from the chairs there. When I am there, I will repair the one that is covered with leather. Remember to bring us the

---

502. During Lent, meat, eggs and cheese were not consumed, and the diet was supplemented by extra vegetables. See Giagnavoco, *Mercanti a tavola*, 74.

silver salt cellar as well as some spoons, if you can, because there are only six here—and a knife box. We also need a little lamp oil, and you had better come here as soon as you can if you don't want us to run out. As I am in a hurry, I will say no more. May God protect you always.

From your Margherita.

Francesco di Marco himself, in Prato.
Received from Florence, 20 February 1399. Answered.

Letter 199 (1401919)
21 February 1399
Florence

In the name of God. Amen. 21 February 1399.

I sent you a letter yesterday with Argomento, and I have not had a reply from you.

Argomento brought me two letters; one went to the bank and the other to Niccolò da Izzano. He brought me a large knife, a cushion, a footstool, a knife box with four knives from our collection, another knife box containing two knives, a jar of oil, and a sack of wheat. Don't send me any more footstools as there are too many. In my opinion nothing else is required. Tell Monna Ghita that I have had to look after the house but that next week I will buy her caps without fail, so she won't have to do without. Tell Guido to go and greet her on my behalf.[503] I will say no more because I hope you will be here any day now. Send my regards to Barzalone and Niccolò and to Monna Nanna and Monna Lapa, and tell her I am expecting her at the time of the special indulgence that is rumored to be coming. May God protect you.

Your Margherita, in Florence.

To Francesco di Marco himself, in Prato.
Received from Florence, 22 February 1399.

---

503. Almost a month later, this promise to Francesco's housekeeper remained unfulfilled. See letter 202.

Letter 200 (1401920)
23 February 1399
Florence

In the name of God. Amen. 23 February 1399.

I sent you a letter yesterday with Argomento. I am writing this merely to advise you that Nanni arrived here as the bundles were being prepared, and I arrived with the others. Nanni told me that he thought you would be very worried, because in his view he was leaving too late. He thought that you would find out and would be very concerned, so I have decided to send him back to stop you worrying. Agnolo arrived here and said that Nanni was to remain here this evening but that you were very upset because he left Prato so late. This is why I want him to return there this evening.

Ser Lapo's son is eager for company. I am sending you plenty of spinach, two bunches of leeks, and two bunches of mint. If you lack any of these things, tell me and I will send them, as long as you are in Prato. You would do well to finish your business as quickly as you can, because I think you are living very poorly and I would have preferred you to have followed my advice to keep Lucia there. The spinach is from Lapa. Have it fried. And please: for the love of God stop this staying up late because it is very bad for you. Try to do what you can during the daytime. If you decide to take a nap, you won't be committing a sin. Staying up so late will bring great sorrow to those who love you. So as not to keep Nanni waiting, I will finish now. May God protect you.

From your Margherita, in Florence.

To Francesco di Marco himself, in Prato.
Received from Florence, 23 February 1399.

Letter 201 (1401921)
27 February 1399
Florence

In the name of God. Amen. 27 February 1399.

I received a letter of yours from Nanni that requires only a short reply. As for visiting Monna Ghita di Vieri, I did not go because it has been raining hard and I was also waiting for you to be here before doing that and the other things that need to be done.[504] Regarding Lucia's cat, we will look after it as best we can. We have only a small amount of washing, and I don't want to send it there. We have very few dirty clothes and I don't want to send them there because they are so few. I will send you Guido's underlinen. As for your coming here on Sunday, that would be good and we will expect you at dinner. I am extremely sorry about Niccolò Ammannato. Please write to them, as you told me you would, so they understand this; and I will do likewise.[505] I am sending you four bunches of spinach, three of mint, and some lupines; and I am sending you back five sacks, two of which came with the oats, two that were here, and the two belonging to Monna Taddea.[506] Send back the panniers we have sent you in the last few days, and some of those baskets with a handle. Please write to me to let me know if, and how, you will send them so I know if, and how, I will get them. God be praised, but He has left me without any baskets. Send me that cloth that I asked for as soon as you can. If there is washing to be done, we would not do it but leave it to Monna Gaia—who could get Monna Fiore to do it when you have left. Send us some of the garlic from Prato. As Nanni wants to leave, I won't say any more. May God protect you always.

From your Monna Margherita, wife of Francesco.

---

504. In a letter of the same day (FD 146), Francesco reminded Margherita to visit Vieri Guadagni's wife, but his reminders were to no avail. See note 500, above.

505. Niccolò dell'Ammannato's son Tommaso (Maso) had been sent to Majorca as an apprentice. Francesco's partner there, Cristofano di Bartolo Carocci, reported that the boy lacked concentration and showed little promise. See letter 209, and FD 146 and 147.

506. Margherita's poor arithmetic suggests that she dictated this letter hastily.

To Francesco di Marco himself, in Prato.
Received from Florence, 27 February 1399.

Letter 202 (1401922)
17 March 1399
Florence[507]

In the name of God. Amen. 17 March 1399.

This morning Nanni brought me your letter and with it several other letters that have been delivered to their addressees. Concerning Manno's mother, I will say what you have told me and get her the things you mention, and she will be satisfied.[508] As for returning here, because you live poorly there in Prato during Lent, it would be best for you to come back soon. Do what you like about the underlinen and other things. Convey my apologies to Monna Ghita, because the cap seller has not been back. I will not answer you about Nofrino because I don't want to get the overgown made before Easter.[509] I will make a decision about it afterward. Nanni came early, as the packages were being tied.

From your Margherita in Florence.

Look in my chest and send me all the white hose—they must be there—because I want to mend the girls' undergowns. If I have to buy anything new, it would be best to get new hose and use the old ones to fix the undergowns. So send me the worst ones.

Now to begin the joust! Don't send me any more letters unless Guido writes them, because your scribe is bad and the person dictating is worse.[510] I will finish now. May God protect you.

---

507. In its text this letter is dated 17 March 1399, but according to the annotation at its end it was received on 16 March 1399. The source of the discrepancy is unknown.

508. Manno d'Albizo degli Agli's mother was Monna Bice Marini. See letter 170. Margherita had been purchasing goods for Manno's baby. See FD 149.

509. For the caps, see letter 199. Nofrino was a tailor. See letters 27 and 204.

510. Francesco did not take up the gauntlet thrown down by Margherita here.

To Francesco di Marco himself, Prato.
Received from Florence, 16 March 1399.

Letter 203 (1401923)
5 April 1399
Florence

In the name of God. Amen. 5 April 1399.

I received your letter, which required a brief reply. In regard to hastening to receive those women, I will do so properly in a way that will please you.[511] As regards living unhappily, I am absolutely sure you are, because it is too much to look after men's affairs and household matters, and only the person who does it can know what running a household involves. I see that you are living with many sorrows, and I am not living happily. I would like to be able to accompany you when you go to Prato, along with some of our serving women, because I think you would live with more tranquility and could look to whatever tasks you have to do; and if I didn't have so many problems to deal with here, I would be better off. Get your business done as soon as you can. You will be doing yourself good, and a favor to the person who loves you. Because Argomento wants to leave, I will say no more. May God protect you. I have given food to the poor.

From your Margherita, in Florence.

To Francesco di Marco himself, Prato.
Received from Florence, 6 April 1399.

511. Margherita's neighbor in Prato Monna Simona, and perhaps the neighbor's daughter Caterina, were to visit Florence. See letter 207, and FD 152.

Letter 204 (1401924)
7 April 1399
Florence

In the name of God. Amen. 7 April 1399.

I received your letter as well as one addressed to Ser Lapo. I answer yours here. I spoke to Francesco the carpenter and told him you will be here in a few days, and that you beg him to make sure the wood is ready for the platform and that things are ready by your return, so work can be started. He answered that all his sons have gone to haul timber today, but they should return this evening and he will get the work done in good time and to your satisfaction. The servant of the Signoria was sent here this morning by Vieri Guadagni, to say that the permit you asked for was ready and should be collected. I answered that you had not returned from Prato but that I would speak to one of your friends about it, because I did not know who the permit was for, and I would advise you about it. I spoke about it with Stoldo, and he says he will do what needs to be done. There is nothing else to be said about the affairs of Monna Simona. As for Nanna, she seems to me to be in good health, and up until now they are well satisfied with her. I don't need to tell Monna Ghita anything. I reminded Guido about some skeins of thread that she has and how she should treat it. He should advise me when Piera wishes to start weaving my cloth. You are right to finish up your business in Prato. Make sure you do it properly so you don't have to return there too soon. I told Stoldo about the affairs of the girl to whom you promised money out of Christian charity, but you will be here before she needs it.[512] As for what we want here, you should bring that fine cloth from which I usually make your undershirts. You should also bring me that cloth belonging to the brick maker from Carmignano, because I want robust cloth for the pillow cases, like the ones I made for here; and bring things like over-gowns and hoods. You also need to have two summer-weight doublets made for yourself. You could obtain some of that fine cloth, and you could use the brick maker's cloth for lining it. You could get Nofrino, who is in Prato, to make them for you.[513] If there is any cloth in your

512. Francesco had promised money for the girl's dowry.

513. This is Nofrino, the tailor mentioned in letters 27 and 202.

chest for making cuffs, bring that too. I need about twelve yards of raw flax to spin into thread. I cannot sew with what we gathered. Speak about it to Niccolò di Piero, whose friends will get me good quality. Yesterday I asked Guido for news about Niccolò and Monna Lapa. He told me Agnolo has had the fever, which is worrying. I am amazed you did not write anything about it to me. Perhaps it wasn't a serious matter. Please God it is so. If there is any need for medicinal cachets or anything else from here, let me know, and send my apologies to Lapa and Niccolò and tell them that you did not write to me about it. We need a lot of small pieces of wood. When you get the chance, remind Mastriscia about the girls' shoes. I gave the sizes to Nanni. Tell him to make one white pair and some black ones for Ginevra. For now I cannot recall anything else I have to say. May God always protect you.

Your Margherita, in Florence.

To Francesco di Marco himself, in Prato.
Received from Florence, 7 April 1399. Answered.

Letter 205 (1401927)
8 April 1399
Florence

In the name of God. Amen. 8 April 1399.

I sent you a letter with Argomento yesterday, and I received a reply from you. It does not matter that you could not answer fully. Concerning Agnolo, I understand that he also has the fever, which concerns me. You were right to apologize for me.[514] We are making sure the cat is well looked after.

Early this morning Bernardo Guadagni presented you with a deer, a fine big animal. As the weather is hot, I thought I would decide what to do with it, because if I had taken the time to send you a message or to send it there to you it would have gone bad. I decided to

---

514. See the preceding letter.

send it to Guido, and I immediately sent to find out whether he was in Florence.[515]

He was in the country, but they were sure he would come back and they expected him for dinner. So I waited until dinnertime and I had a note written in my name telling him who had sent the deer to you. I told Guido you were still at Prato and that I dearly wished to carry out Francesco's wishes, and I was sending it to him because I was sure this was your desire. After this I sent my greetings to him and all the women of the household. I said no more. A poor speaker says best when he says least. If you want to write anything about it, do so as you see fit. Because the bearer of this letter wishes to leave, I will finish now. May God protect you always.

From your Margherita, in Florence.

To Francesco di Marco da Prato himself, Florence.[516]
Received from Florence, 8 April 1399. Answered.

Letter 206 (1401925)
8 April 1399
Florence

In the name of God. Amen. 8 April 1399.

Your letter was delivered by the lad from the bank early this morning. It was brief and required only a short reply. I sent a reply with Allegrino, and if you have not received that letter, try to get it. You told me that Agnolo had only a slight fever and there was no need to be worried, and I was very pleased to hear this. Then, at the twenty-second hour, I received another letter from you, and with it a letter addressed to Ser Lapo and another I sent to the bank. We had them delivered. Now you tell me that Agnolo is much worse. I had a very bad evening because of this; I have always considered him not just a relative but my own son, and he has always respected me as a mother.

515. This is Guido del Palagio.

516. It is clear from this letter that Francesco was in Prato. The scribe evidently made a mistake.

I think of the sorrow and anxiety you will suffer, and I have great sympathy for his father and mother.[517] I pray to God that He will answer their prayers and those of their friends. I think that the best remedy is to recommend oneself to our God, from whom all benefits and graces come. May God in His holy mercy assist them. Before I finished reading the letter, I sent for Master Giovanni.[518] He came immediately and I told him what you had written to me, explaining to him that you considered this relative your own son.[519] As he is looking after many sick people and is reluctant to leave them, I reminded him of the faith and trust we have in him. He replied that, despite the difficulties, he was ready to do your every bidding, considering how much you loved this young man, but that he did not have a horse. I answered that we would get him a horse and an escort and everything necessary for him to get there soon. I immediately sent to Piaciti's household to ask for a mount, but I could not get one because he had gone to the country. Afterward I sent to the house of Vieri Guadagni to see whether they could lend me one, explaining the reason. However, Bernardo had gone to the country and had taken all their riding animals. I sent for Meo di Cambione and Domenico di Cambio as well and I asked all our friends, but we could not obtain a horse at all.[520] Meo did not think it right to take a packhorse because he thought it would be disrespectful to the doctor. Thinking that there was no time to be lost, we turned to Guido, informing him of the case and the need, and telling him that it seemed rude to ask for a horse, seeing that you have his horse there. He answered as you know, in his typical way, showing great sorrow about the case. If you were thinking of sending back his horse tomorrow, please do so. About my coming there, I agree completely with you. I will wait for Master Giovanni to come back, and in the

517. Agnolo, the son of Niccolò di Piero di Giunta and Monna Lapa, died a week after this letter was sent. See Francesco's letter of 15 April 1399 to Niccolò d'Andrea (ASPo, D.1111, 6000809). Niccolò di Piero followed his son to the grave soon after this date. See Melis, *Aspetti della vita economica medievale*, 288–89.

518. This is the doctor Giovanni di Banduccio.

519. See FD 153, where Francesco talks about his love for the descendants of his relative and guardian, Piero di Giunta del Rosso.

520. Bartolomeo di Francesco Cambioni was a partner in Francesco's Florentine bank. He died of the plague in 1400.

meantime I will put things in order to your satisfaction. You can send me a message with him about what you think I should do. I will be ready at any time. May God grant that this does not become necessary. Remember that there is some rosewater there. Send some to them. Remember to ask Giovanni whether he needs any distilled water. I will say no more. May God protect you.

Your Margherita, in Florence.

Francesco di Marco himself, in Prato.
Received from Florence, 9 April 1399.

Letter 207 (1401926)
9 April 1399
Florence

In the name of God. Amen. 9 April 1399.

I received your letter, delivered by Martino di Niccolò, as well as one for Ser Lapo, and two others that I have sent to the bank. I am very glad that you are pleased about what I did with the venison. I received your letter from Niccolò di Piero's relative and sent a reply with Master Giovanni. I have done everything in my power to get him there as soon as possible. I beseeched him to hurry, as if I were asking for my own sake, as I do indeed consider I am. I see from your letter of today that Agnolo is still in danger and that you are waiting until this evening because it is the ninth day. I have faith in God, in the prayers of Agnolo's mother and of the people who love and pray for him, and Master Giovanni will do everything possible for him. I truly hope that God grants us His grace. May it please God to do so.

I know about Monna Simona coming here and I will wait to hear from her how Agnolo is faring. I am ready to come whenever it is necessary; I will come and do what you wrote about in a way that will satisfy you. I leave it up to you to decide. Yesterday I went to Bernardo Guadagni's house because the servant who brought the venison told me that Bernardo's little girl was close to death. So as soon as I had eaten, I went there and discovered that the child had been buried. It has been a terrible blow.

And Bernardo had no more children. He mounted his horse and went off to the country very, very slowly. I offered my condolences to the women and thanked them for the venison, and I asked Monna Margherita to pass on your greetings and your gratitude to Vieri for all his affection and for every service he has done you.[521] She was very insistent that I dine with them, but I didn't want to stay because I would have been worried that letters would arrive from you while I was there. Indeed they arrived as I was taking off my mantle. It was just as well I didn't stay there. I won't say any more. May God protect you.

From your Margherita, in Florence.

To Francesco di Marco himself, in Prato.
Received from Florence, 10 April 1399.

Letter 208 (1401868)
25 April 1399
Prato

In the name of God. 25 April 1399.

After you left here, a load of Barbary lambskins arrived at nones from Pietrasanta. They weighed 505 pounds at a price of twenty-two *soldi* per hundred, plus the usual taxes, and I paid accordingly. For this I borrowed two sealed florins from Ser Conte to give to the carter and we gave him five *lire*, as this was the total of his account: that is, thirteen *lire* and four *soldi*. I made a proper record of it all in the book, but I made a note of Ser Conte's money on a sheet of paper until you arrive, and then it can be recorded as you see fit.

The toll gatherer here says the toll gatherer in Pescia made a mistake because the charge for a load is seven *lire*, seventeen and a half *soldi*, and he was given seven *lire*. This was the sum I gave to the carter, so according to him, he still needs to be paid seventeen and a

---

521. Bernardo Guadagni was Vieri's brother and Monna Margherita's brother-in-law. See note 500, above.

half *soldi*. I told him to wait for you and you will settle the matter with him. He agreed. So now you can clarify how much was charged for the load and confirm whether it was the same as he says.

Tell us what we have to do with these skins and what else we have to do.

The letters for Pistoia have gone and Nencio says he gave them to a trusted man who is his next-door neighbor, so they must have been delivered, but he can't remember his name.

Barzalone came to me today at vespers and told me you had instructed him and Niccolò to speak to the *Podestà*. Niccolò was sick this morning so they decided not to go. Barzalone asked me what I thought he should do. I answered that he knew better than I what was to be done, but that if I were in his shoes, I would not do anything without consulting Ser Schiatta. He knows how these things are done, and I think he understands your feelings. Barzalone did not agree, and I was concerned about telling him what he should do, but if I hadn't answered at all, he would not have done anything. So, bearing in mind the invitations to [the *Podestà*] that you told me you had made, and that time was short, I said it would perhaps be best not to delay any further and to pass on the message as you had ordered. So he made up his mind and went He says that he gave the *Podestà* your message, and he also gave him the letter from Vieri. The *Podestà* thanked him very much, saying that he considered your property his. When you offered him the house he had not given a definite answer, because he had not yet made up his mind what to do. Now he says he has decided. Because it is not the custom of public officials to stay at citizens' houses, he will return to the house of the prior of San Fabiano, because he says he has been his friend for a long time. So you have nothing to be concerned about. May God grant him a long life. I will always like him because he has saved me a lot of work. In my view, you should wait until the end of April before coming back. I say this for the best.

I am sending you a pannier that has onions and herbs for a pie and twenty fresh eggs and two cheeses. The pannier belongs to Miniato del Sera. Send it back to him because he asked me for it when I was in Florence.

I am also sending you a basket of onions, almonds, a cheese, twelve eggs, and strongly flavored herbs for omelets for Caterina and

Ginevra. Tell Francesca to have some made for them, because they are the right herbs for that.

Today we have started to take stock of the household goods. May God protect you always.

From your Margherita, in Prato.

To Francesco di Marco, in Piazza Tornaquinci, Florence.
Received from Prato, 26 April 1399. Answered.

Letter 209 (6300383)
2 May 1399
Florence

In the name of God. Amen. 2 May 1399.

I am writing because Stoldo said yesterday that Ser Giovanni di Barletta had told him that our brother Bartolomeo had arrived there in Prato, which was a great surprise to me.[522] I thought he must have made a mistake. I thought it must have been Maso and that Cristofano had sent him back, and I spent the entire night worrying for a reason I will explain when I see you.[523] Meo Cambioni was here and read me a message and as [...] Bartolomeo is there. He says he intended to go to the convent of St. Anthony and that you don't know, would you believe? This made me very worried. Please, if you are not coming here in the next couple of days, tell me if you bought anything from him that would have given him cause to come here. I would not bring him here until I had consulted with Niccolò and the others so he couldn't be arrested for tax debts. You know what this commune is like. You know what I mean. The last thing we need is for him to be arrested. Because you are wise, behave as you think best. I will inform myself about it as soon as I can, and will advise you immediately. I will send you the cachets and our clothes with Argomento, if he comes;

522. Bartolomeo Bandini, Margherita's brother, had fallen on hard times and was in danger of being arrested for debt and tax arrears. See letters 210 and 211, and Margherita's letter to Bartolomeo in note 529, below.

523. The fourteen-year-old Maso dell'Ammannato was in Majorca. See note 505, above.

the rosary beads belonging to Messer Piero's Caterina, and the [...] for Guido's horse. Bring me those veils of mine that I left inside the chest where the pillow slips are. I didn't remember to bring them when I left. The soles for the Perpignan hose are inside the small chest in the ground-floor bedroom where your small bed is. You will want me to repair them. Monna Margherita says that Lapa wants to leave because she doesn't like to be away from her family. If she were to leave tomorrow or the next day, she would come willingly with her brother. If he decided to come with Nanni, it seems to me she would travel more pleasantly and it would reflect upon us more honorably. She could come on the horse, and Nanni and Andrea on foot.

These are two feast days when we won't be idle. Do what you think best.

Send me that woolen cloth if you want me to have the cuffs made for your doublets, and tell the tailor how big they should be [...] as I have never seen tailors making doublets. Send me back the tablecloth and the basket in which I sent the cachets. Send us some of those pomegranates. May God protect you.

From your Margherita, in Florence.

To Francesco di Marco, in Prato.

Letter 210 (1401928)
2 May 1399
Florence

In the name of God. Amen. 2 [May] 1399.[524]

I answered your queries in a letter sent with Argomento. Now this letter is simply to tell you that I clarified with Niccolò how Bartolomeo stood with this commune. He went to where the old and new taxes are recorded. He found that Bartolomeo has been in debt to this commune for three years for the amount of 200 florins, apart from the penalties, and that for three years he has not paid taxes. Niccolò

524. The month is written as January in the manuscript, but the date of arrival and the content show this to be an error.

believes that if he came, he would be liable for both of these sums. So take care that he is not seized, as he could be taken both in Prato and here. Show this letter to him and tell him from me to avoid getting himself and others into trouble. I have worries enough without seeing him in prison. That's all I need! I had this thought by the grace of God. In haste I will say no more. May God protect you.

From your Margherita, in Florence.

To Francesco di Marco da Prato himself.
Received from Florence, 2 May 1399.

Letter 211 (1401929)
3 May 1399
Florence

In the name of God. Amen. 3 May 1399.

I received a letter of yours from Nanni and one from Bartolomeo.[525] I was very surprised that you had not written to me after you left here, and now I see why you didn't.[526] If you had listened to me, you would not have gone to Prato for the reason that you did, because one should try to pay respect only to God, and all other respect is false. Considering the things you have to do and how much they cost, every time you lose an hour it seems to me you are wasting a thousand, if they are things that others could do for you, and it seemed to me that this was one such matter; and I think nothing is so valuable to body and soul as time is to you, but it seems to me you set little store by it. If you want to continue paying your respects to people, you will never conclude any business of your own, and you need the friends you have already made and whom it is worth trying to keep, but you don't need to make too many new ones. You know what I mean. As for the completion of your business there and what I say about it when I am asked, I say what I believe brings you honor. I am well aware that you are not

525. This is Bartolomeo Bandini. See note 529, below.

526. Checco di Ghinozzo Amedei had become ill as he arrived in Prato and was not able to return to Florence that day. See FD 154.

there for pleasure, and this is what torments me: not everyone can talk about his private business. I was sorry about Checco di Ghinozzo because I know that you are very worried about Nofri's affairs.[527] I looked for our friend in Via dei Servi and everywhere else I thought I might find him, but I could not discover where he was. I waited a morning, an entire morning, at Piazza Annunziata, but he was not to be seen.

At the Annunziata, I found Lorenza, who is a relative of Feraldo de' Pazzi, who you know is a relative of Monna Antonia from Pistoia, and you know that Nofri returned home with his entire household.[528] I wanted to bring her home to dine with me. She told me she was going to eat at Nofri's house and came with me as far as our house. She had already been to Nofri's […] I asked her about the marriage we were trying to organize, and I will tell you what I discovered. We should forget about that young woman who, as you know, could have been a good match for our friend. Lorenza said that her father could never convince her to remarry. She was keeping all her children in Nofri's house. Her mind was not set on marriage, but she wanted to serve God and look after her children. Her mother and father believed she had been sleeping only on a board and they thought she had been fasting so much she had consumption. For this reason I did not think it worth following up this matter any further, and I did not inform you because I did not want anyone to find out. These are matters that should be kept completely secret. I'll do what I can about Monna Ghita. It hardly surprises me that you did not think about Bartolomeo's *prestanza* tax, because you have enough things to think about for twenty people. As for the fact that he did not say anything, I believe that this was simply because he was ashamed, and you are right to say that I should recognize the fact that his situation will always make me sad for as long as I live. I think he is in dire straits, although he hasn't told me anything, and I think the only way he is like the rest of the family is that he has no idea of how to ask for help from me or any of his relatives living here. I enclose here the letter he sent me, and I will answer it as best I can.

527. This is Nofri di Palla Strozzi.

528. Monna Antonia was Feraldo de' Pazzi di Valdarno's daughter and the widow of Paolo d'Andrea della Torre, a merchant from Pistoia who operated in Avignon during the 1370s. Margherita had probably known this couple in Avignon. See Hayez, "'Io non so scrivere a l'amicho per siloscismi,'" 45, note 26.

Francesco, when I found out he was in Prato, far from being happy, I felt sadder than if I had his dead body before me. Not because I would like to see him dead. He is my brother and I cannot but love him, considering whose son he is. If I knew that he was more capable, I would not suffer half as much, because I would think that he could somehow look after himself. The fact is that he seems old, poor, and in bad health, and he has children to look after. Somebody else said to me that he had a most beautiful wife and she was also good and kind. I am as sorry for her as for him. Francesco, you are right to be frightened until he is out of town. I am more frightened than you, because we would be held completely responsible. So please make sure you get him to Pisa as soon as possible and make sure he doesn't get sick in Prato, because it would redouble our sorrow. Nanni says that Gherardini, may God forgive him, had the same experience. The night that he arrived he got the fever. It lasted four months and he had to have a residency permit from the Signoria. When he could not get one, he had to have a servant of the Signoria constantly at his bedside to guard him. Think what a trial that would be. I don't think he has the means to go to Pisa. So, if you ever did or should do anything for me, I now beg you to respond to his needs and my prayer. I realize that you are not obliged to help except as an act of charity and love for God. I know you give to others. It is even dearer to God when a person gives to those whom he is not obliged to assist. In doing this a person gains more merit and is dearer to God. I beg you to reduce your other acts of charity and help him in his hour of need. If I did not believe it were necessary, I would not ask you. I beg you not to send him on foot because he is in poor health, and I would not want us to make matters worse. If he goes to any town, it would involve grave danger. I think that you should get him away from Prato as soon as possible and send him to Pisa. Nanni tells me that Bartolomeo is sick. Do not be anxious about him, and do not ignore the matter. He will get to Pisa soon and will be out of danger. If he does not feel well enough to go to Sant'Antonio, I beg you to commend him to Manno. Tell him not to leave Bartolomeo short of anything that he needs. It is better to have the expense and not be in danger than keep him in Prato and have both the expense and the danger. I will inform him of everything. I won't consider myself alive until I know he is out of the town. I am very busy and don't know where I am, so I will say no more. I will look at your letter this evening, and if you need anything, I will answer you tomorrow. May God protect you. With this I am sending a letter that came from Venice and one for Checco di Ghinozzo, as well as the answer I sent to Bartolomeo.[529]

From your Margherita, in Florence.

529. (1401930) 3.5.1399 Margherita's letter to her brother Bartolomeo:

In the name of God. Amen. 3 May 1399.

I received your letter addressed to Francesca and me. We would have been very happy to see you before you went on that pilgrimage. However, it was not God's will that we meet, and both Francesca and I are sad about this. God, who is in heaven, knows that for several reasons the two of us have passed the worst days of our lives, and we can't give you any help. If we could, you would receive it. I don't know if you know the state Francesca is in. Twenty-eight months ago Niccolò's business failed, and he has no means of support. He has instead a debt of 500 florins. Francesco promised him 200 of these. He did this so that Francesca and her child would not be thrown out on the streets. Niccolò's relatives and friends promised him 300 florins after Francesco's entreaties on his behalf. Francesca has to earn her living with her hands. Niccolò is old and sick and has become a merchant's agent and tries to earn his living as best he can. I keep his daughter in our house, and Francesco has sent his son to work in Majorca. So you can see how many burdens Francesco carries for me. You are well aware that through me each one of Domenico's children obtained something, except myself. You also know that last time you were here, you took away goods and money that were pledged. You did not do what many brothers do who commit themselves in person to look after their sisters as they must. I will not tell Francesco about the manner in which you and my mother behaved. I do not have the courage to mention your needs, nor those of any other relatives, not least because neither you, nor the others, have done what you should. Nevertheless, if the opportunity came, I would not do anything against you. I am in good health and have what I need, so I would like to help you and my other relatives if they are in need. But, as you know, I own nothing, so you must excuse me. I have spoken for you to Francesco to the extent that I can. I can't do any more. Remember that Francesco has to pay sixty florins tax, and I am afraid the commune will ruin him as it has ruined others.

About the matter of the house that Monna Dianora wanted to sell, we always acted so that she couldn't. Seeing that she was unable to sell it, she had Filippo Corsini made her attorney, and he convinced the commune it was hers. Both you and everyone else can stop hoping about it. You say you are coming to Florence and that if you stayed at Santa Maria Novella, it would eliminate all concern. Francesca and I beg you not to put both yourself and us in danger, because the joy of meeting could turn into grief. We are upset and confused. For your own sake, we would like you to write another letter and tell us how you are. We are extremely worried about

To Francesco di Marco himself, Prato.
Received from Florence, 4 May 1399.

Letter 212 (1401931)
6 May 1399
Florence

In the name of God. Amen. 6 May 1399.

Stoldo arrived here and did not bring me a letter from you, but I am not surprised because you don't have Checco and Guido with you.[530] I think that you have enough to do and are very busy with everything, and this upsets me for several reasons. The first is that I think you are badly looked after and are unhappy there. I could not believe anything else. But you can't stop up everyone's mouth, and I would not care much about people's chatter if it did not show us in a poor light.

I beg you to hurry up and return as soon as you can. You will be doing a great favor to the one who loves you, and it will do you honor. Stoldo read me a note regarding what you did about Bartolomeo.[531] May God reward you on our behalf and help me to show my gratitude. I will tell you what needs to be done when I see you.

I told Monna Giovanna that Tommaso has gout. Ser Lapo was told about Monna Giovanna's matter.

Yesterday, in a letter I sent with Argomento, I wrote a complete answer to a previous letter of yours that I had not answered fully. I replied to what I thought was necessary. I fear I was seen speaking to the woman I wrote to you about on account of some things our male friend asked—who, as you know, went to gossip to our neighbor who, I told you, had been a beast. I pretended to know nothing at all, and he

---

what might happen, and we can do little more than pray to God for you. In haste we will say no more. May God protect you.

Received from Florence, 4 May 1399.

530. Checco di Ghinozzo Amadei was ill, and Francesco had sent him to Florence to be purged and bled. See FD 154.

531. On 8 May Francesco reported that Bartolomeo was safely in Pisa. He had supplied his brother-in-law with enough money to leave Tuscany.

was unable to find out anything from me; and I won't tell anyone until you are here. When our friend left, he went to talk to that madman, you know who. I can't speak any more clearly, and you can guess why. If you are going to answer me, get Guido to write, because I read his handwriting well, and that way my scribe won't read anything. Do you understand what I mean? We received the money and the flour, so I think you have received the soles that I sent for your hose. I fixed the other pair to the hose you gave me to be resoled. Remember to bring the fine linen to make your undershirts and that small piece of linen from Carmignano.

Remember to get your new doublets, and if you want any of the overgowns that you have left here since last summer, remember to bring them and some cloth to make cuffs for the doublets. Tell Nanni to bring me a pannier of onions.

Send me those distilled waters because I am waiting for them so I can take the syrup. If you can send them, don't fail to do so. If it is difficult for you to send the large flasks get some of those new small ones that are in the large room, and fill one with fennel water and the other with white water.

Master Giovanni asks where you want him to buy the things. He is happy to get them from Guglielmo,[532] Tell me what you want me to do. Master Giovanni says that one shouldn't wait any longer to be purged. I beg you to finish your affairs so you can be purged too. Now, as time is short, I will say no more. May God protect you.

From your Margherita, in Florence.

To Francesco di Marco da Prato, himself.
Received from Florence, 6 May 1399.

---

532. The shop of Guglielmo the apothecary was in Via Porta Rossa, close to Francesco's business premises in Florence.

Letter 213 (1401932)
7 May 1399
Florence

In the name of God. Amen. 7 May 1399.

Yesterday I sent you a detailed letter with Saccente about the things I thought were most necessary. We sent you Stefano's horse with him, and I sent you back the mule with Argomento. Argomento came by and asked me if I wanted anything. I had given the letters to Saccente. He thought I had also given him the mule. Argomento told me not to give her to anyone except him, and so I promised. I would never have given the mule to Saccente unless you had told me to or I had decided there was a real need. I was very upset about it, because you often need to send her back with Bellozzo's servant. Write to me and say if this is right or not. Stoldo gave me a letter from Majorca that says Maso wants to go to Valencia. I am not surprised, because young people are not very wise and he is simply showing that he is indeed a boy. I remind you, Francesco, that he is only a little more than fourteen, even if he doesn't show it, because he has grown so big that one cannot see how innocent he is. If you want to understand this clearly, I am enclosing a letter he sent to Caterina. Here you will understand how honest he is. I will show it to Niccolò and tell him my opinion.[533] Having written up to this point, I received your letter. I will answer as appropriate. First of all I think you must have a stomach complaint. I think it is much worse than you are telling me because you don't want to upset me. I swear to you that I have never been unhappier to live apart from you than I am today, because I know more than I used to know. I am looking after people I don't have to look after, and the one who should be looked after by me is suffering in health and in reputation. No one can cure this but you. I pray to God to give you the grace to do His will, and to make the person who loves you happy. Tell me in your letter tomorrow how you feel. I remind you, Francesco, the most valuable thing in this world is time. This applies to you more than anyone. As far as Monna Ghita's affairs are concerned, I am more than certain that she treats you as if you were her son. She has every

---

533. Tommaso di Niccolò dell'Ammannato Tecchini had complained about his life in Majorca in a letter to his sister Tina. See note 505, above.

intention of doing so. She demonstrated this to me when I was sick, and she earned my lifelong gratitude. There is nothing distasteful I would shrink from doing in order to assist her. I will reflect on what I know about the matters of our friend and will tell you what I decide to do. I am very pleased that Niccolò Martini is dining with you because I think it will lift your spirits a little. I told Monna Giovanna what you told me.

I did not tell you the reason Niccolò Guasconi cannot look after Monna Giovanna's business.[534] He says it is because of something that happened ten years ago. In my opinion Niccolò is trying, understandably, to avoid getting into hot water, and I think he was forewarned. I am just guessing this. Send me some water for purging myself. I am sending you a small bag in which there are four and a half ounces of cotton wadding and two balls of linen thread. Have them given to Monna Tinga's Lapa for my towels, and tell Monna Ghita to get Piera to work on the cloth because I need it badly. I need twelve measures of raw linen of the best quality to be found to make thread. Bring my riding mantle.

I was very melancholy, but since I heard that Bartolomeo had left, I have been feeling my old self. Tell me how Niccolò and Lapa are and the rest of his household, and how Monna Antonia is. Send my best wishes to them and the women, when you see them. Send my greetings to Barzalone and his women. Send my best wishes to Monna Ghita.

From your Margherita herself, in Florence.

To Francesco di Marco da Prato himself.
Received from Florence, 7 May 1399.

534. See letter 212.

Letter 214 (1401933)
8 May 1399
Florence

In the name of God. Amen. 8 May 1399.

I received your letter as well as several others. I had them all delivered. Concerning the list of clothing, I found everything, and all is in order. I put off visiting the wife of the *Podestà*, who went to Prato: first for one reason, then for another. I did not think she was leaving so soon. I will leave it to you to make my apology.[535] As regards Saccente, you did the right thing for his family, especially because I think he has been wrongly accused. Perhaps I will buy the syrup from our neighbor, as I think there are several reasons why you will be pleased with it. I will send you a sack of barley with Argomento. I received the water flasks. I am happy that Niccolò […] is well. We will expect you on Sunday morning.

Do what you think best about Tommaso's affairs. I see that you have recovered, and I am pleased you are being well looked after by Monna Ghita. I showed Monna Fiore's bread to Lucia. Lucia is praying to God for her. Tell Monna Fiore that if she cannot work out how to do the washing better then I will have to find someone else. She sent me back a tablecloth covered in wine stains. This is not the only time, and she knows I have been complaining about this for a long while.

I have spoken about it several times to Monna Ghita, who says that she is a devil of a woman. Tell Monna Fiore, in a way that Monna Ghita can't, that she seems as scatterbrained as Lucia.

It is not necessary to say anything more about the matters of Monna Giovanna and Niccolò.[536] Monna Giovanna cannot do anything until Tommaso del Bianco has recovered.

I sent you a short letter about the affairs of our friend, so it is not necessary to write it here. I will tell you everything when I see you, before you speak to him. Concerning the flour, I would not send very much, because you have better storage at Prato. I am sending you two sacks as well as the one with the barley. Tomorrow I will send you all

---

535. See letters 195 and following, for Francesco's long-running battle to persuade Margherita to visit Vieri Guadagni's wife.

536. This is Niccolò Guasconi.

the others. Regarding Bartolomeo, I am pleased he has gone to Pisa. We will talk about all this when we meet.[537]

Advise me if anyone is coming early, and if so, I will buy some veal or goat meat. Regarding Francesca's sack that came with the clothes: when Guido finds it—he knows it was left where they slept—he should send it back. Put those cloths for making undergarments inside it. Look after that cloth that was sent to be treated. I will use it to make sheets for the small bed and some undershirts for the household. And I received two basins, two large jugs, two wooden knife cleaners, the basket with the bread, and a package of myrrh. Time is short so I will say no more. May God protect you.

Your Margherita di Francesco herself, in Florence.

To Francesco di Marco himself, Prato.
Received from Florence, 9 May 1399.

Letter 215 (1401934)
2 November 1399
Florence

In the name of God. 2 November 1399.

The reason for this letter is that Ser Guasparre was here with another notary and said the *Podestà* had sent them to us for board and lodging.[538] I think he was lying through his teeth. If I had not been afraid of your reprimand, I would have told him what I thought; but unfortunately for me, he knew you were in Prato with the entire household. There were two women outside. I had the warehouse locked so they could not touch any papers, and had food brought to them and whatever else was necessary; so they received far better treatment than they deserved.

537. See FD 155.

538. This is Guasparre di Ser Bartolo, a notary from Prato.

Antonio Gherardini sent back Piaciti's horse this morning.[539] It was as white as ermine. I will send it back to Piaciti in due course. I am thinking that while Antonio did not send back the horse yesterday, he did send two young men to my house at the second hour after sunset.

Peraccino and Nencio have returned. They left us the horse and the mule. They say that Nanni should be here today, so I will send the animals back with him. He has just arrived.

And things went very well according to Peraccino and Nanni.[540] I was very happy about this. Things could only go well when Barzalone and Niccolò are involved. I beg you to come as soon as you can. It is not the moment to be apart, even though the plague has not spread here. In fact they say there have been fewer deaths in these two days than any other time. I don't know how things are in Prato. They believe that Ludovico Marini has recovered, and so has Piero di Filippo.[541] May God look after us and not consider our sins.

Try to finish up there as soon as you can. Remember what you have to say to Messer Piero, because it would be too upsetting if I lost the forfeit and you criticized me for the rest of my life.[542] Tell my fellow godparent not to start quibbling, as he could, and make sure you say it so you don't mislead your partner, though I trust him enough to believe he would never do it. I don't know what your partner was doing, or what he would have to do, to have that pleasure; but certainly there was never a better time to enjoy oneself than now. At the same time we must keep an eye on God and remember our end, because this is the only way to the greatest of pleasures that I know. Everything else is vain and fruitless. May God give us the grace to be able to recognize the favors He has granted us.

The wet nurse who is looking after the child of Niccolò's wet nurse came for the money she is owed. I told her to come back on Saturday, and I said I would tell Niccolò and when I had heard his reply,

539. Antonio d'Attaviano Gherardini was Margherita's cousin. He was *Podestà* in Prato between May and October 1399. See Hayez, "Le rire du marchand," 425 and 457.

540. This is Piero d'Antonio Zampini.

541. Lodovico Marini was Manno d'Albizo's uncle.

542. There appears to have been some sort of wager between Margherita and her neighbor, Piero Rinaldeschi.

we would give her the amount he told us. Commend me and send my greetings to everyone. May God protect you.

From your Margherita herself, in Florence.

[Added by Stoldo:]
There is no news from anywhere and so I have nothing else to say. I suppose you will be here tomorrow so there is no more to add. Things are going more or less as usual. From what I hear there is even more work to be done in Prato than here, so don't stay there too long. Stoldo, in Florence.

Received from Florence, 3 November 1399. Answered.

Letter 216 (1401714)
4 November 1399
Florence

In the name of God. 4 November 1399.

Agostino brought me your letter addressed to Stoldo and me. It requires only a short reply. In view of the present situation I was very worried that you had not returned.[543] You asked me to inform you how matters are here in Florence. So I sent for Master Giovanni and got him to tell me. As everyone says, the situation is better than when you left, but this is no reason to be complacent.

We hope it will stay unchanged until March. I don't believe there is any advantage to be had by being either here or in Prato. So I will simply tell you my thoughts on what I would do if I were you. I would rather stay in Florence than Prato for the following reason. The plague needs to be treated quickly. The appropriate care should be started within two or three hours. Here in Florence there are better doctors than in Prato. Therefore I believe that if either of us were to fall ill, the best chance of survival would be found here in Florence. You know that here you can look after your body and your soul. Here you would be together with your own, as you dearly wish. So I would prefer to

543. Margherita refers here to the onset of the plague.

stay here, because it seems to me that it is better for various reasons that do not need to be written down. Some people might imagine that I am saying this because I am from Florence. I am certain that you would not believe this is the reason. I stayed away from Florence for six years in a row. You also know very well that I have never wanted to move out to the country, unlike many other people. If I had the choice, I would never go there in these times, because I want both body and soul to be looked after promptly. The right thing is to be prepared to leave immediately, if there is a safe place to go to. However, from what is being said, the disease is everywhere, and I believe that there are people dying in Padua and Venice. So these are not places one could rely on at present. I haven't suggested Genoa for the reasons we have often discussed. If I did see a good place to go, I would urge you to go there immediately. I am writing to tell you what, in my opinion, I think is best. It is up to you to make the decision. May God help you to make one that is good for your body and your soul. Please come back soon. This is not the right time for us to be apart. I also believe that you would be better off where I am now. About bringing your things here, you should bring just the things that are necessary.

We need at least one serge cloth. We could leave the red cloth, but we can't do without the small bowls.

We don't need the tablecloths, as long as there are no guests.

Bring the three caps that you took. I would bring flour and other things a little at a time. I think I left my rings in the chest where the pillow covers are at the time when Agnolo died. May God have mercy on him.[544] Send them to me, and send us a good quantity of the almonds there.

Guido informs you that he has the sheet back from the nuns. After Nanni had left, a packet of letters came from the bank, and we received a letter from Vieri Guadagni. I didn't send it to you because you wrote to me that you would leave Prato yesterday evening, and today I thought that you would be here without fail. The letters are together with this one. I will explain to Vieri why you did not answer him. I will forward the letters to you either with Nanni or with someone else. Try to conclude your business and come as soon as you can, for the good of yourself and those who are with you. You can see

---

544. Agnolo di Niccolò di Piero di Giunta del Rosso had died earlier that year.

that the situation might change from one hour to the next. If anyone should fall ill, you would be trapped there. I am very pleased you sent back Agostino. In the case of sickness, it's best for everyone to stay in his own home.

I think one could compare this plague to what the gospel says about the [Last] Judgment: we don't know whether it will come by day or by night.[545] I wish I had learned virtuous ways from you in the same way I learned to write long letters! I will say no more. May God protect you.

From your Margherita herself, in Florence.

Send us a couple of those medium-sized plates because we need them. If you want to send us even more, do so.

As for the wager that I lost, I am not very upset. Seeing who won it, I don't consider I have lost anything. I really believe my friend is happier than if he had won a pair of capons.[546] I hope to God you haven't greased the judge's palm. If so, let it be on your head.

To the noble gentleman Francesco di Marco, our master in Florence. Received from Florence, 6 November 1399. Answered.

Letter 217 (1401935)
8 April 1400
Florence

In the name of God. 8 April 1400.

Since you left I have not received any letters from you, and I haven't written because you said you would be away only a short time. I am writing this simply to inform you about some things I have sent you.

On the day you left I sent you a pannier with ten loaves of bread—and a small new basket belonging to Ser Schiatta, with a quan-

---

545. Margherita is probably referring to Mark 13:32–33, but the theme is also present in the gospels of Luke and Matthew.

546. See letter 215.

tity of almonds—all with Argomento. Send the small one back to Ser Schiatta. On the 7th I sent you a pot containing some anchovies and a sack with seven pounds of raw flax. If Domenica needs it for the weaving, have it treated and give it to her.

I am not sending you fish from the lake; no good ones arrived here, so I am not sending any, and don't count on receiving any more. You would do well to finish up your business there as soon as you can, because this friar has never preached as well as he is preaching now, so forget about any other sermons. I am extremely sorry you have missed this cycle of sermons, because God knows when there will be another like this.[547] I would have sent you some capons and other items you need if I did not expect you here on Saturday.

Tell Lucia to make sure you are well looked after, and to remember what I said to her when she left here. If she should make any mistakes, forgive her, and remember she is a young woman. She may not have all the wisdom she needs, but even wiser people would not have handled such matters better. Behave patiently if she should not do as well as you would like. Send my greetings to all. I have no more to add. May Christ protect you.

From your Margherita, in Florence.

Postscript:

I had just finished this letter when I received one from you, and I have understood what you say. Regarding sending to the bank for what I need, I will do so, and I will ensure that the household is provided for properly. About you coming here on Saturday, may God let it be so.

I will let you know if I need anything from there. Send someone tomorrow, as early as you can. I had a bottle of oil from Argomento. I sent you the flax for the cloth yesterday with Argomento, and I told you in the letter what I want done with it. I had a letter from Bartolomeo and I will tell you about it when you are here. Argomento wishes to leave, so I will end here. May God protect you.

---

547. Almost certainly, Margherita refers here to Giovanni Dominici (1356–1419), who was preaching in Florence during Lent of 1400. See Nerit Ben-Aryeh Debby, *Renaissance Florence in the Rhetoric of Two Popular Preachers: Giovanni Dominici (1356–1419) and Bernardino da Siena (1380–1444)* (Turnhout: Brepols, 2001), 22; and Mazzei, *Lettere di un notaro*, 1:227–28. See also letters 231 and 233, where Dominici is mentioned as the preacher.

From Monna Margherita, in Florence.

To Francesco di Marco, in Prato.
Received from Florence, 8 April 1400. Answered.

Letter 218 (1401936)
24 September 1401
Florence

In the name of God. 24 September 1401.[548]

On the 22nd I sent you a long letter with the painter, Arrigo; since then I haven't had any of your letters, so I will be brief.

This morning Ser Baldo di Vestro arrived here with the mule. Guido has groomed it properly, so that has been seen to. We heard from the letter you sent to the warehouse yesterday, and from Ser Baldo, that the horse has died—for which I am very sad, more for your sake than for the financial loss, because Ser Baldo told me you were really upset about it, although I could hardly imagine otherwise. I would not be concerned about the loss of the horse and other problems if you weren't so upset, but it seems to me that you and I have many reasons for praising God, considering the immense favor He

---

548. The Datini couple sought refuge from the plague in Bologna between the end of June 1400 and September 1401. Because they were together, there was no need to communicate by letter, and none are extant from this period. See Roberto Greci, "Francesco di Marco Datini a Bologna (1400–1401)," *Atti dell' Accademia delle Scienze dell'Istituto di Bologna* 67, no. 61 (1973): 133–219. In the CD-ROM edition of Margherita's letters, folio 1401879 is misdated as 3 September 1400. It is impossible to place this letter chronologically with certainty because the manuscript is damaged and bears only the date 3 September. It was not sent in September 1400, however, because Margherita and Francesco were in Bologna, and the letter was sent from Prato. It is more likely to have been dictated in September 1398. Because of its very fragmentary state and lack of precise date, the letter has not been translated. It merely asks Francesco to send items of clothing from the household in Florence to Prato. Between 24 September 1401 and 31 July 1406, the couple communicated by letter only sporadically (letters 218–239). Margherita remained in Florence, while Francesco seems to have spent only short periods in Prato without his wife.

has shown, because we all returned fit and well.[549] May God be always praised and may He grant me the grace to be always truly grateful, and especially for the favor He granted me when you arrived safe and sound. Your arrival worried me for a good many reasons, although I didn't want you to notice, in case it scared you. If you think about it a little, you were aware I wasn't very happy, wondering whether you would arrive safely; and yet God had been kind to me in more ways [...] than I would dare to ask for. I can deal calmly with the death of the horse and all the other everyday mishaps, and they wouldn't distress me very much if it weren't for the fact that I see how upset you get. I don't think I can say much to comfort you [...] because you have become obsessed about things like this. I pray to God to give you the grace to accept such events as they should be accepted, and not put your salvation at risk. Ser Baldo tells me that you prepare *vino cotto* and stay up all night, and that you seek out fine grapes [...].[550] I think it would be better not to waste time on this and other such things, because they do more harm than good. Therefore I must remind you to fulfill the good intentions with which you came here. I remind you as well that, in my opinion, you need to do two things: one is to do God's will, and the other is to pass the short span of life that remains to you in such a way that with God's grace you can repay what He has lent you. I believe there can be no good outcome for you from anything else. You are wise, so do what you believe to be right.

I beg you to return soon because I am sure that all you do there is worry, and you are needed here, especially to see to the Malvasia wine, because I won't even touch it if you don't say where you want to put it. The same goes for the wine at Niccolò's house. I don't know what to decide if you don't come. If I have to do something, I will have those sweetened wines there put in two vats in one of the cellars here, and then I will leave them be. There is greater need to deal with more important matters, but these things are of no importance to you.

549. Margherita refers here to the household having survived the plague and its safe return from refuge in Bologna.

550. *Vino cotto* was grape juice that was boiled down to syrup and used to sweeten or flavor other wine.

The house is now ready, so you could be very happy here. Don't neglect big things for little ones.[551]

I had some lamps bought and the house is now in order. We are only lacking some tin containers. If you have more than two mortars in Prato, send us one. If there are only two, leave them there because I have one here and, if necessary, I'll get another one, because I don't want to be left without at least two.

As I am busy tidying up the house, I won't say anything else. May Christ protect you always.

From your Margherita, in Florence.

Together with this letter are several from Venice and from Tommaso. The executors have sent their bill. Look at it and tell me what to answer.

There is also a letter from Giovanni di Ser Nofri who says he has a thousand oak galls, and if you want them they cost twenty-three ducats for the thousand. Stoldo told me to tell him to send them to Ser Conte in Prato, who will see if he is telling the truth about the galls being of a good quality.[552] I will do so today.

I keep writing to Avignon, and last night I stayed awake for several hours, so you can see I am wasting no time doing what I can.

Yesterday we prepared a case of clothing belonging to you and Scolaio for Sarda to bring you. He promised us yesterday he would come here to get it. He did not come, so it is still here. Now I am going out to see if I can find him, and I will send you everything together with a complete list.

There are people here from Giunta del Migliore of Ferrara to collect several sums of money [...] we did not pay them [...]. I will get the register and clarify everything and for the same reason I am keeping [...].

---

551. This phrase recurs in various forms throughout the correspondence because it sums up Margherita's complaint that her husband worried about minor things while serious issues evaded his attention.

552. Oak galls contain tannic acid, and were used for dyeing cloth and for medicine. The ducat was a Venetian gold coin, much used in the Datini business accounts; but this is the only mention in Margherita's letters. It was approximately equivalent to a florin.

I am enclosing a letter from de' Cari.[553] With it was a letter from Catalonia and one from Pisa that we have kept.

We have received your letter from Strozzi's servant, but seeing that Ser Baldo is about to leave I am not answering it here. I will do so fully tonight.

To Francesco di Marco himself, in Prato.
Received from Florence, 24 September 1401. Answered.

Letter 219 (1401937)
24 April 1402
Florence

In the name of God. 24 April 1402.

Your letter was delivered by Argomento, and I received the mushrooms and the embroidered tablecloth. According to Stoldo, Argomento went to the country this morning, and he will come back this evening.

On Sunday letters addressed to "Francesco di Marco and Stoldo di Lorenzo" came from Pisa. Stoldo took them, and the person who brought them said they were very urgent. We thought that he would act on them and reply as required, and this was the reason I did not forward them to you—so as not to lose time.

We found Lapo di Toringo's account, and I am sending it to you with Argomento.[554] It was on the chest. I am sending you the cat with Argomento because she is so frenzied that she can't be kept tied up in any way, and if she got lost, you would tell us that we had been keeping the door open; and so, with regret, we are sending her to you.[555] Get a

---

553. This is Iacopo de' Cari. See letter 224.

554. Lapo di Toringo Pugliesi owed Francesco money. See note 607, below.

555. In his letter of the same day (FD 156), Francesco asked Margherita to send the cat to Nanni Cirioni because he had two male cats. His letter arrived after Margherita had dispatched the cat to him, and on 25 April Francesco expressed resignation about the situation: "I wish you had not sent the cat at this time, but now it is here, I will work out a way of satisfying its needs" (FD 157).

mate for her in Prato, as we can't find one here. When you have done so, you can bring her back here to Florence.

We will forward all letters to you, wherever they come from, and I will say no more, except that you should look after your health. May Christ protect you.

From your Monna Margherita, wife of Francesco di Marco, greetings from Florence.

To Francesco di Marco da Prato himself, in Prato.
Received from Florence, 24 April 1402. Answered.

Letter 220 (1401938)
25 April 1402
Florence

In the name of God. Amen. 25 April 1402.

Yesterday Ser Baldo gave me your letter and I did not send a reply with him because Nanni had just left. I received your letter, one addressed to Stoldo, and another to Ormanno di Iacopo. They have been delivered. I will try to get the notebooks you told me to ask for from Ser Baldo. I see you have received the field peas and other things. I am happy that you like them. The scythe that Nanni should have brought is here, because he forgot to take it. Give back the basket for the mushrooms that Niccolaio Martini sent me. If letters come from anywhere, I will send them to Prato and not give them to anyone else. The man has not yet come from Monna Salvestra for the money. We will send you the bucket you asked for with the first person who can take it to Prato.

Checca's uncle came and told me that he had arranged her marriage, and you know I promised her thirty *lire* when she married.[556] Please do her the favor of giving her this money. I will make sure that she has some other things that I promised her. I have dried all your clothes, and I cannot find your purple-lined overgown of green silk.

---

556. Checca was an ex-servant for whom Francesco had agreed to provide a dowry. See FD 158 and 159.

You must have left it there with your jacket when you returned from Bologna. It would be a good idea when you leave things behind to tell someone else so other people don't get upset about the matter.

I bought an ounce of sweet spices from Guglielmo the apothecary. I will send it on with the first person who arrives. Tommaso del Bianco did not come. If he does, we will do what you say. Here there are fierce arguments about leaving the city. I was told that about five miles away a citizen who fled to the country was seized. I do not know whether it is true. Take great care not to go out of the town gates, because it is not the time to do such things. If you come here, be careful, because it seems that this happened at night.[557] May God, in His holy mercy, not look at our sins [...], because, as far as we can understand, we are facing great tribulations. May God in His holy mercy protect us and not abandon us. Tell Barzalone not to go anywhere because it is not the right time for that.

I foresee that a time will come when economizing will be necessary, whether you like it or not. The greatest satisfaction I have is that I do not think I have spent money carelessly. I always hated unnecessary expenses, whereas it seems to me that many people spend money as if they had stolen it. Happy are those born long ago because today, according to me, whoever has money will need every penny for himself and his family.

Friar Girolamo was here and said you were taxed ten florins.[558] I have not been able to learn anything about Barzalone. I will try to find out, and will let you know by the first letter. I have no more to say except may Christ protect you.

From your Monna Margherita, wife of Francesco di Marco, greetings from Florence.

To Francesco di Marco da Prato himself, in Prato.
Received from Florence, 26 April 1402. Answered.

---

557. In times of plague, civic authorities forbade citizens to enter or leave the town without their permission.

558. See letter 223.

Letter 221 (1401939)
25 April 1402
Florence

In the name of God. Amen. 25 April 1402.

Yesterday evening Nanni brought us your letter and with it a piece of veal and a letter [for Stoldo]. Antonio di Santi was given everything according to your instructions. Nanni reached here trembling all over and seemed nearly dead, and this morning he felt very sick. If Lucia had been here, I would not have sent him to you today. Yesterday I sent you a letter with Argomento, and I enclosed Lapo di Toringo's account.[559]

I am sending you broad beans, field peas, and salad greens. The salad is perhaps not as you would like it because salad is best collected toward vespers. May God grant that we have bread and wine this year. I am sending you two pairs of slippers with Nanni, and I am sending a scythe that they used at Bologna to cut grass. So as not to delay Nanni and have him arrive in the heat of the day, I will say no more. May Christ protect you.

From your Margherita, wife of Francesco, greetings from Florence.

To Francesco di Marco da Prato himself, in Prato.
Received from Florence, 25 April. Answered.

Letter 222 (1401940)
27 April 1402
Florence

In the name of God. Amen. 27 April 1402.

Yesterday I sent you a letter with Argomento as required. Today Nanni delivered one from you that requires only a short reply.

---

559. Francesco had sent detailed instructions about where to look for the records of transactions with Lapo di Toringo Pugliesi and other debtors. See FD 156 and 157.

I received the cheese. I sent the spices with Tommaso del Bianco, and I gave him the message that you sent him.[560] I want to send you the bucket, scythe, candles, Malvasia wine, and walnuts with Nanni.

I don't intend to worry about the fact that you think I am being too generous to Checca. I am giving her what I am obliged to, because she was going to make herself a chemise from some cloth, but I did not let her make it before she left, so as to keep it for her.[561] I gave Nanni Cirioni his letter. Fattorino waited there for the reply and I am sending it to you with our Nanni. I haven't been able to find out anything about Barzalone's affairs because the books are in the bedroom. I told Stoldo to try to find out. Regarding your affairs, Friar Girolamo told me about the ten florins. If Stoldo knows, he should tell you.[562] I am sending you five small flour sacks with Lucia's things in them. So as not to delay Nanni, I will stop writing. May Christ protect you.

From your Monna Margherita, wife of Francesco di Marco, greetings from Florence.

To Francesco di Marco da Prato, in Prato.
Received from Florence, 27 April 1402. Answered.

Letter 223 (1401941)
30 April 1402
Florence

In the name of God. Amen. 30 April 1402.

Yesterday I sent a letter to you with Nanni. I am only writing this because of the letters Stoldo gave me last night to send on to you. Then, at nones, I received a bundle of letters that came from Bologna. Paolo, who hires packhorses, brought them and said they were very

---

560. Francesco's message to Tommaso del Bianco was that he would be sending a mule for him and Stoldo so they could travel to Prato.

561. Francesco regarded the thirty *lire* as sufficient. See FD 158.

562. Stoldo had told Francesco that he would have to pay a tax of fifteen florins, and he asked Margherita to find out who was right about this and also to enquire about how much Barzalone had to pay. See FD 158 and 159.

urgent. I remembered that you had business with Iacopo de' Cari and that you were talking with Domenico di Cambio about some taffeta. You wrote to me that I should send all the letters that come here to Prato. Considering the state of Pisa, and of Bologna as well, I thought that sending them on to Prato would waste too much time, so I decided to open the letters. Inside I found two letters for Master Giovanni di Banduccio; I sent them on to him and one to Domenico di Cambio. The letter that I read spoke about the matters I had anticipated. Domenico received his and he also read the one I am sending to you. If I did the wrong thing in opening them, tell me, and I will not open letters any more but just send them on as they come.

Bartolomeo returned, and he has a permit to stay for all of May.[563] This morning he, Niccolò dell'Ammannato, and Tingo Buondelmonti dined with me.[564] We ate the veal that you sent us. We did not eat omelets with herbs or drink Malvasia wine. We had plenty to eat and there was some left over. A word to the wise suffices: you would do well to return here as soon as you can.

We sent the veal to everyone, according to your instructions, and I will take out the list as soon as I get it.[565] There is nothing to add. May Christ protect you.

From your Monna Margherita, wife of Francesco di Marco, greetings from Florence.

To Francesco di Marco da Prato himself, in Prato.
Received from Florence, 1 May. Answered.

---

563. This is Bartolomeo Bandini, Margherita's brother. See note 529, above.

564. This is the notary Ser Tingo Buondelmonti.

565. Presumably this is the list of the goods Francesco had sent to Margherita.

Letter 224 (1401942)
1 May 1402
Florence

In the name of God. Amen. 1 May 1402.

I wrote to you yesterday, and sent letters from Bologna and elsewhere on to you. I sent them to the city gate. Fattorino says he gave them to Nanni Cirioni's father-in-law. As for the letter that Arrigo the painter brought, it does not seem that he received the other letters that were with it. Stoldo received the letters, and his reply is enclosed. I sent the letter to Cristofano Cirioni, and he tells me he cannot do what he said. Today he will send his reply with someone else. I read the letter. I see there is no need to say any more, except I would like you to return as soon as you can. May Christ protect you.

From your Margherita, wife of Francesco di Marco, greetings from Florence.

To Francesco di Marco da Prato himself, in Prato.
Received from Florence, 1 May 1402. Answered.

Letter 225 (1401943)
5 May 1402
Florence

In the name of God. Amen. 5 May 1402.

Yesterday evening Monna Guiduccia's Filippo delivered your letters, together with other letters that I have had forwarded. About putting Domenica in the house, as well as Lucia, do what you like. As for having matters to settle, the longer you stay there, the more you will have. You will have a good deal of trouble getting away if you start looking at all the things there are to do. I sent you a letter with Neri da Filettole on Wednesday, and we also sent several letters from various people—letters that Ser Lapo had given us to go to Barzalone, and one that Cristofano Cirioni sent. The letter I sent with Filippo was not important. He was very early. He promised me that he would give it to you as soon as he entered the gate. I think he will have done so.

Argomento brought me your letters and other letters addressed to Stoldo and Domenico di Cambio. They were delivered to the warehouse. Because you wrote to me that you would be here this morning, I imagine you have changed it to this evening. You also say that you will come here and go back on Sunday, unless some problem arises here. I would be sorry to see you return there so soon. Just the same, do what you prefer. If you are not coming back now, send me some money because, as you well know, you did not leave me any and I don't want to send to the warehouse for it—because as you know I have been expecting you every day. Because I am hoping you will come back any day now, I will say no more. I enclose with this a letter from Ser Lapo Mazzei and some others.

From your Margherita, wife of Francesco di Marco, in Florence.

To Francesco di Marco, in Prato.
Received from Florence, 5 May 1402.

Letter 226 (1401944)
15 May 1402
Florence

In the name of God. Amen. 15 May 1402.

Yesterday I received your letter from Falcuccio's son.[566] We sent back Piaciti's horse, and yesterday at vespers, Domenico di Cambio sent me another. We received the letters that you mention.

I am writing this simply to send you a pack of letters that came yesterday evening. I am sending them with Chianciano because yesterday I could not find anyone to bring them, and I don't want to give them to just anyone. I decided to send them to you immediately so you would receive them before Stoldo left. Don't be surprised that they are open. When I saw the document I thought it must concern that matter you know about; so I read the letter addressed to you that was on top,

566. This is Michele di Falcuccio. See note 161, above.

and then I understood that it did not. Miniato is not in Florence and will not be here for two days. Therefore I am sending your letter and all the others so you can do what you wish with them. Stoldo's women say that they don't need anything. Tell Barzalone that Marco did not come. Tell him to come here and I will get him to write my reply.

Your Margherita commends herself to you.

To Francesco di Marco himself, in Prato.
Received from Florence, 16 May 1402. Answered.

Letter 227 (1401945)
17 May 1402
Florence

In the name of God. Amen. 17 May 1402.

Yesterday I sent you a reply with Chianciano, and I sent the bundle of letters with him. He gave me your letter and also some letters addressed to Domenico di Cambio, another to Nanni Cirioni, and one to Santa Maria Nuova.[567] I had them all delivered as you told me.

Stoldo came and brought the mule and one letter. In answer to your requests: I will send the mule with Argomento as well as the pack saddle, the saddle, and the bridle. I am not sending the hens because they laid eggs today. Caterina has been difficult since you left [...] this staying shut up inside now that the feast days are here would drive not only her crazy, but even an adult. There is not a soul in this area who hasn't gone to the country or to the festivities.[568] I beg you—please excuse me—to finish up your work there. I seem to see what you already know.[569] I will say no more on this subject, because I think that otherwise I would say something that would not make you happy now, and I also thought deep in my heart that I would not tell you the entire truth, but a time will still come when you will suf-

567. This was the hospital in Florence.

568. Margherita probably refers here to her niece Tina, who was living in the Datini household.

569. This passage seems to refer to the prospect of Francesco's death. He was 67 at this time.

fer greater pains than you do now, and that is one of the things that will kill me, and I cannot help but say it. May God set down the end for us that He sees is good for body and soul. I beg you to pardon me because I cannot say otherwise; you should have pity for me when you realize why I am saying it. I beg you to finish off the business that you went there to do, and I remind you that when you waste time, all those who are with you waste it too. Together with this letter you will receive one from Domenico di Cambio and another from elsewhere. As regards the household and everything else that needs to be done here, it will be managed to your satisfaction. If only God would let me help you in the other things, I would say: "Invite whoever you like and leave these other matters to me"; because not even the Pope would stop me if I wanted to do something. And remember that friar who said to you that if you did not want it, no one would come to your house. How true! I will say no more. May Christ give you the grace to do His will.

Your Margherita commends herself to you.

To Francesco di Marco da Prato himself, in Prato.
Received from Florence, 17 May [1402]. Answered.

Letter 228 (1401946)
18 May 1402
Florence

In the name of God. Amen. 18 May 1402.

Yesterday I sent you a letter with Argomento. I have just received your letters from Argomento as well as the cloths I sent you to be washed, wrapped in the bench cover. I am pleased that you received the mule and the other things I sent because I think you are very unhappy, which concerns me. Similarly, I am sorry for you because of the event that happened, both out of love of you and because I think it will grieve you in many ways. I would like you to be comforted because God took away from you the possibility of having sons. Now he has taken away these hindrances so that you can escape from this evil world, and you see what sort of hope you can place in it. In my opinion it is a matter for regret; but believe me Francesco, God is doing everything for the good of your soul. You know this; if only you were willing to act on what you know. As I believe you are coming here this evening, or tomorrow morning, I will say no more. I pray to God that He has performed a true act of mercy, and may He give grace to that mother to allow her to bear this suffering without speaking ill of Him, as it is a very bitter pill to swallow; and I think now of the favor that God has given me, since I will not have to swallow the same pill.[570] May God give me the grace to be thankful for this and all the other favors He has granted me, and may He give you the grace to do those things that are pleasing to Him. May Christ protect you always.

Your Margherita, wife of Francesco di Marco, Florence.

To Francesco di Marco da Prato himself, in Prato.
Received from Florence, 18 May 1402.

Letter 229 (1401947)
12 September 1402
Florence

In the name of God. 12 September 1402.

I received your letter from Argomento and also a pannier of peaches on Sunday. Master Cristofano's associate brought me some too. You are surprised because I have not written to you. The reason is that I have been sick again and I have no one in the house who knows how to write. I do not want to send for an important person to help me write a letter.[571] Just think that I am in bed and everyone in the household is young. There are people who would come and help me as if they were my brothers, but others would interpret it in a very

570. Margherita appears to be speaking of a mother's losing her child. Being barren, she could not experience the same suffering. Her admonition to Francesco to please God suggests that he may have been the child's father.

571. This letter is in Margherita's hand, and some passages are difficult to read, probably due to her ill health. Francesco replied that he was also sick. See FD 160.

different way, seeing that the greatest pleasure men seem to have is to speak badly about women. If you get the grape harvest in and finish up quickly, I will be very pleased. I had the barrel measured in the way you instructed in your letter, and Argomento will bring it to you. He is bringing one of my cloths. Forget about the house in Bologna. I wanted to send you wine on two occasions. I remind you that Argomento is making wine, but perhaps he won't be willing to bring you any.[572] I think the bowls that I had made for you should be for the household. I will take steps to ensure that all goes well there and see to all the other things so that you will be satisfied.

Master Giovanni has been coming every day and looks after me as much as possible. You ask me to tell you how I am. I would be well if I were God's friend. If I told you everything, I would upset you. Today I was worse than on Thursday. I am resigned to this because it is the will of God. There are two pleasures for me in this world: one is to be content with what God does; the other one, it seems to me, is that those who have a family should not want more from it than what God has granted. They should enjoy their company and not look for faults, particularly when it would be humiliating for others.

Remember that the good and bad we experience in this world are of our own making.

Messer Tommaso Soderini has gone to give his account to God. May the same happen to all those who delight in speaking badly about women.[573] Cilia is here with us. She says Conte has died.[574] May God allow matters to turn out for the best.

I will now finish. May Christ protect you always.

Your Margherita, in Florence.

---

572. It is not clear to whom Margherita refers.

573. Messer Tommaso di Guccio Soderini amassed a fortune in Avignon during the 1360s and had returned to Florence by the 1370s. He became a powerful political figure in the Albizzi regime. See Paula Clark, *The Soderini and the Medici* (Oxford: Clarendon Press, 1991), 14–15. He died on 12 September 1402, as Margherita reports. On his illegitimate son Lorenzo, born in Avignon, see Jérôme Hayez, "Migration et stratégies familiales: Autour de la condamnation de Lorenzo di messer Tommaso Soderini, bâtard et faussaire malchanceux (1405)," *Médiévales* 19 (1990): 43–57.

574. Margherita refers to Ser Conte di Nerozzo Migliorati.

To Francesco di Marco, in Prato.

Received from Florence, 13 September 1402. Answered.

Letter 230 (1401948)
18 January 1403
Florence

In the name of God. Amen. 18 January 1403.

On the 17th of the month I received a letter written by you on the same day, and today, the 18th, I received another letter from you written on the 17th. This is my answer.

I took delivery of the mule and did what you asked and likewise for the letter that you sent me. I got Nanni Cirioni to bring you the mule and the bundle of letters that Domenico di Cambio had sent me. Did you receive them?

I forwarded the letter that you sent me to Domenico di Cambio, so he must know about the money that he has to get from that money changer.

I received the bridle from Argomento and sent it to the house of Nofri d'Andrea. He said he now had the horse, so I think Particino also has his.

I have been told about the pig that you have killed, and you say you will finish up your work as soon as possible. May God help you to do so.

It is a good thing that you are protecting yourself from the cold because it is very bad for your health. I remind you that Bartolomeo is about to get married, so he should be saved from too much toil.

Send Stoldo back to Monna Villana as soon as possible because she says the weather is too cold to be without a husband.

I, Niccolò dell'Ammannato, am staying here and listening to the sermons of the good friar Giovanni Dominici, who preached four times yesterday, which was the feast of Saint Antony.[575] There is nothing new here. May God be your guardian.

From Margherita, your wife.

575. See note 547, above. Fra Giovanni Dominici is also mentioned in letter 232.

To Francesco di Marco, in Prato.
Received from Florence, 19 January 1403. Answered.

Letter 231 (1401949)
20 January 1403
Florence

In the name of God. 20 January 1403.

Yesterday I sent an answer to your two letters with the apothecary Bartolomeo. Then Stoldo arrived, and I did not receive any letters from him. He told me to send Chianciano to you with the big mule, and I will do so and send Nanni Cirioni on the small mule. I lent Chianciano three *lire* from that florin that you left me. Tell Bartolomeo to make him account for it. Ginevra has been slightly unwell, and her face is swollen. I had her examined by Master Giovanni and will do what is necessary. Do you want me to send to Domenico di Cambio for a large sum of money, or do you want to send it to me, as I need some? Look for some material to make undershirts for Andrea and Paolo, as they need them. It must be strong. Just now I received a letter that does not require an answer. There was also one for Stoldo. I read it. I do not see that Chianciano needs to wait here for my reply. I will say no more. Look after yourself so that you may return home fit and well.

From your Margherita, in Florence.

To Francesco di Marco himself, in Prato.
Received from Florence, 20 January 1403. Answered.

Letter 232 (1401950)
22 January 1403
Florence

In the name of God. Amen. 22 January 1403.

I received, on the above date, a letter from you written on the same day and two other letters. One is for Domenico di Cambio and the other for Stoldo, and I had these delivered today. Now I will answer your letter.

I am glad Chianciano arrived there with the mule.

Concerning Ginevra's improvement, I will make sure she is looked after so she recovers properly.

About the money that Chianciano had from me, you say that you approve.

When I need money, I will ask for it from Domenico di Cambio on your behalf.

I had your hose cut down for Nanni d'Andrea, so that has been taken care of.

Regarding the cloth that you bought for Andrea and for Paolo and of which you say you purchased ten and a half yards, I tell you that this is only enough for two undershirts for Andrea or a little more, so buy some more.

[…] the people whom I asked about Nanni Cirioni say they think he left for his destination, as they have not seen him today.

I beg you to get ready to come as soon as you can.

[Added by the scribe Niccolò dell'Ammannato:]
Here people are jousting and enjoying themselves. And I, Niccolò dell'Ammannato, am listening to the sermons of Fra Giovanni.[576] I will urge him to pray to God on your behalf. He is certainly a good and noble man. I am very pleased with all he does.

There is no more to say. May God be your guardian.

From your Margherita, the above date, Florence.

Received from Florence, 23 January [1403]. Answered.

---

576. This is Giovanni Dominici. See letters 217 and 230.

Letter 233 (1401951)
26 January 1403
Florence

In the name of God. Amen. 26 January 1403.

I received a letter from you written on the 23rd of the month. Now I will answer. Because I, Niccolò dell'Ammannato, was a little busy, on account of Filippo dell'Ammannato's mother-in-law, who died—may God grant her forgiveness—we did not write to you.[577] This letter is just to acknowledge the things you sent us, after which we will tell you what we sent:

Eleven pairs of capons.

One basket full of sausages.

Four sacks of flour.

Four sacks of barley.

One bed in four pieces.

One quilt.

One mattress for a small bed. A good quantity of hazelnuts.

And we got him to bring you:

The saddle for the mule.

Two oil barrels.

I will leave it to Stoldo to get the letters you mention.

I sent you with Nanni a set of underlinen that belongs to Guido.

Margherita is suffering from those pains of hers and is in bed. May God help her to recover.

I have no more to say for now. May God be your guardian. I beg you to return as soon as you can.

From Monna Margherita, wife of Francesco di Marco da Prato.

To Francesco di Marco, in Prato.
Received from Florence, 26 January 1403. Answered.

---

577. This letter was not dictated by Margherita, but written on her behalf by Niccolò dell'Ammannato Tecchini.

Letter 234 (1401952)
14 February 1403
Florence

In the name of God. Amen. 14 February 1403.

Yesterday I received your letter written on the 13th of the month. I am answering it with this. I received that letter after Argomento had left here, and it was not at a time when I could answer you.

Martino di Niccolaio took the horses back to Nofri d'Andrea's house.

Argomento was here and could not bring back everything. He took an old sack and put your sandals in it with your leather bag and three registers.

If letters come from anywhere, I will send them to you.

I looked in that basket that you mention. There are few papers in it. I can only find a few short notes in it. However, in that basket where you say not to look, there is one register tied across with string and on the outside is written "Register to send to Francesco di Marco, written in 1382 on 1 December." If you want this, write to me and I will send it to you.

Regarding the two sacks that you mention, I looked in the desk and everywhere else, and I cannot find them. I neither lent them to anyone nor put the clothes in them when I sent them to be washed; there was no need, because until summer this year I had some big old sacks that were suitable. Barzalone told me he had lost one. I know I have seen Nanni and Argomento carrying flour and wheat off in them many times. I often got angry about it. There are ten new ones in that sack that you left here, and altogether there must be eighteen sacks of that type.

I gave the letters to Domenico and to Miniato. Both their replies are enclosed with this letter. If Miniato had had the small mule he would have come there with Zanobi Agolanti.

I have no more to add. May God be your guardian.

From Monna Margherita, wife of Francesco di Marco.

To Francesco di Marco, in Prato.
Received from Florence, 14 February 1403. Answered.

Letter 235 (1401953)
17 February 1403
Florence

In the name of God. Amen. 17 February 1403.

I sent you a letter with Miniato about what was required. It did not need an answer but simply listed the things I had sent you. I have not had a letter from you since then. I never find Niccolò at home when I send for him.[578] This is why I have not answered all your letters. Miniato has returned the small mule and told me to get Argomento to bring it to you, and I will do so. Argomento was here and brought four sacks of flour. I will have it stored in the way you say. I will look after the household and do whatever needs to be done to keep it in order as best as I can. Nothing more needs to be said about Miniato. Argomento is passing on the instructions that Miniato gave him. He will tell the people who are treating the thread that they should not boil it as long as linen. I am sending you two sets of underlinen for the apprentices and two pairs of slippers so that they can put the other ones they are wearing in the wash. I am not sending you any because you have them there. Remember to bring a bench cover, if there is one. I would like to know how Barzalone's wife Monna Vanna is. He was told she was suffering a miscarriage. Tell Barzalone to let me know if there is anything here he would like me to get for her, and I will gladly see to it. Unfortunately these are the rewards this world provides.

As I am in haste, I will say no more. May Christ protect you.

From your Margherita, from Florence.

To Francesco di Marco da Prato.
Received from Florence, 17 February 1403. Answered.

578. This is Niccolò dell'Ammannato Tecchini.

Letter 236 (1401954)
21 February 1403
Florence

In the name of God. Amen. 21 February 1403.

    Yesterday I wrote to you and answered your two letters, but I couldn't find anyone to deliver them to you. This morning Stefano di Ser Piero came and brought a bundle of letters addressed to Nanni Cirioni. There was one for me and I got it at vespers. It would be better to leave the packages open. From now on I will open all the letters that come and will keep my own. I gave a letter of mine to Stefano di Ser Piero, and I am sending one to Monna Zita; and one to Luigi Lottino and one to go to Vernio.[579] He told me he gave them to Mannuccio di Lodovico. I received a load of wood from Argomento. The mule is here; I will have it groomed and Stefano will bring it back there. I opened Luigi's letter to see whether anything had happened about the matter you know about. You do not mention the pills I sent you with Puccio.[580] I am pleased at what you say about coming here on Monday, and you would do well to free yourself for a good while, at least all of Lent, so you could hear Fra Giovanni's sermons.[581] Tell me if I have to buy anything. I will not do so unless you send me a message. Tell me if they have not done the washing, and I will send you plenty of clothes. Take care not to eat so much that you need to take pills. Try to enjoy yourself at the celebrations this Thursday before Lent. Remind Ser Piero that I am his goddaughter, and he should not lead you astray because it would reflect little credit on him. Because Stefano is leaving [I will say no more]. May Christ protect you.

    From your Margherita.

    After I wrote this letter Nanni Cirioni came here. I complained to him that he had not sent me my letter. He said that he received his at the same time as I got mine. So it is not his fault.

---

579. Monna Zita was the wife of Niccolaio Martini while Luigi di Lottino Gherardini was a relative of Margherita. Francesco wrote about his brother-in-law Bartolomeo Bandini. See FD 169, 170, and 171.

580. Puccio di Bonciano was a new carrier.

581. See letters 219 and 221.

To Francesco di Marco da Prato.
Received from Florence, 22 February 1403. Answered.

Letter 237 (1401955)
23 February 1403
Florence

In the name of God. Amen. 23 February 1403.

Casino, our former laborer, brought me a letter from you dated 22 February, as well as several others. One was addressed to Luigi Lottino, and I sent it to Tingo so he could forward it to him at his country house. I sent the letter for Ser Lapo to his house, and I had the letters for Domenico and Stoldo given to them.

You say you will be here on Monday. May God accompany you. You say you have eaten a great deal. I will ensure that here you eat more modestly.

I remind you, when you come, to bring the records so we can settle the baker's account.

Please make sure you remain healthy. If you are going to be here in the next few days, there will be no need to write to you again. Here there is no other news.

The Piaciti sent you letters yesterday, and as Stoldo was here as usual, he took them and has presumably answered them.

There is news from Venice that Bindo Piaciti's daughter Nanna is very sick, and her father is attending her. If you are writing there, say something appropriate about this.[582]

Send my greetings and commend me to everyone there. We are all well here. May God be praised for this, and I pray that He will protect you.

[Added by the scribe Niccolò dell'Ammannato:]
I, Niccolò dell'Ammannato, beg you to write to me if there is anything I can do on your behalf, or for your relatives or friends. I will try to do whatever you wish.

582. For Margherita's cousin Bindo Piaciti, see note 271, above.

There is nothing new to add, so there is nothing more to be said. From Margherita, your wife.

To Francesco di Marco, in Prato.
Received from Florence, 24 February 1403. Answered.

Letter 238 (1401956)
24 February 1403
Florence

In the name of God. Amen. 24 February 1403.

Nanni delivered your letter as well as the package of books and the linen, four pairs of capons, two baskets, and eight letters. After the servant had left, I sent them immediately to Stoldo. I do not imagine that you will return here any later than Monday. As for your having eaten too well, I will feed you in a way to make up for your overeating, as long as it does not harm you.

I sent you a letter with a relative of Niccolaio Martini and also a reply from Domenico to the letter that Casino brought.[583] Nanni told me that you want to put Anna in a convent.[584] I think that is the last thing she has in mind. Her answer to you was of the sort that she is used to giving. She knows that I know what she thinks. Tell her mother that I said she should watch her carefully because she needs it. She should not let her enjoy herself as she did at her place. She should not let her go out with Michele's wife. She would do well to close the front door and keep it bolted when she goes out. She should think carefully about what I say. You should warn her when you leave there, even though she has never been afraid either of you or of me. It would have been better for her if she had been.

I would have written you many letters but I did not want to give them to anyone except you, in case they fell into someone else's hands, because these girls' affairs are very delicate matters. Tear this up as

583. See letter 237.

584. It is possible that this girl was one of Chiarito's four daughters, for whom Francesco provided dowries.

soon as you have read it. There is no more to say for now. May Christ protect you.

Your Margherita, in Florence.

To Francesco di Marco himself, in Prato.
Received from Florence, 24 February 1403. Answered.

Letter 239 (1401957)
31 July 1406
Florence

In the name of God. 31 July.

Today I received your letter from Argomento, and this is my answer. We received the barley from Argomento and placed it with the rest. The wheat was put in the vat above so it is well protected. I am sending you back the bags, both your own and those belonging to Lionardo. We also received the capons and the squabs, so everything is accounted for. We are sending you the wine with Argomento—nine flasks, that is—and we are also sending you your clothes wrapped in a towel. We received twenty florins and gave them to Luca, so that has been attended to as well.[585] I will do what I have to do. I took the young birds yesterday and clipped their wings.

I will say no more for now. May Christ protect you always.

Argomento has not been paid.

To Francesco di Marco, in Prato.
Received from Florence, 31 July 1406.
One pannier.

---

585. Luca del Sera was Francesco's trusted partner. After his recall from Spain in the early fifteenth century, he became head of the Florentine branch. He had worked in Genoa, Barcelona, Majorca, and Valencia. He married Francesco's niece, Tina dell'Ammannato Tecchini. See Melis, *Aspetti della vita economica medievale*, 61, 112.

Letter 240 (1401958)
3 August 1406
Florence

In the name of God. 3 August.

Since you left here, you have not written to me at all, and I have not written to you because there has been no need.

I am writing because I would like to know what is keeping you there; I have been really worried about it, because I am starting to believe it is not giving you any comfort. Forget about food and spending. If only these things gave you some comfort! Even if I knew for certain that you would only live for another year, I would not be so worried. I remind you that Luca is here all alone, and I remind you that when you are here with Checco Naldini and Guido, you have a lot to do. For this reason, if you do not have anything to do in Prato—and I don't think you do—I think it would be better for you to arrange to come here. I am not saying this because Luca is not doing everything he can. He writes and looks after everything. If only you were like him.[586] He came here to attend to your business and he never left the house, even on Sunday, because he was writing all day and slept very little at night. It was much better than if he had gone to Prato. Do not send for him any more, because I think your affairs here in Florence would suffer without him. I am sending you the things that you asked for. Luca will tell you about them. About sending the clothes to Lucia to be washed in the evening, I remind you that I would like her to be wiser than she is. But because I am not about to make her be born again, let her be just as God made her.

I do not want to get rid of people who serve me well. As I have so few, it would not be fair to them, it would not bring any advantages, and it would upset me. So I want to avoid this if I can.

I am very sorry about Barzalone's little one for many reasons, and also for Monna Vanna.[587] I beg you to help ease his difficulties in whatever way you can. He has already had too many.

---

586. This is Luca del Sera. See note 585, above.

587. Margherita refers here perhaps to Barzalone's young relative, mentioned below, who suffered at the hands of the wet nurse with insufficient milk.

I will say no more. May God protect you.

Commend me to Monna Simona and to everyone there. Send my best wishes to Domenica and tell her that Tonina is well. Tell Domenica to go and see her daughter and provide her with what she needs. We have been told that she is very sick. It was not Stefano who told us this, but a woman from there.

We asked Stefano and he said that you did not want her to go there because she was behaving as if she was going off to be entertained. It is not much use for someone to have a white tablecloth and no food. It would be better to have some milk and a dirty tablecloth. But she betrayed and deceived Barzalone because she promised to be a wet nurse for his sister-in-law but provided no milk at all. If I were there, I would treat her as she has treated us.

To Francesco di Marco, in Prato.
Received from Florence, 3 August 1406.

Letter 241 (1401870)
3 January 1410
Prato

In the name of God. 3 January 1410.[588]

The reason for this letter is that we have just received a bundle of letters from the son of Master Giovanni di Banduccio. In the bundle there were two addressed to Ser Francesco D'Agniolo, the other to Chese and partners.[589] We delivered them.

You will have heard what happened from Rome and also that the Marchese is not coming here.

---

588. Francesco had left for Florence the previous day. The last flurry of letters between 3 and 11 January 1410 (Francesco wrote seven letters while Margherita wrote ten) concerns preparations for the reception of important guests at the house in Prato.

589. On Chese di Filippo Saccagnini, see Fiumi, *Demografia*, 472–75.

An emissary of Cardinal du Puy came a short time ago to speak to the Pope and confirmed to us that this was true.[590] As they had heard that you were not here, he came to ascertain whether we were pleased for the cardinal to come here on Sunday. Otherwise he will go to the inn. We answered that you told us to do all we could to place our house at the cardinal's disposal, and we said what an honor it would be for you. He accepted the invitation, and went off to Pistoia saying that he would give us exact information tomorrow evening or the day after.

I am amazed that you have not sent Puccio back to us, and I expected you to tell me about how to provide for the cardinal.[591] I decided to have bread made. As far as wine and firewood and other things are concerned, I will wait for your reply. According to his familiar, his stay will be brief.

Messer Marco dined and slept here last night.[592] We sent for Ser Baldo to keep him company, and similarly we had Monna Bartolomea di Checco for our own company. We received him in the best possible manner. He said it was a long time since he had been treated so well. The Pope sent for him twice yesterday evening. From what one can see, he has great reverence for the Pope. As I am in a hurry, I will say no more. May Christ keep you in His holy grace.

From your Monna Margherita.

To Francesco di Marco, in Florence.
Received from Prato, 3 January 1410.

[Noted on the sheet by Francesco:]
Tell me about the silk thread and the colors available to embroider Ciano's daughter-in-law's garland.[593]

590. Cardinal Pierre Gérard had been bishop of Le Puy. He had participated in the conclave of 1409 at Pisa, which had elected the antipope, Alexander V (Pietro Filargo), on 26 June. This Pope died in Bologna on 3 May 1410.

591. See FD 173.

592. This is Messer Marco from Venice, to whom Francesco had instructed Margherita to offer hospitality (FD 172 and 173).

593. Ciano is mentioned in FD 174.

About Lapo di Toringo's ten florins.

Tell Ser Baldo to send us the record of Benozzo's defense.[594]

Send the deer and kid skins.

Remind Lorenzo di Stefano about the old *Podestà*'s money.

The measurements of the small window.

Letter 242 (1401869)
3 January 1410
Prato

In the name of God. 3 January 1410.

This evening Puccio brought us a letter from you, and we also received the candles and the hemp.

Lando did not come to tell us anything regarding Messer Giovanni Genovardi.[595]

Then, after we had read the letter, I decided to send Lionardo and Ser Baldo to look for him and show him the letter and speak to him in the manner that Ser Baldo thought would bring you honor. We went there, and we were told that he is still at Pistoia and that he will be coming without fail on Saturday, tomorrow morning. So, when he has come, we will stay here and visit him on your behalf and show him what you have written to us in the letter.

This morning we sent you a letter with Grazzino to tell you that Messer Marco had left early today and that the Marchese was not coming here, and that it is believed certain that the Pope is leaving here tomorrow.[596] They told the butchers not to prepare meat for them. Many people have already left.

---

594. See FD 178.

595. The laborer Lando da Leccio had not reported on whether Messer Giovanni Genovardi—a lawyer from Lucca who held office in Aix as an official of the count of Provence, Louis II d'Anjou—would come to Prato.

596. See letter 242. Francesco wanted to offer hospitality to all these dignitaries during their stay in Prato.

We wrote to you about what the Cardinal du Puy's familiar told us. They said he would certainly be here on Sunday or Saturday evening.

We heard once more how it pleased God to call to himself the cardinal of Albano.[597] May God grant him peace.

You know how on the day you left, we spoke about doing some things, and I told you to speak about it with Luca and that he should advise me what I should do. I gave orders to have some bread made, but just the same, we will not do so if we do not hear from you. It seems to me that you should send us one of those young men so if the cardinal comes Lionardo will not be alone. It is not that anything in particular needs to be done, because the house is in order. It seems to me, however, that it looks poorly for a person of your status if only Lionardo is here. I think that the cardinal will only stay for a short time.

This evening they are having a great celebration for the events in Rome, and they will be lighting great bonfires.[598]

Concerning having the letter, that is the memorandum delivered to Nofri di Neri, I saw to it. I told Matteo but he could not attend to that matter because he has a cardinal in the house.[599] I went back there today but did not find him. I will go back as soon as I can and I will send his reply to you. I am sending you with this letter a reply from Nofri di Neri. For now I will say no more. May Christ keep you in His most holy grace.

From your Margherita, in Prato.

To Francesco di Marco, in Florence.
Received from Prato, 4 January 1410.

597. Nicola Brancaccio had been made a cardinal in 1378, and although he belonged to the obedience of Avignon, he had attended the 1409 Council of Pisa that elected Alexander V.

598. King Ladislao of Naples occupied Rome in 1408. His garrison was driven out by a combined army of Florentines and Sienese at the beginning of 1410.

599. Matteo di Ser Niccolaio Inghirami belonged to a wealthy Pratese family.

Letter 243 (6300688)
4 January 1410
Prato

In the name of God. 4 January 1410.

Guido came at terce, and he brought us the pine-nut cake and the note about what has to be done.[600] We understand your wishes exactly, and without going over all the details, we will carry them out so that honor will be reflected on you and the guests will be looked after properly. Barzalone, Ser Baldo, Lionardo, and I, as well as Andrea and Guido, are here and we will manage everything so that it will run perfectly smoothly. The dining room is in proper order, with tables and benches and bench covers.

Yesterday I wrote to you that Messer Giovanni Genovardi had not come yesterday evening; and also that, according to what I had heard, the cardinal of Albano has died.

I wanted to convey a message to Pistoia, and a short time ago as I was writing, his familiar—that is, Cardinal du Puy's—arrived. He says that there is no need to send anyone because he will convey our message perfectly to Monsignore, the cardinal; and that if it is true that the cardinal of Albano is dead, the cardinal will not be able to come for many days because he will have to go to the funeral. In the event that Albano has not died, he does not know whether the cardinal can come tomorrow, but his familiar has promised that he is going there immediately—and that without fail, by this evening or tomorrow morning, we will be told whether he is coming, when, and with how many people. We will be informed in plenty of time so that we can provide what is necessary, and fulfill your wishes in a way that will bring you honor and make them very satisfied. You will be informed day by day of what happens.

The Pope left this morning and is going to Bologna. Lionardo saw Messer Giovanni Genovardi who, at the time, appeared to be coming from Pistoia. He invited him to our house, but he said he wanted to keep the Pope company for part of the way and that he would come to have a word with me afterward. I will find out from him the truth about the cardinal of Albano and if Cardinal du Puy's familiar knows

---

600. See FD 173.

when he is coming. We will offer him and his retinue hospitality here in our house and we will receive him with great honor. You will be informed about what follows.

Regarding provisions for the visit of the Pope, we have simply bought a calf for ten florins, which is still big enough for us to have plenty of food to do him honor should he come tomorrow or the next day. We have poultry and everything else prepared so that everything will go smoothly and in an orderly way. We—Messer Lionardo and the others—arranged with the butchers to get another calf if we need it.

We are getting Puccio to bring you the flasks that we have. If they do not seem suitable, use the ones you have there. I am sending you two pieces of veal.

To avoid delaying Puccio, I will say no more. Everything is being looked after. May Christ protect you.

Grazzino Catino, the man from Leccio, has not come. We are sending some veal for you to taste because it is considered very good here. The animal is one of ours and it is unweaned.

I do not have any good oranges here.

Grazzino has now arrived.

A letter is enclosed from Matteo di Ser Niccolaio, who has accepted.

Monna Margherita, in Prato.

To Francesco di Marco, in Florence.
Received from Prato, 4 January 1410.
Twenty-six and a half pounds of veal.

Letter 244 (1401871)
4 January 1410
Prato

In the name of God. 4 January 1410.

I sent you a letter [earlier] today with Puccio and told you that we have prepared what is necessary to receive Cardinal du Puy honorably, and that his familiar had been here and was to advise us tonight or tomorrow morning when the cardinal will come. He did not come this evening. We are expecting him to contact us tomorrow so we can make sure everything that is necessary is prepared. We will keep you informed.

And we told you that we heard that the cardinal of Albano was dead. Then we went to Messer Giovanni Genovardi and asked him about it. He said that he has almost recovered, so the story can't be true. Guido di Ridolfo was the one who told us, and he was not able to tell us anything about Cardinal du Puy's arrival. We invited Giovanni Genovardi to come here, but he did not want to stay and went off to Florence. Take note of this.

The Pope departed and we were left with the veal that was prepared for him. We supplied ourselves generously and sent you two pieces. We have the poultry and everything else ready.

I got Barzalone and Bernabò and Lionardo to taste the wines that are here, and we have chosen two barrels of red: one from Filettole for the cardinal and the other from the Canals for his retinue, both good wines, as well as some of the white from there for him and our Malvasia wine for the retinue.[601] We also took in supplies of fodder so that we will have everything that is necessary. If we get it at the right price, we will acquire as many bushels for the house as we need. We told Cristofano several times that the price had to be right.

As for the wines from the Canals, the one from the Straits of Messina is going off, according to Barzalone and Bernabò, and is not suitable for making vinegar. So, if you agree, it will be given in charity to the needy before it goes bad. So tell us what you want us to do and it will be done.[602]

Ridolfo di Lanfranco sent an invitation for you to dine on Monday with the bishop. I sent the appropriate excuse.

I was with Ser Amelio to have Biagio Becco's document signed. However, he says it cannot be done if you are not present, because it is written in your name. Otherwise another document would need to be prepared. Because this one is in order, he wants to wait until you are here.

---

601. Francesco sent from Florence eleven flasks of a fine white wine from Lucca. See FD 174.

602. See FD 177.

We cannot look after the debtors and other such matters until these cardinals are out of the house; then we will do what has to be done and keep you informed day by day.

We will look after the stable and the fire and everything else, just as you say.

We will have Lionardo da Calendino make the slippers as soon as possible, and we will make sure they are all delivered at the same time.

When we see Niccolaio from Tavola, we will tell him what you say about the bricks and the tiles.

I told you that there were no good oranges here.

We got all the pieces that we wanted from the veal we prepared for the Pope.

[Added by the scribe:]
I, Guido, took six *soldi* from the money in the writing table this morning to pay the taxes and did not put them in the record. Write it down together with the fifty-two *soldi* recorded.

The bishop of Frejus sent us his luggage today and will be sending other things tomorrow. We will put everything in the warehouse under lock and key to keep it safe.

The rooms are as well supplied with firewood and furniture as when the king was here, if not better.[603]

Lionardo bought two jars from Meo del Carota, each with a capacity of thirty bushels. They have not come yet. The one belonging to Granalosso will be inspected as soon as possible.[604]

When the cardinal comes, we will get some gray partridges and other good things. Some people say he will not come. You will be informed.

---

603. The most important of Francesco's many guests was Louis II of Anjou, the self-styled King of Sicily and Jerusalem, Prince of Capua, and Duke of Puglia. He had availed himself of Francesco's hospitality in 1409 and returned for a stay of eighteen days in July 1410, just weeks before the merchant's death. He granted his host the right to add the royal lily of France to his arms. See Origo, *The Merchant of Prato*, 380–83.

604. Francesco had heard that Granalosso had a large storage jar for sale and wanted Margherita and Barzalone to inspect it. See FD 173 and 177.

There is nothing further to say in this letter, and we did not get a letter from you this evening. We will write to you when we have news. May Christ protect you.

Monna Margherita, in Prato.

To Francesco di Marco, in Florence.
Received from Prato, 5 January 1410. Answered.

Letter 245 (1401872)
5 January 1410
Prato

In the name of God. 5 January 1410.

We wrote you a letter today and sent it with a worker from Porta a Corte called Nanni di Filippo.[605] We told you that we had sent Lionardo to Pistoia to find out about the arrival of the cardinal, because he has not sent any message. Other people came and they said that he will not be here for many days. Now that all is ready he can come at any time. Tomorrow we will have precise details from Lionardo and then we can decide what to do instead of being kept in suspense as we have been until now, and we will keep you informed about everything.

The bishop of Frejus came here thinking you were here and says that, since you are not here, he will go to Pistoia tomorrow. He did not want to prolong his stay. Here we received him well and had a fire lit for him. He went to his room and we kept him company and honored him as best we could, and made the appropriate apologies to him on your account. We asked him whether he wanted us to write anything to you; he said it was not necessary, and that if he needed anything he would tell us tomorrow. You will be told what happens.

We asked him whether he knew when the cardinal is coming. He says it will not be in the next two days because the news from Pistoia is that the Pope has been arrested at Barberino to stop him going to Bologna. Before leaving Pistoia, the cardinal wants to see what the

---

605. Porta a Corte was one of the eight municipal divisions of Prato.

Pope decides to do. We do not believe this story of the arrest is true, because here we have not heard anything about it.

Then Puccio di Bonciano arrived, and he gave us the wine as well as the oranges and apples that you sent. Everything was put in proper storage so that it is safe. We will now reply to your letter.

Nanni Cirioni came. Tomorrow he is going to Florence and will bring you this letter.

There is no need for you to say any more about receiving the cardinal and the other people who happen to come here. Everything will be done properly and with due honor.

It seems that the story of the cardinal of Albano's death is untrue, and as you were told today, you have his coat of arms painted over your doorway. You have that special relationship with Lello.[606] He asked you for hospitality last time, and I do not doubt that he will ask you for it again when he is better. I think this will happen after the visit of this Cardinal du Puy. So write to me and tell me what my answer should be. I think this business might last longer than we thought.

You were told that Giovanni Genovardi has gone to Florence.

Together with this letter there is the record obtained from Ser Baldo regarding the Benozzo affair. If you need anything else, say so.

As regards the letter we sent with the cobbler this morning, he says he gave it to his brother-in-law to give to you because he had forgotten. Tell me whether you received it.

Puccio will come tomorrow when Lionardo has returned, and you will hear about the response from the cardinal. Puccio will bring the horse and the mule, and will bring the windows and all the other things for which you asked. As for the veal that is here, we will make our decisions after we find out when the cardinal is coming, and we will inform you of everything we do.

Regarding the tax for the salary of the *Podestà*, Lorenzo di Stefano, the treasurer, says the due date is the 20th of this month and that he does not know if the amount includes the tax for this month. When it does have to be paid, he will do as he promised.

We spoke to Iacopo the carter about the wood, and also to Monna Maria's Nanni. Neither of them can bring it. We asked the man from Colonica whether he is able to go there. He says Iacopo has no

---

606. This is Lello di Matteo Orsini.

suitable oxen and he himself has some but they are at Colonica. Nevertheless, if we see him, we will find out when he can come there, and you will be told.

As for the carriers who will come with the salt, we will organize to send you a load as you say. It is at Ser Iacopo's house. Lorenzo or someone else will bring it.

Messer Torello will be told what you say about the ten florins, and Roncone about the wood.[607]

The measure of the skylight window is included. The entire sheet gives the length, and the mark near the top of the longer side, where the writing is, marks the inside width taken in the same way as Nencio did it the other time. Take note.

We gave nine new *lire* to Botto da Casale today, and, as you instructed, we gave the money for the tax to the man who supplied the millet. We lent Puccio 161 *soldi* and one *denaro* for his tax.[608] Monna Margherita paid it all.

Barzalone made his payment. May Christ protect you.

Monna Margherita, in Prato.

Nanni Cirioni will tell you personally about Cardinal du Puy, because he met his servants.

To Francesco di Marco, in Florence.
Received from Prato, 6 January 1410.

A message from Messer Torello for Master Lorenzo.
Lionardo then returned at terce and says that the cardinal has decided not to come until he discovers the truth about whether the Pope has been arrested at Barberino, although nothing has been reported about it here. And he also says that before he comes, he will send his party ahead to let us know. He does not know when. For this reason I have not yet decided what to do about the veal. A decision will be made before Puccio comes, and you will be told everything. Nanni also heard what Lionardo said and the reply he received, so if anything should

607. In his letter of 5 January, Francesco Datini had instructed Margherita to tell Torello tactfully that if he did not get ten florins from Lapo di Toringo Pugliesi, the amount would be added to Torello's own account. See FD 174.
608. This is the carter, Puccio di Bonciano.

be unclear in this letter, he will be able to tell you everything when he sees you.

Papero di Vanni brought us an account for payment of his dowry for the sum of 165 *lire*, and asks you to get it paid to him and to give him the receipt.

Letter 246 (1401873)
5 January 1410
Prato

In the name of God, 5 January 1410.

I wrote a letter and sent it to you this morning with the cobbler, the husband of the woman who sings. But I have not received a letter from you, and Puccio has not arrived. It is the twentieth hour so I will not say much.

This is just to advise you of what we have done. We were waiting this morning either for the cardinal to come or for him to send us a message about when he would come, as that familiar of his promised. However, he did not send any message at all. For this reason I decided to send Lionardo just a short time ago so that he could go and find out about the cardinal's arrival. We have bought a calf, and if he delays coming then we can decide what to do with it. The fowl are still alive and we will not kill any birds until we know he is coming. Lionardo will come back tomorrow morning and we will find out for certain and you will be told.

Then those familiars of the bishop came, and we asked them about the cardinal and if they know about his arrival. They say they do not and that they think he will stay put for many more days. So unless we tell you otherwise, there will be no need for you to supply anything for his arrival. When Lionardo returns, he will tell us how matters stand.

We have been told that the cardinal of Albano is certainly not dead. Considering that you have his arms painted on the doorway and that Lello asked you for the house, and considering what you mean to him, I imagine that when the cardinal is better, Lello or someone else will probably ask you for the house for him when he passes by here. So please tell us what you think we should answer if we are asked. There is no need for you to be in a hurry, as I do not think he will be here for many days yet.

The servant of the bishop who left his case here came and asked me to lend a mule to the bishop, who is intending to come here. He tells us that the bishop's animals are sick. I made the appropriate excuse. We asked him how long the bishop would stay. He says it will be ten days or more because his horses are sick.

A man arrived who said he was a servant of Messer Guido di Pestiglia, and he wanted to speak to you about a certain trial that has begun at Montpellier. He says he will come to you in Florence because he needs to speak to you. I think he is a charlatan who wants you to lend him some money. Just the same, because he wished to speak to you, I decided to tell him your whereabouts. If this trial is something you need to know about, he should not fail to know where you are.

At Pistoia they say there are still eight cardinals. People are coming here continually. They are asking about you every day, and I think for their own need rather than for yours. For this reason I am glad that you are in Florence rather than here. I feel that you should stay there for your own good until this fuss is over, as it would not fail to harm you.

Messer Torello has been here; they ordered that if this cardinal comes he should be with Messer Piero, and that he will make the speech as necessary in your honor.

I don't think I have any more to say to you. I think you must have kept Puccio until evening. May Christ protect you,

Monna Margherita, in Prato.

To Francesco di Marco, in Florence.
Received from Prato, 6 January 1410.

Letter 247 (1401874)
6 January 1410
Prato

In the name of God. 6 January 1410.

I wrote as long a letter to you as was required this morning and sent it with Nanni Cirioni. Then today we were given your two letters by a person from Porta a Corte. My reply to the matters in them now follows.

You were told that Lionardo had returned and that he had not been able to find out about the arrival of the cardinal. The cardinal was supposed to let us know when he was about to arrive; so he is keeping us in suspense and has still not sent us word. We have no idea when he is coming, which is bad news as far as this calf is concerned; given the expense, we wouldn't like to have to give it away to anyone else. So as not to keep it any longer, we had already given orders for it to be divided up in the manner we thought would bring us most honor. Margherita was going to give some to the wife of the *Podestà*, some to Messer Torello's wife, some to Messer Piero and some to the provost, and some to Ser Amelio and to the friars. And when we had given this order, one of the servants of the bishop of Frejus came, and we asked him about this cardinal and he said, "I think he will be here tomorrow." On account of this we stopped and had the veal examined to see how long it would keep. The butcher inspected it, and he thought that it would last until Thursday and would be even better than today. Therefore, if the cardinal comes tomorrow, we will keep it for its original purpose, and if he does not come and we do not receive any message, then we will divide it and will tell you everything we do. This waiting from one hour to the next is more tiring and troublesome for us than anything else. I do not think that you need to send any food from there, unless we tell you.

Messer Giovanni Genovardi did not return this evening. If he comes, we will do what you say.

There is no more to say about wine and fodder. It is ready and in order just like everything else required. If only the man would come. It seems like we have been waiting a thousand years.

We are giving the wine from the Canals away to the needy, which is better than letting it go bad.

While we were writing shortly after sunset, Messer Giovanni Genovardi arrived at Cambio's inn with your two-line letter.[609] We went to him immediately with two torches to escort him from the inn so he could come with all his company, horses and all, to eat and sleep here. We did and said all we could, but he graciously begged us to leave him be, by God, as he did not want to leave the inn this evening and there was no need for all the fuss on his account. So we could only do as he wished. We returned home and sent him some white wine from Lucca, some cheeses, and some of those apples. He was very pleased and said that we had been so kind that he would be most obliged to us always and would make a favorable report of it to the king. Tomorrow he is leaving. We will try our best to give him a meal first.

The same Messer Giovanni says that tomorrow he will be with Cardinal du Puy. He will let us know when the cardinal is coming, for which we will be grateful, and you will be told.

We did not send Puccio today because we were waiting so we could tell you if we had any news from this cardinal. The weather was wet too, and I did not think it was necessary. Now, because we do not know whether you need him, we have decided to send him tomorrow with the two pack animals, as you instructed, as well as the cloth windows you asked for and two pairs of hens. Tell us if you need more, or anything else.

And, as we said to you, if there is no more news of this cardinal, do not send any food here, because it could be that he will put off coming or not come at all. Biagio di Becco's document will be delayed. As far as the other matters are concerned, we will do what we can.

I got back the five *soldi* that Grazzino had received, and they have been spent.

The bishop sent a case of clothes, and all day long they take them out and put them in as they please. We are letting them do what they like.

We saw Granalosso's jar. I think it can be repaired, and then it will be worth more. His son is asking for twelve *denari* per bushel. It is worth six.

609. FD 176.

I enclose the list of items from Avignon.

Messer Torello has asked for the horse and says that he may go to Florence tomorrow morning, the 7th.

I decided later to keep Puccio here today and send him this evening, or tomorrow morning, with the two pack animals and he will tell you if we have any more news about the cardinal. Here we will do what has to be done. May Christ protect you.

I would have given the windows to Argomento, but he cannot carry them.

Monna Margherita, in Prato.

To Francesco di Marco, in Florence.
Received from Prato, 7 January 1410.

Letter 248 (1401875)
7 January 1410
Prato

In the name of God. 7 January 1410.

Today we got Puccio di Bonciano to deliver you a letter, and sent veal, pork, poultry, windows, and skins, and you must have received it all. Then we got a letter from you that requires a brief answer. Here is our reply.

About the matter of these cardinals, we do not know what to say any more. People are continually coming and going. A short time ago a cardinal came who is returning to see the bishop's representative. We asked this man what they are saying about Cardinal du Puy. He thinks he is coming tomorrow, or in the next few days. We have also been told that he is the sort of man who says "I am leaving now" and then, unless everything is ready, he stays two or three days, and you cannot rely upon him in any way. Now we have decided what to do about the veal. It seems that it is in good condition and we will not do anything unless we know for certain about the cardinal's arrival. You will be told what happens.

There is nothing more to say about Messer Giovanni Genovardi. He has left and may God keep him safe.

You have Benozzo's document, so that is in order, and Papero's account.[610] Tell us if you will have the customs tax paid for him. Lorenzo di Stefano will be reminded about the money.

You cannot count on getting the wood from Curradingo brought to Prato, as they are unable to load it. It will be done as soon as possible.

The man from Colonica never brought any money and we have not seen him. If we do see him, we will pass on the message.

Checco brought the wood from Filettole. Roncone will be told what you say.

When money is paid, we make an appropriate record.

Messer Torello went to Florence, so we cannot give him the doctor's message that you mention. You will find out about it from him in Florence and tell us whether Lapo should be asked for the ten florins, as he has not paid them.

Mannuccio is getting better, they say.[611] I see we made the right decision about the veal.

I was very pleased to hear that Monna Francesca is there with Pippa; I was worried because she had said she was coming here but didn't come.[612] Please remember my aunt, Monna Giovanna, sometimes as well.

We sent Puccio with two pack animals as you said, thinking you needed him and also so the meat would not be wasted.

Your letter needs no further reply and there is no news to add. May Christ protect you.

It seems clear to us that barley will not go below twelve *soldi* a bushel, and good-quality barley thirteen *soldi*.

Two letters are enclosed from Messer Piero in Pisa.

---

610. See letter 245.

611. This is Mannuccio di Lodovico Mannucci.

612. Pippa may be Pippa dei Peruzzi, of the prominent Florentine family, who seems to have been related to the Gherardini family. Piera di Filippo di Tommaso Lisca Peruzzi had married Amideo del Pelliccia Gherardini, Margherita's uncle. According to Jérôme Hayez, it is possible that the Francesca mentioned here was the maternal half-sister of Amideo and Accerito del Pelliccia Gherardini.

Monna Margherita, in Prato.

To Francesco di Marco, Florence.
Received from Prato, 8 January 1410.

Letter 249 (1401876)
7 January 1410
Prato

In the name of God. 7 January 1410.

I wrote you a letter this morning to tell you our news and had it delivered by Monna Pina's Lodovico di Niccolò. He is in Florence, at Piazza San Michele. If you have not received the letter, send for it. As we have not had a letter from you, I will be brief.

We lent Messer Torello the horse and he is going to Florence at this moment.

I still have no news from Pistoia regarding the cardinal, and because he seems to be coming later than we imagined and the veal is still fine, we have decided to divide it up and send the best pieces to you in Florence. You will be able to make better use of it there than we can here. The *Podestà* and the provost can go without, as we heard they would not really welcome it, the reason being that they thought the meat had been kept too long.[613] However, we had been advised that it could not have been better. Because Messer Torello is not here either, we divided it up as you see. Those who do get it will be grateful, and it is probably a more useful gift there than here.

I am also sending you some wild-boar meat, a present from Toringo Pugliesi, as well as three gray partridges, a present from Domenico di Giovanni Tarpuccia, the cobbler.

Of the veal that remained, we gave one piece to the friars, one to Ser Amelio, one to Messer Piero, one to Ser Baldo, and also gave some to other deserving people, and they appreciated it very much, and we kept some for ourselves. We think we have taken the best course of

---

613. The provost of Santo Stefano was the leading ecclesiastical dignitary in Prato, which had not yet become a bishopric.

action and you will be pleased, mostly for the reasons I have said, but also because it was done judiciously.

You will receive everything this evening from Puccio, who at present is loading the said goods. He is coming with a light load so he can get there more quickly, and thus allow you to decide what to do this evening.

I will say no more, so as not to delay Messer Torello's servants any further. May Christ protect you. Tell me if you want to make a start on pruning the garden or anything else.

Monna Margherita, in Prato.

To Francesco di Marco, in Florence.
Received from Prato, 7 January 1410.
One blanket.
The horse.

Letter 250 (1401877)
8 January 1410
Prato

In the name of God. 8 January 1410.

We received your letter tonight from Ser Ammannato, and Puccio has arrived. Excuse us, but we will be brief because we are busy.

Two of Cardinal du Puy's servants arrived this evening and they told us he will be here early tomorrow, so we are making the necessary preparations. They say that there will be perhaps forty people, and we will provide for them so they do not have any living expenses. We have already killed the chickens they wanted and offered all our poultry for them to take as they see fit, and we have ordered the meat they want from the butcher. They will be given everything and we will pay for bread, wine, sweets, and other things. We have everything ready to treat him with great honor. We do not know how long he will stay. You will be told everything, and we will make the appropriate apologies for you. These servants who came here were amazed at such hospitality.

Now, no matter how many come—they, their animals, and all the others—be confident that everything will run smoothly.

Until this visit is over, remember that we cannot see to our own affairs. We can do nothing apart from being available here to look after their needs. We will do for the present what we must, and afterward we will attend to other matters. When they have gone we will write a more leisurely reply to your letter. May Christ protect you.

Monna Margherita, in Prato.

We received sixteen sealed florins from Ser Tingo: that is, three from him and thirteen paid by him on behalf of Lionardo d'Agostino; and twenty-seven gold florins, twelve *soldi*, six *denari* from Paolo Saccagnini; and from Ridolfo, as I said, four gold florins, one *soldo*, three *denari*. I would have sent all the money to you tomorrow but I do not have time to look for someone to bring it; and if it is needed here, I will spend it.

His people say the cardinal will stay all tomorrow and Friday morning. I think that he will come to see Florence without fail and then go to Bologna. You will be told what is happening.

To Francesco di Marco, in Florence.
Received from Prato, 9 January 1410.

Letter 251 (1401878)
9 January 1410
Prato

In the name of God. 9 January 1410.[614]

I wrote to you this morning and sent the letter to the town gate early, because Pippo di Monna Guiduccio says he is bringing you the letter. I told you that the cardinal should be here this morning. He did come this morning and we have been, and are, honoring him and his retinue as much as is possible. Messer Bonaccorso, Ser Baldo, Barzal-

---

614. This is Margherita's last surviving letter to Francesco, who became ill at the end of July 1410 and died on 16 August.

one, and Stefano di Ser Piero and their assistants were present at his arrival. Messer Bonaccorso and Ser Baldo gave the welcoming speeches and made appropriate apologies on your behalf. Messer Piero could not be present but it was of little importance as all went well, and is going well. The cardinal was here at mealtime, and he had all his food prepared in the proper manner by his cooks. We supplied them with poultry, meat, bread, wine, and Malvasia wine, and fodder and straw, so they did not have to spend anything. They consider they have been treated extraordinarily well and are paying us many compliments. They really all seem well-mannered people, and I think every courtesy done to them has been well worth it. There are fifty people between horsemen and those on foot, and all have been well provided for. Tomorrow, he says, they will go along the road from here to Barberino before proceeding to Bologna. I think they will leave early, as they have already sent a cook on ahead. You will be told everything that happens. When they have been seen off, we will attend to the other things that you mention in your letter.

This morning I told you about the money we collected and that it would be sent as soon as possible. I will do this.

We also received a short letter from you this morning from Friar Ventura's servant Tommaso, and a brief reply is needed.

We will set up the vat of white wine tomorrow as you say. It holds fifty-one barrels, according to what is written on it, and we will get Buono and Michele Benozzi to fill it.

I will say no more to Piero di Guiduccio. Piero di Geri will be coming to Florence.[615] The carter from Campi did not come. When he does we will load the wood for him.

The bishop did not ask for ginger or anything else. Tell me if you want us to offer it to him or to say nothing. He has had lunch and dinner with this cardinal and is with him all the time.

Lionardo is looking for jars all the time, and if he finds good ones, he will buy them. Lionardo has made supports for the jars.

It seems that Mannuccio has been getting sicker, and has called Master Ugolino.[616]

---

615. Piero di Geri di Ghetto Buonristori, one of the richest men in Prato, had been Gonfalonier of Justice in June and July 1407. See Vestri, *Istituzioni e vita sociale a Prato*, 12–13.

616. See letter 248.

The cardinal saw the Madonna's girdle today.[617] The cheese is a brushed one.

We received thirty-five bushels of barley to sell on behalf of the commune. We did not receive the rest from the others.

Tomorrow we will resolve the Biagio di Becco affair in the way you say.

We will say no more in this letter. May Christ protect you.

Monna Margherita, in Prato.

This morning Messer Bonaccorso and Messer Torello dined with the cardinal at his table.

To Francesco di Marco, in Florence.
Received from Prato, 10 January 1410.

---

617. The holy *cintola*, or girdle, of the Virgin Mary, preserved to this day in its own chapel in the church of Santo Stefano, was accorded great religious devotion and was carefully guarded as a symbol of Pratese civic pride.

Appendix 1

Conventions for Names and Titles

Monna, a shortened form of *Madonna*, was a title given to married women. Its etymological origin is *mia donna* ("my lady"). The modern equivalent in Italian is *Signora*.

Ser was a title given to notaries or priests. **Messer** indicated a lawyer or knight.

Di ("of "), when used of males, is a patronymic. For example, the name Cristofano di Mercato di Giunta tells us that Cristofano is the son of Mercato, who in turn is the son of Giunta. When *di* is used in association with a married woman's name, it indicates and precedes the name of the husband. "Monna Tina di Betto Ridolfi" means "Tina, the wife of Betto Ridolfi." But Lorita di Aldobrandino Bovattieri, widow of Monte d'Andrea di Ser Gino Angiolini, is named for her father; and so are some other women.

Da ("from") is used when referring to the family's town of origin. So "Francesco di Marco Datini da Prato" reveals that Francesco's father was Marco and his town of origin was Prato.

Nicknames are occasionally added to baptismal names. They should not be mistaken for family names. For example, Domenico di Giovanni di Puccino's nickname was "Tarpuccia." He is referred to on some occasions as "Domenico Tarpuccia," and on others simply as "Tarpuccia." A women might be referred to by a female variant of her husband's name. Giovanni di Luca Bencivenni bears the nickname Fattorino, so his wife is sometimes called Fattorina; Bellozzo Bartoli's wife is sometimes Bellozza.

Appendix 2

Measurements, Money, and Time

A cask (translating *barile* in the letters) normally contained 45.5 liters. A *metadella* of wine was equivalent to 1.14 liters. A *fiasco* ("flask") of wine contained 2.3 liters, and a *fiasco* of oil contained 2.1 liters. For both oil and wine, a *fiasco* contained about two *metadelle*.

One *moggio* was equivalent to about eight bushels, or about 290 liters. (The plural *moggia* is used in this text, as opposed to *mogge* or the common modern plural, moggi.)

The *denaro* was the smallest common unit of currency. Twelve *denari* equaled one *soldo*, and twenty *soldi* equaled one *lira*. *Soldi* and *lire* did not exist as coins, but were monies of account. The value of the gold florin (*fiorino*) was about four *lire*; but it fluctuated, and was usually expressed in terms of *soldi di piccioli*. In 1400, it cost ten *soldi di piccioli* to pay an unskilled construction worker for a day.

The seven canonical hours were marked by the ringing of church bells. These were used alongside the "solar hours," extended to be counted from sunset, which were struck by the municipal clocks that were beginning to appear in urban centers. Margherita refers to both systems. There was great flexibility by regional custom, and seasonal variability as the day's length changed through the year. The canonical hours, in an approximate and standardized way, fitted like this:

Canonical	Hour from sunset	Modern time of day
matins	(various pre-dawn hours; not used in the letters)	
prime	12th hour	6 a.m.
terce	15th hour	9 a.m.
sext	18th hour	12 noon
none(s)	21st hour	3 p.m.
vespers	24th hour	6 p.m. ("sunset")
compline	3rd hour	9 p.m. ("nightfall" or "bed time")

Prime, terce, sext, and nones could also include the subsequent three-hour period; when Margherita refers to "mid-terce" (see letter 162), she means about 10.30 a.m. The Angelus (see letters 99 and 180) was rung at 7 p.m.

Bibliography

Primary Works

Boccaccio, Giovanni. *Decameron*. Edited by Antonio Quaglio. Milan: Garzanti, 1974.

Davis, Norman, ed. *Paston Letters and Papers of the Fifteenth Century*. 2 vols. Oxford: Oxford University Press, 1971–1976.

Datini, Francesco. *Le lettere di Francesco Datini alla moglie Margherita (1385–1410)*. Edited by Elena Cecchi. Prato: Società Pratese di Storia Patria, 1990.

Datini, Margherita. *Le lettere di Margherita Datini a Francesco di Marco (1384–1410)*. Edited by Valeria Rosati. Prato: Cassa di Risparmio e Depositi, 1977.

_____. *Per la tua Margherita—: lettere di una donna del '300 al marito mercante*. Edited by Diana Toccafondi and Giovanni Tartaglione. Prato: Archivio di Stato, 2002.

Mazzei, Ser Lapo. *Lettere di un notaro a un mercante del secolo XV, con altre lettere e documenti*. Edited by Cesare Guasti. Florence: Le Monnier, 1880.

Pitti, Buonaccorso. *Cronica*. Edited by Alberto Bacchi della Lega. Bologna: Romagnolo dall'Acqua, 1905.

Strozzi, Alessandra Macinghi. *Lettere di una gentildonna fiorentina dal secolo XV ai figliuoli esuli*. Edited by Cesare Guasti. Florence: Sansoni, 1877.

_____. *Selected Letters of Alessandra Strozzi*. Translated by Heather Gregory. Bilingual edition. Berkeley: University of California Press, 1997.

Secondary Works

Altman, Janet. *Epistolarity: Approaches to a Form*. Columbus: Ohio State University Press, 1982.

Battaglia, Salvatore. *Grande dizionario della lingua italiana*. Turin: Unione Tipografico-Editrice Torinese, 1961–2008.

Bensa, Enrico. "Margherita Datini." *Archivio Storico Pratese* 6 (1926): 1–14.

Boffee, Julia. "Women Authors and Women's Literacy in Fourteenth- and Fifteenth-Century England." In *Women and Literature in Britain, 1150–1500*. Edited by Carol M. Meale. Cambridge: Cambridge University Press, 1993. 159–82.

Brambilla, Simona. *Itinerari nella Firenze di fine Trecento: fra Giovanni dalle Celle e Luigi Marsili*. Milan: Edizione Cusi, 2002.

_____ and Jérôme Hayez. "La maison des fantômes: Un récit onirique de ser Bartolomeo Levaldini, notaire de Prato et correspondant de Francesco Datini." *Italia medioevale e umanistica* 47 (2006): 75–192.

Broomhall, Susan. "'Burdened with small children': Women Defining Poverty in Sixteenth-Century Tours." In *Women's Letters across Europe, 1400–1700: Form and Persuasion*. Edited by Jane Couchman and Ann Crabb. Aldershot: Ashgate, 2005. 223–37.

Brucker, Gene. *The Civic World of Early Renaissance Florence*. Princeton, NJ: Princeton University Press, 1977.

_____. *Florentine Politics and Society 1343–1378*. Princeton, NJ: Princeton University Press, 1962.

Brun, Robert. "Annales avignonnaises de 1382 à 1410: extraites des Archives de Datini." *Mémoires de l'Institut Historique de Provence* 12 (1935): 17–142; 13 (1936): 58–105; 14 (1937): 5–57; 15 (1938): 21–52, 154–92.

Byrne, Joseph. "Crafting the Merchant Wife's Tale: Historians and the Domestic Rhetoric in the Correspondence of Margherita Datini (1360–1425)." *Georgia Association of Historians* 16 (1996): 1–17.

_____. "Reading the Medieval Woman's Voice: Reflections on the Letters of Margherita Datini, an Italian Housewife on the Eve of the Renaissance." *West Georgia Review* 25 (1995): 5–13.

_____ and Eleanor Congdon. "Mothering in the Casa Datini." *Journal of Medieval History* 25, no. 1 (1999): 35–56.

Catitani, Aurora Fiorentini and Stefania Ricci, eds. *Il costume al tempo di Lorenzo il magnifico. Prato e il suo territorio*. Milan: Charta, 1996.

Cavaciocchi, Simonetta. "The Merchant and Building." In *Francesco di Marco Datini: The Man, The Merchant.* Edited by Giampiero Nigro. Florence: Firenze University Press, 2010. 131–63.

_____, ed. *La donna nell'economia secc. XIII–XVIII.* Istituto Internazionale di Storia Economica "F. Datini." Prato: Le Monnier, 1990.

Cherewatuk, Karen and Ulrike Wiethaus, eds. *Dear Sister: Medieval Women and the Epistolary Genre.* Philadelphia: University of Pennsylvania Press, 1993.

Cherubini, Giovanni, ed. *Prato storia di una città.* Vol 1. Prato: Le Monnier, 1991.

Ciappelli, Giovanni. "Il cittadino fiorentino e il fisco alla fine del Trecento e nel corso del Quattrocento: uno studio di due casi." *Società e storia* 11, no. 46 (1989): 823–72.

Clark, Paula. *The Soderini and the Medici.* Oxford: Clarendon Press, 1991.

Constable, Giles. *Letters and Letter Collections.* Turnhout: Brepols, 1976.

Couchman, Jane and Ann Crabb, eds. *Women's Letters Across Europe, 1400–1700: Form and Persuasion.* Aldershot: Ashgate, 2005.

Crabb, Ann. "Gaining Honor as a Husband's Deputy: Margherita Datini at Work, 1381–1410." *Early Modern Women: An Interdisciplinary Journal* 3 (2008): 225–32.

_____. "'If I could write': Margherita Datini and Letter Writing, 1385–1410." *Renaissance Quarterly* 60 (2007): 1170–1206.

_____. "Ne pas être mère: l'autodéfense d'une Florentine vers 1400." *Clio: Histoire, Femmes et Sociétés: Maternités* 21 (2005): 150–61.

Daybell, James. "Women's Letters and Letter Writing in England, 1540–1603: An Introduction to the Issues of Authorship and Construction." *Shakespeare Studies* 27 (January 1999): 161–86.

_____, ed. *Early Modern Women's Letter Writing, 1450–1700.* Basingstoke: Palgrave, 2001.

Debby, Nerit Ben-Aryeh. *Renaissance Florence in the Rhetoric of Two Popular Preachers: Giovanni Dominici (1356–1419) and Bernardino da Siena (1380–1444).* Turnhout: Brepols, 2001.

De Blasi, Nicola. "La lettera mercantile tra formulario appreso e lingua d'uso." *Quaderni di retorica e poetica* 1 (1985): 39–47.

Doglio, Maria. *Lettera e donna: Scrittura epistolare al femminile tra Quattrocento e Cinquecento.* Rome: Bulzoni, 1993.

Doglio, Maria. "Letter Writing, 1350–1650." In *A History of Women's Writing in Italy.* Edited by Letizia Panizza and Sharon Wood. Cambridge: Cambridge University Press, 2000. 13–24.

Ferguson, Margaret. "Renaissance concepts of the 'woman writer'" In *Women and Literature in Britain 500–1700.* Edited by Helen Wilcox. Cambridge: Cambridge University Press, 1996. 143–68.

Fiumi, Enrico. *Demografia, movimento urbanistico e classi sociali in Prato: dall' età comunale ai tempi moderni.* Florence: Olschki, 1968.

_____. "Sulle condizioni alimentari di Prato nell'età comunale." *Archivio Storico Pratese* 42 (1966): 3–26.

Frangioni, Luciana. "Avignon: The Beginnings." In *Francesco di Marco Datini: The Man, the Merchant.* Edited by Giampiero Nigro. Florence: Firenze University Press, 2010. 249–280.

_____. *Chiedere e ottenere: L'approvvigionamento di prodotti di successo della bottega Datini di Avignone nel XIV secolo.* Florence: Opuslibri, 2002.

_____. *Milano fine trecento: Il carteggio milanese dell'Archivio Datini di Prato.* 2 vols. Florence: Opuslibri, 1994.

Frick, Carole Collier. *Dressing Renaissance Florence: Families, Fortunes and Fine Clothing.* Baltimore, MD, and London: Johns Hopkins University Press, 2002.

Giagnavoco, Maria. *Mercanti a tavola: Prezzi e consumi alimentari dell'azienda Datini di Pisa (1383–90).* Florence: Opuslibri, 2002.

Goldsmith, Elizabeth, ed. *Writing the Female Voice: Essays on Epistolary Literature.* Boston, MA: Northeastern University Press, 1989.

Goldthwaite, Richard. *The Economy of Renaissance Florence.* Baltimore, MD: The Johns Hopkins University Press, 2009.

Greci, Roberto. "Francesco di Marco Datini a Bologna (1400–1401)." *Atti dell' Accademia delle Scienze dell'Istituto di Bologna* 67, no. 61 (1973): 133–219.

Guarducci, Piero and Valeria Ottanelli. *I servitori domestici della casa borghese toscana nel basso medioevo.* Florence: Libreria Editrice Salimbeni, 1982.

Guillén, Claudio. "Notes toward the Study of the Renaissance Letter." In *Renaissance Genres: Essays in Theory, History and Interpretation.* Edited by Barbara Kiefer Lewalski. Cambridge, MA: Harvard University Press, 1986. 70–101.

Guzzetti, Linda. "Donne e scrittura nel tardo trecento." *Archivio veneto* 152 (1999): 5–31.

Hayez, Jérôme. "Francesco di Marco Datini et ser Bartolomeo di messer Nicola Levandini." *Italia medioevale e umanistica* 47 (2006): 75–128.

———. "'Tucte sono patrie, ma la buona è quela dove l'uomo fa bene'. Famille et migration dans la correspondance de deux marchands toscans vers 1400." In *Eloignement géographique et cohésion familiale (XVe–XXe siècle).* Edited by Jean-François Chauvard and Christine Lebeau. Strasbourg: Presses Universitaires de Strasbourg, 2006. 69–95.

———. "Le rire du marchand: Francesco di Marco Datini, sa femme Margherita et les *gran maestri* florentins." In *La famille, les femmes et le quotidien (XIVe–XVIIIe siècle): Textes offerts à Christiane Klapisch-Zuber.* Edited by Isabelle Chabot, Jérôme Hayez and Didier Lett. Paris: Publications de la Sorbonne, 2006. 407–58.

———. "L'Archivio Datini: de l'invention de 1870 à l'exploration d'un système d'écrits privés." *Mélanges de l'école française de Rome* 117 (2005): 121–91.

———. "Un facteur siennois de Francesco di Marco Datini: Andrea di Bartolomeo di Ghino et sa correspondance (1383–1389)." *Bollettino dell'Opera del vocabolario italiano* 10 (2005): 203–397.

———. "La voix des morts ou la mine de données: Deux siècles et demi d'édition des correspondances privées des XIIIe–XVIe siècles." *Mélanges de l'École française de Rome* 117, no. 1 (2005): 257–304.

———. "'Veramente io spero farci bene … ': Expérience de migrant et pratique de l'amitié dans la correspondance de maestro Naddino d'Aldobrandino Bovattieri médecin toscan d'Avignon (1385-1407)." *Bibliothèque de l'École des chartes* 159 (2001): 413–539.

_____. "'Io non so scrivere a l'amicho per siloscismi': Jalons pour une lecture de la lettre marchande toscane de la fin du Moyen Âge." *I Tatti Studies: Essays in the Renaissance* 7 (1997): 37–79.

_____. "La gestion d'une relation épistolaire dans les milieux d'affaires toscans à la fin du Moyen Age." *La circulation des nouvelles au Moyen Age.* No editor. Paris and Rome: Publications de la Sorbonne, École Française de Rome, 1994. 63–84.

_____. "Migration et stratégies familiales: Autour de la condamnation de Lorenzo di messer Tommaso Soderini, bâtard et faussaire malchanceux (1405)." *Médiévales* 19 (1990): 43–57.

_____. "Préliminaires à une prosopographie avignonnaise du XIVe siècle." *Mélanges de l'École française de Rome: Moyen Âge, temps modernes,* 100 (1988): 113–24.

_____ and Diana Toccafondi. *Il palazzo di Francesco Datini a Prato: Una casa fatta per durare mille anni.* Florence: Edizioni Polistampa, 2011.

Herald, Jacqueline. *Renaissance Dress in Italy 1400–1500.* London: Bell and Hyman, 1981.

Hoshino, Hidetoshi. *L'Arte della Lana in Firenze nel basso medioevo.* Florence: Olschki, 1980.

Ilardi, Vincent. *Renaissance Vision from Spectacles to Telescopes.* Philadelphia, PA: American Philosophical Society, 2007.

James, Carolyn. "Woman's Work in a Man's World: The Letters of Margherita Datini (1384–1410)." In *Francesco di Marco Datini: The Man, the Merchant.* Edited by Giampiero Nigro. Florence: Firenze University Press, 2010. 53–72.

_____. "A Woman's Path to Literacy: The Letters of Margherita Datini, 1384–1410." In *Practices of Gender in Late Medieval and Early Modern Europe.* Edited by Megan Cassidy-Welch and Peter Sherlock. Turnhout: Brepols, 2008. 43–56.

Johnson, Lynn Staley. "The Trope of the Scribe and the Question of Literary Authority in the Works of Julian of Norwich and Margery Kempe." *Speculum* 66, no. 4 (1991): 820–38.

Kent, Francis W. "Prato and Lorenzo de' Medici." In *Communes and Despots: Essays in Memory of Philip Jones.* Edited by John Law and Bernadette Paton. Aldershot, UK: Ashgate, 2010. 193–208.

Kent, Dale V. and Francis W. Kent. *Neighbours and Neighbourhood in Renaissance Florence: The District of the Red Lion in the Fifteenth Century.* Locust Valley, NY: Augustin, 1982.

Klapisch-Zuber, Christiane. *Women, Family and Ritual in Renaissance Italy.* Trans. Lydia Cochrane. Chicago and London: University of Chicago Press, 1985.

Luzzati, Michele. "Datini, Francesco." *Dizionario biografico degli Italiani.* Vol. 33. Rome: Istituto della Enciclopedia Italiana, 1987. 55–62.

Martines, Lauro. *The Social World of the Florentine Humanists 1390–1460.* London: Routledge & Kegan Paul, 1963.

McLean, Alick. *Prato: Architecture, Piety and Political Identity in a Tuscan City-State.* New Haven, CT, and London: Yale University Press, 2008.

Melis, Federigo. *I vini italiani nel medioevo.* Edited by Anna Affortunati Parrini. Florence: Istituto Internazionale di Storia Economica "F. Datini" di Prato, 1984.

_____, ed. *Documenti per la storia economica dei secoli XIII–XVI: con una nota di paleografia commerciale a cura di Elena Cecchi.* Florence: Olschki 1972.

_____. *Aspetti della vita economica medievale.* Vol. 1. Siena: Monte dei Paschi di Siena, 1962.

Merisalo, Outi. "L'omissione del relativizzatore *che* nel toscano del fine Trecento alla luce delle lettere di Francesco Datini." *Neuphilologische Mitteilungen* 101 (2000): 279–85.

Miglio, Luisa. *Governare l'alfabeto: Donne, scrittura e libri nel Medioevo.* Rome: Viella, 2008.

_____. "Scrivere al femminile." In *Escribir y leer en Occidente.* Edited by Armando Petrucci and Francisco Gimeno Blay. Valencia: University of Valencia, 1995. 63–87.

_____. "Leggere e scrivere il volgare: sull'alfabetismo delle donne nella Toscana tardo medievale." *Civiltà comunale* 103 (1989): 357–83.

Nanni, Paolo. *Ragionare tra mercanti: Per una rilettura della personalità di Francesco di Marco Datini (1335ca–1410).* Pisa: Pacini, 2010.

Nigro, Giampiero. *Il tempo liberato: Festa e svago nella città di Francesco Datini.* Prato: Istituto Internazionale di Storia Economica, 1994.

_____, ed. *Francesco di Marco Datini: L'uomo, il mercante.* Florence: Firenze University Press, 2010. Also in English: *Francesco di Marco Datini: The Man, the Merchant.* Florence: Firenze University Press, 2010.

Origo, Iris. *The Merchant of Prato: Francesco di Marco Datini 1335–1410.* New York: Knopf, 1957.

Panizza, Letizia, ed. *Women in Renaissance Culture and Society.* Oxford: Legenda, 2000.

_____ and Sharon Wood, eds. *A History of Women's Writing in Italy.* Cambridge: Cambridge University Press, 2000.

Passerini, Guia. "Dora Guidalotti del Bene: Le lettere (1381–92)." *Letteratura italiana antica* 4 (2003): 101–59.

Pezzarossa, Fulvio. "'Non mi peserà la penna'. A proposito di alcuni contributi su scrittura e mondo femminile nel Quattrocento fiorentino." *Lettere italiane* 41 (1989): 250–60.

Piattoli, Renato. "Gli Agli a Prato, e cinque lettere di Agnolo di Lotto." *Archivio Storico Pratese* 7 (1927): 29–37.

Petrucci, Armando. *Writers and Readers in Medieval Italy: Studies in the History of Written Culture.* New Haven, CT, and London: Yale University Press, 1995.

Radanova-Kuseva, Neli. "Sui valori del condizionale nell'antico italiano (il Trecento)." *Rassegna italiana di linguistica applicata* 19 (1987): 55–65.

_____ and Maria Kitova-Vasileva. "L'espressione della posteriorità nell'italiano e nello spagnolo del Trecento." *Studia slavica hungarica* 35 (1989): 133–47.

Renzi, Lorenzo, and Antonietta Bisetto, eds. "Linguistica e italiano antico." Special issue, *Lingua e stile* 35, no. 4 (2000).

Scott, Karen. "'Io Caterina': Ecclesiastical Politics and Oral Culture in the Letters of Catherine of Siena." In *Dear Sister: Medieval Women and the Epistolary Genre.* Philadelphia: University of Pennsylvania Press, 1993. 87–121.

Serianni, Luca. *Testi pratesi della fine del Dugento e dei primi del Trecento.* Florence: Accademia della Crusca, 1977.

Stott, Deborah. "'I am the same Cornelia I have always been': Reading Cornelia Collonello's Letters to Michelangelo." In *Women's Letters Across Europe, 1400–1700: Form and Persuasion.* Edited by Jane Couchman and Ann Crabb. Aldershot: Ashgate, 2005. 79–100.

Tesoro della lingua italiana delle origini. Available at: http://tlio.ovi.cnr.it/TLIO .

Tomas, Natalie. *"A Positive Novelty": Women and Public Life in Renaissance Florence.* Clayton: Monash Publications in History, 1992.

_____. "Woman as Helpmeet: The Husband-Wife Relationship in Renaissance Florence." *Lilith: A Feminist History Journal* 3 (1986): 61–75.

Tylus, Jane. *Reclaiming Catherine of Siena: Literacy, Literature and the Signs of Others.* Chicago: Chicago University Press, 2009.

Valori, Alessandro. "L'onore femminile attraverso l'epistolario di Margherita e Francesco Datini da Prato." *Giornale storico della letteratura italiana* 175, no. 569 (1998): 53–83.

Vestri, Veronica. "Istituzioni e vita sociale a Prato nel primo Quattrocento." *Prato, Storia e Arte* 84, supplement (1993).

Villain-Gandossi, Christiane. *Comptes du sel (Libro di ragione e conto di salle) de Francesco di Marco Datini pour sa compagnie d'Avignon, 1376–1379.* Paris: Bibliothèque Nationale, 1969.

Vivarelli, Enrico. "Aspetti della vita economica pratese nel XIV secolo; con trascrizione delle 459 lettere di Monte d'Andrea Angiolini di Prato." *Tesi di Laurea,* University of Florence, 1987.

Zarri, Gabriella, ed. Per lettera: La scrittura epistolare femminile tra archivio e tipografia secoli XV–XVII. Rome: Viella, 1999.